Knowing, Teaching, and Learning History

Knowing, Teaching, and Learning History

National and International Perspectives

EDITED BY

*Peter N. Stearns, Peter Seixas,
and Sam Wineburg*

New York University Press

NEW YORK AND LONDON

NEW YORK UNIVERSITY PRESS
New York and London

Library of Congress Cataloging-in-Publication Data
Knowing, teaching, and learning history : national and international
perspectives / edited by Peter N. Stearns, Peter Seixas, and
Sam Wineburg.
p. cm.
Papers presented at a conference.
Includes bibliographical references and index.
ISBN 0-8147-8141-1 (alk. paper) —
ISBN 0-8147-8142-X (pbk. : alk. paper)
1. History—Study and teaching. 2. Historiography. I. Stearns, Peter N.
II. Seixas, Peter C., 1947– III. Wineburg, Samuel S.
D16.2 .K59 2000
907'.2—dc21   00-008810

New York University Press books are printed on acid-free paper,
and their binding materials are chosen for strength and durability.

Manufactured in the United States of America
10 9 8 7

Contents

Acknowledgments

This book was prepared on the basis of a conference that was funded by the Spencer Foundation and the Carnegie Foundation for the Advancement of Teaching. The editors wish to thank both these agencies for their support and guidance. The American Historical Association and its Teaching Division sponsored the conference and this book, and the project has benefited immensely from this collaboration. A number of individuals played indispensable coordinating roles: Noralee Frankel, of the American Historical Association; Susan Mosborg, of the School of Education at the University of Washington; and Darlene Scalese, Karen Callas, and Joanne Ursenbach, of the Dean's Office, College of Humanities and Social Sciences, Carnegie Mellon University. To all, our thanks.

PNS
PS
SW

Introduction

On January 18, 1995, the "History Wars," to that point confined largely to skirmishes on op-ed pages of the *New York Times* and *Washington Post*, erupted on the floors of the United States Congress. In a debate on national history standards, Senator Slade Gorton (R-Washington) presented his colleagues with a portentous choice that, according to Gorton, would fix the national character for generations to come.

"George Washington or Bart Simpson," Gorton asked his colleagues—which figure represented a "more important part of our Nation's history for our children to study?" Gorton's question, asked with graven seriousness, symbolized how far issues of history had spilled beyond schoolhouse walls and become part of the national agenda. No longer the concern of a small group of educationists and their historian consultants, the history curriculum had by the mid-1990s become an issue for presidential aspirants, talk-show hosts, and, seemingly, anyone willing to express an opinion.

Public interest in history was reciprocated in historians' new interest in the public. Recognizing the complex entanglement of history and memory, historians have offered scholarly examinations of nearly every practice in which nonhistorians invoke, narrate, or display representations of the past, including commemoration, museum displays, historical fiction, and popular film. Historians' interest in what David Lowenthal (chapter 4, this volume) has called heritage (in contrast to history) had never been greater. Moreover, as they engaged in these inquiries, historians found themselves crossing disciplinary lines, using reception theory from cultural studies, working next to anthropologists, and confronting epistemological issues thrust upon them by philosophers and literary critics. Yet, just at a time when the larger society was deeply engaged in questions of teaching history to the young, there was one gaping hole in historians' scrutiny of memory practices: the teaching and learning of history in the schools.

It could plausibly be argued that schools are the major site for the construction of collective memory in contemporary society. With universal, compulsory schooling, and with history classes compulsory for at least some years of that schooling, the entire U.S. population is exposed to school accounts of the past during its formative, impressionable years. Prima facie, schools must have considerably more impact on our collective memory than, say, monuments or museums. Yet, historians have generally been drawn more to the latter than the former as objects of scholarly study. Perhaps, even in this era, when the texts of low culture—from comic books and popular romance to TV sitcoms and theme parks—attract their share of scholarly interpretation, schools, or at least classrooms, still remain uncomfortably beyond the fashionable pale.

The reasons for this relative neglect may reflect a deeper problem than the low status accorded to precollegiate education. Perhaps the problem is that historians fail to see what happens in elementary and high school history as a memory project, as heritage. Perhaps they prefer to understand the subject of school history less as practice of public memory than as the first steps toward a critical, disciplinary practice of history. Herein lies an interesting conundrum: Is school history primarily an uncritical heritage exercise—again, in Lowenthal's terms—intended to convey a particular version of the past? Or, is it an elementary version of the critical, disciplinary history that some will encounter in undergraduate or graduate programs, meant to prepare young people to think critically about the past and its legacy for the present? In practice, of course, school history bears some elements of each and in different teachers' hands can be molded into one or the other.

While the recent spate of work on history and memory has only rarely addressed what it means to learn or teach history, academics in related fields have undertaken research that trains its attention directly on these questions. Indeed, in the past ten years a new field has come into being that focuses on what it means to learn and to teach history in classrooms and university seminars, in museums, and in society at large. The core assumptions at the heart of this work stand in contrast to the assumptions that many historians and history teachers take for granted.

For example, a long-standing belief at the heart of history teaching is that the instructional act can be neatly carved into the two separate spheres of "content" and "pedagogy" (or, alternately, "content" and "process"). Accordingly, any topic can be taught using a variety of "techniques" (sometimes called "tricks"), from lectures to demonstrations to role plays to simulations to new CD-ROM interactive presentations. The selection of techniques by an instructor is thought to be guided by "effectiveness," a conception of aims informed primarily by common sense, leavened, perhaps, with a sprinkling of insights from learning theory, psychology, or some other sphere of knowledge thought to be beyond the purview of the historian.

In contrast, the guiding assumption of the new work on history teaching and learning is that the process of communicating knowledge about the past is, above all, an epistemological and cultural act that conveys deep and sometimes unintended messages about what it means to be historical in modern society. There is, to paraphrase Hayden White, a great deal of content embedded in the form. As an example, consider some of the common ways used to assess historical knowledge, whether a multiple-choice test, a term paper, an oral history assignment, or the "test" given to doctoral students—the dissertation. None of these is a neutral or interchangeable device. Each "teaches" students about the certainty (or uncertainty) of historical knowledge; each conveys messages about the students' agency in the face of historical knowledge; each guides students toward a particular conception of what counts in framing a historical argument—even whether argument has a place in knowing history! Thus viewed, history teaching moves from a technical act for conveying knowledge to a cultural act that teaches students about warrant, about the nature of understanding, and about their own role in making historical knowledge. Classrooms, not just monuments and commemorations, become the places where the contending voices in the debate over what history means, or should mean, in a democracy come together.

Over the past decade, history teaching and learning has been the subject of considerable research that has put flesh on the issues of culture and epistemology in the history classroom. This research has sampled broadly from the available methodologies in the humanities and social sciences, from in-depth interviews to ethnographies of classroom life, from anthropological and psychological tasks on how students deal with historical evidence to field-based experimental research. Three converging developments have contributed to the coalescing of this new field of interest.

First, the "cognitive revolution" in learning and teaching, as Howard Gardner has called it, has shifted the focus from behavior, the central construct in learning theory for the first half of the twentieth century, to acts of meaning and sense-making. More than anything else, the cognitive revolution has problematized the "copy model" of mind, in which learning was thought to be an unquestioned reflex of teaching, something that sprang forth automatically from a well-planned lecture or carefully crafted textbook narrative. By focusing on the inevitable gaps between teachers and learners, and on the human propensity to formulate meaning in the face of incompleteness and uncertainty, the cognitive approach has cast a suspicious eye on the behavioral proxies used as stand-ins for learning. Research in the cognitive tradition alerts educators to the cognitive architecture behind a given response—the thought patterns, beliefs, misconceptions, and frameworks students bring to instruction and that influence (and often determine) what they take from it.

The second development that has given impetus to the new work on history teaching and learning has to do with changes in the discipline of history itself. Broad public debate over questions of nation, race, gender, culture, and identity have numerous implications for what and how history is taught in schools and universities. But, as supporters and critics have noted, historiographic challenges have run deeper than the question of inclusion of previously marginalized groups. In the past decade, heightened attention has been paid to the nature of historical knowledge, inspired not only by the inclusion issue but by the historicization of history, narrative theory, and feminist, postcolonial, and cultural studies. These developments have opened up the conversation about not only the nature of historical knowledge but who in society gets to decide, all of which has resulted in a receptivity to thinking anew about the epistemological terrain of the history classroom.

Finally, in North America as well as internationally, there has been heightened interest in the problems of historical consciousness, collective memory, and the public presentation of the past. Historians and philosophers of history, as well as lay people, museum directors, filmmakers, and scholars from a broad array of fields have participated. The focus on a usable past has often brought schools into the debate, even if historians themselves have not always been at the forefront, and sparked important conversations about the relationship between nation building and the teaching of history in schools.

Together, these developments have led to the recognition that the history curriculum is no longer the province of any single group and that multiple constituencies must come together to address problems that are by definition beyond the capabilities of any single faction. It was precisely this realization that led to the editorial alliance behind this volume, an alliance that would have been unthinkable even twenty years ago.

The roots of this volume go back to Peter Stearns's tenure as vice president of the Teaching Division of the American Historical Association. In 1995 Stearns, a historian at Carnegie Mellon University, asked Sam Wineburg, a cognitive psychologist at the University of Washington, to organize a session for the 1997 meeting of the American Historical Association devoted to the new developments in history education research. In that session, Wineburg presented work on how students read historical texts. He was joined by Peter Seixas, a historian and teacher educator at the University of British Columbia, who presented research on how teacher trainees used (and misused) primary-source documents with their students. The third member of the symposium was Robert Bain, a high school teacher at Beachwood (Ohio) High School, who holds a Ph.D. in history from Case Western and who has been a prominent teacher leader in the history reform movement. The historian Amanda Podany, the fourth panel member, discussed interactions between historians and teachers; her presentation was based on her experience as director of the California History Social Science Project, a multisite collaboration between universities and schools throughout the state. Acting as discussants for the symposium were Stanley Katz, of the American Council of Learned Societies, and the psychologist Jerome Bruner, whose pioneering research on understanding and problem solving helped to launch the cognitive revolution. In its composition, this symposium sought to model the many voices that had come together in the new enterprise known as research on history teaching and learning.

Out of this AHA panel a three-way collaboration emerged among Stearns, Seixas, and Wineburg. Together, our efforts to forge a collaborative path were given a boost with an invitation to a working conference hosted by Peter Lee, Alaric Dickinson, Rosalyn Ashby, and Denis Shemilt at the University of London. Since the mid-1970s, these individuals and their colleagues have spearheaded the Schools Council History Project, one of the largest curriculum reform projects in history education and arguably one of the most successful, replacing the traditional chronological curriculum with a thematic-based curriculum that focuses on history as a distinct form of knowing and understanding. Drawing on the wisdom of our British colleagues, we realized that the time had come to try to do something that had not yet been done in a North American context: to bring together representatives from the constituencies that influence the teaching of history—historians, history teachers, teacher educators, cognitive and cultural psychologists, education researchers, and staff developers.

The radicalism of this gesture should not be overlooked. Throughout much of the 1980s and 1990s, the history curriculum was in ferment, but the conversations about it were disparate, episodic, and conducted largely within distinct thought collectives. Historians, many of whom were brought to the conversation of schooling by the battle over national standards, saw the debate as one of content ("the battle over the curriculum") and not one that could benefit from empirical research on teaching or learning. Researchers in history education, most of whom had disciplinary backgrounds in psychology or education, wrote and published in venues typically ignored by members outside their community and largely stayed out of the standards debate. Teacher educators, those individuals most directly responsible for preparing future teachers, were for the most part left out of the loop. And teachers, who must try to synthesize new developments in the discipline of history as well as new insights into the nature of learning, were often viewed as beneficiaries rather than full-fledged collaborators and conversation partners.

The idea of bringing together around a single table members of these groups found a receptive audience among two individuals who themselves embody the spirit of collaboration and innovation. Patricia Graham, a historian of education and president of the Spencer Foundation, was in the audience at the original AHA panel in 1996. With her sharp questions and synthetic insights, she pushed us to think about our aims both in the short and in the long term and generously provided us the funds to convene an international conference. We received additional funding from the Carnegie Foundation for the Advancement of Teaching, headed by Lee S. Shulman. An educational psychologist by training, Shulman was one of the pioneers in the field of research on teaching, who helped spur that field to address the subject-specific demands of teaching across the disciplinary spectrum. With the help of these benefactors and the foundations they head, we brought together on the campus of Carnegie Mellon University in November 1998 twenty-five leading history educators from North America and Europe. The present volume is one of the fruits of that conference.

Choices, Beliefs, and Understanding

In recent years, one central debate about history in the schools has been galvanized by the movement to develop National Standards: Which history should be taught? Chapters in this volume from Gary B. Nash (chapter 6) and Ross E. Dunn (chapter 7), both active contributors to the U.S. National Standards, address this question. These chapters do not, however, reenact the standards controversy of the past several years but examine the foundations of this question: What is the relationship between exposure to particular narratives of national (or world) development on the one hand and the learning of disciplinary practices and habits of mind on the other?

The teaching of history, like all aspects of historical study, involves choice and selection: One cannot avoid choices, one cannot simply "include more." The question then becomes on what grounds choices are made. The chapters in this volume point toward a resolution of this dilemma. The criteria for choices of inclusion can themselves be made explicit and become the subject of teachers' and students' discussions. While historians make these choices consciously, teachers often proceed without a forum for deliberation, and students too often assume that their task is simply to learn what has been taught.

Shared Understanding

A second fundamental issue that emerges from these chapters involves the role of history in what some have called "the identity project." How do beliefs about the past, including unconscious projection, shape ordinary citizens' understanding of themselves and the contemporary world? In chapter 2, the cultural psychologist James V. Wertsch distinguishes between *belief* and *knowledge* about the past, drawing from his research on historical consciousness in Estonia during the collapse of the Soviet regime. He found that people can store elaborate constructions of "official" history, while actually deeply believing alternative, opposition accounts of the past. The latter, though often less coherent, contribute more to individuals' identity formation and to their moral and political outlook.

Beliefs about the past are the subject of two large-scale research projects, Roy Rosenzweig's survey of American adults (chapter 14), and Bodo von Borries's European "Youth and History" project, which surveyed 32,000 students in twenty-seven European and Middle Eastern countries (chapter 13). Other chapters examine young people's beliefs at closer range. In chapter 15, Linda S. Levstik describes the disjunctures between students' beliefs about historical significance and the events and issues that teachers feel prepared to take up in class. Levstik found that students' interest in "negative" and "coercive" aspects of U.S. history is systematically sidetracked by teachers eager to fit events into a progressive narrative of national development.

The task of understanding students' beliefs and understandings is addressed in chapters by Gaea Leinhardt (chapter 12), James Voss and Jennifer Wiley (chapter 19), and Sam Wineburg (chapter 16), who show that these beliefs cover a wide range of issues, not all of which are immediately obvious, including what historical sources to believe, how to handle conflicting sources, and the very nature of historical argument. How to handle students' different beliefs generated important differences among conference participants.

On the one hand, Rosenzweig celebrated his respondents' "intimate uses of the past," and Levstik favored students' "vernacular" version of history, in contrast to "official views justifying the contemporary social structure." On the other hand, the British participants, veterans of the Schools History Project of the 1970s and 1980s, downplayed the "identity project" as a variant on Michael Oakeshott's "practical past."

The history education researchers Peter Lee and Rosalyn Ashby (chapter 11), for example, focus on students' developing sophistication in handling conflicts among differing historical accounts. They advocate a view of learning history as "coming to grips with a discipline." The aim of their research is ultimately to help schools enhance students' historical thinking. In this effort, they recall David Lowenthal, who noted the "sustained effort and judgment" required by history, or points made by Sam Wineburg, who has distinguished the difficult and "unnatural act" of historical thinking from students' facile beliefs about the past.

Between Collective Memory and Critical History

The poles of a usable versus a critical past represent an irreducible tension in history education. If history teaches us anything about the school curriculum, it is that history, qua school subject, has a hard time avoiding present political purposes. Given the inherent moral implications of any historical narrative, insofar as school history engages with and shapes a collective memory, it is inherently political, whether the agenda is focused on national progress, the struggle for human rights, global awareness, ethnic identity, or something else. And so a third underlying issue that emerges from these chapters is the question of the political purposes of history education. This question always threatens to push fine-grained history education research to the sidelines, as conflicting political purposes for the teaching of history are much more easily understood, deeply felt, and reducible to the media soundbite.

In chapter 3, Desmond Morton addresses these issues with reference to history education in Canada. Quebec school history, he reports, is alive and well. Yet, those who are pushing history as a means to foster Canadian unity outside Quebec do not necessarily regard this as good news. Morton questions whether they—or, for that matter, teachers, parents, or the public in general—can get excited about a disciplinary approach to historical thinking, one that fosters caution rather than passion, critique rather than celebration. The view from Canada, like the views from the United Kingdom and Europe, offers an important comparison for American readers.

In chapter 1, Peter Seixas offers a third way to address the dichotomy between collective memory and critical history by asking whether postmodern perspectives offer a productive middle ground for the school curriculum. Although postmodernist theory opens a way for students to understand the relationship between the narratives about the past and the political interests of those who construct them in the present, Seixas strikes a wary chord about the side effects of pedagogical postmodernism, including problems of excessive relativism and nihilism.

Recommendations for Reform

Three relationships—between learning particular accounts and learning the discipline, between historical knowledge and historical belief, and between history education and the political motives that lie behind its presence in the school curriculum—inform not only the chapters that report research in this volume but also those that address classroom practice. In chapter 18, Christine Gutierrez, who teaches high school in South Central Los Angeles, draws attention to the community within the school, and the community beyond, and their implications for the teaching and learning of history. Robert B. Bain, using his knowledge of both the history classroom and history education research, explores in chapter 17 what it means to be a "scholar of history teaching." He shows how history education research, informed by cognitive science and cultural psychology, has shaped what he does as a teacher and how his classroom practice generates new questions and opportunities for further research.

Like those by Gutierrez and Bain, several other chapters describe innovations that might serve as models for deeper historical thinking among students. The history education researcher Veronica Boix-Mansilla notes in chapter 20 that the links that students make between historical and contemporary events are often simplistic, if not altogether mistaken. Similarly, Peter N. Stearns (chapter 21) identifies particular tasks of historical analysis, including intercultural comparison, theory testing, and assessment of historical change, that students encounter in his undergraduate world history course. These tasks require understanding that college instructors frequently neglect or assume that students already possess.

The psychologist Charles A. Perfetti's computer program, "The Sourcer's Apprentice" (chapter 22), helps high school students to read historical documents in ways closer to those practiced by historians. Perfetti's work stands out in that it draws heavily on the core insights of cognitive scientists working in domains other than history. But, like each of the teaching innovations presented in this volume, Perfetti's program rests on a more explicit definition of the tasks involved in historical reading, thinking, and writing than is customarily entertained in history curricula and classrooms. Only with such definition can learning history be systematically advanced beyond the simple accumulation in memory of more historical facts.

These innovations cannot stand on their own as a reform program; they require broader structures of support. One of the key avenues of reform of the teaching of history, if it is to come, will be in teacher education. Diane Ravitch's quantitative study (chapter 8) points to the history-poor backgrounds of many of the nation's social studies teachers, raising the question of how teachers who themselves lack knowledge can teach what they do not know to students. Of course, any call for more undergraduate history courses for future teachers must have as a corollary a commitment to investigate what actually goes on in those courses. Further, investigators need to question the kinds of connections future teachers make between their undergraduate history education and their tasks of teaching in the schools. Aiming to make these connections explicit, and at the same time to ensure that they take place, G. Williamson McDiarmid and Peter Vinten-Johansen (chapter 9) provide an account of a history teaching methods course taught by a historian and a teacher educator at Michigan State University. The collaboration generated a dynamic and productive interplay between disciplinary knowledge and procedures on the one hand and pedagogical considerations on the other.

Successful reform, however, will be broad and multifaceted. Much energy has been devoted to the articulation of standards, at the national, state, and local levels. Equally important, and less well developed at the present moment, are assessment tools that will measure what students do and provide opportunities for teachers to talk about their practice. There will need to be new classroom materials not only in the form of new textbooks like those from the School's Council History Project and document collections like those being produced by Nash's UCLA National Center for History Education but also in the electronic forms like that being pioneered by Roy Rosenzweig's "History Matters" on the Web (www.historymatters.gmu.edu). Shelly Weintraub, in chapter 10, describes the Oakland (California) School District's history education reform efforts, giving the reader a glimpse of what an interlocking set of reform initiatives might look like and tying together professional development, history standards, materials development, and student assessment.

Finding Consensus

In a volume that draws together papers that represent national, ideological, institutional, and disciplinary diversity, can we speak of consensus? As we take a step back from these papers, we see several unifying themes:

• First, these chapters speak to the productivity of talking across these many divisions. Almost every chapter here exemplifies this productivity. This is not to say that bridging our divides has been, is, or will be easy. In particular, talking across disciplinary boundaries raises problems of vocabulary and outlook that we have only begun to explore. But, it is clear from this array of contributions that multiple perspectives enrich the conversation and begin to address the complexity of educational change in ways that go beyond a single disciplinary perspective.

• Second, these chapters convey a sense of the opportune moment for change, derived from at least two—and possibly more—broad intellectual sources. Psychology's cognitive revolution has called attention to the need to attend to young people's ideas, their structures of understanding, and their processes of conceptual change. On the other hand, the historiographic revolution of the past few decades has provided a sense of opportunity for the historians involved. Together, the two movements generate a powerful dynamic.

• Third, as a collection, these chapters reflect the complexity of issues in history education and, in that sense, stand in contrast to the public debates over the U.S. History Standards, which tended to occupy only one layer of a multilevel set of issues. The authors represented here speak to the importance of articulating the contending purposes of history education; the relationship among history in the schools, public memory, and disciplinary history; students' beliefs about the past and the relationship of those beliefs to their own identities; the processes of conceptual change and growth in historical understanding; and the multiple avenues through which educational change might be sought. Which history should be taught is only one (albeit important) question among many.

• Fourth, if we were to search for a simple way to differentiate the educational agenda embodied in these chapters, in contrast to the status quo in history education, it might be best articulated by the words of Denis Shemilt, the British history educator responsible for the evaluation of the School's Council History Project (chapter 5). Shemilt notes that the contributors seek both a deep understanding of the past and a deep understanding of history. That is, students should gain facility with understanding the variety, the difference, and the strangeness of life in the past, the interplay of continuity and change, the multiple causes and consequences of events and trends, the role of individuals, collectivities and states, and so on. But, they should also understand the processes of knowledge-making, the construction of a historical narrative and argument, the uses of evidence, and the nature of conflicting historical accounts. This second level of understanding acts as the best insurance against the dogmatic transmission of a single version of the past, a practice that violates the core tenets of the discipline.

• Fifth, these chapters highlight the fact that history is one special and specialized practice in a whole array of what we might call memory practices. Awareness of this should help us to situate the particular tasks of teaching history in the schools, where the public's and the politicians' desire for a reinforcement of tradition and memory will continue to compete with a critical disciplinary history for space on the curricular agenda.

• Finally, this collection of chapters exemplifies what both Robert Bain (chapter 17) and Lee Shulman have termed a "scholarship of teaching." As scholars of history teaching, we are working toward a deep and considered understanding of a core cultural practice. Whether this understanding will yield immediate solutions to particular problems of instruction is not a question on which all else hinges. As Lee Shulman pointed out in our deliberations in Pittsburgh, no one expects historians' scholarship to yield immediate solutions to contemporary problems of state and society. Educational scholarship should be seen in the same light. Its purpose is to broaden and deepen discussion, to teach us how to ask questions with greater acuity and insight. These goals, then, frame the chapters that follow.

Part I

Current Issues in History Education

School history has been challenged by profound social and cultural changes over the past thirty years. In the academy, these were first expressed in the "culture wars" and subsequently in new debates over the nature of historical knowledge. In school history, there is now attention to a broadened scope of activity, inclusion of more diverse historical actors, and representations of a greater range of historical perspectives. While these changes offer welcome challenges to an earlier, more monovocal and linear trajectory of history as human progress, they simultaneously pose many new problems.

Every school textbook, curriculum guide, CD-ROM, and classroom exercise carries implicit notions about what history is, how it should be organized, and why it is worth learning. But, these assumptions are not generally made explicit, so their conflicts and inconsistencies, their strengths and weaknesses, escape systematic examination. The essays in this section take a step back, to bring underexamined assumptions under scrutiny. The fact that the section comprises papers based in four different national contexts—the United States, Canada, the United Kingdom, and Estonia—offers a limited but important comparative dimension to the discussion.

Peter Seixas's essay introduces the question of the nature of historical knowledge in the schools by asking how history curriculum practitioners handle conflicting historical accounts of the same historical phenomenon. He suggests dividing the field into three broad orientations, which he calls "collective memory" (the predominant approach in North America), the "disciplinary" orientation (more prominent, as Denis Shemilt explains later in the volume, in British classrooms), and a "postmodern" orientation. He weighs the contributions and liabilities of each.

In the second chapter, James Wertsch uses a different approach to conflicting historical accounts. In his research in Estonia in 1991, he found an opposition between the official accounts that people had learned—

often very well—in the schools of the Soviet Union and the accounts that they *believed*, drawn from family, friends, underground literature, and other informal sources. Wertsch uses the opposition to define two concepts: "mastery," the ability to reason within and about historical narratives, and "appropriation," which involves an emotional commitment to narratives as a kind of "identity resource." He argues that, while mastery has been the subject of most history education research, investigators need to address a host of questions about appropriation, as both a psychological and a sociocultural problem.

Desmond Morton's meditation on Canadian history education was written in the wake of a publicity campaign aimed at calling attention to students' ignorance of the facts of Canadian history. Set against Seixas's typology, Wertsch's analytical divide between mastery and appropriation, and Morton's own insights, the publicity campaign appears to raise issues far more complex than its designers probably realized. There is no easy connection between knowing a list of historical facts and being able to reason about the past. Nor is there one between being able to reason about the past and using history in the cause of patriotic identity- and nation-building. Morton challenges not only Canadians but all history educators to think deeply about simple prescriptions for mining the past as a solution to contemporary political problems. On the other hand, he asks whether a rarified conception of critical and rational history can generate widespread public interest and support.

David Lowenthal shares Morton's concern about the uses of the past. His chapter develops ideas that he introduced earlier in two widely read books.[1] The seemingly paradoxical juxtaposition of the "foreignness" of the past and its "immediacy" gives rise to a host of problems and promises for the study of history, particularly for young people, and particularly in the current cultural moment. Remembering his own education, Lowenthal laments the loss of a "story of humanity that had a length and a form within which one could find one's bearings." If this is gone— and it is—then Lowenthal suggests a number of measures to help fill the gap. Among them is the notion of hindsight, the understanding that all historians view the past not "as it was" but with the benefits and liabilities of the backward view.

The problem of "finding one's bearings" through history is addressed, as well, by Denis Shemilt. Shemilt's efforts to help students find their bearings are, however, responses to a somewhat different disorientation from Lowenthal's. In Britain, the widespread Schools History Project reforms, in Shemilt's view, have been relatively successful on one front, and a dismal failure on a second. In what Seixas would call a "disciplinary" model, British history teachers have attempted "to develop pupils' understanding of History as a logical and evidence-based means of making sense of the past." But, while British students may be methodologically sophisticated with regard to historical inquiry on a small scale, they are apparently unable to offer a large, coherent mapping of the past and even further from being able to offer flexible, broadly based, multiple narrative frameworks, of the sort that would help them use the past to "find their bearings."

The last two papers of Part I deal in different ways with those large, narrative frameworks that both Lowenthal and Shemilt call for. Gary Nash traces the pictures of the early American past drawn by textbooks since the late eighteenth century. He celebrates the relatively recent emergence of an interpretation based on the "convergence" of "red, white, and black," supplanting a succession of interpretations that located historical agency solely among the European-American population. Similarly, Ross Dunn presents three successive models for the teaching of world history, "Western Civilization," "Different Cultures," and "Patterns of Change." He argues for the last of these, on the grounds that, like Nash's "convergence" paradigm, it is more socially inclusive and also firmly based in recent historiographical developments.

What history is, how it should be organized for schools, and why it is worth learning: As readers will see, the authors in this section offer no consensus, but they do deepen the discussion.

NOTE

1. Lowenthal, *The Past Is a Foreign Country* (Cambridge, 1985) and *The Heritage Crusade and the Spoils of History* (London, 1996).

Chapter 1

Schweigen! die Kinder!

or, Does Postmodern History Have a Place in the Schools?

Peter Seixas

In August 1998, British Columbia's first negotiated treaty since Confederation was signed by representatives of the Nisga'a people and the federal and provincial governments. It provides for treaty settlement funds, land, property ownership, and self-government for the Nisga'a, within the limits prescribed by Canadian law. The treaty has yet to be ratified; the debates over it provide an avenue into an examination of the legacy of the past, the nature of history, and its uses today. These concerns are at the center of any discussion of history education.[1]

Those who oppose the treaty see its history in this way: When whites came to BC, the land was relatively empty, the inhabitants technologically backward. Progressive, cosmopolitan British North Americans developed the undeveloped land. In so doing, they made various attempts to assimilate the native people, while setting aside reserves for those who resisted assimilation for one reason or another. The political order they created, though not perfect, was increasingly democratic, and increasingly ready to accept native people on its own terms. The treaty thus represents an unnecessary giveaway of land and tax-revenues that belong to all the people of British Columbia and creates a restrictive and race-based franchise in the native-controlled areas. Moreover, it is an attempt to redress possible wrongs that were set in motion more than century ago and that are best left behind. These views are articulated by opposition parties, talk-show hosts, opinion columnists, and others.

Those who support the treaty paint a very different picture of precontact native culture. They note the substantial precontact population in the region and its complex social and political structures, particularly along the coast. Strict codes of property ownership, succession, and civil order were handed down through oral tradition. This version highlights the Royal Proclamation of 1763, which guaranteed that Aboriginal rights to land and self-government were to be respected. Any changes were to be effected through negotiations with the Crown. From the time of the gold rush, which brought British Columbia's first major wave of white settlement, a resource-hungry white population, supported by provincial governments that were contemptuous of the First Nations' rights, steadily eroded both the land base and the legal redress available to Indians. In so doing, they not only overrode, ignored, or confused the principles that had shaped the Nisga'a legal codes but also violated the principles laid down by the British Crown for governing native-white relations in the region. In this version, the treaty represents a long-awaited return to these principles. Variations of this version are articulated by Nisga'a representatives, provincial government leaders, and the preponderance of current academic historical scholarship.[2]

As teachers confront the task of teaching history, there are three ways of dealing with these conflicting interpretations of the past, reflecting three fundamentally different orientations toward historical pedagogy and epistemology. The first is simply to teach the best story as the way it happened, an approach I will call "enhancing collective memory," since it does not engage students in the historical disciplines' modes of inquiry. The second is to present both versions and to teach students to reach conclusions about which one is the better interpretation on the basis of a series of documents, historians' assessments, and other materials. In a classroom with this orientation, rather than being *told* simply to believe a single story, students come to understand what makes a valid historical account. In the process, they learn disciplinary criteria for deciding what makes good history; thus, I will call this approach a "disciplinary" one. The third orientation reflects uncertainty about the notion of a "best story." Here, students consider both versions with the supporting documentation but then relate the versions of the past to their political uses in the present. The task for students in the third orientation is not so much to arrive at a "best" or most valid position on the basis of historical evidence as to understand how different groups organize the past into histories and how their rhetorical and narratological strategies serve present-day purposes. This I will call the "postmodern" approach.

This paper uses these three alternative approaches, collective memory, disciplinary, and postmodern, as an entry into a discussion of the philosophical and pedagogical issues that confront history educators at the turn of the millennium, not only in British Columbia but around the world.

The Best Story about the Past: History in the Schools to Shape Collective Memory

There is a compelling logic to the argument that we should teach the best possible interpretation of the past to students. In fact, recent debates over history curriculum in the United States have largely *begun* by assuming this stance and then concentrated on fighting over which interpretation is the best one.[3] Similar struggles have taken place over museum displays that presented stories that challenged traditional interpretations of the settlement of the West and the dropping of the atomic bomb.[4] Jack Granatstein has recently precipitated a parallel debate over history curriculum in Canada.[5] All of these arguments over history education are conducted as if the question "Which historical interpretation should we teach?" were *the* central question. Clearly, there is a lot at stake. What is it that the different sides are seeking to control?

Quite simply, it is the power of the story of the past to define who we are in the present, our relations with others, relations in civil society—nation and state, right and wrong, good and bad—and broad parameters for action in the future. Again, there is a lot at stake. If British Columbia's schools present the region's history over the past hundred and fifty years as a part of the progressive story of "Building the West" (as a widely used school textbook is entitled), then many aspects of the historical record fit into place. White settlers become the central protagonists in developing the land, engineering technological progress, and promoting economic growth. These aspects of progress are intimately tied to political affairs. The negotiation that brought British Columbia into the Canadian Confederation in 1871 rested on a promise to extend the railroad to the Pacific coast. The decision allowed British Columbians to see themselves as part of an imperial story of Canadian progress, with consequences for the nature and role of the state, as well as for patterns of settlement, demographic change, and immigration.

School history's story of progress has been modified over the past twenty-five years, most notably with the marginal and episodic inclusion of women and the much more central inclusion of non-British immigrants.[6] Thus, the role of Chinese workers on the Canadian Pacific Railroad, the exclusion of Sikh immigrants in 1907, and the Japanese internment during World War II are highlighted. But, while these complicate the nation-building story, they do not necessarily upset it. That is—not without some difficulty—they can be incorporated in a more inclusive best story of the past. This allows the modified story to have somewhat different meanings for newly important groups in British Columbia. A struggle against racism and exploitation—and for inclusion—provides the schools' frame for viewing British Columbia's past immigrant relations as prelude to contemporary multiculturalism. A revised best history thus continues to provide a framework for answering questions of identity and social purpose.

Returning to the Nisga'a, shaping a new story without excluding or marginalizing Aboriginal people involves a more fundamental revision of the nation-building story than what has already occurred in the school system to date. Such a revision may be possible. A recent journalistic interpretation discusses the history of native-white relations in British Columbia as a struggle between imperial loyalists who recognized the principles of the Proclamation of 1763 and a "Yankee faction" who were "disposed to ignore altogether the rights of the Indians and . . . who hold the American doctrine of manifest destiny in its most fatal form" (Glavin, 1998). But, the serious inclusion of First Nations ultimately entails moving beyond Canada as the "nation" whose development provides the governing narrative framework. Because "nation," as a concept, is so tied to "progress" and to "history" itself, such a narrative introduces multiple perspectives on historical judgments and quickly threatens to move beyond the tight sphere that I have defined in this first section as the *single* best story.

It is not my intention here to weigh alternative versions of the past. Rather, the question is what the single best version provides for students in the school, and for the society as a whole. There are three interrelated answers: identity, cohesion, and social purpose (provided the history is taught, and taught well). First, the single best version helps to shape a group identity defined by common experience and belief. Group identity is given shape by who is marginalized and who is excluded from the group. Second, by defining a group identity, history education can provide social cohesion. The group can hypothetically be defined as broadly as all of humanity itself, but the nation has typically provided the framing group for history in the modern era. Other group identities provide competing possibilities: ethnicity, as well as gender, class, ability, and sexual orientation. Yet, history framed in any of these orientations provides identity and cohesion within the group (however defined), even if it leads, as conservative critics fear, to fragmentation of the national story.[7] Learning the best version of history provides a compelling moral framework, the third benefit. It offers a trajectory that ties individuals' decisions and actions in the present to the longer course of events, whether expressed in the struggle for human rights, sacrifice for the national good, moral uplift or economic well-being through hard work, class struggle, or gender equality. One cannot mobilize for any social or national purpose without invoking the best version of history to support it.[8] Indeed, the idea of social change (or even the conscious ideal of social conservation) makes no sense without a historical orientation in which to frame it.

All this explains why people care so deeply about which version of history students learn: If effective, schools can operate to shape the consciousness which guides social change over the next generation. It is also why textbooks, whose mandate it is, generally, to present the best version, undergo the kind of review process that they do.[9] What, then, is the problem with this conception of history in the schools? First, it is difficult and contentious to decide which is the right version of the past to teach. And, second, there is a problem with history as dogma. If historians, curriculum experts, textbook writers, and school authorities make all the decisions about the right version of the past, then the students' only job is to absorb it. What started out as a contentious, debate-ridden investigation about truth, right, and meaning in the past and present ends up before the students as a catechism to be memorized. At best, it comes in the form of gripping and vivid stories with a moral trajectory; at worst, it is a desiccated version of the past, a relatively meaningless batch of names, dates, and events, in which case the social project of history learning is lost in any case. In either instance, historical knowledge appears as something fixed by authority rather than subject to investigation, debate, and its own system of warrants.

History in the Schools as an Exercise in Disciplined Knowledge: History as a Way of Knowing

David Lowenthal distinguishes between heritage and history. In his dichotomous definition, "heritage" is a use of the past to support or oppose interests in the present. It is not subject to critique but is held as "a dogma of roots and origins that must be accepted on faith."[10] It establishes rights of one group or another and becomes "history as a weapon."[11] In contrast, "history" is disinterested. It is universal, in the sense that no group bears exclusive claim to particular stories or to "truth." It aims for—though, of course, it never achieves—"meticulous objectivity."[12] It is public, subject to debate, and falsifiable. Its truth claims rest on historical method and the historical record through documentary and artifactual sources.

If we accept this dichotomy, "history" as practiced in the schools is actually closer to the practices of heritage, in that students spend most of their time getting "the story." Only marginal attention, if any at all, is devoted to learning how to question a historical account, understand the evidentiary base upon which it rests, and to assessing it in relation to competing accounts. The introduction of history—as opposed to heritage—into the schools would mean doing all those things. In the case of the Nisga'a treaty, schools would have students examine the historical documents, the records of early British Columbia settlement, and the oral and artifactual history of the Nisga'a. Students would then weigh the competing versions.

To follow Lowenthal's dichotomy further, this exercise in history would be an objective, disinterested investigation. Students would be careful not to superimpose late-twentieth-century notions of racism on nineteenth-century actors, who lived with different assumptions. Nor would identity politics shape the historical investigation. Rather, students would be asked to see the difference and uniqueness of the past, not necessarily its relation to the present, particularly if its relation to the contentious contemporary issues clouded students' ability to understand what happened in the past.[13]

What are the benefits of this approach? While the single authoritative interpretation of the past, conveyed as what really happened, is consistent with an authoritarian political culture, the epistemology that underlies this educational approach is suited to the education of critical citizens in a liberal democracy: It should help them to develop the ability and the disposition to arrive independently at reasonable, informed opinions. This orientation toward school history provides students with active exercise in building historical knowledge and criticizing others' historical accounts. Rather than promoting identity fissures in a multicultural, multinational, and multiply gendered world, it offers the promise of deliberative distance, which only a broad historical view can achieve.[14]

Criticism of this approach can be divided into four sets of concerns. Politically committed advocates, who look to history education as an intervention into collective memory—national, ethnic, or other—see attention to historical method as a distraction at best and a threat to the efficacy of the project at worst. If one wants school history to promote Canadian national unity, for example, then what purpose is served by placing before students conflicting interpretive possibilities? Granatstein divides "process" from "content" in an attack on this approach: "At a time when most students are exposed to only one or even a half course in Canadian history, such methodological nonsense stressing process above content is simply destructive. . . ."[15]

A related question suggests that students will be lost to relativism once we tell them that history is not "just the facts." There is considerable reason to believe that this will not be the consequence of this course. Students are already exposed to conflicting historical interpretations in popular culture. They need the means to assess the relative strengths and weaknesses of these interpretations. For this reason, schools' *failure* to teach history's disciplinary procedures is more likely to lead to relativism. Empirical evidence of the soundness of this approach comes from research programs growing out of the British Schools Council History Project and the project's widespread influence throughout the British school history curriculum.[16]

From a different direction come questions about the historical epistemology that underlies such an approach. Chris Husbands, who has been heavily influenced by the disciplinary approach, admits, "From the perspective of the mid-1990s, the claims made for both developments in social history and constructivist approaches to school history now appear somewhat unsophisticated." He notes how postmodernists' attention to "the social context under which historical knowledge is constructed" undermines earlier assumptions about the relationship between the academic and school history.[17] I will explore this further later in this essay.

Finally, there is a question whether an exercise in historical knowledge-building that consciously excises identity issues from the study of history can satisfy the deeply felt needs that lead people to learn history in the first place. How much support will be forthcoming for a history project that does not make a central concern people's drive for connections to their roots, their quest to define a common identity forged in the vicissitudes of a common past, or their need to bring historical perspectives to their understanding of current struggles for social justice?

These two orientations toward history education—collective memory and the disciplinary—have shaped much of what has been said and written about the field. The third orientation is less well explored. It results from the postmodernist challenges to historical methodology as a way of knowing. Few of the postmodernist historiographers have specifically addressed pedagogical issues.[18] The remainder of this essay is devoted to sorting out the consequences of their work for a theory of history education, with a discussion of what positive contribution they might make where the first two orientations fall short, and the potential drawbacks of this third approach.

The Postmodern Challenge to History in the Schools

Why do the Nisga'a have one story of the past, and the right-wing populist radio talk-show host Rafe Mair another? From what do such differences arise? What are their consequences? These questions provide an opening to move from the disciplinary orientation into questions about the relationship between historical knowledge and power and thus into the thick of postmodernism. Nobody—not the Nisga'a participants, nor Rafe Mair, nor the purportedly objective and disinterested historian of Lowenthal's ideal—is exempt from these questions.

To characterize the predicament, both proponents and opponents invoke metaphors of crisis and danger: Both sides speak of being on the edge of the cliff, of falling into the abyss, of taking a plunge into uncertainty, and of murdering history.[19] Others attempt to get the discipline back to the safety of solid ground by promising to "tell the truth about history," by offering a "defense of history," or by advocating a "return to essentials."[20] As in the debates over collective memory, a lot is at stake.

Jonathan Culler sees contemporary cultural theory as serving primarily to destabilize and call into question each layer of certainty on which one might attempt to stand. He identifies the contribution of theory (and Foucauldian theory in particular) across the humanities and social sciences in its encouragement "to be suspicious of what is identified as natural, as a given."[21] Jenkins identifies postmodernists by the way in which they greet this uncertainty: "the best guides to history today are those who not only know all about the collapse . . . into uncertainty, but who like it and can accept it." He adds, with a flourish, "Historians respond favourably to the postmodern condition if they care nought for the foundational certainties of modernity, feeling that they can effectively construct something on the 'basis' of nothing (for when—in fact—was it ever different?)."[22] There is something salutary—even scientific—about questioning foundations, examining assumptions, and doubting authority. The question is how much is enough.

In what follows, I survey four aspects of the postmodern critique: the narrativity of history, the positionality of historians, the limitations of progress, and the textuality of sources. One way to start to comprehend the postmodern impossibility of bridging the gap between present and past is through an examination of the narrative form of historical writing. Historical accounts are organized as narratives, with a beginning, middle, and end, with a meaning expressed through language that conforms to its own rules. The past, on the other hand, is not organized at all; it has no beginning, middle, or end (except as chosen by the historian), nor does it have meaning (except as imposed by the historian), and it exists beyond linguistic rules. It is, as David Harlan has argued, immense, infinitely polysemous, sublime, and gone. Historiography is the attempt to impose "a meaningful form (or narrative) onto a meaningless past. . . ."[23]

Hayden White and his followers do not deny historians' abilities to state facts about the past or to assemble chronicles (lists of facts in chronological order). It is when the historian starts to make judgments about what all the facts add up to that the imposition of narrative forms becomes crucial. And, without this imposition there is no meaningful history. In this account, historiography becomes more a literary or poetic act and less a social scientific act. The historian makes these choices (consciously or unconsciously) on the basis of linguistic, aesthetic, ideological, or moral criteria. At this level—in the construction of the narrative (as opposed to the listing of facts)—the historian is constrained, according to the postmodernists, only by language, and not by the record of the past.[24]

Roger Chartier objects: "If history is no different from fiction," he asks, "then is the historiographical operation a waste of time?"[25] Without denying the ubiquity of narrative in historiography, Chartier calls attention here to the other crucial aspect of the historian's work: that which takes place in the archive. The archive and the past whose traces it holds are the basis for the historical narrative; they place limits on interpretation. The archive and the limits it sets distinguish history, even when written in literary form, from literature. Chartier thus denies that history is

> one mode of fictional invention among others. Against that dissolution of the status of history as a specific knowledge . . . one must insist forcefully that history is commanded by an intention and a principle of truth, that the past history has taken as its object is a reality external to discourse, and that knowledge of it can be verified.[26]

The postmodernist stance toward historical knowledge does involve logical inconsistency. Jenkins, for example, quotes Rorty approvingly, in order to counter the charge that postmodernist thought will lead to social fragmentation and nihilism.

> The idea that liberal societies are bound together by philosophical beliefs seems to me ludicrous. What binds societies together are common vocabularies and common hopes. . . . To retain social hope, members of such a society need to be able to tell themselves a story about how things might get better, and to see no insuperable obstacles to this story's coming true. If [such] social hope has become harder lately, this is not because the [philosophers] . . . have been committing treason but because, since the end of World War II, the course of events has made it harder to tell a convincing story of this sort.[27]

What is problematic here for Jenkins (though he does not recognize or acknowledge it) is Rorty's statement about the relationship between "the course of events" and the telling of a convincingly hopeful story. If, as Jenkins argues throughout, "events" can be configured into any story form, then how can postwar "realities" exert this kind of constraint on the stories we wish to tell about them? Here we see the difficulty of trying to talk in a consistent way about the past without a strong notion of its placing constraints about what can be said about it. Yes, there are choices, but within limits.[28]

Corollary to the postmodernist attention to emplotment and narrative is scrutiny of the position of the historian. In their disciplinary orientation, historians excuse themselves from the historicization that they apply to all other human phenomena. Postmodernism undercuts the historians' Archimedean stance, calling into question their implicit claim to

stand outside the flow of history and their abilities to be impartial ob-
servers of the past: All historical accounts are fundamentally positioned
and politicized. In this way, postmodernists challenge the division between the discipline of history and collective memory. History is just one
of a number of ways of remembering the past. Historians' accounts are
distinguished from others, not on the grounds of epistemology or
method but because of their ability as "experts" to exercise "a regulatory
function in relation to the 'public past.'"[29] Reviewing the failure of past
historians' "objectivity," Peter Novick has driven the field at least toward
epistemological humility.[30] But, moving too easily and too far, the postmodernist is caught in a widely recognized bind: "How . . . can you theorize your own position in a way that escapes the critique you want to
make of those who have been historians before you?"[31] The problem of
making a claim of knowledge recedes infinitely.

Also closely related to the question of narrative emplotment is the
problem of progress. Progress and decline provide large-scale, evaluative
frameworks for historical narratives. Jenkins identifies the central role of
the notion of progress in modern historiography: Both radical (Marxist)
and liberal (bourgeois) modernists saw history as "a way of looking at the
past in terms that assigned to contingent events and situations an objective significance by identifying their place and function within a general
schema of [progressive] historical development."[32] Postmodernism, in
Jenkins's argument, arises from an appraisal of "what has gone wrong"
with the trajectory of progress, which was fundamental to the modern
sense of historical development and also to the discipline of history.

Like many of the other postmodern assertions, this one ends in para-
dox. The "trajectory of progress" is held to be problematic because a certain volume of common sense evidence appears to stack up against a
judgment of things getting generally better—or, this, at any rate, is the
reason the assertion resonates with our "sense" of things. But such a judgment, "the end of progress in the postmodern era," is precisely the kind of
contextualizing grand narrative that postmodernists call into question.[33]
If the "end of progress" is no more than Jenkins's choice of emplotment,
why should we care?

Like the postmodern attention to narrative, positionality and progress,
scrutiny of the problem of textuality runs into self-contradiction when
taken to an extreme. Yet, as with the other aspects of postmodernism,
there is something highly salutary about the focus on the textualization
of the past. It reminds us that the past is distant and that the only way

that we can construct an interpretation is by means of its textual remainders. It reminds us that historical documents demand interpretation: They need to be studied not only for the information they yield directly but also for their discursive organization, the conditions of their production, and the ways in which they have been used over time. Moreover, once we are finished with this process, all we have is an interpretation, never the past itself.

In this regard, postmodernism reinforces the mainstay of traditional historiography—the close reading of historical documents. At the same time, it draws systematic attention to the limitations of historians' readings, by pointing to the forces that have shaped the archive itself, its gaps and its silences.[34] Further, it calls attention to the limitations of the conceptual lenses through which we examine the texts that have survived. In these ways, postmodernism pushes historians further down the paths they have always traveled.

Beyond these salutory effects lies Chartier's "cliff." As he states it, "Recognizing that past reality is usually accessible only through texts intent on organizing it, dominating it, or representing it is not the same thing as postulating that the logocentric and hermeneutic logic governing the production of discourse is identical to the practical logic ruling conduct and actions."[35] The task, then, is not simply to give up and drown in the sea of discourse but, again, as Chartier puts it, "to link the discursive construction of the social to the social construction of discourse."[36]

Where does the postmodernist sensibility take us in relation to the contradictory stories of the Nisga'a? It points to the limitations of the authority of the written historical record, which rested in the control of only one party in the native-white conflicts. By so doing, it opens consideration of other sources of evidence—oral tradition most importantly.[37] Moreover, postmodern theory draws attention to the historical roots of the concepts of race, property, nation, civilization, which have shaped so much of that history. Postmodernism also helps to position all historical accounts in relation to the current interests of their narrators. Concurrently, it helps to hold up to critical examination assumptions of linear development and progress as the basis of accounts of native-white interactions.

But these positive contributions have a downside. If all historical knowledge is understood *simply* as a weapon in a power struggle, if all accounts of the past are epistemologically equivalent, all history is turned into collective memory. As an expression of one party's interests, collective memory bears no moral authority for other parties. If one party dominates, what grounds are there for critique or opposition? If two parties conflict, their respective collective memories provide no assistance in resolving their differences. And so postmodernism has limitations for dealing with the very problems of power and knowledge that inspire its theorists. It is only when we make our best—and always inadequate—attempts to stand beyond the blinders of collective memory that we can critique accounts that are important enough to us that we care about their truth value.

Postmodernism and the Schools

Happily, the debates among academics are ongoing. But what of others in the culture about which the academics theorize? Young people are exposed to ideas about the past in film, on television, and through a multiplicity of extracurricular sources.[38] What are *their* methods for adjudicating among different historical narratives? Do they imagine that divergent messages are entirely matters of form, cultural convention, or the social location of the narrator? In my own study of young people's viewing two films about the American West in the 1860s, *Dances with Wolves* (1990) and *The Searchers* (1956), some students explained the narrative differences between the films as the result of progressive accumulation of new facts about the past; others saw the contrasting emplotments as a consequence of the different ideological milieux of the two filmmakers.[39] While young people's ideas about the past may have strong extracurricular sources, schools, more than any other institution, are in a position either to reinforce or to counteract systematically their notions about the nature of historical knowledge.

Possibly the most creative explication of the educational possibilities of narrative theory is that presented by Tom Holt. He demonstrates ways to bring students into the process of history-making by showing them the choices available for emplotting history. Discussing a student's construction of her own autobiography, he notes:

> The facts . . . are not self-evident: their resonance, acceptance, and comprehension depend on the author's creative manipulation and insight. . . . Here she realizes that it will be different if told chronologically or as a memoir or as a movement back and forth in time. No, the facts do not

speak for themselves. Order alters meaning. It conveys to the reader what's important and what is not. To make sense, the narrative must have a point.[40]

The history student, like the historian, has an active role, even after the documents and facts are in. There are choices about the meanings to be conveyed by an historical account, and these shape the facts and documents to be mobilized. Yet, the archive can rise up and place limits. And Holt, as a practicing historian, never moves far from the archival materials. Indeed, his exercises are based on a wealth of documents; students go back and forth between the creative narrative construction and the constraining archival documents.

Holt gives us an initial hint of the impact of such work on high school students, but there is room here for more systematic study of the impact of such programs on various ages of students. What sense of the world, of knowledge, of history, does the open-ended free play of argument, plot, ideology, and narrative trope offer students? How do they become aware of the limits? Holt, for good reason, advocates opening up historiography for students, for whom it is usually a closed and finished process. But how, in this kind of program, do they learn when an account is bad history? When do they learn how to compare two accounts of the same chronicle of events? And when they do so, what kinds of explanatory means do they need in order to deal with their differences? All of these questions require different answers for different ages of students. Peter Lee and Rosalyn Ashby's current research on students' understandings of historical accounts should provide important answers to these questions.[41]

The concept of progress—a view that plots the past as a positive and interdependent development of science, technology, politics, culture, and moral life—has provided the metahistorical plot for most school textbooks. We might legitimately ask, though, whether students themselves have some sense of "the collapse of the Enlightenment project."[42] It may be that students do have a post-Enlightenment pessimism about the future, as well as a skeptical view of the knowledge that scientific expertise can produce. But, if this is the case, then the question remains what should be taught in the schools. Can one possibly serve worthwhile social goals by teaching that there is no progress in knowledge, that struggles for liberal ideals of democracy, human rights, tolerance, and economic well-being are illusory, no more than rhetorical word-play? And would a program of history so conceived have any chance of broad public support?

Applying the postmodern to a different end, there may well be tenable purposes served by a school program that teaches students to examine historical narratives for implicit notions of progress or decline. They might be taught to interrogate both the criteria that an author appeared to be using to convey a sense of historical progress (or decline) and to identify the structure of the narrative argument (i.e., the evidence upon which an implicit sense of progress or decline was based). An examination of school textbooks might yield interesting subtexts of progress, not previously made explicit to students. If these were held up to question, on the basis of the validity of their assertions, the teacher would have led the students into a disciplinary inquiry. If they were questioned in terms of the reasons that school authorities would want students to be exposed to a story of historical progress, then they would have moved into the postmodern terrain.

Conclusion

None of us would care about history education if it were not important to know the past. So, let us teach it with the best techniques for engaging students and having them retain it in memory that curriculum specialists and educational psychologists can devise. Or so the collective memorialist would argue.

But the problem is that knowing the past is both difficult and contentious on other levels. Someone must adjudicate among the different accounts of the past that might be taught in schools. Moreover, students encounter other interpretations in extracurricular culture. So, let us provide them not only with interpretations of the past but with the tools of historiography, allowing them to engage, at some level, in the ongoing debates and conversations about about the past, rather than uncritically accept any particular version. Or so the disciplinary approach to history education would have it.

But the next problem is that the tools of historiography are themselves historically contingent and positioned. If we expose students to the challenges of historical knowledge, how can we stop before we go all the way, and show them what Foucault, White, and others have unleashed on the discipline? Or so the postmodernist would argue.

This succession of epistemological stances toward history education thrusts us inexorably down a blind alley. At the end, there are two possibilities:

    a. The postmodernist arguments are flawed, refutable, and we must simply turn back and proceed on the basis of one of the other orientations to school history.
    b. The postmodernist arguments are valid: All knowledge is relative. Therefore, we can teach whatever serves our purposes in schools: history as collective memory, disciplinary history, postmodernist history, or none at all.

Neither of these possibilities itself justifies the teaching of postmodernism in the schools. A call for teaching postmodern history can never rest on the grounds that it tells the truth about the nature of historical knowledge.

Thus, at the end of a discussion about the problems of historical knowledge, the question of how to teach history in schools ironically turns back to the realm of the political. To what ends shall we teach history? If we had an easy consensus on collective memory, a knowledge of the past through tradition, then school history could be mobilized for a coherent social purpose. But, the lack of consensus is precisely what thrusts us beyond school history as consensual tradition, into the realm of history as a disciplinary practice. Disciplinary history provides students with standards for inquiry, investigation, and debate. History taught through this approach exemplifies the liberal, open society and should prepare students to participate more fully in one. Postmodernism, in turn, calls up the flaws and limitations of our own liberalism and objectivity, while resting on assumptions that destabilize the foundations of all knowledge.

Is the blind alley of my own making, a consequence of too-rigid boundaries, as I have drawn them, among the three orientations to history education? Understanding their interplay, can we find ways to introduce their various insights at different levels of schooling, while mitigating their weaknesses by being alert to their dangers and flaws? Perhaps, but only with scrutiny and discussion of history education, sustained with an intensity—and on a scale—that we are only now beginning to envision.

To historicize history is to understand that today's methods for establishing truth are no more than today's methods. And yet, that is not to say that we have no way of establishing a complex, multiperspectival historical truth for our time. To deny students an education in those methods, then, is to exclude them from full participation in contemporary culture.

NOTES

1. Cole Harris and Jean Barman, eds., *The Nisga'a Treaty*. Special issue of *BC Studies*, 120 (1998/99).

2. Paul Tennant, *Aboriginal Peoples and Politics: The Indian Land Question in British Columbia, 1849–1989* (Vancouver, BC, 1990); Joseph Gosnell, "Speech to the British Columbia Legislature, Dec. 2, 1998," *BC Studies*, 120 (1998/99), pp. 5–10.

3. Gary Nash, Charlotte Crabtree, and Ross E. Dunn, *History on Trial: Culture Wars and the Teaching of the Past* (New York, 1997).

4. Edward T. Linenthal and Tom Engelhardt, eds., *History Wars: The Enola Gay and Other Battles for the American Past* (New York, 1998).

5. Jack L. Granatstein, *Who Killed Canadian History?* (Toronto, 1998).

6. Susan McIntosh, "Re/presenting Women: The Dilemma of Social Studies Curriculum Change in B.C.," unpublished M.A. thesis, University of British Columbia (1998).

7. Arthur M. Schlesinger, Jr., *The Disuniting of America* (New York, 1992); Gertrude Himmelfarb, *On Looking into the Abyss: Untimely Thoughts on Culture and Society* (New York, 1995); Granatstein, *Who Killed?*

8. It is not surprising, in this regard, that one half of Chief Joseph Gosnell's speech to the Legislature consisted of a historical account of Nisga'a relations with White settlers. Joseph Gosnell, "Speech."

9. Alexander Stille, "The Betrayal of History," *New York Review of Books*, 45(10) (June 11, 1998), pp. 15–20.

10. David Lowenthal, *Possessed by the Past: The Heritage Crusade and the Spoils of History* (New York, 1997), p. 2.

11. Schlesinger, *Disuniting*.

12. Lowenthal, *Possessed*, p. 106.

13. See Sam Wineburg, "Historical Thinking and Other Unnatural Acts," *Phi Delta Kappan* 80(7) (1999), pp. 488–499.

14. It is also consistent with the positions advocated by Shemilt (1996) and Lee (1994, 1998). See also Lee and Ashby, and Shemilt, this volume.

15. The disciplinary advocate would reject Granatstein's dichotomy of "process" and "content" in history. Granatstein, *Who Killed*, p. 46.

16. Denis Shemilt, *History 13–16 Evaluation Study* (Edinburgh, 1980).

17. Chris Husbands, *What Is History Teaching? Language, Ideas and Meaning in Learning about the Past* (Buckingham, UK, 1996), p. 132.

18. Keith Jenkins's theoretical work is somewhat of an exception, in that it is addressed to postsecondary students: *On "What Is History?" From Carr and Elton to Rorty and White* (London, 1995). As discussed later, Husbands's *What Is History Teaching?* uses postmodernist insights to inform his exploration of school history teaching.

19. Roger Chartier, *On the Edge of the Cliff: History, Language, and Practices* (Baltimore, 1997), pp. 13–27; Himmelfarb, *Into the Abyss*; David Harlan, *The Degradation of American History* (Chicago, 1997); Granatstein, *Who Killed?*

20. Joyce Appleby, Lynn Hunt, and Margaret Jacobs, *Telling the Truth about History* (New York, 1994); Richard J. Evans, *In Defence of History* (London, 1997); Geoffrey R. Elton, *Return to Essentials: Some Reflections on the Present State of Historical Study* (Cambridge, 1991). Much of what I have to say about this orientation relies on the account of the linguistic or postmodern turn as explicated and defended by Jenkins, *Rethinking History* (London, 1991) and *On "What Is History?"* and as attacked in Chartier's *On the Edge of the Cliff*. Jenkins is a leading British commentator and one of the few who have written on the topic with an explicitly pedagogical orientation. In part because *Rethinking History* is intended as an introduction for students, Jenkins has taken care to write in as straightforward a way as the genre allows. I prefer his text to the idiosyncratic *Degradation*, by Harlan, Robert F. Berkhofer, Jr.'s obscure and convoluted *Beyond the Great Story: History as Text and Discourse* (Cambridge, 1995), and the more specialized work by Michael S. Roth, *The Ironist's Cage: Memory, Trauma, and the Construction of History* (New York, 1995). Chartier's critique is knowledgeable and moderate. He has dealt with the challenges of French theory at close quarters and acknowledges the real contributions and invigoration that they provided.

21. Jonathan Culler, *Literary Theory: A Very Short Introduction* (Oxford, 1997), p. 7.

22. Jenkins, *On "What Is History?"* p. 38.

23. Harlan, *The Degradation*.

24. Hayden White's scheme involves explanation by various forms of argument, emplotment, and ideology, all of which are related through one of four tropes: metaphor, metonymy, synecdoche, or irony. The scheme itself is beyond the scope of this paper. For the definitive discussion, see White, *Metahistory: The Historical Imagination in Nineteenth-Century Europe* (Baltimore, 1973), pp. 1–42. See also Hayden White, "New Historicism: A Comment," in Aram Veeser, ed., *The New Historicism* (London, 1989); Richard Vann, Nancy Partner, E. Domanska, and F. R. Ankersmit, "Hayden White Twenty-five Years On," *History and Theory* 37(2) (1998), pp. 143–193; Alan Munslow, *Deconstructing History* (London, 1997).

25. Chartier, *On the Edge of the Cliff*, p. 35.

26. Ibid., p. 8.

27. Jenkins, *On "What Is History?"* p. 41.

28. See Saul Friedlander, ed., *Probing the Limits of Representation: Nazism and the "Final Solution"* (Cambridge, MA, 1992).

29. Bennett, quoted in Jenkins, *On "What Is History?"* p. 17.

30. Peter Novick, *That Noble Dream: The "Objectivity Question" and the American Historical Profession* (Cambridge, 1988.)

31. Stanley Fish, "Commentary: The Young and the Restless," in Aram Veeser, ed., *The New Historicism* (New York, 1989).

32. Jenkins, *On "What Is History?"* p. 9.

33. See Berkhofer, *Beyond the Great Story*.

34. These problems are central for postcolonial and subaltern theory. See, e.g., Gyan Prakash, "Subaltern Studies as Postcolonial Criticism," *American Historical Review,* 99(5) (1994), pp. 1475–1490; Robert Young, *White Mythologies: Writing History and the West* (London, 1990); Bart Moore-Gilbert, *Postcolonial Theory: Contexts, Practices, Politics* (London, 1997).

35. Chartier, *On the Edge of the Cliff*, p. 19.

36. Ibid., p. 25; see also Mark Lilla, "The Politics of Jacques Derrida," *New York Review of Books*, 45(11) (1998), pp. 36–41.

37. For a brilliant presentation of oral and written stories, and the light that they shed on conflicting cultural values, see Julie Cruikshank, *The Social Life of Stories: Narrative and Knowledge in the Yukon Territory* (Lincoln, NE, 1998).

38. Wineburg, this volume; Peter Seixas, "Historical Understanding among Adolescents in a Multicultural Setting," *Curriculum Inquiry*, 23(3) (1993), pp. 301–327.

39. Peter Seixas, "Confronting the Moral Frames of Popular Film: Young People Respond to Historical Revisionism," *American Journal of Education,* 102 (1994), pp. 261–285. See also David Lowenthal, this volume.

40. Holt, *Thinking Historically*, p. 5. See also Husbands, *What Is History Teaching?* pp. 44–53.

41. See Peter Lee and Rosalyn Ashby, this volume.

42. The collective memorialist will have a quick retort here: Teach them what the Enlightenment is, and *then* worry about its collapse.

Chapter 2

Is It Possible to Teach Beliefs, as Well as Knowledge about History?

James V. Wertsch

In 1991, as the Soviet Union was undergoing the final stages of its disintegration, I conducted a set of interviews with ethnic Estonians in Estonia about their history. Among the topics I raised were the events in 1940 that had resulted in Estonia's becoming part of the Soviet Union. Responses to my questions varied somewhat, depending on the interviewee's life history, but in certain respects they were strikingly similar. In particular, it became clear that all the interviewees actually knew *two* accounts of the events of 1940: the official version as presented in schools, the media, and other institutions controlled by the Soviet state, and at least one unofficial version that had been learned from family, friends, underground literature, and other informal sources.

The official and unofficial histories of the events of 1940 differed along several dimensions. For example, whereas the official history was centrally produced by the Soviet state and took the form of a monolithic, coherent narrative at any particular time,[1] the unofficial history—or histor*ies*—emanated from a variety of sources and took a variety of forms. And, whereas renditions of official history texts were performed in the public sphere (e.g., at school and at commemorative events), public discussion of unofficial history was strictly banned; it was a topic to be discussed only in private settings.

These forces resulted in a situation where the structure and content of official and unofficial historical texts were quite distinct. Yet, they were related in complex ways as well: A set of dialogic processes gave rise to unofficial histories that stood in stark opposition to official ones. Rather than taking the form of coherent, independent narratives, the unofficial accounts consisted of loose collections of counterclaims to assertions found in official texts.[2] For example, whereas the official account asserted that in 1940 the vast majority of peasants and workers in Estonia demanded to join the Soviet Union, unofficial accounts often included vignettes about how rare such cases were.

Perhaps the most striking difference between these official and unofficial histories concerns the stance that the Estonians took toward the two sorts of texts. Almost without exception, they asserted that the official account of the events of 1940 was false and the unofficial ones were true. This judgment about the official history applied to some of the specific claims or propositions it included, but it applied most obviously to its "narrative truth."[3] Interviewees generally reacted quite strongly and negatively to the overall story line, or "emplotment"[4] of the official text, that is, how the text represented—or misrepresented—events, characters, and motives.

A somewhat surprising and ironic additional detail in all this is that the interviewees—or at least those who had completed their higher education before perestroika began in the 1980s—tended to know the official account as well as, if not better than, the unofficial account. These interviewees could produce a version of the official narrative almost automatically, and they could employ it with great facility when reasoning about events and the actors and motives that gave rise to them. In short, they demonstrated many of the skills we normally associate with higher-order historical thinking. Conversely, their knowledge of the unofficial accounts tended to be partial and fragmented and was often coupled with an inability to organize coherent interpretations and lines of reasoning about the past.

These interviewees demonstrated what might be called a pattern of "knowing but not believing" in the case of the official history and perhaps even "believing but not knowing" in the case of the unofficial history. These patterns stand in sharp opposition to what had been intended by the Soviet authorities, whose objective clearly was to provide instruction that would result in little, if any, conflict between knowing and believing narratives about the past.[5]

Of course, one does not have to go to the former Soviet Union to find a pattern of knowing but not believing historical narratives. It probably can be found in at least some segment of the population just about anywhere. For example, a Native American student in a U.S. university once told me in a semihumorous way: "Oh yes, what you found with the Estonians is just like our case. The only difference is that no one had the gall to tell us that we invited others here in the first place!" Similarly, Holt[6] has observed that minority students in the United States may take the stance that history is made up of "someone else's facts," suggesting a distinction between knowing and believing accounts of the past. And, authors in this volume such as Seixas and Morton raise similar issues even when dealing with history instruction in a relatively open, pluralist setting such as Canada. In general, then, one need not go far to find profiles of knowing but not believing narrative accounts about the past.

This profile of knowing but not believing raises questions about what constitutes knowledge and belief in the case of historical texts in general and how such knowledge and belief are related. I will take up these issues from the perspective of a sociocultural analysis that focuses on forms of "mediated action."[7] From this perspective, human action, including speaking, thinking, and remembering, inherently involve an irreducible tension between active agents on the one hand and the "cultural tools" they employ to carry out action on the other. Just as speaking necessarily involves the use of a particular language, with all the "affordances" and "constraints"[8] imposed by its grammar, vocabulary, and so forth, such factors come into play when representing and interpreting the past— something that is done with the help of cultural tools in the forms of texts provided by a sociocultural setting. This is not to say that human agency is not important in this process; it is simply to say that individuals and groups always act in tandem with cultural tools. In this view, representing the past is dialogic rather than a monologic production by an independent agent.

In analyzing the relationship between agents and the narratives used to represent the past, one often encounters the term "internalization." For example, we ask whether an individual or group of individuals has internalized the account of the past provided by the state. While wishing to address issues that are usually formulated in these terms, I will seek to avoid using "internalization" in what follows for two reasons. First, it is a notion that often introduces conceptual baggage, if not confusion to be avoided in my view. By employing the spatial metaphor of internalization, we are all too often tempted to search inside individuals, minds, consciousness, or some*where* else to find a concept, a value, and so forth. I have outlined elsewhere[9] some of the conceptual pitfalls this entails.

The second reason I wish to refrain from using the term "internalization" is that it conflates two relatively distinct notions that need to be differentiated, at least in discussions of whether people know and believe narratives. Elsewhere,[10] I have discussed these notions under the headings of *mastery* and *appropriation*. The mastery of a cultural tool involves knowing how to use it. For example, the mastery of historical narratives may be reflected in being able to reproduce them or in the ability to employ them to reason about the causes of events or the motives behind a group's actions. This focus on "knowing how" to use a cultural tool involves fewer and less philosophically questionable commitments to internal mental representations than accounts that focus on "knowing that."[11] For my purposes, however, the main point is that mastery of a cultural tool falls primarily under the heading of cognitive functioning and has relatively little to do with emotional commitment to narratives as "identity resources."[12] In the case of national historical narratives mastery is concerned with the ability to "think the nation"[13] but tells us little about the emotional ties and forms of attachment required in the formation of "imagined communities."[14]

An example of what I am calling mastery in connection with history can be found in the research of Beck and McKeown.[15] In a study of U.S. elementary school students' responses to questions about the American Revolution, they identified several patterns of change in knowledge between fifth and eighth grades. Some students began with sketchy but basically correct information and then improved over the fifth grade and maintained this knowledge until eighth grade; some students began with incomplete but accurate information and then improved over fifth grade, only to regress by the beginning of the eighth grade; some began with little or no accurate information and never made progress; and so forth.

The general—and generally sobering—findings reported by these authors were that "the single most striking pattern across all the data was the amount of confusion that was manifested in students' responses after fifth-grade instruction and before eighth-grade instruction."[16] While these findings were not formulated in terms of the distinction between mastery and appropriation, the focus on the cognitive abilities involved in remembering texts and using them as foundations for reasoning about events means that they fall under the heading of the former.

The process of appropriating historical narratives involves a different sort of relationship between agent and cultural tool than does cognitive mastery. The construct of appropriation that I am employing derives from the Russian term *prisvoenie* as used by Bakhtin.[17] The root of this term and the associated verb *prisvoit'* are related to the reflexive term *svoi* ("one's own"). The prefix *pri* carries the meaning of "movement toward." Hence *prisvoit'* means bringing something toward or into oneself or making it one's own, and the noun *prisvoenie* means something like the process of making something one's own. This sense of making a text one's own involves an emotional dimension that may operate quite independent of cognitive mastery; hence, the need to avoid reducing appropriation to mastery.

The opposite of appropriation in this sense is resistance, which involves distancing oneself from a text.[18] Just because someone is exposed to a cultural tool—and just because the person has mastered it—does not mean that the individual has made it his or her own. This seems to be precisely the case with the Estonians' knowing but not believing official Soviet history. As evidenced by their ability to recite and otherwise use official historical narratives, the Estonian interviewees demonstrated mastery of these texts. However, instead of believing or appropriating them, they resisted them, partly through their knowledge of alternative, unofficial accounts.

As I outline them in this chapter, the issues of mastery and appropriation are part of an analytic framework concerned with mediated action. However, much of what I have to say about them is related to observations made from other theoretical perspectives as well. For example, "history" and "heritage" as used by Lowenthal[19] do not map directly onto mastery and appropriation, but the distinctions are related. Specifically, it is not unusual for "history" to be mastered but not be fully appropriated, whereas the opposite pattern often emerges for "heritage."

Psychological and Sociocultural Aspects of Appropriation

In what follows, I will explore some aspects of appropriation (as well as its opposite, resistance). This focus does not reflect the assumption that we have a complete account of how people master historical texts. Instead, it stems from the fact that, in contrast to the concept of mastery, on which there is an existing body of research,[20] the issue of how texts are appropriated has hardly been explored at all, at least in psychological research. In order to outline how one might go about examining this issue, I shall review appropriation first as a psychological issue and then as an issue of sociocultural context.

Psychological Aspects

Some useful insights about the appropriation of historical texts can be gleaned from the research of "self-determination theory."[21] In their review of studies of familial socialization from this perspective, Grolnick et al.[22] argue that it involves "inner adaptation to social requirements so that children not only comply with these requirements but also accept and endorse the advocated values and behaviors, experiencing them as their own."[23]

The theme of accepting, endorsing, and experiencing values and behaviors as one's own runs through the writings on self-determination theory. While a perspective concerned with mediated action differs in that it would focus on narrative texts and other cultural tools (as opposed to values and behaviors) as the objects to be accepted, endorsed, and experienced as one's own, there are some interesting parallels to be found between the two approaches. In both cases, the emphasis is primarily on what de Certeau[24] has termed "consumption." Indeed, Grolnick et al. implicitly address how consumption contrasts with production when they note the "potential contradiction between the forces of socialization that attempt to promote compliance with culturally transmitted behaviors and attitudes, and the children's need to actively assimilate new values and behaviors if they are to accept them as their own."[25]

One of the most important implications of self-determination theory for my purposes is that it provides a nuanced account of internalization, or what I am terming appropriation. From its perspective:

> Internalization . . . concerns the processes by which individuals acquire beliefs, attitudes, or behavioral regulations from external sources and progressively transform those external regulations into personal attributes, values, or regulatory styles. . . . [T]his definition highlights that full or optimal internalization involves not only taking in a value or regulation but also integrating it with one's sense of self—that is, making it one's own—so the resulting behavior will be fully chosen or *self*-regulated.[26]

From this perspective, different types and degrees of internalization exist. Grolnick et al.[27] stress that "internalization is . . . not an all-or-nothing phenomenon. Rather, it concerns the degree to which an activity initially regulated by external sources is perceived as one's own and is experienced as self-determined."[28] These authors outline a developmental path that begins with external regulation and moves to introjected regulation and regulation through identification, and they argue that the most mature form occurs "when the identification as been *integrated* . . . with other aspects of one's self."[29] In general, then, levels of internalization have to do with

> whether a value or regulation that has been taken in by the person, has been fully integrated and thus has what we . . . refer to as an internal (rather than an external) perceived locus of causality. If a behavior is experienced as fully chosen and autonomously undertaken, it would have an internal perceived locus of causality, whereas if it is experienced as pressured or coerced by an internal force, it would have an external perceived locus of causality. In the latter case, the regulatory process would be within the person but would not have been fully integrated.[30]

The major message to take away from these comments about self-determination theory is that any complete account of the appropriation of historical texts must address the issues of levels of appropriation and how these levels exist in a dynamic system. Believing, appropriating, or resisting texts is perhaps never a simple, all-or-nothing affair, and statements such as my own about "knowing but not believing" official accounts of history accordingly stand in need of revision.

While recognizing the important insights offered by self-determination theory, I would like to sound a cautionary note as well—one that perhaps has more to do with harnessing this theory in new areas than with where it was originally formulated. This cautionary note has to do with avoiding the pitfalls of "methodological individualism."[31] With regard to the issues being addressed here, the point is to avoid the temptation to reduce appropriation to an individual psychological phenomenon or attribute, a temptation that is heightened by discussions of integration into self systems and so forth.

A form of methodological individualism that is of particular concern when considering historical texts is the "essentialism" that so often plays a role in nationalism and national identity. As authors such as Calhoun[32] note, essentialism has played a particular and a particularly dangerous role in nationalism almost since its beginning. In spite of numerous warnings that nations are not "a natural, God-given way of classifying men"[33] but are instead more on the order of "invented traditions,"[34] there continues to be a powerful tendency among people in the modern world to assume that nationality is some sort of inalienable essence or attribute of individuals (almost like IQ in the popular imagination). This has played out with disastrous consequences in connection with racial, ethnic, and religious criteria and, ever since the efforts by figures such as Herder[35] and Fichte[36] to find the spirit of a people in language, folklore, and literature, the implications for historical narratives are clear as well.

In short, major theoretical as well as ethical and political problems arise when we begin to view the appropriation of a historical narrative as creating some sort of inalienable psychological essence of the individual. In contrast, I wish to emphasize that it is crucial to invoke some sort of sociocultural analysis as well.

Sociocultural Aspects

One of the most obvious ways to avoid the pitfalls of methodological individualism in this case is to take into consideration the contextual variability of appropriation. This means approaching belief systems as dynamic and contextually specific rather than as static attributes of individuals. Even in the case of a single individual, what is said and thought in one setting may vary greatly from what is said and thought in another. Who is not familiar with the experience of finding oneself in a rhetorical setting where one ends up defending a position that one had never really thought about or had even rejected? In such cases, we find ourselves saying things like, "I never thought I would say this, but . . . "

Of course, this is not to argue that there is no such thing as appropriating texts in a psychological sense or that individuals are totally malleable, depending on the context in which they happen to find themselves. Instead of accepting this radical alternative to the assumption that beliefs are static essences of individuals, the point is to explore an intermediate, yet principled, framework in which texts serve as "identity resources"[37] to be mastered and to be employed in particular contexts in a variety of flexible ways.

A complete account of these matters would involve addressing issues about the contexts of speaking and thinking and, indeed, about human nature that go far beyond what I can undertake here. Hence I shall restrict my focus to one dimension and one comparison of how political and cultural settings influence the appropriation of official history.

In my earlier discussion of official history in Soviet Estonia, I noted that adherence to a single, monolithic view of the past was strictly enforced in the public sphere. The tight central control of instruction, the media, and other sources of information was complemented by harsh sanctions for publicly discussing alternative interpretations. The mere possession of a competing account of the past such as a book by Aleksandr Solzhenitsyn could be punished by the loss of one's job or a lengthy prison term, depending on the period and circumstances. The overall effect of such repression is still far from understood, but one thing that is clear is that, at least among certain circles, this system resulted in making history a highly contested matter and resulted in the emergence of unofficial accounts that stood in clear opposition to the official version.

In Estonia, as well as in Russia and other parts of the Soviet Union, the 1970s and 1980s were characterized by growing cynicism about official history and an increasingly active and public production of unofficial histories through the underground press, jokes, drama, and other avenues. One upshot of all this was a growing salience of unofficial accounts of the past and an intensified opposition between official and unofficial histories. In this context, the debate was often heated, and as a result the opposing sides and accounts emerged in very sharp ways.

Such a sociocultural setting stands in contrast to the context for learning and discussing history in the West over the same period. In this latter context, numerous efforts have been made in the public sphere to provide counterforces to state control over history instruction. For example, investigators such as Lee[38] have outlined ways of incorporating genuine and active process of historical knowledge-building in instruction. Such efforts seek to introduce a far wider range of perspectives than characterized public political debate and instruction in the former Soviet Union.

Of course one should not overlook the power of the state everywhere, including in the West, in these matters. One has only to consider the consequences for a student of failing to pass mandatory examinations on American and state history—*official* history, to recognize that states everywhere have the interest and the means to compel students to master an official account of the past (with the intention of appropriating it as well). To note such parallels, however, should not blind one to the major differences between the Soviet Union and places like the United States in terms of the impact of centralized control over information and discourse in the public sphere.

Some hint of how these differences might play out in history instruction can be found in studies by investigators such as Seixas[39] and Barton and Levstik.[40] The results of their studies suggest that, instead of having a single, coherent account of the past, North American middle and high school students often hold multiple, vaguely competing, and often somewhat confused views. Much of this heterogeneity takes the form of the contestation between "vernacular" and "official" culture as outlined by Bodnar,[41] but even with this in mind it is striking that students seem not to be particularly aware of, let alone concerned with, the fact that several different accounts emerge in their understanding of history.

It is precisely on this issue of how competing accounts of the past arise and are interrelated that the situation in the West seems to differ from that in the former Soviet Union. For the ethnic Estonians I interviewed, competing accounts stood in stark opposition as official and unofficial histories, an opposition characterized by strong resistance to the former and appropriation of the latter. We still do not fully understand the political and cultural forces that gave rise to this state of affairs, but my strong hunch is that the strict imposition of a single, tightly coherent historical narrative provided a good "target" for opposition and a wellspring of alternatives. Determined, prolonged resistance to official accounts of the past (accounts that, again, underwent many abrupt "revisions") seems to have resulted in a kind of clear, if not stark, opposition between it and unofficial histories.

The findings with North American students reported by Seixas and Barton and Levstik suggest an alternative scenario. In this case, students seem to have mastered, at least partially, more than one account of the past, but these multiple accounts were apparently not organized into clear-cut, oppositional categories of narratives to be appropriated or resisted. By the standards of the Estonian interviewees, there is a kind of indifference or agnosticism toward historical narratives, both those produced by the state and those emerging out of vernacular culture. In short, both the public discourse and the psychological representation of history seem to be organized in quite different ways in the two settings.

Conclusion

Understanding the impact of history instruction is a complex issue that will require contributions from many theoretical perspectives. In this chapter I have outlined one such perspective having to do with mediated action. From this standpoint, human action is understood as involving an irreducible tension between active agents and cultural tools provided by a sociocultural setting. The specific cultural tools that I have considered when examining knowledge and belief about history are narrative texts.

As suggested by the Estonian case reviewed earlier, we have told only part of the story when we assess the cognitive knowledge generated through history instruction. In addition, there is the question of being committed to, or believing, particular texts. The distinction between such knowledge and belief becomes very clear when considering cases such as Estonians' interpretation of the events that led up to their becoming part of the Soviet Union in 1940. Specifically, they showed considerable mastery of a basic official history of these events, but it ended up being a target of resistance rather than appropriation. In short, appropriation did *not* follow mastery in the way intended by Soviet authorities.

Such findings raise a host of general questions about the nature of mastery and appropriation. I have argued that these two processes can be adequately understood neither in purely psychological nor in sociocultural terms. Although the forces of appropriation and resistance operate in both spheres, this does not suggest that some kind of simple parallel exists between them. Instead, we are looking at a situation that involves interlocking, complementary systems at the level of sociocultural context and individual psychology, and the temptation to reduce one to another must be avoided.

Whatever the outcome of detailed investigation of these issues, what is clear already is that we will need to introduce the notion of appropriation as well as mastery into our discussions of history instruction and its consequences. Much of our current research is grounded in the implicit assumption that, if we can encourage and assess the mastery of historical texts, we have encouraged and assessed their appropriation. This clearly was not the case for the Estonians I interviewed, and we don't really know whether it is the case for anyone else. Exploring the various possibilities will be an important part of the process of trying to understand whether we can teach belief as well as knowledge about history.

NOTES

The writing of this paper was assisted by a grant from the Spencer Foundation. The statements made and the views expressed are solely the responsibility of the author.

1. Even though it took on the appearance of permanence, the official account changed from time to time, a fact reflected in the standard joke "Nothing is so unpredictable as Russia's past."

2. Peeter Tulviste and James V. Wertsch, "Official and Unofficial Histories: The Case of Estonia," *Journal of Narrative and Life History*, 4(4) (1994), 311–329; James V. Wertsch, *Mind as Action* (New York and Oxford, 1998).

3. Louis O. Mink, "Narrative Form as a Cognitive Instrument," in Robert H. Canary and Henry Kozicki, eds., *The Writing of History: Literary Form and Historical Understanding* (Madison, 1978), pp. 129–149.

4. Paul Ricouer. *Time and Narrative*, vol. 1 (Chicago, 1984) (translated by Kathleen McLaughlin and David Pellauer).

5. Wertsch, *Mind as Action*.

6. Thomas Holt, *Thinking Historically: Narrative, Imagination and Understanding* (New York, 1990).

7. Wertsch, *Mind as Action*.

8. Ibid.

9. James V. Wertsch, Commentary on J. A. Lawrence and J. Valsiner, "Conceptual Roots of Internalization: From Transmission to Transformation," *Human Development*, 36(3) (1993), pp. 168–171; Wertsch, *Mind as Action*.

10. Wertsch, "Conceptual Roots of Internalization"; Wertsch, *Mind as Action*.

11. Gilbert Ryle, *The Concept of Mind* (New York, 1949).

12. James V. Wertsch. "Vygotsky and Bakhtin on Community," unpublished paper, Washington University, 1998.

13. Benedict Anderson, *Imagined Communities: Reflections on the Origin and Spread of Nationalism* (London, 1991).

14. Ibid.

15. Isabel L. Beck and Margaret G. McKeown, "Outcomes of History Instruction: Paste-Up Accounts," in Mario Carretero and James. F. Voss, eds., *Cognitive and Instructional Processes in History and the Social Sciences* (Hillsdale, NJ, 1994) 237–256.

16. Ibid., p. 250.

17. Mikhail M. Bakhtin, *The Dialogic Imagination: Four Essays by M. M. Bakhtin* (edited by M. Holquist; translated by C. Emerson and M. Holquist) (Austin, 1981).

18. Wertsch, *Mind as Action*.

19. David Lowenthal, *Possessed by the Past: The Heritage Crusade and the Spoils of History* (New York, 1996); David Lowenthal, this volume.

20. Beck and McKeown, "Outcomes of History Instruction: Paste-Up Accounts," Margaret G. McKeown and Isabel L. Beck, "The Assessment and Characterization of a Young Learner's Knowledge of a Topic in History," *American Educational Research Journal*, 27 (1990), pp. 688–726.

21. Edward L. Deci, Harold Eghrari, C. Patrick Bruce, and Donald R. Leone, "Facilitating Internalization: The Self-Determination Theory Perspective," *Journal of Personality*, 62 (1994), 119–142; Wendy S. Grolnick, Edward L. Deci, and Richard M. Ryan, "Internalization within the Family: The Self-Determination

Theory Perspective," in Joan E. Grusec and Leon Kuczynski, eds., *Parenting and Children's Internalization* (New York, 1997), pp. 135–161.

22. Ibid.

23. Ibid., p. 135.

24. Michel de Certeau, *The Practice of Everyday Life* (Berkeley, 1984) (translated by Steven F. Rendall).

25. Grolnick, Deci, and Ryan, "Internalization," p. 135.

26. Ibid., p. 139.

27. Grolnick, Deci, and Ryan, "Internalization."

28. Ibid., p. 140.

29. Ibid., p. 141.

30. Ibid., p. 140.

31. Steven Lukes, "Methodological Individualism Reconsidered," in *Essays in Social Theory* (New York, 1977), pp. 177–186; Wertsch, *Mind as Action.*

32. Craig Calhoun, *Nationalism* (Minneapolis, 1997).

33. Ernest Gellner, *Nations and Nationalism* (Ithaca, NY, 1983), p. 49.

34. Eric Hobsbawm and Terrence Ranger, *The Invention of Tradition* (Cambridge, 1983).

35. Johann G. Herder, *On the Origin of Language* (Chicago, 1966).

36. Johann G. Fichte. *Address to the German Nation* (New York, 1968) (first published in 1807–1808).

37. Wertsch, "Vygotsky and Bakhtin on Community."

38. Peter Lee, "Historical Knowledge and the National Curriculum," in Hilary Bourdillon, ed., *Teaching History* (London, 1993), pp. 41–48.

39. Peter Seixas, "Historical Understanding among Adolescents in a Multicultural Setting," *Curriculum Inquiry*, 23 (1993), pp. 301–337.

40. Kenneth C. Barton and Linda S. Levstik, "'It Wasn't a Good Part of History': National Identity and Students' Explanations of Historical Significance," *Teachers College Record*, 99 (1998), pp. 478–513.

41. John Bodnar, *Remaking America: Public Memory, Commemoration, and Patriotism in the Twentieth Century* (Princeton, 1992).

Chapter 3

Teaching and Learning History in Canada

Desmond Morton

July 1 is Canada Day, the anniversary of the proclamation of the new Dominion of Canada in 1867 as a confederation of three self-governing colonies, from then on to be four provinces and, eventually, today, ten provinces and three territories. It is a statutory holiday, celebrated with modest enthusiasm in much of the country. In Montreal, most of the city's tenants observe it as their annual moving day.

An Ignorance of Historical Facts

In 1997, 130 years after Confederation, the Canada Day celebration was marked by the cross-country release of a poll by the Angus Reid organization, financed by the Donner Foundation and sponsored by the brand-new Dominion Institute. From a sample of 1,104 young Canadians, 18–24 years old, the Institute reported truly lamentable ignorance of Canada's history. Barely half could name our first prime minister, almost two-thirds did not know the date of confederation, and 36 percent could not identify the century in which confederation took place. Two-fifths of the sample did not know the enemy in the First World War: more than a third guessed that it included Britain, France, and Russia. Most thought the first Canadian astronaut was Neil Armstrong.

As published by most of Canada's daily papers and as a news feature for holiday news packages on radio and television, the Dominion Institute survey produced much "viewing with alarm" and demands for better performance from a much-abused public school system.[1] While conventional wisdom, based on juvenile memories, insists that Canadian history is dull, it must nonetheless be learned. Schools and their teachers were obviously falling down on the job.

The Dominion Institute provided the guidance. An essay by Daniel Gardner, a young, conservative editorialist for the Ottawa *Citizen*, acknowledged that knowledge of history facts did not constitute historical understanding but asserted that they were part of the common cultural heritage. While history had acquired a dreary reputation among school children, the current ignorance was a result of its disappearance from the curriculum in four of Canada's provinces and the exiguous rations provided in most of the remainder—a single compulsory high school course in Ontario, Canada's biggest province.

Across Canada, "social studies"—dismissed as "kiddie sociology" by one of the Institute's consultants—had displaced history. The culprit, of course, was "progressive pedagogy," with its acquiescence in child-centered choices.[2] The answer, supplied by Gardner and endorsed by the Institute's young president, Rudyard Griffiths, was a "National History Framework," "a minimal list of the people and events to which every child educated in Canada's schools must be introduced" as "the basis upon which more profound historical understanding would be pursued."

Viewing with Alarm

Since the Dominion Institute's first survey in July 1997, other surveys have followed at intervals. In November, the Institute reported that most young Canadians would have failed the rather elementary quiz applied by Citizenship Courts to people who want to be naturalized. In July 1998 the Institute featured results of a basic test of civic knowledge. Young Canadians, it announced, "hadn't a clue." They might be proud of their national health insurance system, but few could say when it had begun and in which province. At first, most historians and teachers disdained the Dominion Institute's history quiz. The questions themselves were at the lowest level of Bloom's Taxonomy, and two of the official answers were actually incorrect.[3] However, the teaching of history rapidly became an issue, usually on terms framed by the Dominion Institute. In the face of citizen protests, led by war veterans, Manitoba's Conservative government dropped plans to abolish the subject. L. R. Wilson, the retiring chief executive of Bell Canada International, pledged half a million dollars of his own money to promote the cause of history in the schools. J. R. Miller, president of the Canadian Historical Association, complained that professional historians had been sidelined and ignored in the debate.[4] Professor J. L. Granatstein, recently retired from Toronto's York University, promptly responded. In *Who Killed Canadian History?*, he identified the killers as politicians, bureaucrats, and many of his former university colleagues, especially social, feminist, and multicultural historians. By ignoring political, military, and diplomatic topics, they had confused, misled, and bored most students.[5] The book was a Canadian best-seller in the summer of 1998.

As ever, French-speaking Quebec marched to its own drummer. True to the provincial motto, "Je me souviens" (I remember), history has regained a once-threatened place in the curriculum, reinforced by a compulsory exam at the end of Secondary 4 (10th grade). Indeed, in the wake of a report by a task force headed by popular historian Jacques Lacoursière,[6] the education minister, Pauline Marois, promised to double the number of hours devoted to history and to spread its study through all school years. To find time, home economics would suffer. She would, claimed Marois, prefer to teach her sons to cook. The political response was divided. Diehard sovereignists condemned the Lacoursière group's recommendations for the study of world history and for more attention to Quebec's English minority and Aboriginal peoples. Monique Nemni, editor of the federalist *Cité Libre*, warned that additional history courses would merely add separatist propaganda.[7] Marois's business-minded successor has frozen her reforms for a year.

Textbooks in English-speaking provinces certainly include the history of French Canada, though the results may not be conducive to national understanding. On the basis of polling by the SOM organization, the November 1998 issue of *l'Actualité*, Quebec's news magazine, reported that Quebeckers have a much more sympathetic stereotype of English-Canadians than the reverse. Why do Quebeckers appear more careless, hypocritical, and ignorant and less patriotic, open-minded and realistic than "les Anglais"?[8] One explanation, claimed historian Daniel Francis, could be found in history textbooks, where students receive their only systematic introduction to their fellow citizens. Francis reported the depiction of cheerful, childlike *habitants*, dominated by their seigneurs and priests until British invaders imposed democracy, commerce, and progress.[9]

History Wars with a Canadian Spin

Hearing about the debate over the teaching of Canadian history, Americans may have a sense of déjà vu. Comparative historians have produced evidence that Canada is about a decade behind its neighbor to the south. Historically minded Canadians will recognize the latest round of an enduring struggle. At ten- or twenty-year intervals, Canadian students have been found ill informed, their teachers have been judged incompetent, and their schools have been deemed in need of some variant of the current ideology. In the 1960s, the recipe was imaginative pedagogy; in a more conservative age, the answer is a Canadian version of national standards. Professor Granatstein, now director of Canada's War Museum in Ottawa, demands a return to the study of politics, battles, and heroes and federal intervention to rescue history from "educational theorists and the timid provincial politicians."[10]

Canadians have some reason to worry about the level of historical consciousness among their fellow citizens. Constitutional reforms, based largely on Quebec's historic claim to "distinct" status in Confederation, failed in 1990 and again in 1992 because of a widespread refusal to heed "old-fashioned" Quebec concerns that challenged the individual equality enshrined in Canada's 1982 Charter of Rights and Freedoms. The resulting frustration in Quebec sent support for secession soaring from 30 to 60 percent by the summer of 1990. In 1994 Quebeckers elected their second sovereignist government. On October 30, 1995, 49.4 percent of Quebeckers voted yes on an elaborate and mystifying question that could have given Premier Jacques Parizeau a mandate to secede from Canada. Would proper instruction in Canada's history have inoculated Quebeckers from disloyalty? Alternatively, would proper teaching have rallied Quebeckers to reverse the verdict of 1759?

Federalist historians argue that francophones have exercised enormous power in Canada since 1867 and that their language, culture, and distinctive institutions are stronger than ever. A compulsory course on Quebec and Canada, reinforced with a province-wide exam, emphasizes the status of French Canadians as a minority and Quebec's endless struggle for its rights in an indifferent or hostile Canada. Outside Quebec, young Canadians seldom hear of the French-English partnership on which Confederation was based in 1867 or of Quebec's view of what follows when the principles of partnership are ignored. Few students anywhere in Canada learn how the Royal Proclamation of 1763 has become a charter of Aboriginal rights in what remains of the territories of George III and his heirs.

History is a "user's manual" for a Canada dependent on accommodation and compromise. If, like many such manuals, it is tossed into a bottom drawer and forgotten, who will know how to cope with problems? The Quebec-Canada debate on secession has become essentially ahistorical. If few Canadians know even elementary facts about their history, what community of national experience can they share? "Those who would rend the country asunder," proclaimed Gardner, "will make another attempt soon and the pressures which so buffet national memory will only grow in strength."[11] In the Prime Minister's office and among business leaders, the Dominion Institute's message has been received, studied, and filed for action.

Ten or More Histories to Teach

While Professor Granatstein seeks resolute federal action, education remains the most jealously guarded of provincial jurisdictions. In 1864 most Fathers of Canadian Confederation wanted a strong central government. They agreed with Lincoln that, more than slavery, an excess of states rights had led to the U.S. Civil War. The major powers of a nineteenth-century government—railways, canals, banking, tariffs—were entrenched in Ottawa. Over a century, social change, judicial interpretation, and regional politics have gradually reversed the original intention. Canada is now among the most decentralized of federations. In 1867 responsibilities too trivial for Ottawa—roads, schools, direct taxation, and "charitable and eleemosynary institutions"—were left to the provinces. Today, health, education, and welfare are among the most costly responsibilities of government. Canada's provinces collectively spend far more than Ottawa. Some of Ottawa's biggest expenditures are transfers to the provinces to deliver jointly funded health, social, and educational programs and to level up the quality of services delivered by the poorer provinces.

In the 1860s only Ontario and Nova Scotia had public school systems, but, even then, education was a sensitive issue. The rights of religious and linguistic minorities were salient concerns of the Confederation era. As

Fathers of Confederation, D'Arcy McGee and George-Étienne Cartier spoke of protecting "cultural nations"—English, French, Scots, and Irish—in a single new "political nation." To his fellow French-Canadians, Cartier insisted that their rights as French-speaking Catholics would be secure because in Quebec they would control every issue that mattered to their cultural survival, from the solemnization of marriage to schooling. So it has proved. What Cartier's fellow confederates failed to foresee was that other provinces would become almost as firm as Quebec in asserting and even expanding their authority.

As a tool for shaping citizens, public education was a nineteenth-century invention, and history was its sharpest blade. In English-speaking provinces, national identity was initially British. From Lunenburg to Esquimalt, school history initially meant memorizing the kings and queens of England and the significance of 1066, 1214, and 1588. The cost of British allegiance came home to Canadians after they lost 62,000 men in the First World War. A new, more strictly Canadian nationalism became fashionable. In the 1920s, Canada's own history emerged in the schools. Former students recall an often monotonous emphasis on explorers and pioneers and a nervous avoidance of the near present. The program became politically charged. British Columbia banned its first Canadian history text; the author, W. L. Grant, headmaster of Upper Canada College and a decorated veteran, had dared to explain Quebec's "un-British" opposition to the war effort.[12] All provinces have maintained the tradition of political and community control of history and social studies teaching. As in the United States, regional patterns may be discernible, but each province has a distinct program.[13] As a child in socialist Saskatchewan in the late 1940s, I learned the virtues of cooperatives and absorbed the doctrine that the West's problems were largely caused by the financial barons of Montreal and Toronto. Later governments, of a more right-wing bent, approved textbooks that taught that the sinners had moved to Ottawa and woefully expanded the government. In pre-1960s Quebec, wisdom was represented by the Vatican. History focused on the struggle of French Canadians to survive imperial follies and English-speaking prejudices.[14] To this day, Canada's schools close for the 24th of May holiday; in English-speaking Canada, children explode fireworks to evoke a faint memory of Queen Victoria; Quebec students parade for la Fête de Dollard des Ormeaux, remembering a man killed in battle with the Iroquois in May 1660 and popularized by the historian Canon Lionel Groulx as a devout martyr who saved Montreal.[15]

Was It Better in the Past?

Wherever taught, Canadian history soon acquired a dreary reputation in schools. Exceptional teachers will always inspire students, but the cautious or the ill qualified avoid trouble through such time-honored strategies as copying notes on the blackboard and drilling students for predictable examination questions. Principal Maurice Hutton, of Toronto's University College, once declared that Canadian history was "as dull as ditchwater": generations of students agreed.[16]

The problem has been rediscovered often. In an essay for the Massey-Lévesque Commission on the state of Canada's culture, one of the members, Professor Hilda Neatby, condemned school history, a foretaste of her much-read condemnation of Canada's public schools, *So Little for the Mind*. In 1962 a prominent literary critic, Professor Northrop Frye of Victoria College, told the Toronto School Board that not much would be lost "if history, as presently prescribed and taught, were dropped entirely from the curriculum." A decade later, after a study funded by his employer, Trinity College School, Bernard Hodgetts published *What Culture? What Heritage?*, a savage denunciation of how young Canadians were taught their history. His crusade for Canadian Studies fitted the nationalist mood of the 1970s. Funding for the resulting Canadian Studies Foundation did not survive the decade. Speaking in 1996, Professor Ken Osborne, a respected observer of the history and social studies scene, concluded that "it seems reasonably clear that most students are not being led to think about the Canadian past . . . in any coherent or systematic way." Osborne had to add that he knew of no "golden age" for Canadian history teachers or learners.[17]

Like others, many Canadians believed history to be "scientific," full of objective, officially sanctioned truths. The federal Royal Commission on Bilingualism and Biculturalism in the 1960s was shocked to find that sharply different versions of history were being taught to English and French-speaking students.[18]

Some Commission members also insisted that Canada was "multicultural," not "bicultural," a proposition formally accepted by Ottawa in 1972 and much earlier in some western provinces, where francophones were a small minority. Outside Quebec, bilingualism was official policy, but multiculturalism became incompatible with traditional attempts to squeeze Ukrainian, Polish, German, or Native memories into conformity with Anglo culture. Rather than face the challenge of incorporating multiple perspectives or the dreariness of "recognition history," most education departments found safety in social studies. History diminished or vanished, its departure hastened by an emphasis on language, mathematics, and other job-readying skills.

In the Present

Like many history teachers, the Dominion Institute deplored the social studies trend.[19] Its motives were patriotic. But does the study of history inculcate patriotic citizenship? The evidence is mixed. As Laval University education professor Christian Laville wryly notes, the generation that created Quebec's sovereignty movement in the 1960s was educated by the Christian Brothers in the 1940s and 1950s to be loyal Canadians.

And how important is the school role? It is not solely or primarily because we sat through history classes that we understand the past. As David Lowenthal has elegantly reminded us, we encounter the past in a host of guises, in the street, when we shop and when we travel, and when we walk past a cemetery, the county courthouse, or a war memorial.[20] It emerges in all but the most determinedly featureless suburb. The past may be a foreign country, but it shares our present through place names, cherished knickknacks, or our own family roots, however short or damaged. In a classroom, the past is seldom real. To share it, youngsters must be exposed to special places or times: museums, heritage sites, Black History Month. As the managers of the Disney Corporation and their competitors demonstrate, history is good for tourism. Canadian taxes rebuilt Louisbourg and L'Anse aux Meadows in hope of drawing travelers to the bleak and impoverished extremities of Cape Breton Island and Newfoundland. Few towns or villages have allowed the flow of travelers to ignore whatever they have that is ancient, quaint or merely curious.

Cultivating Historical Understanding

Through history, students can learn "historical understanding": the fundamentals of causation, sequence, and relationships that distinguish "history" in its full intellectual rigor from that magpie's nest of diamonds and baubles called "heritage." Such an approach, as Quebec's leading popular historian, Jacques Lacoursière, argued, is rich in the "skills" that preoccupy contemporary educational policymakers. In his working group report, Lacoursière summarized the benefits of teaching "historical thinking":

> It is through history that we understand the mechanisms of change and continuity, and the many ways in which problems are posed and resolved in society. We learn to recognize and weigh the different interests beliefs, experiences and circumstances that guide human beings inside and outside their own societies, in the past and in the present. History enables us to understand how such interests, beliefs and experiences drive human beings to construct knowledge, and makes us aware of the value of knowledge and of its relative nature.[21]

That learning does not necessarily occur in schools. We can learn much about the past from a film on the Plains Cree leader Big Bear or from a museum visit or from the reminiscences of an elderly war veteran, but when these interludes are over, what remains are memories, unassociated with any broader pattern of evidence or experience.[22] Only through the systematic, fully informed study of history can we discover the tragic dilemma of western treaty-making, the meaning of a wealthy family's silverware, or the social context of joining the Canadian Army in 1939.

Without sequence, context, and linkages, without thoughtful examination of the evidence, the past becomes episodic, romanticized, and ultimately meaningless. Without history, we may have a host of memories, but we lack the tools to transform memories into the logical pattern we call experience. Without experience, we remain children, prone to repeat even our most painful mistakes. The benefit of applying intellectual discipline to our past, not the obligation to cram selected dates and facts into young heads, provides the best case for reviving school history.

Is This What History Teachers Understand?

Of course, this is not the argument currently being made for history in Canada any more than it was the inspiration for the Bradley Commission in the United States. Indeed, if "historical thinking" displaced the memorization of approved facts and an approved "framework" as a major goal for the history promoters, would some of the official and corporate enthusiasm for school history fade? In Canada, the Dominion Institute, the Prime Minister's Office, and business leaders are not mobilizing resources for history to encourage awkward questions about

French-English relations or the recurrent failures of business orthodoxy, or whether the Royal Proclamation of 1763 granted Aborigines title to the land under their homes, farms, or businesses.

Is "historical understanding" a practical goal for most history teachers in Canadian classrooms? However valuable to a civilized human and an involved citizen, "thinking historically" is a sophisticated concept, an outcome of professional training, insight, and time. These are all scarce assets. In most Canadian provinces, teacher training now favors professional courses offered within faculties of education. Distinct in other ways, Quebec has joined a trend. Following a pattern evident in Canada's western provinces, new Quebec teachers will henceforth complete degrees in pedagogy, not in arts or science. They will require explicit academic qualifications only to teach languages and mathematics. As a rally of teachers and historians at the University of Montréal complained in 1997, Quebec expects teachers to deliver a larger, more sophisticated history program without requiring them to know any history.[23] Self-taught enthusiasts can teach history brilliantly, but who can bring enthusiasm, insight, and synthetic skill to a subject he or she barely knows?[24]

School history has plenty of supporters in contemporary Canada. An Environics poll at the end of January 1999, just before McGill's well-attended conference on "Giving the Past a Future," found that 86 percent of Canadians considered it very important that students learn history in school, and almost as many claimed that they wanted to learn more themselves.[25] The current enthusiasm for school history—heaviest among older and influential Canadians—may not necessarily benefit students. Memorizing a few hundred facts will not, in Fernand Dumont's phrase, persuade the young that they are free "to *read* history and to *make* it as well."[26] While many current curriculum documents bow to the significance of context and chronology and even mention the challenge of "historical thinking," themes and issues and concepts dominate.

Under current pressure, Canadian educational authorities may impose more history instruction on the young, but, as in so many other changes in education, reformers have good reason to worry about their success. More of the old style of history could conceivably kill the subject. But, the new, critical style demands a preparation and a commitment only a minority of current or prospective teachers may be able to deliver. Yet, without that kind of training, the past will serve as raw material for the kind of "heritage" Lowenthal eloquently and legitimately deplores.[27] As a Scots proverb warns: "God save us from having our wishes fulfilled."

NOTES

1. See Sam Wineburg, "Making Historical Sense," this volume.

2. Daniel Gardner, *Youth and History: A Policy Paper for the Dominion Institute of Toronto* (Toronto, 1997), pp. 8–10.

3. Despite the official answer sheet, the poet Robert Service was not Canadian, and Canadian women who happened to be Asian or status Indian had to wait long after 1918 for the right to vote.

4. J. R. Miller, "The Invisible Historian," *Journal of the Canadian Historical Association*, St. John's (1997), pp. 3–18.

5. J. L. Granatstein, *Who Killed Canadian History?* (Toronto, 1998).

6. Jacques Lacoursière et al., *Learning from the Past: Report of the Task Force on the Teaching of History* (Quebec, 10 May 1996).

7. See Monique Nemni, "L'education au Québec: Comment on abrutit nos enfants," *Cité Libre*, 22(6) (novembre-décembre 1994).

8. "Québec/Canada sondage: les frères siamois, *L'Actualité*, 23(17) (1er novembre 1998), pp. 27–36.

9. "C'est la faute à l'histoire," *L'Actualité*, 23(17) (Ier novembre 1998), pp. 38–40; Daniel Francis, *National Dreams: Myth, Memory and Canadian History* (Vancouver, 1997), pp. 88–110 passim. At the turn of the century, texts by Sir Thomas Chapais proclaimed such a view. In the 1920s, it began to be overturned by Canon Lionel Groulx in a series of passionate books that portray British democracy as a plot to undermine *le fait français*.

10. Granatstein, *Who Killed*, p. 149. For his program, see chapter 6.

11. Gardner, "Youth and History," p. 14.

12. Charles Humphries, "The Banning of a Book in British Columbia," *B.C. Studies*, 1 (1968–69), pp. 1–12.

13. See Appendix A: *History/Geography/Social Science Curricula across Canada*, from the Social Program Evaluation Group, Queen's University, 1996. Significant efforts have been made among both eastern and Atlantic provinces to develop a common social studies curriculum, but progress has been limited. Ontario and Quebec are both in the throes of major curriculum change.

14. See C. Bilodeau, "L'Histoire nationale," in *Royal Commission Studies: A Selection of Essays Prepared for the Royal Commission on National Development in the Arts, Letters and Sciences* (Ottawa, 1951), pp. 217–230.

15. In practice, the holiday marks the beginning of a frostfree summer in most of Canada; families get busy planting flowers and vegetables.

16. Cited by F. H. Underhill in *Canadian Historical Review*, 16 (September 1935). Hutton was a British-born, Oxford-trained classicist.

17. Ken Osborne, "Teaching Heritage in the Classroom," pp. 165, 171. On other references, see Northrop Frye, *Design for Learning* (Toronto, 1962);

Bernard Hodgetts, *What Culture? What Heritage?* (Toronto, 1972); and Hilda Neatby, "National History," in *Royal Commission Studies* (Ottawa, 1951).

18. Marcel Trudel and Geneviève Jain, *L'Histoire du Canada: enquête sur les manuels* (Ottawa, 1969). Trudel, Jean Hamelin, and Paul Cornell attempted to solve the problem with *Unity in Diversity* (Toronto, 1969), a first-year university text in both languages that sank without trace in a few years. Significantly, the title in French translated as "Unity and Diversity," contrasting Quebec and the rest. One of the coauthors, Marcel Trudel, a distinguished specialist on New France, asserted a common view at the time: "It is persistently maintained in certain circles that it is impossible to write a Canadian history of equal validity for our two main language groups. This amounts to saying that history should serve the particular ends of each of them. But history's prime function is to convey an understanding of society as it was in the past, and more specifically in this case, to acquaint both French and English Canadians with the adventure they have shared on North American soil." Marcel Trudel, *Canadian History Textbooks: A Comparative Study: Studies of the Royal Commission on Bilingualism and Biculturalism* (Ottawa, 1970).

19. Ironically, the best performance in the Institute's 1997 questionnaire came from Alberta, where history vanished from the curriculum in the 1970s; the worst results came from Quebec, where history learning is reinforced by a compulsory provincial exam.

20. David Lowenthal, *The Past Is a Foreign Country* (Cambridge, 1985).

21. Lacoursière et al., *Learning from the Past*, p. 3.

22. See Denis Shemilt, "The Caliph's Coin: The Currency of Narrative Frameworks in History Teaching," this volume.

23. René Durocher, José Igartua, et al. "L'enseignement de l'histoire: une réforme à poursuivre," *La Presse*, Opinions, 8 juillet 1998.

24. The centrality of teacher education has been raised by Diane Ravitch, most recently in *Harpers*, 298(1785) (February 1999), p. 4.

25. Environics poll, "Interest in Canadian History: Preliminary Findings," released 28 January 1999. (A private Ontario government poll in 1997, leaked to Canadian Press in 1999, reported that adults in Ontario believed mathematics and English to be indispensable but viewed history and French as "more disposable." See "History and French Rank Low in Survey," *Toronto Star*, 25 January 1999.)

26. *Histoire sociale*, 4 (November 1969), p. 16.

27. See David Lowenthal, *Possessed by the Past: The Heritage Crusade and the Spoils of History* (New York, 1996).

Chapter 4

Dilemmas and Delights of Learning History

David Lowenthal

History holds unparalleled problems and promises for student and teacher alike. In this chapter, I first suggest why history may be harder to learn than is commonly thought. One reason is that it is a uniquely amateur and particularistic realm; other reasons arise from or are magnified by modern trends in historical understanding—notably an erosion of common historical referents, a vogue for essentialist apologetics, and postmodern denials of judgmental value. I then discuss three reasons why it is crucial to study history: the contribution of historical understanding to everyday affairs; the benefits of recognizing the foreignness of the past; and the virtues of hindsight, seeing the past's ongoing consequences. I end by suggesting how history teaching may be enlivened by stressing history's immediacy.

History as Amateur Scholarship

More than any other academic profession, history is amateur in its approach, its appeal, and its apparatus. Unlike the physical and social sciences, history has no technical jargon and requires no grounding in some arcane aspect of nature or human nature. Its practitioners generally strive to be accessibly straightforward, even to the point of eschewing theory entirely. Many historians share Richard Cobb's old-fashioned aversion to "the methodology of history as the invention of solemn Germans and . . . the ruination [of] future historians."[1]

Not only are we inclined to think that anyone *can* learn history; we are inclined to feel that everyone *should* learn history. Only geography among other disciplines makes similar claims to universality, and geographers have lately become more and more narrowly professional, addicted to scientism, social or natural. The days when historians preened themselves on the arduous opacity of historical *science* are happily for the most part past.[2]

History's amateur character leaves it highly vulnerable, however, to assaults on the integrity of historical knowledge. Nonhistorians misconceive amateur as dilettante. And because it is open to all and matters so passionately to so many, history is readily seized on as a weapon for this or that cause, this or that faith—it continually risks being turned into civics or heritage.[3] But just because history is amateur does not mean it is easy; just because it is ideally open to all is not to allow that one historical opinion is as good as any other. We forget at our peril, as Diane Ravitch's essay in this book points out, that to fathom history demands sustained effort, and to teach it calls for experience and judgment.

Special Demands of Historical Understanding

The skills that history requires are in many ways unlike those necessary for the natural and social sciences. This is no place for an epistemological exegesis, but it is worth noting a few modes of thinking specially needed in history:

Familiarity: Ability to recognize and situate a substantial common store of references about a consensually shared past.

Comparative judgment: Ability to absorb and critique evidence from a wide range of variant and conflicting sources.

Awareness of manifold truths: Ability to understand why different viewers are bound to know the past differently.

Appreciation of authority: Ability to acknowledge debts to forerunners and to tradition while avoiding blind veneration or unquestioning adherence to earlier views.

Hindsight: Awareness that knowing the past is not like knowing the present and that history changes as new data, perceptions, contexts, and syntheses go on unfolding.

What follows touches on these five skills, although I dwell explicitly here only on the first and the last.

Enduring Impediments to Historical Learning

The traits of historical insight just noted have one principle in common: they call for some degree of maturity. History may involve young people intensely, but it is a mode of discourse traditionally central to their elders. As a young historian, I was discouraged (though not dissuaded) from writing a biography as my doctoral thesis, on the ground that no callow juvenile had the experience needed to limn a life from cradle to grave.

Immaturity

Early childhood does preclude historical insight. At the start of life we are immured in the present. No time exists except now; past and future are unimaginable. Self-absorbed, self-centered, we appreciate only the immediate. As we grow, memory and expectation provide awareness of our personal past and future, but history, that remote epoch before our own being, long remains shrouded in obscurity, even in disbelief. Youngsters scarcely conscious there has been a past give little thought to what it may have been like. To engender empathetic interest in the past, teachers need magic skills to transmute the substance of their own maturity in the cauldron of young minds.

Many remain historically apathetic as well as ignorant. For Tracy, the English sixteen-year-old school-leaver of an exemplary tale, "history" means coloring eighteenth-century costumes. Tracy not only knows little history but has no notion of historical time: "Was the eighteenth century before or after the war?" she asks her teacher.[4] (An actual American student worried that if Socrates lived from 469 to 399 he must have died before he was born.[5])

Most of us at length become aware that other times have happened and that it makes sense to view them in sequence. But the autonomy of past epochs remains dubious, as with Virginia Woolf's Mrs. Swithin, who could not believe there ever was a nineteenth century, "only you and me and William dressed differently."[6] That denizens of past times were actual people, yet unlike us in countless important ways, is not an unstudied intuition; it is a hard-gained reflective insight.

Presentism

For many, awareness of historical difference remains partial and tentative. Folk of past times are usually viewed in comparison with our own, as better or, more commonly, worse than ourselves: benighted, corrupt, evil, or just plain stupid, as Peter Lee and Ros Ashby's essay in this volume shows. Even bright students are ahistorical. Their own moralities become universal values, from which deviance is infamy. College history students are apt to take equality as a given: They condemn any society, past or present, that fails to honor it. Slavery and servitude are not historical conditions but unnatural perversions.

"Students who have been properly introduced to Western civilization will know that inequality has not only been a fact but also a norm throughout most of history," contends the Stanford historian Daniel Gordon.[7] But how many are properly introduced? The assertion that "*all* the students are egalitarian meritocrats," as Bloom charges, unable even to imagine "any substantial argument in favor of aristocracy or monarchy, [those] inexplicable follies of the past," may exaggerate.[8] Yet, Gordon himself admits that many Stanford students refused to discuss "the values of these antiquated beings."[9]

Young and old, we all risk being blinkered by present lenses. Young Derek, in Sam Wineburg's study, denies the patent historical evidence before him, because he cannot conceive that American colonists would choose to emulate the suicidal etiquette of eighteenth-century English soldiers. In conforming what he sees "to the shape of the already known,"[10] Derek resembles Marco Polo, who conflated the rhinoceros he saw with the unicorn he expected.[11]

Efforts to make social history at Colonial Williamsburg more sophisticated show how persistent presentism can be. Trying hard to be nonjudgmental, guides still end up displaying the past as an aberrant present—sometimes superior, usually inferior to today in aesthetics, behavior, and beliefs. When change is noted, visitors are invited to pity the past, to laugh at its absurdities or mock its backwardness. Past motives are explained in terms of present morality, past social hierarchy palliated by a Horatio Alger mystique of upward mobility. Craftspeople who "selfconsciously set out to puncture visitors' notions about both the superior simplicity and the inferior crudity of the past" scarcely dent ingrained assumptions of nostalgia and progress.[12]

These dilemmas are not confined to living-history sites. They go to the heart of an ahistoricism that pervades textbooks and the media, Stanford and the Smithsonian.[13] But Americans are not alone in being unable to shed present-day lenses or put themselves in others' shoes. Responses to queries posed to fifteen-year-olds throughout Europe show students "neither willing nor able to accept pre-modern reality and morality, even in theory. . . . The human-rights argument is accepted without doubt for an era before the invention of human rights. [Un]aware of the existence of another logic . . . for decision-making five hundred years ago, [they] argue only from their modern viewpoint of individualism, secularism and autonomy."[14]

It is an enduring fallacy to believe one's own epoch singularly significant, eventful, or critical. Churchmen discerned in sacred annals a purposive preparation for mankind to take charge; paleontologists divined from fossil sequences the anatomical perfection reached in their own time; moderns fancy their epoch critical because it is millennial.[15] Students need to realize that every present seems especially salient to self-centered denizens, who skew history to prove their point.

Sacred versus Secular Time

Sacralizing some chosen time in the past likewise impedes historical understanding. Most societies attach special virtue to a point of origin. Plucked from the stream of history, founding moments become transcendent verities. Thus, Americans decant the Declaration of Independence and the Constitution from history into sacred time.[16]

Events so privileged confound chronological thought, disjoining the stream of history before and after the sacred moment. The effect in Christianity and Islam is obvious. Two life-stories, fourteen and twenty centuries back, fix the calendar and structure historical time for much of humanity. Bidirectional counting, backward before and forward since Christ or Mohammed, affects perceptions of the past in myriad ways yet little studied.[17]

Though embedded in secular history, scriptural history is uniquely invested with eternal truth. But how can sacred time be reconciled with historical understanding? No wonder history is hard to teach; its tenets contest sacred faith in the same temporal arena.[18] Most of us live with but do not resolve this dissonance. Yet similar smudging by pagans, for example, renders their history suspect in our eyes. Ancient Greeks' "view of mythology as a sort of history is difficult for modern minds," notes a classicist.

> We find it hard to see . . . how the Athenians could attribute to . . . Theseus both a famous battle against centaurs and the foundation of some of their revered religious and democratic institutions. These seem to us actions in two completely different spheres, and the fact that the first kind of story can be told about an individual seriously undermines his claim to be "historical."[19]

Beyond the secular-sacred quandary, historical quests often conflict. Academic historians strive to understand the past and the emergent present as truly and impartially as possible; nations, tribes, ethnic groups, and other factions use history to affirm identity and to inculcate loyalty—"to make nations out of peasants."[20] These two aims are at odds: the first relies on consensually attested evidence, the second on faith devoid of empirically testable data. One is the bedrock of historical insight, the other of civic self-assurance. Partisan passions inflame the division. When the Smithsonian Institution's proposed Enola Gay exhibition was aborted as offensive to patriots, its organizer rued how hard it was to celebrate and to educate at the same time.[21] Yet history teachers are in fact committed to doing just that. To marry civic with pedagogic duties is our most arduous and unending task.

Current Obfuscations of History

These impediments to historical understanding are not new. But, they seem aggravated today by the dwindling common stock of historical referents, the rise of anachronistic apologetics, and the cult of postmodernism.

Erosion of Terms of Discourse

The loss of common referents is a recurrent lament given new force in our time. Personalities, phrases, and events pass into oblivion ever more swiftly. Media dispersion that makes fame and infamy global also makes them ephemeral. At Sainte Chapelle in Paris, a young visitor asked the historian Alethea Hayter what the place celebrated.

"Well," I began, "it was built by Saint Louis . . ." "Saint Louis?" was her puzzled reply . . . "Yes, it was built by a king of France who went on a crusade . . ." "Crusade?" she asked, bewildered. Despairingly I persevered. "Yes, he went on a journey to the Mediterranean, and brought back a sacred relic, the Crown of Thorns . . ." "Crown of Thorns?" she queried, still more at sea. At that point I gave up; I felt unable to insert any idea of the significance of the Sainte Chapelle into a mind which had been given no context of European history or Christian belief at all. Will Clio soon be not merely eclipsed but extinguished in general consciousness?[22]

The erosion of canonical names, dates, and events isolates us from fellowship with any common past. In England the famous spoof *1066 and All That* is no longer funny because few now have even heard of the names and dates it ridicules.[23]

To be sure, other common referents exist; mass-media audiences share a sports, music, and pop-culture repertoire. But that store is ephemeral, inchoate, and trivial; it nourishes no discourse beyond its own short-lived icons; it bridges us with only the recent past; its communal stock is too thin to enrich the social fabric. It does not compensate for "the loss of the historical frame of reference, the amputation of the time dimension from our culture." Being "in the swim" is not equivalent, notes a famed art historian, to "being in the culture."[24]

Some argue that with history, as with arithmetic, new modes of retrieval reduce our memory needs—why store away names and dates easily gained from data bases? But having historical references at our fingertips is not the same as having them in our heads. To converse, to compare, to contrast, to consult an encyclopedia requires a stock of common knowledge not merely on tap but ingrained, part of our own and our coevals' general consciousness.

Huge charts of Western history from 395 to 1815, dating events in six regional and topical realms, were prerequisite in my 1940 Harvard freshman history course. "No student should think of memorizing this chart as a whole," we were told; just "the most significant material." It is easy to mock the simplistic hubris of such aides-mémoire. Yet, they held out a sanguinary confidence, however delusive, that the past was commensurable. We could never know it all, but we had some idea of where to begin to look for it.

No more. Such an approach is now risibly Eurocentric and factoidal. Memorizing dates is boring, pointless. Historians whose concerns now embrace wider worlds realize that aligning, say, twelfth-century China and Koblenz tells little about either. And along with history's expanded ethnic scope, its enlarged social content makes still more passé a chronological crutch once most useful in military and imperial contexts.

In scuttling our precursors' framework we hope to shed their ethnocentric arrogance. But we have also lost their optimism that history was assimilable, that the story of humanity had a length and a form within which one could find one's bearings. With no such prop, students today are wholly at sea. History has no shape, no pattern, no consensually fixed guideposts. Such patterns are, to be sure, selectively contrived. But without them we have no common historical ground, no arena of discourse, save for generic topics thought universally applicable—conquest, slavery, hegemony, imperialism, resistance. More constricting than the old decontextualized chronologies, these themes impose presentist blinkers. Pasts scrutinized mainly in terms of fragmentary set topics cannot be viewed in their historical fullness, as many-sided, multifarious, often self-contradictory realms.

History as Essentialist Apologetics

A vogue for historical guilt valorizes presentist spins on past events. A culture of contrition condemns past iniquities. A rage for restitution—of land, art objects, grave goods, skeletal remains, bars of gold, languages, history itself—sweeps the world. I do not deny its legitimacy where heirs of the victimized are indubitably agreed and amends are more than windy rhetoric. But restitution and repentance fog historical understanding. They lump present groups as sole inheritors *en bloc* entitled to receive, or required to yield up, this or that ancestral good. Heritage so viewed exalts group purity, continuity, single-mindedness to the detriment of commingling, creolization, flexibility. It encourages people to essentialize history, giving particular groups special claims on "their" past and privileging their interpretive views. When every entity is specially privileged to interpret "its own" history, consensual truth succumbs to minority credos.

History thus becomes a cluster of separate pasts ideally uncontaminated by outsiders, instead of the chronicle of mixing it actually is. And the past serves as a moral echo accrediting two fallacies: that we incarnate ancestral virtues and that those back then would feel as we do, given the chance.

Because we want our ancestors to mirror ourselves, we feel the need to clean up their act. Hence the spate of official apologies—in Rome for the torture of Galileo, in America for slavery, in Britain for the Irish famine, among Christian penitents (and even the Vatican) for the Crusades. Heads of state have the hardihood to broadcast that their precursors were "wrong" and the hubris to assume it helpful to repent ancient misdeeds. To thus elide present morality with past miseries sows false hopes about setting history right. "What makes us authentic . . . is our sense of trauma, and thus our status as victims," writes an historian. And school history becomes "history as it is felt, especially by its victims." This impedes understanding. For "feelings can only be expressed, not discussed," leading either to "mute acceptance of whatever people wish to say about themselves, or in violent confrontations. . . . You cannot argue with feelings."[25]

Relativist Nihilism

Postmodern relativism poses further obstacles to history learning, as Peter Seixas's essay in this book shows. That historical bias is omnipresent, objectivity a never-achieved dream, no good historian denies. But the postmodernist stance goes further, denying all claims to historical truth and rejecting any judgments that sanction some versions over others. In the past, critics oppressed by mainstream history supplied their own revised views; today's critics trust *no* version of history. Relativist egalitarianism invalidates historical consensus based on scholarship. "Not only is historical truth irrelevant, but it has become a common assumption that there is no such thing."[26] But if all history is ipso facto dubious, why bother to learn it?

So concluded Tracy's teacher. What did it matter that she was clueless about the eighteenth century? Tracy would soon get a job, run a household, have a family—and probably do all this at least as well as her teacher. She had no need of the eighteenth century. The next day her teacher quit history to teach English, where chronology was of no moment.[27]

She was wrong about both English and history—not because it was vital to place the eighteenth century, or for that matter any other datum of history, although some fund of knowledge shared with her coevals might be helpful. The main reason Tracy, like all of us, needs history is not to have specific nuggets of data; it is to know how to think historically—to acquire, screen, and weigh evidence about anything past. Lacking such apprehension, we can scarcely cope with the simplest social transaction.

Why We Need History and What History We Need

It is often said that without memory we would be idiots, lacking any sense of retrospect or prospect, and that without history societies would likewise be marooned in the shallow present. It is less commonly realized that historical thinking—as distinct from historical content—is essential to manage everyday affairs. We continually reshape our private memories to meet the rigorous truth standards of a public past. To reach a consensual understanding of what has happened and why, we must check our own recollections and records against those of others.

The classic case for historical thinking is Carl Becker's 1931 AHA presidential address, "Everyman His Own Historian."[28]

> Mr. Everyman, when he awakens in the morning, reaches out into the country of the past and of distant places, . . . pulls together things said and done in his yesterdays, and coordinates them with his present perceptions and with things to be said and done in his tomorrows. Without this historical knowledge, this memory of things said and done, his today would be aimless and his tomorrow without significance.

But "unaided memory is notoriously fickle," and on occasion Everyman's falters. "Uneasily aware of something said or done he now fails to recall," he begins hunting for sources, reaches into the private record office of his vest pocket, and finds a note he had written: "December 29, pay Smith's coal bill, 20 tons, $1017.20." He has an image of having done so, but a hunt through his files yields no evidence. So he goes to Smith, who reminds him, after searching his own records, that he had bought his coal not from Smith, who did not have what he needed, but from Brown. Everyman now goes to Brown, who "takes down a ledger, does a bit of original research . . . which happily confirms the researches of Smith." Everyman pays his bill, of which he eventually finds a duplicate in his own papers, properly drawn.

> Mr. Everyman would be astonished to learn that he is an historian, yet . . . he has performed all the essential operations involved in historical research. . . . The first step was to recall things said and done. Unaided memory proving inadequate, a further step was essential—the examination of certain documents . . . Unhappily the documents were found to give conflicting reports, so that a critical comparison of texts had to be instituted in order to eliminate error.

Finally he forms a more or less true and complete picture "of a selected series of historical events—of himself ordering coal from Smith, of Smith turning the order over to Brown, and of Brown delivering the coal," thanks to which "Everyman could, and did, pay his bill." Had all the records and actors failed to concur he would have rechecked archival sources with Brown. "If Mr. Everyman had undertaken these researches in order to write a book instead of to pay a bill, no one would think of denying that he was an historian." So, Becker concludes, "in a very real sense it is impossible to divorce history from life. Mr. Everyman cannot do what he needs or desires without recalling past events; he can not recall past events without . . . relating them to what he needs or desires to do." Most vital, he can do this properly only by meshing his own memory and records with those of others.

> If Mr. Everyman lived quite alone . . . he would be free to affirm and hold in memory any ideal series of events that struck his fancy. [But] Mr. Everyman has to live in a world of Browns and Smiths, . . . which has taught him the expediency of recalling certain events with much exactness

—an exactness congruent with the memories and archives of his fellows, whose own private fancies may be quite different. As an English historian more recently remarked, "if history was thought of as an activity rather than a profession, then the number of its practitioners would be legion."[29]

The particular "history" in Becker's tale is important to very few people; it survives only as an example of why and how to *do* history. What history mostly gives us is such examples, but they are not enough: we also need the lesson Becker draws—that is, to acquire the habit of historical exploration. That habit proves vital when the past becomes important to us, either to clarify some debatable or conflictual present circumstance or to satisfy an incessant itch to understand what it was like and how we came to be what we are.

Becker's lesson reveals history's salient vitality: it is never dead, not even sleeping, at worst napping. We can never entirely let go of the ongoing past, for it never lets go of us. Historical involvement is not only essential but inevitable. To say dismissively "that's history," or "history is nothing to do with me" is a profound error. We are fully historical creatures, our consciousness and memory bound up with pasts both near and remote. And rational present action demands insight into other people's pasts as well as our own.

Becoming Aware of the Past's Ineffable Strangeness

Our hardest task as teachers is to keep antiquity accessible while stressing its ineffable strangeness. Such understanding requires not only empathy with the past but awareness of its unbridgeable difference. The past was not only weirder than we realize; it was weirder than we can imagine. However much we strive to know them, past minds remain opaque to us. To link us with precursors while accepting the unlikeness of their worlds, we must somehow convey the past's mysterious affinity.

But how? Because his students were turned off by the past's remoteness, the California classics professor Victor Davis Hanson recast ancient Greece as "raw, relevant history." Thucydides came alive when the students saw how much they resembled this hard-nosed, pugnacious pragmatist who lied, slaughtered, and turned historian only when he could no longer be a warrior. "He was a man more like themselves than their professors, . . . a tough guy who shows how their brutal experiences are universal, even banal, and thus explicable."[30]

But, this is not history; it is fictional empathy. Likening Thucydides's brutality to their own did not "explain" these students' own experience but voided it of personal and social context. To stress human universality by lumping *Star Trek* with the Peloponnesian Wars engenders delusive hopes of domesticating the present as a replay of the past. And it forecloses awareness of difference, of change, of contingency.

That all humans are in some ways alike—biologically, socially, perhaps psychologically—is probable. But these universals are historically trivial and reductive. Diversity constitutes the core of history. Historians' most difficult but also rewarding task is to persuade audiences—students, readers, interlocutors—that every past was uniquely *un*like the present.

How can teachers convey an awareness of distance, of strangeness too great ever wholly to grasp? Glimpses into uncannily dissimilar pasts can be had through encounters with dynamically inspired portrayals of them. "Experience has taught us," concludes Colonial Williamsburg's research chief, "that museum visitors learn best when they are invited to enter into the day-to-day circumstances of real people from the past."[31] Such experience can be a vital adjunct to history teaching. "This person brought the Revolution alive for me," a Williamsburg visitor told an interpreter. "If only I could have had you in the classroom."[32]

At their best, first-person historical interpreters can foster conscious immersion in what is foreign. In Plimoth Plantation's replica 1627 village, I watched "William Bradford" thus engage a midwestern booster of individualism and free enterprise. Like many Americans, this visitor grew up in the faith that the Pilgrim Fathers were true begetters of his own values. Now he was finding *this* prototype Father's views diametrically opposed to his own: Bradford was a Calvinist predestinarian, a believer in community to whom secular capitalist enterprise was blasphemous, selfish individualism anathema.

Seething with indignation, the visitor could not just dismiss pious Bradford as a crank or a Communist. He would normally have spurned or even struck him—but you do not commit mayhem on historic sites. The venue demands tolerant colloquy, facing up to discomfiting, even unnerving difference. For the first time in his life, this visitor confronted a world view fundamentally at odds with his own and had to engage with it as an idea. Analogous engagements might be multiplied in museums, at memorials, in foreign travel, even at home. Diffidence about the ethics and propriety of painful or shocking historical reenactments can be alleviated by advance planning, overcome by honest artistry. Intending to boycott the staging of a slave auction at Colonial Williamsburg as a tasteless affront to black dignity, NAACP chief Jack Gravely stayed to laud the event for amplifying historical understanding, black and white. In Gravely's words, in this performance "pain had a face, indignity had a body, suffering had tears. We saw all of that."[33]

Our most fruitful encounters with alien pasts come from their literary chroniclers, celebrants, mourners, moralizers, and analysts. To apprehend realms remote from present-day life, I commend six texts, each engrossing and visionary in some distinctive way.

1. *Revelation of Saint John the Divine.* The last book of the New Testament unnerves most readers by its arcane remoteness from their own world, its deliberately opaque imagery of wonders and terrors. We are dazed by breastplated horses with scorpions' tails and lions' teeth and women's hair, reiterated sequences of sevens, the three woes announced by angels, the number of the beast, and the blood of saints and harlots. We waver between St. Jerome's tribute—"Revelation has as many mysteries as it does words"—and Bernard Shaw's dismissal—"curious record of the visions of a drug addict." With its perplexing prevision of a coming millennium of banqueting and fornication, *Revelation* lends authority now to apocalyptic millenarians, now to Church Fathers or to antipapal Protestants, now to evangelicals, to fundamentalists, or to historical skeptics. This great symbolic poem warrants Herder's accolade:

> When a book, through thousands of years, stirs up the heart and awakens
> the soul, and leaves neither friend nor foe indifferent, . . . in such a book
> there must be something substantial, whatever anyone may say.[34]

Revelation is a book for all time. But it is also very much a Judaic book of
its own intertestamental time, fantasizing contemporary events to fore-
cast the imminent apocalypse.

2. *Montaillou*.[35] Emmanuel Le Roy Ladurie's classic account of religious conflict in a medieval French village is a marvelously detailed depiction of peasant life eight centuries ago. It is also a deeply focused presentation of modes of thought and action in a society riven by passions,
some so strikingly familiar to us they seem our own, others so utterly unlike as to seem from another universe.

3. *Out of Egypt*.[36] The chronicle of André Aciman's own Sephardic
family depicts with intense intimacy the interdigitated worlds of early-
twentieth-century Alexandria, its segmented and sheltered religious communities alike shuttered apart yet converging in myriad realms of life—a
ghettoed world now banished into history by ethnic cleansing and by
identity politics.

4. *Akenfield*.[37] In Ronald Blythe's portrait of his native Suffolk village,
octogenarian neighbors relate their own early lives. Turn-of-the-century
youngsters waited, age 11 or 12, to be plucked out of the local school,
the girls sent into domestic service, the boys into the fields. But the
patent inequity of their prospects, compared with the gentry or farmers
for whom they labored, aroused no sense of injustice; to the contrary,
these children felt lucky to find work and their families to feed one less
mouth. Life was *naturally* hierarchical. After the First World War had
jumbled master and servant together in the same enterprise, if in different ranks, doubts did arise that so wide a gulf was justified, engendering
grievances that culminated in Britain's General Strike of 1926. Even half
a century later Blythe's villagers did not expect equality; ingrained by
tradition and experience were hierarchical niches of caste and birth distinguished by disparate rewards and duties.

5. *Surviving the Holocaust*.[38] Avraham Tory's diary of two and a half
years in Lithuania's Kovno ghetto is a day-by-day account of lethal risks
and unimaginable hardships, endured by Jews forced within claustropho-
bic limits by anti-Semitic fiat. Ceaselessly shadowed by threats of extermination, the several thousand ghetto dwellers are depicted at work and
in quest of food and clothing, bargaining over labor and livelihood with

the SS, the German army, Lithuanians, and their own leaders. Tory's measured narrative of everyday trauma conveys the aura of determination that makes these confined Jews more rational than their persecutors, whose weakness and venality they must circumvent and manipulate to save their own lives. The matter-of-factness of these lives, under the looming menace of mass slaughter, makes this story more realistically uncanny than the hideous brutalities of the extermination camps.

6. *Patterns of Intention.*[39] Michael Baxandall shows how our view of Piero della Francesca departs from that of Piero himself and of his contemporaries and explains *why* historical distance makes such perspectival gulfs inevitable. We who now love Piero's paintings try to understand what the artist and others of his time made of them, but we can never see the paintings as they did back then. Perceptions that for them stemmed from innate ways of being for us become self-consciously studied and foreign.

Admiring Piero's paintings, we long to understand them as fifteenth-century Italians did. We must resist the temptation to think we can ever do so, lest we forget the gulf that divides us from them. To remind us of that impassable gulf, Baxandall commends the continued use of obsolete descriptive terms, words whose very strangeness signal meanings and interactions foreign to us. His book brings the Renaissance past alive not by minimizing but by stressing its ineffable distance. And it shows, better than any other text I know,-how to engage with the ultimate frailty of all historical understanding.

The Benefits of Hindsight

Many seek to know the past by imagining themselves living back then. Historical empathy is tempting, but, as noted for Thucydides wannabes, it imparts limited light. Hindsight is a mode of apperception that makes us aware we both diverge from the past and progress beyond it. It enables us to see past events not only as filtered through contemporary eyes and voices but also in terms of what has later unfolded—the *consequences* of Socrates, the Crusades, the French Revolution, the Civil War, or whatever. Such insights keep on and on unfurling, enriching insights at every stage, while at the same time further distancing us from how things were originally seen. The historian discovers "what, until he discovered it, no one ever knew to have happened at all."[40]

Hindsight carries risks as well as benefits, to be sure. Knowing much about past times that those living then could not have been privy to gives us an illusion of superiority. "Can we really be fair to men of the past," wondered the historian A. F. Pollard, "knowing what they could not know?" Indeed, hindsight knowledge so departs from that of eye witnesses that the two seem incommensurable.[41] Historians and biographers are accused of bringing people of the past to life only to "arrange them in all sorts of patterns of which they were ignorant."[42] Moreover, hindsight lends the past an apparent coherence, consistency, and reliability it never possessed for its denizens, tidying chaos into order, often into predestined sequence, as though things could not have happened otherwise.[43] Knowing how things *have* turned out removes us still further from those for whom the past was a messy and confusing present. "With our minds prepossessed by a knowledge of the result, can we, indeed, understand them at all?"

Yet we cannot eschew hindsight; it is inescapable in our perception of the past. "We are bound to see the Second World War differently in 1985 than in 1950," as I once wrote, "not merely because masses of new evidence have come to light, but also because the years have unfolded further consequences—the Cold War, the United Nations, the revival of the German and Japanese economies."[44] Fifteen years on we view that war through additional lenses of Vietnam, Soviet collapse, new genocides, European unification, revisionist analysis of everything from the Final Solution to the *Enola Gay*.

To understand what happened long ago, it is not enough to know what people thought back then; we have to add thoughts of our own time. We cannot understand Caesar without knowing what he believed, but it is no less important to realize that Caesar was ill-informed and self-deluded and lacked prevision.[45] Concepts like "the fall of Rome" or "the Renaissance" were "not perceived to exist, at the beginning of the process, and . . . could only be fully recognized and articulated at the end of it."[46]

Not only is hindsight essential to how we see the past; it is indispensable to how we describe and explain it to others. "Documents are ripped out of their original context . . . to illustrate a pattern which might well not have been meaningful to any of their authors." The shape of the narrative reflects the historian's retrospective knowledge, "for he must not only know something of the outcomes of the events that concern him; he must use what he knows in telling his story." In J. H. Hexter's telling example, the chronicler of the 1951 National League baseball pennant race, when the New York Giants pulled up from last place at midseason to a first-place tie on the final day, had to have the outcome in mind as he wrote the story.[47]

Hindsight's additions are no substitute for lost immediacy, but they enormously amplify what we learn of the past. They also throw a laudably humbling light on the present. While it may thrill students to realize that their own insights are uniquely privileged, compared with all their predecessors', it is also sobering to reflect that time will similarly outdate what they know, too. In this regard, history is much like family life. Of the many things about which we know more than our grandparents, perhaps the most significant is knowing *them* as they never knew themselves. The chastening corollary is that our grandchildren will run similar historical rings around us. Updating the past recurrently illuminates. But we must remember that the lamp of history needs refueling all the time.

It is therefore prudent as well as politic to treat our students as the historians they are bound to become. The deficiencies of youth noted earlier can best be outgrown by instilling in those we teach the conviction that they are already participants in history. As Wertsch, Wineburg, Levstik, and Rosenzweig also imply in this book, students thereby become both more comfortable with and more competent in history. Not only are they embedded in time; they are destined to shape it. They should feel not only privileged but entitled to share its thrills, its trials, and its heady freedoms. Public historians—those who engage the public at museums, historic sites, monuments, memorials—can help convey a sense of immediacy and involvement that enable student and teacher alike to see history as both active and reflective.

Historical enlightenment requires being receptive to astonishment. The best-taught past is unendingly surprising. It is full of tales at once true and false, tales given added salience by being translated into our own words and for our own eyes. But to be worth seeing and studying at all, it should be encountered as simultaneously bizarre and wonderful.[48]

NOTES

1. Richard Cobb, "Becoming a Historian," in his *A Sense of Place* (London, 1975), pp. 5–48, at 47. Cobb holds that "one just went to the archives, read them, thought about them, read some more, and the records would do the rest . . . All

the historian had to do was to be able to read, and, above all, to write clearly and agreeably."

2. Carl Schorske, "History and the Study of Culture," in his *Thinking with History: Explorations in the Passage to Modernism* (Princeton, 1998), pp. 229–230. Although laments about scientific history recurrently resurface (e.g., John Demos, "The Resurrection of Clio: History Is Re-emerging as Literature," *International Herald Tribune*, January 1, 1999, p. 7), few historians nowadays profess to be scientists. See Keith Windschuttle, *The Killing of History: How Literary Critics and Social Theorists are Murdering Our Past* (New York, 1997), pp. 215–221.

3. See my *The Heritage Crusade and the Spoils of History* (London, 1996).

4. Jenny Diski, "On the Existence of Mount Rushmore and Other Improbabilities," in her *The Vanishing Princess* (London, 1995), pp. 169–177.

5. Evelyn Edson, "The Historian at the Community College," AHA *Perspectives* (October 1996), p. 17.

6. Virginia Woolf, *Between the Acts* (New York, 1941), pp. 174–175.

7. Daniel Gordon, "Teaching Western History at Stanford," in Lloyd Kramer, Donald Reid, and William L. Barney, eds., *Learning History in America: Schools, Cultures, and Politics* (Minneapolis, 1994), pp. 44–52, at 52.

8. Allan Bloom, *The Closing of the American Mind* (New York, 1987), p. 90.

9. Gordon, "Teaching Western History."

10. Sam Wineburg, "Historical Thinking and Other Unnatural Acts," *Phi Delta Kappan*, 80 (1999), pp. 488–499, at 491–492.

11. Umberto Eco, *Serendipities* (New York, 1998), pp. 54–55.

12. Richard Handler and Eric Gable, *The New History in an Old Museum: Creating the Past at Colonial Williamsburg* (Durham, NC, 1997), pp. 99–100.

13. David Lowenthal, review of Handler and Gable, *The New History*, in *William and Mary Quarterly*, 55 (1998), pp. 490–492.

14. Andreas Körber, "Can Our Pupils Fit into the Shoes of Someone Else?" in Joke van der Leeuw-Roord, ed., *The State of History Education in Europe* (Hamburg, 1998), pp. 124–38, at 136.

15. Stephen Jay Gould, *Wonderful Life: The Burgess Shale and the Nature of History* (London, 1989), pp. 43–45.

16. Lowenthal, *Heritage Crusade*, pp. 135–136, 152; Michael Kammen, *A Machine That Would Go of Itself: The Constitution in American Culture* (New York, 1987), pp. xxiii, 36.

17. The usage of B.C. in historical chronology dates only from 1627, with the French Jesuit-astronomer Denis Petau (David Ewing Duncan, *The Calendar* [London, 1998], pp. 101–102). Recent research suggests that because people naturally think from past to present, it is harder to understand sentences that present information apparently out of sequential order (Thomas Münte, cited in Alison Motluk, "First Things First," *New Scientist*, September 5, 1998, p. 11).

18. Could a genuinely good Christian be a good historian, wondered the

American historian Charles S. Sydnor in 1953; Sydnor's doubts bore not on the ahistorical nature of the Nativity but on the inability of Christians to understand the selfish ambitions and other motives of such influential non-Christians as Franklin, Napoleon, and Caesar (Michael Kammen, *In the Fast Lane: Historical Perspectives on American Culture* [New York, 1997], pp. 16–17).

19. Lesley Fitton, "Looking for a Hero? Greek Mythology and the Greek Bronze Age," *British Museum Magazine*, no. 30 (Spring 1998), pp. 11–15, at 15.

20. William McNeill, quoted in Joyce Appleby, "The Power of History," *American Historical Review*, 103 (1998), pp. 1–14, at 10.

21. Edward T. Linenthal, "Struggling with History and Memory," *Journal of American History*, 82 (1995), pp. 1094–1101; Martin Harwit, *An Exhibit Denied: Lobbying the History of the Enola Gay* (New York, 1996).

22. Alethea Hayter, "The Rise and Fall of Clio" (review of Schorske, *Thinking with History*), *Spectator* (London), July 15, 1998.

23. W. C. Sellar and R. J. Yeatman, *1066 and All That* (London, 1930); Raphael Samuel, "One in the Eye: *1066 and All That*," in his *Island Stories: Unravelling Britain* (London, 1998), pp. 209–212.

24. Ernst Gombrich, *The Tradition of General Knowledge: Oration at the London School of Economics* (London, 1962), pp. 11, 21. Gombrich blamed this loss on academic overspecialization and dread of "smattering"; he proposed a three-minute secular Athanasian creed, to be learned by all, which began with "I belong to Western Civilization, born in Greece in the 1st millennium B.C. It was created by poets, artists, historians and scientists, who freely examined the earlier myths and truths of the Orient," and was later transformed by Christianity and by "renewed faith in the progress of human knowledge." That faith had "endangered and transformed, in our century, most other cultures of the globe . . . I hope there will be a 21st century, Amen" (pp. 22–23).

25. Ian Buruma, "The Joys and Perils of Victimhood," *New York Review of Books*, April 8, 1999, pp. 4–9.

26. Ibid., 8. See, for example, Windschuttle, *Killing of History*; John Warren, *The Past and Its Presenters* (London, 1998), pp. 3–31.

27. Diski, "On the Existence of Mount Rushmore."

28. Carl Becker, "Everyman His Own Historian," *American Historical Review*, 37 (1932), pp. 221–236, reprinted in Robin W. Winks, ed., *The Historian as Detective: Essays on Evidence* (New York, 1969), pp. 3–23.

29. Raphael Samuel, *Theatres of Memory: Past and Present in Contemporary Culture* (London, 1994), p. 17.

30. Victor Davis Hanson, "Raw, Relevant History," *New York Times*, April 18, 1998.

31. Cary Carson, ed., *Becoming Americans: Our Struggle to Be Both Free and Equal: A Plan of Thematic Interpretation* (Williamsburg, VA, 1998), p. 16.

32. Carol Dozier, interviewed by Marie Tyler-McGraw, "Becoming Americans

Again: Re-envisaging and Revising Thematic Interpretation at Colonial Williamsburg," *Public Historian*, 20 (1998), pp. 53–76, at 68.

33. Jack Gravely cited by Monique Braxton, Channel 10 News Broadcast, Norfolk, VA, 10 October 1994, quoted in Cary Carson, "Colonial Williamsburg and the Practice of Interpretive Planning in American History Museums," *Public Historian*, 20 (1998), pp. 11–51, at 51.

34. Bernard McGinn, "Revelation," in Robert Alter and Frank Kermode, *The Literary Guide to the Bible* (Cambridge, MA, 1987), pp. 523–541.

35. Ronald Blythe, *Akenfield: Portrait of an English Village* (London, 1969).

36. André Aciman, *Out of Egypt: A Memoir* (New York, 1994).

37. Avraham Tory, *Surviving the Holocaust: The Kovno Ghetto Diary* (Cambridge, 1990). Tory's narrative is excerpted, along with other materials, in the United States Holocaust Museum, *Hidden History of the Kovno Ghetto* (Boston, 1997).

38. Emmanuel LeRoy Ladudrie, *Montaillou: Cathars and Catholics in a French Village* (London, 1978).

39. Michael Baxandall, *Patterns of Intention: On the Historical Experience of Pictures* (New Haven, 1985).

40. R. G. Collingwood, *The Idea of History* [1946] (New York, 1956), p. 238.

41. A. F. Pollard, "Historical Criticism," *History*, 5 (1920), pp. 21–29, at 29.

42. Virginia Woolf, "I Am Christina Rossetti," in her *The Common Reader: Second Series* (London, 1932), pp. 237–244, at 236.

43. Scott A. Hawkins and Reid Hastie, "History: Biased Judgment of Past Events after the Outcomes Are Known," *Psychological Bulletin*, 107 (1990), pp. 311–327; Lowenthal, *Heritage Crusade*, 115.

44. David Lowenthal, *The Past Is a Foreign Country* (Cambridge, England, 1985), p. 217.

45. Peter Munz, *The Shapes of Time: A New Look at the Philosophy of History* (Middletown, CT, 1977), pp. 80, 93.

46. R. Stephen Humphreys, "The Historian, His Documents, and the Elementary Modes of Historical Thought," *History and Theory*, 19 (1980), pp. 1–20, at 12.

47. J. H. Hexter, "The Rhetoric of History," *International Encyclopedia of the Social Sciences*, vol. 6 (New York, 1968), pp. 368–94, at 378–80.

48. Caroline Walker Bynum, "Wonder," *American Historical Review*, 102 (1997), pp. 1–26, at 26.

Chapter 5

The Caliph's Coin

The Currency of Narrative Frameworks in History Teaching

Denis Shemilt

> Taking leave of the good hermit, I pressed into his hand
> a small brass coin the superscription of which was un-
> known to me and which I therefore feared I might have
> some difficulty in passing. I assured my kind host that it
> was a coin of the Second Caliph Omar, and of value far
> superior to any modern gold piece of a similar size. As
> the hermit, like many other saintly men, was ignorant of
> letters his gratitude knew no bounds."
> —Hilaire Belloc, "The Mercy of Allah"

The claim of history teachers to pass coinage of real and enduring value is
persuasive. It is easy to argue, first, that the capacity of adolescents to play
worthwhile roles within free societies is, in part, a function of the depth
and quality of their understanding about how and why things happen in
human affairs and, second, that the depth and quality of this understanding is, to some extent, conditional upon their knowledge of history and of
the ways in which contemporary forms of life and experience are developmentally related to those of their predecessors. Pupils, it may be proposed, should grasp that consequences are frequently unintended by the
very people whose actions are instrumental in their realization. The
tragedy of good intentions, the lesson that the errors and evils of the
modern world do not always follow from folly and self-serving greed but
often derive from heroic and self-sacrificing attempts to set things right,

may be readily learned from history but is difficult to convey within citizenship courses without resort to crude propaganda. Other unique and enduring outcomes of school history might include an understanding of how it is that, while the future is indeterminate, future possibilities are limited and skewed by the actualities of past and present. We can make our future, but, because we cannot remake our past, the realistically available futures are no more than a subset of those that we might wish to imagine or to bring about. Of equal importance is an understanding that we perceive more easily the fact than the flux of change because significant transformations in the nature and quality of life follow from slight shifts in the relative incidence or values of a few unconsidered variables.

These illustrations could be elaborated and many others could be advanced to argue for the unique and powerful contribution that school history can and should make to the cultural currency and intellectual economy of the curriculum. The problem is that we typically wish school history to serve more local and partisan purposes: to enhance national identities, to persuade the dispossessed to exercise the right to vote, and so on. It is difficult to achieve consensus about such purposes or about the content and organization of history (or social studies) syllabuses necessary to fulfill them. Nor is it easy to agree about the extent to which the promise of school history is fulfilled in practice, although few people appear to be fully satisfied with what is or seems to be achieved.[1]

Debate about the purposes and outcomes of school history has been joined in many countries. The British debate has many dimensions and elements, most of which are parochial but which, in three respects, may prove to be of more general interest. The first and most singular feature of recent British experience is the strength of the academic challenge to the use of history to engineer social responsibility or to redefine national or group consciousness. This is not to deny that school history has the potential to intensify or to focus the patriotic impulse or group identity; it is to posit an inverse relationship between the certainty with which such outcomes can be ensured and the integrity of the means by which they can be realized. It is also to claim that the values underpinning History as an academic discipline in an open society are more important than any particular representation of the human past. If we are true to the values of History per se, we cannot answer for the views that adolescents will express about the contemporary social and political agenda, but we may nonetheless expect such views to be more rational and informed than would otherwise be the case.[2]

The second salient feature of the British scene is that over the past twenty-five years large numbers of history teachers have, more or less wittingly and to varying degrees, attempted to induct pupils into History as "a form of knowledge." Students of the Schools History Project (SHP) (ages 13–16) and of the Cambridge A' Level History Project (16-18) learn how to use evidence to adjudicate between competing accounts; to evaluate explanations of actions, events, and states-of-affairs; and to determine the relative significance of events within developmental narratives of varying durations and ranges. In reality, the teaching of these projects is as radical or conventional as the practices of the teachers themselves. This notwithstanding, to a greater or lesser degree, British history teachers attempt to develop pupils' understanding of History as a logical and evidence-based means of making sense of the past.

The third element of the recent British experience is less optimistic. It is that although school history has come to be regarded as more "a thinking" and less "a rote-learning" subject, and while many adolescents are better equipped to make rational sense of the past and perhaps even to bring historical perspective to bear upon the analysis of contemporary events and options, few possess the knowledge or even the sense of the past necessary to exploit this understanding.[3] The logical and methodological apparatus of historical enquiry can be applied to fragments of and episodes in the past, but not to the past as a whole. This remains shadowy, mysterious, and, in its broader aspects, given. It is as if odd scenes of a play could be variously interpreted and even, with benefit of scholarship, new lines substituted here and there, but the plot as a whole remain both unknown and immutable. Worse still, constructivist research into pupils' historical thinking suggests, but does no more than suggest, that students conceive the aim of History to be the presentation of a uniform "picture of the past."[4] At best, the optimum "picture" is conceived to be complex and multidimensional, to possess meaning and narrative logic, and to be determined by the patient application of logic and the evaluation of evidence. It is, however, assumed that there should be one "best picture."

For the most able adolescents, the past seems to be construed as an "event-space" populated by concurrent and consecutive events that already possess boundaries demarcating them from and connections linking them with other events.[5] Over the past twenty-five years, British teachers have sought, with some success, to teach pupils that statements of historical fact must be justified against evidence; that such statements are at best "more likely than not" and at worst "more likely than the alternative statements on offer"; and that evidence derived from relics and records may be challenged and variously interpreted. What has not been attempted in Britain is to teach pupils how to handle the past as a whole. In consequence, few fifteen-year-olds are able to map the past; even fewer can offer a coherent narrative; and virtually none can conceive of anything more subtle than a single "best" narrative.

Investigations into pupils' constructs about the past undertaken as part of the initial evaluation of SHP and subsequent reform of the Study in Development[6] component indicate not only that few British fifteen-year-olds develop useful and historical narrative frameworks but that, for many, the "event-space" within which such narratives form and grow is *incoherent* and lacking in order or meaning. One girl interviewed in an SHP postevaluation study and asked to describe medical practices at the time of the Battle of Hastings struggled to do so: "The Battle of Hastings was some time between Robin Hood and when Alfred burnt the cakes," she opined.[7] It is significant that:

- she could construct from memory a simple if inaccurate timeline for the history of medicine.
- she could *not* relate other scraps and fragments of historical knowledge (e.g., about the Battle of Hastings) to this timeline.
- her History of Medicine timeline comprised *a list* of notable physicians, inventions, and discoveries that had no more narrative logic than the alphabet. Hippocrates comes before Galen much as "G" precedes "H." Meaning might be attributed to individual events and items in the timeline, but the timeline itself is meaningless; it is a list not a historical narrative.

The essential meaninglessness of nonnarrative lists is evident in the following excerpt from a post-SHP evaluation transcript. The sixteen-year-old in question had written an outline history of medicine as an alphabet-like list of names and items:

INT: Did Galen learn anything about medicine from Hippocrates?
SUB: No
INT: Why not?
SUB: Galen had his own ideas.
INT: Why is Galen important in the history of medicine?
SUB: He was a good doctor for the Roman soldiers.

INT: Let's go back to Hippocrates and to this idea about the four humours getting out of balance, too much phlegm gives you a cold and so on . . . Is that what causes colds?

SUB: No, it's the cold that makes the phlegm.

INT: If the theory of the four humours is wrong, why is it important in the history of medicine? Why do you have to learn about it?

SUB: It's what they did in them days.

INT: Is it possible that modern medicine could have been in any way different if Galen and Hippocrates had never lived, or if they come up with different ideas?

SUB: No.

INT: Why not?

SUB: They're dead and gone.[8]

This pupil possesses some sense of chronology and can construct a timeline, albeit one limited to people and events connected with the history of medicine, but in her written work and oral responses she shows no signs of construing this timeline as a *history*, as a meaningful narrative into which present and future can be incorporated. Imagine a child who has never seen a movie or a play. Show this child the trailer for a movie: a set of disconnected ten-second clips. The child might learn the sequence of clips, but the trailer as a whole will mean nothing. Lacking the concept of a movie, the child will not be able to conceive what the clips could mean. This is how some adolescents *seem* to construe the history they learn; the problem is not so much failure to understand bits of content in isolation as failure to conceive of event-space in ways that allow them to construe each part in relation to the whole and the whole as more than the sum of the parts. More encouraging is the fact that the Study in Development appears to have *some* positive impact inasmuch as the incidence of incoherent event-space constructions among participants is almost 45 percent lower than for pupils who follow non-SHP syllabuses. Indeed, for the majority of fifteen-year-old SHP pupils, the history of medicine, at least, has meaning and narrative logic and connects with present and future. The problem remains that, for many, this narrative is limited to medicine and is monothetic in character. By this is meant, first, that the narrative is construed to have the same epistemological status as the "facts" incorporated within it; second, that for pupils, "what changes" is the same as "what happens"; and, third, that history is seen as a one-way street that does not admit of multiple traditions or lines of development, of dead ends, false dawns, or might-have-beens. As one boy remarked:

> *SUB:* We know where medicine will be in the future: there'll be cures for cancer, electric hearts, brains even.
>
> *INT:* O.K. Are you saying that these things *might* happen? Or do you think that they will happen *for certain*?
>
> *SUB:* For certain! It's the way its got to go.
>
> *INT:* Why has it "got to go" this way? Suppose we run out of money for medical research? Suppose that World War III breaks out and people lose faith in science?
>
> *SUB:* I'm not sure how long it'll take. It might get held up like you say, but it might be quick since history has speeded up since 1900.[9]

This boy, and others like him, can debate the reasons for and causes of particular actions, events, and outcomes, but he seems to construe the greater narrative that links the distant and recent pasts, the present and future as occupying an event-space that is monothetic in nature, mechanical in operation, and monolithic in outcome. The apparent contradiction between their constructions of the past on the small scale, over short periods of time, and on the large scale, over spans of time that extend across taught topics and periods, is noteworthy.

It is possible that the contrast between the ways in which teachers present history at the lesson level (to be researched, debated, and argued) and at the curriculum level (to be accepted as an unquestioned and unproblematic sequence of topics and themes) leads pupils to construe the big picture very differently from the little pictures. Truffle-hunting in lessons is a thorny and uncertain enterprise, but the parachutist's perspective implicit in the history curriculum is just how it is! It would follow that event-space is construed as monothetic because there is a "ghost in the syllabus" rather than in the machine. History is to be debated and constructed in class and over short time spans; the syllabus moves on in the nature of things.

Pupils who have acknowledged the uncertainty of outcomes and who reason in terms of necessary rather than sufficient conditions over the short term may nonetheless conceive of long-term developmental and causal processes in mechanical terms. Students required to play "black box" games in physics also tend to acknowledge uncertainty—"It could be this! It could be that!"—and to argue the necessary features of the unseen mechanism—"You must have a potentiometer somewhere in there or you couldn't have this output!" But, for all their uncertainties, physics students never doubt the *nature* of the unseen mechanism. It is just possible that history students, aware of antecedents and consequences but unable to observe the developmental, intentional and causal processes at work over the long term, also assume that they are dealing with inputs and outputs and are required to work out what happens inside the historical black box. If so, discussion of alternative outcomes may involve the consideration of *logical* but not of *causal possibilities*. Pupils who believe in mechanical causality and monothetic lines of development may sometimes consider what would have happened to outputs had inputs been other than they were and may even perform mind experiments wherein "black box" processes are systematically varied.

Evidence from the SHP evaluation and from subsequent investigations that led to the reform of the Study in Development unit suggests that, for a significant number of pupils, this possibility should be entertained. Indeed, there is evidence to suggest that many British fifteen-year-olds (6 percent of those following SHP and 28 percent following non-SHP courses) conceive history as a one-way street over even short time spans. For example, one boy wrote that World War II necessarily followed Hitler's invasion of Poland because "the war could not have been caused by something else."[10] The argument is interesting: War is given, *so its antecedents must be inevitable*. The subsequent interview makes it clear that he perceives further questioning to be pointless:

INT: What's the connection that makes the one follow from the other? Why did the invasion of Poland lead to World War II?

SUB: It just happened.

INT: How can it *just* happen? . . . Do you mean there was no reason?

SUB: It just did.

INT: Do you mean it was luck?

SUB: Well . . . it was just what was meant to happen and it did.[11]

There is a divinity in the sequence of events that requires no causal mechanism.

Of greater interest still are pupils who appear to construe monothetic event-space in binary terms. Such pupils equate change in history with headline actions and events, rather than with the consequences thereof for people in general. Thus, a change in medicine is seen as a result of John Snow's 1854 study of a cholera outbreak, rather than of the shifts in public health policy and practice to which it contributed or the impact these changes had upon subsequent mortality rates from cholera and other infectious diseases. The historical narrative comes to be seen as a series of changes (actions and events, inventions and discoveries) separated by periods of quiescence in which nothing happens. The event-space is occupied by alternating events (1s) and temporal spaces (0s). The following extract from a post-SHP evaluation transcript reflects this view or something close to it:

INT: What might have happened to medicine if Hippocrates had not come up with the Theory of the Four Humours?
SUB: Nothing, you'd have nothing.
INT: Why?
SUB: If he'd done nothing you won't get anything.
INT: Are you saying that Greek medicine would have been different than it was?
SUB: No, you wouldn't have medicine.
INT: But suppose that Hippocrates had come up with a different theory, say that sickness comes from bad smells, dirty water, and dirty food?
SUB: He wouldn't do that, would he? It was the Four Humours or nothing.
INT: Has there ever been a time in history when absolutely nothing happens?
SUB: Yes. In the Middle Ages nothing happened for hundreds of years.[12]

It is almost certain that, like almost all adolescents, this girl knows full well that people got sick and were treated during these "holes in history" when "nothing" is said to have happened. It seems to be the case, however, that some pupils fail to relate this commonsense knowledge to the monothetic narratives constructed on the basis of what they are taught in history classes. (In like manner, pupils charged with sundry offenses will insist that they did "nothing" during the whole of a lunch break or in response to direct and prolonged provocation by another pupil). This and similar views are consistent with the "ghost in the syllabus" postulate but also suggest a deeper failure to distinguish between contingency and necessity. The "ghost" is a mechanical spirit whose choices are limited to 1 or 0, something or nothing.

A final example illustrates how deeply this binary something-or-nothing assumption may enter into the fabric of constructed event-space. The following written response was recorded by a non-SHP pupil on an ECT (personal construct) instrument administered as part of the SHP evaluation study:

The statement says, "It [Hitler's invasion of Poland in September 1939] could have caused something else . . . Britain and France could have let him get away with it." If that is so, nothing would have happened, so the statement contradicts itself.[13]

This pupil rebuts the postulate of alternative outcomes on the grounds of logical inconsistency: Had Britain and France let Hitler get away with it, "nothing would have happened," so the suggestion that the invasion of Poland "could have caused something else" is nonsense. The alternative to something (World War II) is nothing (a hole in history or empty event-space).

It must be noted that many adolescents think in more sophisticated ways. Significant numbers of British fifteen-year-olds are able to discuss what *did* occur in the context of what *could have* occurred, but even so it is often difficult to distinguish arguments that refer to *causal possibility* from those that simply admit of other *logical possibilities*. The distinction is crucial insofar as it is one thing to conceive of alternative but logically coherent pasts and quite another to consider in what respects *our past* (and hence perhaps, though not necessarily, our present) could have been different. Physicists engage in the first type of mind game when they ask whether it is possible for a universe to exist in which the value of Planck's constant is twice or a half that in our universe. The subject in the following transcript extract clearly distinguishes between mind games played with logical and causal possibility:

> *SUB:* . . . although anything *could* happen . . . different things would need different lengths of time spans, and this makes some very unlikely . . .
> *INT:* How quickly can things happen?
> *SUB:* Not so fast. . . . As fast as people can do things or change their minds.[14]

Other adolescents show some, albeit inconclusive, signs of a disposition and ability to construe the polythetic complexity of historical event-space. The following comment was written by a non-SHP pupil critical of the ways in which history is taught. Two statements about the origins of World War II are contrasted: one "considers the problems of the past by suggesting what might have been the consequence of an event and not merely what was the consequence; . . . [whereas the other statement] only describes an event without there being any room for discussion of possible results, in much the same way as we, ourselves, are taught history as a subject which is completely sealed and cannot be changed."[15] Much hangs upon what this boy means by "completely sealed and cannot be changed." Does he mean "could not have been other than it was," or "cannot be reconceptualized," or "cannot be validly construed in more than one way"? It is unfortunate that this ambiguity was not followed up at interview.

Few British fifteen year olds go much further than this, and no more than 43 percent of SHP and 19 percent of non-SHP pupils show any sign of conceiving actuality as a special case of causal possibility. Given the difficulty of determining when pupils are arguing from logical and when from causal possibility, the real proportions may be significantly lower. More certain is that, for around 36 percent of SHP and a mere handful of non-SHP pupils, narrative frameworks occupy a multifaceted but still monothetic event-space in which discrete if overlapping and interrelated narrative strands are construed. For the original SHP Study in Development, these may relate to pharmacology, surgery, and public health through time.[16] Apart from the fact that they pertain to a relatively minor aspect of human history, these narratives are limited, first, in that pupils construe them as "natural narratives" (i.e., natural categories) inherent in the fabric of the past rather than imposed upon it by the historian's activities, and, second, in consequence of this, pupils strive to produce definitive narratives for each strand or category of concern.

This is as good as it gets. There is no evidence to suggest, let alone to demonstrate, that by the end of compulsory education British adolescents use genuinely polythetic and broadly based narrative frameworks to structure their knowledge of the past or to relate that knowledge to the present.

The problem remains that, on the basis of existing evidence, we can offer only suggestions about pupils' constructs that are tentative and lack precision. Further research is required to determine

a. the scope, content and structure of pupils' constructions of event-space;
b. the extent to which the nature and sophistication of pupils' constructions of event-space is contingent upon the quality of pupils' understanding of History as a form of knowledge;
c. how pupils' narrative frameworks of the past inform analyses of and judgements about the present.

It may be anticipated, however, that systematic investigation into adolescents' constructs of the past will do no more than replicate the findings illustrated, albeit with greater refinement and security, because very few teachers attempt to give pupils a conspectual framework of human history that enables them to articulate elements of the past with each other and with the present in any meaningful fashion. And what we fail to teach adolescents they are unlikely to develop for themselves. It follows that research would prove most valuable were it to follow and assess a thoroughgoing attempt to foster the development and use of large-scale narrative frameworks by pupils. Research might then inform what can be achieved by whatever means. Such a project has obvious dangers. By accident or design, pupils might be taught to accept a privileged "picture of the past," rather than how to construct and use meaningful narratives of their own devising. This danger is all the more real since an initial framework must be directly taught and will, of necessity, favor certain mimetic possibilities while preempting others. We can aim to teach an elemental and elementary framework that will serve pupils as a scaffold, not a cage, but the contents and configuration of the scaffold will make it easier for pupils to construct some narrative frameworks rather than others. The best we can hope for is constructions of the past that are meme-dependent but not meme-dictated. In order to maximize opportunities for pupils to develop valid and usable narrative frameworks while minimizing the likelihood of prescribed or privileged "pictures of the past" being taught with intent or learned by default, it is necessary, first, for history syllabuses to address the human past in general, and, second, to revisit this general framework throughout pupils' historical education. In short, whatever history we decide or are compelled to teach, some time should be set aside each year for the development of a conspectual framework within which other outlines and topics can be located and from which they can derive meaning.

As I have noted, the research necessary to inform the progression of narrative frameworks could most usefully be undertaken were systematic attempts to develop such frameworks to become commonplace in schools. This notwithstanding, a crude and simplistic scheme may be derived from the data reviewed earlier in this chapter.

Level 1: A Chronologically Ordered Past

This level of history is typically taught by means of timelines of varying kinds and degrees of sophistication. In Britain, timelines usually focus upon national histories, cover relatively short spans of time, and include landmark events like the deaths and accessions of monarchs, the defeat of the Spanish Armada, and significant occurrences such as the Gunpowder Plot and the Fire of London. Pupils often forget the sequence of events while, as a rule, remembering something or other about the events themselves. They also make sense of what is portrayed in timelines in ways that fail to connect with what is known about the contemporary world. For example, when presented with a timeline that depicts people between 1066 and the present ordered by reigning English monarch, significant numbers of eight- and nine-year-olds opine that "everyone looked like that" in the reigns of Elizabeth I and James I and, moreover, they fix the change in fashions precisely in 1603.

The utility of timelines and of other means of organizing the past in chronological terms is not disputed. These devices are not sufficient, however. It is necessary, in addition, for pupils to acquire a basic chronology that embraces the whole of the past and is represented in terms of significant phases of human history. These phases may be particularized with reference to what holds for *some people* and for *most people* without reference to geographical location. For example, the start of the Neolithic Revolution could be noted as a period of time in which "*Some* people started to farm for food, although *most* people still lived by hunting and foraging." (The point at which *most* people could be said to live by farming should also be noted.) The same distinctions should be made with respect to heat-based industry, writing, urbanization, and so on. Geography should enter into the synoptic timeline in two ways: first, to record the diffusion of population into previously vacant areas of the world, and, second, to note when isolated peoples came into regular contact with others for the first time.

The scope and generality of such a chronologically ordered map of the past are its diacritical features. They must add perspective and scale to the temporally and spatially narrow syllabuses and timelines taught as part of state and national curricula, and they must be sufficiently general to distinguish history from soap opera, to delineate the deep currents that shape the lives of millions upon millions rather than the frothy antics of the few. Above all, chronologically ordered maps of the past must contain the seeds of coherent historical narratives.

Level 2: Coherent Historical Narratives

There is a degree of difference between picturing the past as "map" and as "story." A map has order and defines relationships; a story has logic and meaning. In history as narrative, the spread of urban settlements in the fourth century B.C. does not simply follow the spread of agriculture but follows *from* it. The fact that the populations of the Roman and Chinese empires fell during apparently separate crises of classical and Han civilizations in the fourth and fifth centuries A.D. makes for convenient generalization in a chronological map but for uncomfortable coincidence in a historical narrative, not because everything in history must be neat and tidy with a complete and perfect explanation for why the past is as it is— a sure sign that we are dealing with lies, with fantasy, or with both—but because narrative frameworks work with connections, patterns, and colligatory generalizations as well as with time and space.[17] Indeed, it is only when pupils are able to relate historical contents of present concern to preexistent but ever-developing narrative frameworks that we can begin to explain that such colligatory concepts as the Industrial Revolution or the General Crisis of the Seventeenth Century are not events, nor even categories of event. In the United Kingdom, even sixteen- to eighteen-year-old adolescents experience some confusion when asked to fix precise locations for the Industrial Revolution (even more for the General Crisis) in time and space. They may also construe the relationship of individual inventions, transportation developments, factory systems, and capitalizations to the Industrial Revolution as that of part to whole, much as the fateful charge by Cromwell's Ironsides is part of, or an episode within, the Battle of Naseby. Nor can such adolescents easily explain why such questions as "Was there an Industrial Revolution? Or a General Crisis in Seventeenth Century Europe?" are reasonable in ways that questions like "Was there a Spinning Jenny? Or a Long Parliament?" are not. The Long Parliament is a whole that has parts; it is the sum of individual and the product of collective actions in ways that the General Crisis is not. In like manner, it is commonsense to say that Fairfax and Ireton participated in the Battle of Naseby, but to claim that they participated in the General Crisis would be no more meaningful than to say that they played their part in seventeenth-century history.

It is here that the distinction between "what happened" and "what was going on" is pertinent. The historian must not be false to the chronicle of events but must also construct meaningful accounts that impute narrative significance to events by means of quantitative and colligatory generalizations, analysis of trends and turning points, and intentional and causal explanations. It follows that the vast majority of "facts" for which historians possess satisfactory evidence are not mentioned in their accounts. The significance of each "bit of the past" is determined by the meanings immanent within the historical narrative. The "singular particulars" (evidence based reconstructions of "what happened") only signify, or more usually fail to signify, to the extent that they inform or illustrate "what was going on."

It is not difficult to teach sixteen-year-old adolescents to look for common factors that underlie and explain such seemingly disparate phenomena as the English Civil War and Interregnum, the Frondes in France, the 1650 coup d'état in the United Provinces, the Catalonian, Portuguese, and Neopolitan revolts, and the Thirty Years War in Germany and Bohemia—although few get very far with their investigations. What is difficult is for adolescents to challenge the concept of a General Crisis, once introduced, without at the same time challenging the local significance of the phenomena themselves. Perhaps there was no general crisis because the English Revolution was no more than a Great Rebellion, and one that failed? Maybe the Frondes was a little local difficulty of no great moment? At best, adolescents can be persuaded to criticize the General Crisis concept as a category mistake, a promiscuous lumping together of phenomena more different than similar. What they find exceedingly difficult to do is to criticize the concept of a General Crisis without either diminishing or denying lower-level generalizations or baseline data on the one hand or resorting to an extrahistorical critique of linguistic categories on the other hand. (The colligatory concept "Industrial Revolution" is frequently analyzed with reference to the defining features of "revolutions"). To go further than this requires adolescents to possess a valid and usable narrative framework such that, first, the concept of General Crisis can be evaluated as a generalized description and explanation within an ongoing story that connects antecedent and succeeding phenomena in ways that are more meaningful than would otherwise be the case without violence to accuracy of description, and, second, that they can make of historical narrative an object of consciousness in opposition to the construed past such that debate as to how we might most validly describe and explain the past has no necessary implications for beliefs about what actually happened. Only when adolescents are able to distinguish history from the past and to see that debates about the validity of narratives are not solely about the truth or fidelity of images and pictures of the past can they genuinely understand what is being debated.

Level 3: Multidimensional Narratives

The third stage in the development of pupil constructs is neither as radical nor as difficult to engineer as the second. It is, however, of equal consequence. Any worthwhile narrative framework should embrace at least three interlocking and interpenetrating dimensions: means of production and population history (economics, technology, and people); forms of social organization (social structures, institutions, and politics); cultural and intellectual history (commonsense, religion, and institutionalized knowledge). The extent to which the third dimension of cultural and intellectual history can be woven into a coherent framework accessible to the majority of adolescents without being so simplified as to be counterproductive is debatable. It may be that a sufficiently complex framework could be developed from distinct but interrelated sociopolitical and technoeconomic narratives.

Level 4: Polythetic Narrative Frameworks

As might be anticipated, this is the most difficult step for adolescents to take and is possible only once their constructs of history and of History as a form of knowledge have reached high levels of sophistication and elaboration. Physicists strive to formulate a GUT—a Grand Unified Theory of everything (or of everything that really matters). Historians ceaselessly research and reanalyze, reappraise, and rewrite accounts, but there is no comparable quest for a GUN—a grand unified narrative. Views do change, theories and accounts do fall from favor, but old dialectics spawn new dialectics, not settled syntheses. To ask which one account of world history (or any fraction thereof) I should read would be tantamount to a child asking for the correct setting on a kaleidoscope before venturing to peer through the eyepiece. This is difficult for adolescents to understand and, to a considerable extent, must be experienced on the basis of attempts to construe the past as a whole rather than apprehended as a philosophical proposition.

Once pupils understand that we can never play truth games with historical accounts (if only because these accounts are *about* the past, not the evidence that we extract from sources, and because there is no way in which we can access, rerun, or replicate the past in order to check the fidelity of the correspondence between account and that which is accounted) but must debate the validity of what we say about the past, it is natural to assume that there can be a perfectly valid, or at least a most valid, account. Indeed, the Cambridge A' Level History Project aimed and to some extent succeeded in teaching sixteen- to eighteen-year-olds how to adjudicate between competing accounts. Adolescents can also be taught that the validity of accounts varies with temporal and spatial scale—for example, that the notion of an English Revolution may be more defensible over the timescale 1558–1714 than 1640–1685. They do, however, tend to construe the problem as one of matching questions to the most appropriate timescales; in short, they still believe in *a best* answer and hence in a *most valid* account.

We do, in truth, demand that pupils perform an unconscionable number of reverse somersaults. First, we say that there is no single right answer to any of the really significant questions in history and that pupils must work things out for themselves. Then we say: "But not any answer will do. Some answers are indefensible even if no one answer is clearly right! And some admissible answers are not as good as other admissible answers." Pupils then spend considerable time and effort learning how to determine which answers and accounts are better than others. If they succeed, we say: "But even though some accounts are better because more valid or coherent or parsimonious than others, there is no one best account, since we find it useful to vary questions, assumptions, and perspectives." This is difficult to appreciate unless—to recycle a convenient simile—pupils are able to view the past as through a kaleidoscope: the patterns are ordered and determinate but do not yield a single stable picture. Individual pupils may express personal preferences for patterns or narratives for whatever reason, but the view and understanding of the whole would be impoverished were all other possibilities to be discarded. To be truly useful, the frameworks employed by pupils must not just be ordered and coherent, complex and multidimensional; they must be polythetic and admit of alternative narratives.[18]

This four-level model is highly speculative and goes beyond the evidence. As I have said, it may be possible to acquire the necessary research data only if and when systematic attempts to develop pupils' narrative frameworks are made. How might this be done? The following desiderata may be suggested:

a. History must be taught as "a form of knowledge" that equips pupils to evaluate knowledge claims, to distinguish description from explanation, and to debate the significance of events within historical narratives.

b. Pupils must be taught and retaught a conspectus of the whole of human history. This need take no more than a fraction of syllabus time but must be revisited and elaborated throughout a pupil's historical education.

c. History syllabuses should include thematic studies (studies in development) over long spans of time. Such themes should address the material, social, and organizational aspects of human history. (This is not to preclude major roles for local, national, and in-depth studies).

d. It is important not just to advance chronologically through a syllabus but to review and to analyze overviews of varying degrees of resolution—twenty years, 160 years, 700 years—as and when appropriate. More important still, such overviews should be located in and related to narrative frameworks taught at levels 1–3.

e. When planning lessons and schemes of work, it is important to identify data that we wish pupils to retain for incorporation within emergent narrative frameworks. Such data should be distinguished from those used to provide color, to maintain interest, and to assist in the generalization and articulation of higher-order learning outcomes. Key data should be reinforced by means of advance subsumers and frequent reviews and summaries.

More, much more, could be written about this than space permits, but the most fundamental question of all remains to be answered: "So what?"

The answer to this final question is based upon the hunch that unless and until people are able to locate present knowledge, questions, and concerns within narrative frameworks that link past with past and past with present in ways that are valid and meaningful, coherent, and flexible, the uses that are made of history will range from the impoverished to the pernicious. At worst, adolescents will seek to find parallels between past and present and, with reference to known outcomes, to justify preferred policy options over others. Or, they may draw universal lessons about the manifest destinies of nations or groups; about the obligations to keep faith with the sacrifices made by predecessors (usually an obligation to shed yet more blood); or about the historic, hence unalterable, characters and intentions of other groups and nations. Cicero remarked that to be ignorant of history is to remain forever a child. We might add that to subscribe to populist and mythic constructions of the past is to remain trapped in the codes and culture of the street gang, to invoke persuasive and partial histories that reinforce simple truths and even simpler hatreds.

History cannot be disaggregated and plundered for bits and pieces that can validly and usefully inform the present. Its value is as a big picture (and a complex, polythetic picture) that, first, gives perspective to the present by prompting us to take the long view and to look beyond what is happening to what might be going on, and, second, allows us to fit present phenomena within a narrative and polythetic framework. This is not too dissimilar to dropping a new piece of colored glass into the kaleidoscope, turning the barrel and observing the new patterns that emerge.

This, of course, is no more than a hunch. But we have argued for generations about what bits of history pupils should learn with whatever consequential benefits to the pupils as individuals and to the societies of which they are members. Might it not be time to consider the possible benefits of history as a whole rather than of selected fragments? Might this not enable pupils to spurn the Caliph's coin and to see through the mythical history that attaches to it?

NOTES

1. See Veronica Boix-Mansilla, this volume.

2. Peter Lee draws an elegant analogy with Heisenberg's Uncertainty Principle. Lee argues that we can either answer for the beliefs and attitudes that pupils form on the basis of the history we teach or we can answer for the integrity of the history itself. P. J. Lee, "History in School: Aims, Purposes and Approaches," in P. J. Lee et al., *The Aims of School History* (London, 1992).

3. See the unpublished SHP *Evaluation Report* submitted to the British Schools Council (Council for Educational Technology).

4. SHP *Evaluation Report*.

5. By "event space" is meant no more than "the rules and parameters presumed to govern the contents of the past." For example, actions, events, and states-of-affairs may be construed as thing-like entities with precise boundaries in time and space. Generalizations may be construed as "big things," as "complex wholes with many parts," or as categories of action or outcomes. The contents of the past may be presumed to exhibit various sorts of order—temporal and spatial, causal and contingent, natural and necessary—or no order at all. Models of action may be individual, institutional, collective, or all of these.

6. The original Study in Development, *Medicine Through Time*, addressed one aspect of history from prehistoric to modern times. It was taught over a period of six to eight months to fourteen- to fifteen-year-old pupils and was intended to promote understanding of change and development. Options dealing with energy and with crime and punishment were added at a later date.

7. These and other data are taken from previously unpublished research materials relating to the reform of the SHP Study in Development units.

8. SHP Study in Development research.

9. SHP Study in Development research.

10. SHP *Evaluation Report*.

11. SHP *Evaluation Report*.

12. SHP Study in Development research.

13. SHP Study in Development research.

14. SHP *Evaluation Report*.

15. SHP *Evaluation Report*.

16. The phrase "narrative framework" lacks elegance and transparency but is difficult to improve upon. It refers to a scaffold of fact, generalization, and interpretation that (a) imposes meaning upon the past, (b) represents the present as part of an ongoing process, and (c) is capable of extension and elaboration in the light of further study.

17. The concept of "colligation" is derived from W. H. Walsh, *Introduction to the Philosophy of History* (London, 1951), pp. 23–24.

18. A different and more powerful analysis of the properties of narrative frameworks may be found in P. J. Lee, "Historical Knowledge and the National Curriculum," in R. Aldrich, ed., *History in the National Curriculum* (London, 1991).

Chapter 6

The "Convergence" Paradigm in Studying Early American History in the Schools

Gary B. Nash

Sixty-three years ago, the editor of *American Anthropologist*, discouraged by American provincialism, floated a wry essay explaining how much American culture owed to people from faraway parts of the world. The "unsuspecting patriot" who touts his "precious heritage" awakens "garbed in pajamas, a garment of East Indian origin; and lying in a bed built on a pattern which originated in either Persia or Asia Minor. He is muffled to the ears in un-American materials: cotton, first domesticated in India; linen, domesticated in the Near East; wool from an animal native to Asia Minor; or silk whose uses were first discovered by the Chinese. . . ." Other "foreign ideas," the author explained, "have already wormed their way into his civilization without his realizing what was going on. . . . " The awakened American "glances at the clock, a medieval European invention, uses one potent Latin word in abbreviated form, rises in haste, and goes to the bathroom. . . . In this bathroom, the American washes with soap invented by the ancient Gauls. Next he cleans his teeth, a subversive European practice which did not invade America until the latter part of the eighteenth century. He then shaves, a masochistic rite first developed by the heathen priests of ancient Egypt and Sumer. The process is made less of a penance by the fact that his razor is of steel, an iron-carbon alloy discovered in either India or Turkestan. Lastly, he dries himself on a Turkish towel. . . . "[1]

For those who wrote history textbooks for young learners, it would be a long time before they paid attention to this notion of interpenetrating worlds. Textbooks, in particular, presented American Indians and Africans in ways that today seem quaint at best and vicious at worst. This essay traces how historical scholarship, most of it done after World War II, gradually constructed a more realistic, sensitive, and anthropologically informed understanding of early American cultural encounters and very slowly seeped into schoolbooks. Without attempting an exhaustive survey of high school and college textbooks, I postulate that not until the late 1950s did young American learners began to see that Africans and Indians were more than primitive savages with strong backs and valuable land to contribute to the American way and that their plight in a white-dominated society was not nature's dictum. With roots in the pre–World War II "progressive education" movement, this halting change occurred only when innovative academic scholarship began to achieve a critical mass that textbook writers could no longer ignore. The essay also reflects on the relationship between school textbook writers and academic historians and the meaning that students take from textbook explanations of the course of history.

For more than a century, young Americans in public schools learned what may be called an "inevitabilist explanation" of relations among Europeans, American Indians, and Africans.

In the two generations before the Civil War, as the public school movement began to bring basic education to American youth, the first textbooks drove home the theme of inevitable Indian-white relations. The first schoolbooks of the early republic, such as Jedidiah Morse's *Geography Made Easy* (1791), perpetuated the notion that the rapid mortality of the Algonquian peoples in New England was God's undertaking. "The hand of Providence is noticeable in these surprising instances of mortality among the Indians to make room for the English," wrote Morse. "They waste and moulder away; they in a manner unaccountable disappear."[2] Another schoolbook, published during the War of 1812, assured students that "the religion of nature, the light of revelation, and the pages of history, are combined in the proof, that God has ordered that nations shall become extinct, and that others shall take their place."[3]

By the mid-nineteenth century, the search for a scientific history brought forth a secular version of inevitability reasoning. An angry Jehovah did not dictate the course of history, but larger forces did, whether environmental and geographic, moral and political, or economic and social. The view arose, as Isaiah Berlin has written of modern history in general, that "the behaviour of men is . . . made what it is by factors largely beyond the control of individuals."[4] History textbooks became suffused with terms such as "the march of events," the "spirit of the age," the "laws of history," "manifest destiny," and the "tide of human affairs"— all phrases connoting the inevitability of events, the irresistible rhythms of human life, the unswervable forces that dictate the ways humans act.

In this kind of historical explanation, historians planted "mental depth-charges," to use James Axtell's telling phrase, in the minds of young learners. "When heard or read," Axtell reminds us, these loaded words "quickly sink into our consciousness and explode, sending off cognitive shrapnel in all directions, . . . showering our understanding with fragments of accumulated meaning and association."[5] This aptly describes the furtive power of words such as "inevitable," "inexorable," and "unstoppable"—or, in Isaiah Berlin's elegant formulation, the transferring of guilt about sordid parts of history to cosmic forces beyond the power of individuals to alter:

> No sooner do we acquire adequate "natural" or "metaphysical" insight into the "inexorable" or "inevitable" parts played by all things animate and inanimate in the cosmic process, than we are freed from the sense of personal endeavour. Our sense of guilt and of sin, our pangs of remorse and self-condemnation, are automatically dissolved; the tension, the fear of failure and frustration disappear as we become aware of the elements of a larger "organic whole," of which we are variously described as limbs or elements.[6]

In the decades bracketing the Civil War, when the first multivolume histories of the United States reached the public, the presumption of inevitable conflict and conquest came strongly to the fore. Mention of Africa and Africans was hardly contemplated for public or school reading. George Bancroft's heroic history of the United States, which began appearing in 1856, casually dismissed Indian culture. The native people were "ignorant of the arts of life" and suffered from "the hereditary idleness of the race." John Gorham Palfrey's *Compendious History of New England*, published in 1873, devoted a chapter to depicting the Indians as biologically inferior, insolent, and lacking in mental capacity. Influenced by the general acceptance of phrenological certitudes, which had swept the country in the middle decades of the nineteenth century with the notion that the various branches of the human family were ordered hierarchically by nature, Palfrey portrayed New England's Indian wars as entirely the fault of savage people.[7] For John Fiske, popular lecturer in the centennial year of 1876, nature's arrangement of the races made genocide defensible. "As a matter of practical policy," he wrote, "the annihilation of the Pequots [in 1637] can be condemned only by those who read history so incorrectly as to suppose that savages, whose business is to torture and slay, can always be dealt with according to the methods in use between civilized peoples."[8]

Imbued with the scientific racism of the late nineteenth century, textbook writers harped on the lesson that Indian decline was caused by the Indians' own inability to rise above the lesser endowments bestowed by nature. "The Indian will not learn the arts of civilization, and he and his forest must perish together," wrote one turn-of-the-century textbook writer. Another explained that "the red race is rapidly passing away in accordance with a well-established law of nature, that causes an inferior race to yield to a superior when one comes in contact with the other."[9] Such statements conform closely to Berlin's description of the inevitability complex: "Acts hitherto regarded as wicked or unjustifiable are seen in a more 'objective' fashion—in the larger context—as part of the process of history which, being responsible for providing us with our scale of values, must not therefore be judged in terms of it; and viewed in this new light [our historical actions] turn out no longer wicked but right and good because necessitated."[10]

By the early twentieth century, when an increasing percentage of the nation's youth received a basic education in American history, students were encouraged to consider the plight of African Americans in the same light. Both American Indians and African Americans, children learned, suffered from behavioral defects acquired at birth. This in itself made any serious study of Africa or the pre-Columbian American societies irrelevant. Since nature had arranged the races of man hierarchically, who could argue with the consignment of black Americans to the lowest positions in society? American children grew up with the understanding that in a democracy the portioning out of unequal opportunities and rewards according to race was perfectly natural because nature had endowed Americans of different skin hues unequally.[11]

A few dissenters raised their voices, insisting that when two races met, the outcome was not inevitable or caused by people who simply acted like savages. Helen Hunt Jackson reached a considerable audience with her book *A Century of Dishonor*, issued in blood-red covers in 1881. Excoriating the federal government's genocidal Indian policies in the century after the writing of the Constitution, Jackson attacked the notion that the victors had no responsibility for the plight of the vanquished.[12]

Jackson's *Century of Dishonor*, which played a role in the establishment of the Indian Rights Association in 1882, might have led to a reconsideration of textbook treatments of Indian-white relations. But her book did not move members of the budding historical profession. More to their liking was work of one of their own—the Harvard-trained Theodore Roosevelt, whose highly popular *Winning of the West* was a classic of inevitabilist argument. In his multivolume series, Roosevelt organized all of American history around the notion of "a series of mighty movements" that had begun in the Saxon forests of the previous millennium. All history moved teleologically toward the dominance of the English race. Tied to this premise, all Indian wars, from the early seventeenth century through the post–Civil War wars of the Great Plains, were part of the inexorable "race-history of the nations," as Roosevelt called it.[13] Contemptuous of Indians as a racial type, Roosevelt justified genocide as "necessary to the greatness of the [white] race and to the well-being of civilized mankind. It was as ultimately beneficial as it was inevitable." It was "wholly impossible to avoid conflicts with the weaker race," and the extermination of Indians should be acknowledged with national pride because "the most ultimately righteous of all wars is a war against savages . . . " for it establishes "the foundations for the future greatness of a mighty people."[14]

Though not as strident as Roosevelt, most textbook writers in the early twentieth century reflected the Bull Moose's mindset on what happened when cultures met. David Muzzey, king of textbook writers by the 1920s, taught students about "the stolid stupidity [of Indians] that no white man could match" and how they "loved to bask idly in the sun, like the Mississippi negro of to-day." Indians almost everywhere in North America, he counseled, were "sunk in bestial savagery" and "contributed almost nothing to the making of America." "It was impossible," he wrote, with inevitabilist implications, "that these few hundred thousand natives should stop the spread of the Europeans over the country. That would have been to condemn one of the fairest lands of the earth to the stagnation of barbarism."[15]

The "pragmatic revolt" in historical writing, positing that historical judgments should be tentative and arguing that more than one perspective on the past is fairer to the variety of people involved in any historical situation, brought fresh approaches to Indian-white and African American–white relations in the 1930s. Leading the way just before World War II was Harold Rugg, a staunch member of the progressive education movement and a person well read in the work of anthropologists and sociologists such as Robert Park, Franz Boas, and Melville Herskovits, who were trying to rescue Indian and African cultures from the oblivion heaped upon them by historians. Urging teachers to help students acquire indispensable qualities of "open-mindedness" and "critical-mindedness," Rugg asked unusual questions about Indian-white relations in his many textbooks. In one chapter, entitled "The Red Man's Continent," he asked: "In what spirit did the Indians and the Europeans receive each other?" "Did the white many buy the Indians' land that they settled upon?" "Or did they ruthlessly conquer it as the Spaniards had done in Central and South America?" "Was it right for the more numerous Europeans to drive back the scattered tribes of Indians?"[16]

After World War II, a mix of scholars began to develop the basis for challenging the reigning nationalist narrative in which Indians and Africans functioned mainly as foils for the European settlers' ceaseless march of progress.[17] These trailblazers emphasized the many ways in which Indian culture contributed to the development of an uniquely American culture in the colonial period.[18] Also rethinking the controlling paradigm was the popular writer Bernard DeVoto, who made a passionate plea to shift the story line of American history from its dismissal of Native Americans as little more than a hindrance to the course of progress. "Most American history," he wrote,

> has been written as if history were a function solely of white culture—in spite of the fact that till well into the nineteenth century the Indians were one of the principal determinants of historical events. Those of us who work in frontier history—which begins at the tidal beaches and when the sixteenth century begins—are repeatedly nonplused to discover how little has been done for us in regard to the one force bearing on our field that was active everywhere. . . . American historians have made shockingly little effort to understand the life, the societies, the cultures, the thinking, and the feeling of the Indians, and disastrously little effort to understand how all of these affected white men and their societies.[19]

In 1956, Kenneth Stampp, laying siege to the U. B. Phillips "Plantation Legend," held aloft a similar banner, turning passive and primitive enslaved Africans into active and far-from-savage people as they negotiated their way through the ordeal of slavery.[20]

The efforts of De Voto, Stampp, and many others might have brought textbook writers snappily to attention. But, in fact, with Americans consumed with Cold War fevers, pioneering scholarship faced a protracted struggle. For more than a decade after a rush of mold-breaking studies, only a few students began to encounter material that explained who the Africans and the Native Americans were, what their past was, how their cultural characteristics differed from those of European settlers, and how this might have affected Indian-white relations and the practice and experience of slavery by both Europeans and Africans.[21] Those students who read Daniel Boorstin's widely assigned book *The Americans: The Colonial Experience* would have concluded that there were no Africans in North America before the American Revolution—in fact they represented about one-fifth of the population and about half of the southern colonies' population—because slavery and slaves were never mentioned at all in the book.[22] Huge numbers of other students continued to be schooled on depictions of Africans as rescued from the primitive savagery of jungle Africa, a proposition that made the enslavement of millions of Africans seem like a fortuitous occurrence. Henry Steele Commager and Samuel Eliot Morison's best-selling *The Growth of the American Republic* was typical in its presentation of slavery and Africans. All Africans, in their textbook, had one name. "Sambo," they wrote, "whose wrongs moved the abolitionists to wrath and tears . . . suffered less than any other class in the South from its 'peculiar institution.' . . . The majority of slaves . . . were apparently happy. . . . There was much to be said for slavery as a transitional status between barbarism and civilization."[23]

Textbooks on colonial American history mirrored this relegation of enslaved Africans to grateful, if involuntary, immigrants. For example, Oliver Chitwood's *A History of Colonial America*, first published in 1931 and issued in new editions in 1948 and 1961, must have made students feel good about slavery and believe that any study of pre-contact Africa was useless.[24] "Generally when the master and slave were brought into close association," he wrote,

> a mutual feeling of kindliness and affection sprang up between them, which restrained the former from undue harshness toward the latter. . . . Good feeling between master and slave was promoted in large measure by the happy disposition or docile temperament of the Negro. Seldom was he surly and discontented and rarely did he harbor a grudge against his master for depriving him of his liberty. On the contrary, he want about his

daily tasks cheerfully, often singing while at work. . . . The fact that he had never known the ease and comforts of civilization in his homeland made it less difficult for him to submit to the hardships and inferior position of his condition. In this respect, the American Negro was better off than the slave of ancient Rome, who was often the intellectual equal and sometimes the superior of his master.[25]

Not until about 1959 did large numbers of postwar high school and college students imbibe a more realistic, less self-justifying treatment of slavery and Indian relations. In a passage that might have shocked parents weaned on a different set of lessons about what happened when Europeans and Indians met, Richard Hofstadter, William Miller, and Daniel Aaron wrote that "the Indians were confronted by a people who would be satisfied with nothing less than complete ownership of land and for whom a contract was a contract." King Philip's War in 1675–76 and many subsequent wars followed a certain cycle of events: "first, friendly overtures from the Indians, then open war, and finally the expulsion or extermination of the natives."[26] Similarly, these textbook authors took cognizance of Stampp's pathbreaking work, presenting slavery as brutal rather than benign and telling students that Reconstruction was "a tragic era" not "because of excesses in its treatment of whites but because it stopped so far short of effective emancipation of the Negro."[27]

If the Cold War atmosphere delayed the emergence of an antiracist presentation of American history, it could not stop a new generation of historians from studying Indian and African history intently. But, while the monographs piled up, most textbooks clung to old ways, though glacial creep was under way. Measuring the impact of a particular book on textbook writers and publishers is nearly impossible, but it is clear that the accumulated weight of scholarship by the 1970s was having an effect. By 1971, C. Vann Woodward, the titular dean of southern historians, was emphasizing the degree to which "the two great hyphenate minorities" in America—white southerners and black Americans—"shaped each other's destiny, determined each other's isolation, shared and molded a common culture."[28] After the publication of Alfred Crosby Jr.'s *The Columbian Exchange: Biological and Cultural Consequences of 1492* in 1972, it became difficult to ignore how profoundly European diseases had decimated native peoples and how importantly Indian food, pharmacopeia, and agricultural knowledge contributed to the making of colonial culture. Similarly, Peter Wood's *Black Majority* (1974) and Eugene Genovese's *Roll, Jordan, Roll: The World the Slaves Made* (1976) raised the consciousness of many textbook writers about how African knowledge of rice cultivation transformed South Carolina's economy, how the practice of slavery was always mediated between slave and master, and how Africans in general subtly Africanized European societies in a number of ways.[29] The Indian fur trade and Indian wars, though by no means first studied in the 1970s, received much new attention in that decade in ways that made more noticeable the centrality of the trade to the settlers' economy and the importance of Indian allies in the context of the struggle for empire in North America among the contending European powers.

In 1972–73, in writing *Red, White, and Black: The Peoples of Early America*, I made the first attempt to synthesize a growing literature that showed the severe limitations of traditional accounts of the colonial period that employed arguments about historical inevitability and implicitly justified their inattention to Africans and Indians by characterizing these immensely varied and changing peoples as if they had been frozen for centuries in a kind of primitive amber. Relying on historically informed anthropological studies as much as on the still inchoate scholarship in Indian and African history, I attempted to show that it mattered a great deal who the Indians were, how they had evolved for centuries before 1492, how they varied in the Americas, and how their own histories were part of the equation when Europeans invaded their lands and encountered them continuously for several centuries. Likewise, I argued that it mattered a great deal where the African slaves came from, how they varied in language and cultural background, and how these variations affected their adaptation and resistance to European enslavement.[30] The book urged students to understand the shared history of Europeans, Africans, and native Americans.

By the early 1980s, newly written college-level American history textbooks began to incorporate the burgeoning scholarship on African and Indian history.[31] *A People and a Nation* (1982), written by six distinguished Americanists, led the way.[32] The book had a brief description of early Indian peoples, another page on "cultural differences between the Indians and the English," and a sketch of Olaudah Equiano, with quotes from his *Interesting Narrative of the Life of Olaudah Equiano . . . Written by Himself* (1789), that at least allowed students to glimpse life in an Ibo village in West Africa.

Going farther were three textbooks published in 1984: Robert A. Divine et al.'s *America: Past and Present*; R. Jackson Wilson et al.'s *The Pursuit of Liberty: A History of the American People*; and Gary B. Nash, Julie

Jeffrey, et al.'s *The American People: Making a Society and a Nation*. Other new textbooks that slowly found favor among instructors who had been using politically oriented textbooks such as John Garraty's *The American Nation* and John Morton Blum et al.'s *The National Experience* began treating Indian and African peoples as more than so much clay to be molded by Europeans. Both in single-author texts, such as Stephan Thernstrom's *A History of the American People* (1985) and in jointly authored textbooks such as James West Davidson et al.'s *Nation of Nations* (1990) and James Kirby Martin's *America and Its People*, authors began to weave material on Indian lifeways and perceptions of Europeans into accounts of the European colonization process while treating Africans in short sections with titles such as "The World the Slaves Made."

These efforts by no means satisfied prominent Indian historians. In 1984, Fred Hoxie, director of the D'Arcy McNickle Center for the History of the American Indian at Newberry Library, examined thirteen currently used U.S. History books (all published in the previous three years) and found them full of misinformation, not particularly informed on current scholarship, and plagued by the problem of molding the "Native American experience to fit the upbeat format of their books."[33] James Axtell, similarly surveying sixteen best-selling college textbooks in 1987, gave a scathing account of errors, half-truths, and serious omissions.[34] Two years later, James Merrell noted that recent monographic work on American Indians was not changing the textbook presentation of colonial history nearly enough and was being ignored "by the larger community of scholars studying early America."[35]

Not until the 1990s did college textbooks prepare students for understanding tricultural interaction in the Americas, and it was only in that decade that precollege textbooks left behind inevitabilist and deeply Eurocentric formulations. For conservatives, this represents an attempt to be politically correct or to satisfy publishers' desires to cater to a multicultural market. To the contrary, the books have merely incorporated sound scholarship derived from closely argued monographs such as Edmund Morgan's *American Slavery, American Freedom: The Ordeal of Slavery in Colonial Virginia* (1975); Mechal Sobel's *The World They Made Together: Black and White Values in Eighteenth-Century Virginia* (1987); James Merrell's *The Indians' New World: Catawbas and Their Neighbors from European Contact through the Era of Removal* (1989); Daniel K. Richter's *The Ordeal of the Longhouse: The Peoples of the Iroquois League in the Era of European Colonization* (1992); and James Axtell's many essays.[36]

In 1990, *The Enduring Vision*, written by six distinguished historians, greatly expanded coverage of Indian and African peoples, emphasizing the richness and variety of human encounters in early America.[37] In a long introduction titled "American Land, Native Peoples," students learn of "an ancient heritage" and "the Indians' continent." The first chapter surveys "North American Indian Societies at the Moment of European Contact." The discussion of the peoples of West Africa before the Atlantic slave trade began helps students learn about agricultural practices, religious beliefs, ancient trading practices, family structure, and attitudes toward land and property of these diverse groups.

Other books since *The Enduring Vision* have followed suit.[38] All build on the mounting scholarship showing that the colonial experience of Europeans can be fully comprehended only by studying all three of the internally diverse culture groups that converged in the Americas—Europeans, Africans, and Native Americans. Many historians now make claims for studying Africans and Indians that go far beyond mere inclusiveness. For example, James Axtell insists that we have greatly underappreciated the influence of Indian culture on Europeans as native peoples and intruding settlers interacted. Axtell builds a case that, for three centuries after 1492, "both the natives themselves and the colonial Southeast remained unmistakably 'Indian' throughout."[39] In other parts of the continent, he maintains that, notwithstanding European attempts to missionize Indians, it was "the Indian defenders of the continent [who] . . . were conceded to be, in effect, the best cultural missionaries and educators on the continent."[40] Although this may overstate the case, other historians have carefully documented how native peoples, in hearing the missionaries' preachments, mediated between old and new beliefs. In the Southwest, for example, the Indian converts to Catholicism "simply added Jesus, Mary, and Christian saints to their rich pantheons and welcomed Franciscans into their communities as additional shamans."[41]

The maturation of scholarship that presents a thoroughly intermixed history among Europeans, Africans, and American Indians is displayed in Richard White's rich analysis of the *pays d'en haut*, the Great Lakes region where for over two centuries, Europeans and Indians "constructed a common, mutually comprehensible world" in "the middle ground." In the *pays d'en haut* "the older worlds of the Algonquians and of various Europeans overlapped, and their mixture created new systems of meaning and of exchange"—an accommodation that occurred because for many generations "whites could neither dictate to Indians nor ignore them." "The boundaries of the Algonquian and French worlds melted at the edges and merged" because "Algonquians who were perfectly comfortable with their status and practices as Indians and Frenchmen, confident in the rightness of French ways, nonetheless had to deal with people who shared neither their values nor their assumptions about the appropriate way of accomplishing tasks. They had to arrive at some common conception of suitable ways of acting; they had to create . . . a middle ground."[42]

Similarly, Daniel Usner Jr. has shown how the world of colonial Louisiana and West Florida was constructed in the seventeenth and eighteenth centuries out of complex economic and social linkages "between seemingly disparate sites within a region—Indian villages, colonial plantations, winter hunting camps, military outposts, and port towns."[43] Colin Calloway, a prolific historian of Indian-white contact, speaks of "the new worlds that Indians and Europeans created together in early America and . . . how conquest changed conquered people and conquerors alike." In chapters on healing and diseases, material culture, religion, warfare, diplomacy, and racial intermarriage he makes a compelling case for the emergence of hybrid cultures.[44] James Merrell punctuates the point about how Anglo-Indian diplomacy was conducted. "Native etiquette—woods' edge ceremonies and wampum belts, the exchange of gifts and the talk of paths cleared and fires kindled—set the tenor, tone, and tempo of foreign relations on the colonial frontier." Indians adopted European toasts and salutes in treaty-making with European colonists, "but the basic fabric is undeniably native American in origin, as colonists, having lost the battle, ruefully understood."[45]

On the African side, parallel lines of argument have stressed the impossibility of understanding the European experience in the Americas without assaying the African presence. John Thornton's deft synthesis of recent scholarship shows how African language, art, music, dance, decorative traditions, cuisine, and pharmacopeia "helped to form the newly developing culture of the Atlantic world."[46] Cultural receptacles in older historical accounts of Africans in the Americas, the millions of Africans brought across the Atlantic are here seen as cultural donors.

That scholarly study of a triangular melding of cultures has begun to transform the precollegiate study of history is found in the National Assessment of Education Progress U.S. History Consensus Project. Created under the auspices of the U.S. Department of Education, the Project was responsible for creating a framework for studying American history from which examinations would be constructed in order to measure the historical literacy of young Americans. The Project employed a steering committee of twenty-six academic historians, veteran school teachers, educational administrators, representatives from the private sector, and members of the public, as well as a planning committee of twenty-three similarly varied individuals. Sitting on the steering and the planning committees were historians representing most parts of the political spectrum and whose specialties spanned intellectual and cultural history, social and economic history, political and religious history, women's and African American history, and so forth.

In constructing the United States History framework, the NAEP architects reached consensus on adopting eight chronological periods of which the first was "Three Worlds and Their Meeting in the Americas (Beginnings to 1607)." "What," asked this framework, "were some of the political ideas, institutions, and practices of Native Americans, Western Europeans, and West Africans before the meeting of these three peoples in the Western Hemisphere?" Other questions it posed included these: "What were the family patterns, religious practices, and artistic traditions of Native Americans, Western Europeans, and West Africans on the eve of Columbus' voyage?" "How did Europeans, Native Americans, and West Africans live and make a living on the eve of Columbus' voyage." In essence, this national framework—a kind of rehearsal for the National History Standards that were already being developed—urged that students learn a good deal about Africans and Native Americans *before* the planting of Jamestown, Virginia, or Plymouth, Massachusetts, in order to establish a basis for understanding that Africans were not reduced simply to units of labor and Indians were not simply driven west but that both peoples were part of a dynamic interaction with Europeans out of which early American culture emerged. This in no way implied that European, American Indian, and African institutions and cultural forms constituted a kind of trilateral commission through which early American political and economic institutions were formed. Rather, it recognized the validity of massive scholarship that shows how in much subtler ways, the interaction of Europeans, Africans, and Native Americans altered agricultural practices, crop regimens, diet, the practice of war, and material and expressive culture.[47]

Few are the college or high school textbooks that still inculcate lessons about the inherent inferiority of American Indians, African Americans, and other groups, the insidious message of Nature's unchangeable sorting out of intellectual and social capabilities. Most textbooks published in the past decade have cast aside explanations about the inevitable fate of American Indians and enslaved Africans, partly because of effective protests by people of various backgrounds and partly because of the coming of age of a rich new scholarship on previously neglected topics.[48] Typically, students getting their first lesson in American history read a chapter entitled "The First Americans," where they learn about the populousness of indigenous people on the eve of the Columbian voyages; about the broad diversity of native cultures; and about the ways in which Indian peoples often were as skilled in water engineering, agriculture, and town planning as Europeans of the fifteenth century.[49] If they lacked literacy, Native Americans passed stories from generation to generation. If they had no written laws, they had codes of conduct carefully observed and enforced. If they lacked Iron Age technology, gunpowder, and compasses, Indians conducted intracontinental trade over vast territories. When history is approached this way, the vast cultural gap portrayed in the polar opposites of civilization and savagery—the incubator of inevitabilist thinking—yields to a meeting of cultures where almost nothing was inexorably determined and almost everything was contingent, negotiated, and, in the end, the result of human agency.

By studying early American history in this way, students may learn that basic fairness to all peoples involved in the national story requires abandoning a univocal American story and that the *unum* cannot be produced out of the *pluribus* if many elements of the latter are ignored or demeaned. Students may also come to understand that challenging a hoary set of meanings is not unpatriotic but in fact captures the richness of American history and celebrates what the fiery abolitionist Wendell Phillips liked to call "the United States of the United Races." They may also learn about the danger of teleological thinking in history and how it vitiates the lesson that most teachers think invaluable—that the individual, even when constrained in myriad ways, matters in the way he conducts his life, in the way she believes in the ability of a single person to change the many. Finally, students may learn to differentiate among cultural fusion in some arenas of human life, cultural adaptation and absorption in others, and elsewhere continuing cultural tension and even conflict. This is not a bad situation for young students learning to live in a democracy.

NOTES

1. Ralph Linton, "One Hundred Per Cent American," *American Mercury* 40 (1937), pp. 427–429, reprinted in Alain Locke and Bernhard J. Stern, eds., *When Peoples Meet: A Study of Race and Culture Contacts* (New York, 1942), pp. 27–29. Linton was a colleague of Franz Boaz at Columbia University and a leading cultural anthropologist of his day.

2. Morse, *Geography Made* Easy, quoted in Ruth Elson, *Guardians of Tradition: American Schoolbooks of the Nineteenth Century* (Lincoln, NE, 1964), p. 78.

3. Joseph Richardson, *The American Reader* (1813), quoted in Elson, *Guardians of Tradition*, p. 79.

4. Berlin, *Historical Inevitability* (London, 1954), p. 7.

5. Axtell, "Forked Tongues: Moral Judgments in Indian History," in Axtell, *After Columbus: Essays in the Ethnohistory of Colonial North America* (New York, 1988), p. 35.

6. Berlin, *Historical Inevitability*, p. 7.

7. Palfrey, *Compendious History*, 2 vols. (Cambridge, MA, 1873), I, pp. 131–132, 184–186, 194; II, p. 122.

8. Fiske, *The Beginnings of New England* (New York, 1889), p. 134.

9. James A. Bowen, *English Words as Spoken and Written* (1900); Henry E. Chambers, *A Higher History of the United States* (1889), quoted in Elson, *Guardians of Tradition*, p. 80.

10. Berlin, *Historical Inevitability*, pp. 39–40. Such formulae subtly cross-cut the textbook insistence on the power of the individual to make a difference and the celebration of the American individual, Horatio Alger writ large, as essential to American uniqueness.

11. For a full discussion of early twentieth-century textbooks on this theme, see my "The Concept of Inevitability in the History of European-Indian Relations," in Carla Pestaña and Sharon Salinger, eds., *Inequality in Early America* (Hanover, NH, 1999).

12. George Washington Williams was writing *The History of the Negro Race in America, 1619–1880*, 2 vols. (New York, 1883) at the same time, but this compendium had no apparent influence on textbook writing.

13. Roosevelt, *The Winning of the West*, vol. 10 of *The Works of Theodore Roosevelt*, 11 vols. (New York, 1924), p. 8.

14. Ibid., pp. 388–389, 275.

15. Muzzey, *An American History* (Boston, 1911), pp. 23, 25; *History of the American People* (Boston, 1927), pp. 2, 228. Muzzey was a Progressive on many issues, such as labor and business monopoly, but not on race.

16. Rugg, *History of American Civilization* (Boston, 1930), p. 198; *Teachers Guide and Key* (Boston, 1932), pp. 80–83. In his *The Conquest of America: A History of American Civilization—Economic and Social* (Boston, 1937), Rugg rumi-

nated that "perhaps the warfare that developed out of disputes over land could not be avoided because the civilizations of the red man and the white man differed so greatly." But, in using the plural, Rugg showed that he was breaking from the savagery-civilization polarity.

17. See, for example, the anthropologist Clark Wissler's *Indians of the United States: Four Centuries of Their History and Culture* (New York, 1949), especially chs. 19 and 22; the lawyer-activist Felix Cohen's "Americanizing the White Man," *American Scholar*, 16 (1952), pp. 177–191; and the anthropologist A. Irving Hallowell's "The Impact of the American Indian on American Culture," *American Anthropologist*, 59 (1957), pp. 201–17.

18. The initial exploratory essay seems to have begun with Alexander F. Chamberlain's "The Contributions of the American Indian to Civilization," published in 1903 in the *Proceedings of the American Antiquarian Society*, New Series, 16 (1903), pp. 91–126. Another early foray was Leo J. Frachtenberg, "Our Indebtedness to the American Indian," *Wisconsin Archaeologist*, 16 (1915), pp. 64–69. This was followed two decades later by the agricultural economist Edward E. Everett's "American Indian Contributions to Civilization," *Minnesota History*, 15 (1934), pp. 255–272.

19. DeVoto, "Introduction," in John K. Howard, *Strange Empire* (Toronto, 1965), pp. 15–16. Between 1965 and 1973, at least five essays appeared that expanded on DeVoto's point and called for responsible scholarship to correct the malicious depictions of American Indians or to remedy studied inattention to their role in the development of colonial American society. William Brandon, "American Indians and American History," *American West*, 2 (1965); Virgil J. Vogel, *Indians in American History* (Chicago, 1968); Rupert Costo, ed., *Textbooks and the American Indian* (San Francisco, 1970); Robert Berkhofer, "Native Americans and United States History," in William C. Cartwright and Richard L. Watson Jr., eds., *The Reinterpretation of American History and Culture* (Washington, DC, 1973); and Wilbur R. Jacobs, "The Indian and the Frontier in American History—A Need for Revision," *Western Historical Quarterly*, 4 (1973), pp. 43–56.

20. Stampp, *The Peculiar Institution: Slavery in the Ante-bellum South* (New York, 1956).

21. With the G.I. Bill enabling millions of Americans to go to college for the first time, the gates of the historical profession gradually opened to people of diverse class, religious, and racial backgrounds in the 1950s. Although known as the period when the "consensus school" of American history emphasized the homogeneity of American society and its lack of conflict, the postwar decades also produced important new interpretations of early Indian-white relations and bold new formulations of African American history.

22. Boorstin, *The Americans: The Colonial Experience* (New York, 1958). Boorstin provided a stern lesson on the dangers of the Pennsylvania Quakers' pacifism in dealing with Indians. In a section entitled "How Quakers Misjudged

the Indians," Boorstin rang the bell of historical inevitability loudly: The Quakers' "view of the Indian was . . . unrealistic, inflexible, and based on false premises about human nature. . . . The increasing, west-flowing population of the Province was passing like a tidal wave over Indian lands. The troubles of the Indians could no longer be reduced to niceties of protocol, to maxims of fair play, or to cliches of self-reproach. Here was one of those great conflicts in history when a mighty force was meeting a long-unmoved body; either the force had to be stopped or the body had to move" (p. 54).

23. Commager and Morison, *Growth of the American Republic* (New York, 1930), 415, 418. Passages of this sort remained in subsequent editions (in 1937, 1940, 1942, 1950, and 1962); not until the 1969 edition did the text change.

24. This essay makes no attempt to assay how much young learners over the years have absorbed from textbooks or how much they have challenged textbook interpretations of history. Other essays in this book provide useful reflections on this, notably those by Linda Levstik, Peter Seixas, and Samuel Wineburg.

25. Chitwood, *History of Colonial America* (New York, 1961), pp. 351–352. Max Savelle's *A History of Colonial America*, first published in 1942, went through a second edition in 1964 with gaping silences on Africa and Africans (though not portraying Africans as Sambo-like grateful recipients of Western civilization) and little on the dynamics of Native American societies. This was not remedied until 1972, when Darrold Wax, a specialist on the slave trade, added considerable material on the place of Africa in the expansion of Europe, the slave trade in British America, the Africans and slavery in eighteenth-century colonial America, and the place of African Americans in the American Revolution. Wax explicitly addressed these changes in the introduction to the third edition: *History of Colonial America* (Hinsdale, IL, 1972), ix. Robert Middlekauff made changes for the second edition published in 1964. David Hawke's *The Colonial Experience* (Indianapolis, 1965) had only a few paragraphs on the beginnings of slavery in the seventeenth-century colonies, not a word on who these Africans were or what cultural attributes they brought with them in the slave ships, and nothing on the resistance of captured Africans to lifelong slavery. However, Hawke did not describe the Indians as savages and at least quoted Bernard de Voto: "The wonder is that the Indians resisted [European] decadence as well as they did, preserved as much as they did, and fought the whites off so obstinately and so long."

26. *The American Republic* (Englewood Cliffs, NJ), p. 33.

27. Peter Novick, *That Noble Dream: The "Objectivity Question" and the American Historical Profession* (Cambridge, 1988), p. 351.

28. Woodward, *American Counterpoint: Slavery and Racism in the North-South Dialogue* (New York, 1971), pp. 5–6.

29. Other influential books were Philip Curtin, *The Atlantic Slave Trade: A Census* (Madison, WI, 1969); Richard S. Dunn, *Sugar and Slaves: The Rise of the Planter Class in the British West Indies* (Chapel Hill, NC, 1972); Gerald W. Mullin,

Flight and Rebellion: Slave Resistance in Eighteenth-Century Virginia (New York, 1972); and the seminal books, though not based on seventeenth- and eighteenth-century documents, of John Blassingame, George Rawick, and Herbert Gutman.

30. *Red, White, and Black: The Peoples of Early America* (Englewood Cliffs, NJ, 1974). Second and third editions, striving to keep abreast of the burgeoning scholarship, were published in 1982 and 1991. A fourth edition appeared in 2000.

31. Without doing a systematic survey, I believe that only freshly written textbooks incorporated new scholarship on Indian and African/African American history, while very few earlier textbooks, revised for new editions, paid much attention to this work.

32. Mary Beth Norton, David Katzman, William Tuttle, Paul Escott, Howard Chudacoff, and Thomas Paterson, *A People and a Nation* (Boston, 1982).

33. Hoxie, "The Indians versus the Textbooks: Is There Any Way Out?" *Newberry Library, Occasional Papers in Curriculum Series*, 1 (Chicago, 1984), p. 2.

34. Axtell, "Europeans, Indians, and the Age of Discovery in American History Textbooks," in Axtell, *Beyond 1492: Encounters in Colonial North America* (New York, 1992), pp. 197–216. The essay was first published in the *American Historical Review*, 92 (1987), pp. 621–632. Even in 1995, James W. Loewen indicted precollege textbooks' treatment of American Indians, though this analysis examines twelve high school textbooks of which only two were published later than 1987. Loewen, *The Lies My Teacher Told Me: Everything American History Textbooks Got Wrong* (New York, 1995), ch. 4.

35. Merrell, "Some Thoughts on Colonial Historians and American Indians," *William and Mary Quarterly*, 3d Ser., 46 (1989), pp. 94–119. The quotation is on p. 95. Merrell argues that studies of African Americans and women percolated more quickly "across the boundaries between specialists and generalists" than new research on Native Americans and wonders whether the Indianists' self-description as "ethnohistorians" has been part of the problem (a view with which I disagree). See ibid., pp. 113–117.

36. An appreciation of the outpouring of new scholarship on nontraditional topics can be gained by simple quantification. The forthcoming *Harvard Guide to African-American History* will list more than 250 books and more than 470 articles on African American history for the period from 1765 to 1830 published since 1965.

37. Paul S. Boyer, Clifford E. Clark Jr., Joseph F. Kett, Thomas L. Purvis, Harvard Sitkoff, and Nancy Woloch, *The Enduring Vision* (Lexington, MA, 1990). In subsequent editions, Neal Salisbury replaced Thomas L. Purvis as the early Americanist author.

38. Some textbooks continue to ignore the present generation's scholarship on African and Indian history. Bernard Bailyn et al.'s *The Great Republic* has gone through four editions since its first publication in 1977 without giving students a clue that it mattered how African and Indian peoples understood their world,

how they were parts of dynamic societies that had changed over centuries, and how this might have affected the colonial experience of Europeans. John Garraty has adopted a different approach. Rather than incorporating the rich scholarship of the last quarter-century into the narrative itself, he has inserted "visual portfolios that show the aesthetic richness of Benin and Dahomey."

39. Axtell, *The Indians' New South: Cultural Change in the Colonial Southeast* (Baton Rouge, 1997), p. 4.

40. Axtell, *The Invasion Within: The Contest of Cultures in Colonial North America* (New York, 1985), p. 302.

41. David J. Weber, *The Spanish Frontier in North America* (New Haven, 1992), p. 117.

42. White, *The Middle Ground: Indians, Empires, and Republics in the Great Lakes Region, 1650–1815* (Cambridge, 1991), pp. ix–x, 50.

43. Usner, *Indians, Settlers, and Slaves in a Frontier Exchange Community: The Lower Mississippi Valley before 1763* (Chapel Hill, NC, 1992), p. 8.

44. Calloway, *New Worlds for All: Indians, Europeans, and the Remaking of Early America* (Baltimore, 1997), xlv.

45. James H. Merrell, *Into the Woods: Negotiators on the Colonial Pennsylvania Frontier*, unpublished ms., ch. 1, p. 10.

46. Thornton, *Africa and Africans* (Cambridge, 1992).

47. For a discussion of the criticisms of the National History Standards that in the main follow the NAEP framework, see Gary B. Nash, "Early American History and the National History Standards," *William and Mary Quarterly*, 54 (1997), pp. 579–600.

48. James Loewen, in *The Lies My Teacher Taught Me*, takes high school textbooks to task for their abusive treatment of American Indian history, but Loewen's analysis is based on textbooks published more than ten years ago.

49. For example, Herman Viola, *Why We Remember: United States History through Reconstruction* (Menlo Park, CA, 1997); Joyce Appleby, Alan Brinkley, and James McPherson, *The American Journey* (New York, 1997); Sarah Bednarz et. al, *We the People: Build Our Nation* (Boston, 1997). All of these books give limited space to American Indian history after the first chapter, but they do not plant in the minds of schoolchildren "a story of the inevitable triumph by the good guys," as Loewen puts it in *Lies My Teacher Told Me*, p. 129.

Chapter 7

Constructing World History
in the Classroom

Ross E. Dunn

During the past century and a half, American educators have repeatedly rewritten the definition of world history as a school subject. This construction and reconstruction is apparent in the educational literature. A text published in 1874 for courses in "general history" offered this definition:

> Viewing history as confined to the series of leading civilized nations, we observe that it has to do with but one grand division of the human family, namely, with the Caucasian, or white race. . . . Thus we see that history proper concerns itself with but one highly developed type of mankind; for though the great bulk of the population of the globe has, during the whole recorded period, belonged, and does still belong, to other types of mankind, yet the Caucasians form the only truly *historical* race.[1]

After World War I, textbooks dropped such overt pseudoscientific racism. World history as the story of Aryans gave way to world history, at least in the modern centuries, as the story of "civilization," that is, of Europe and its cultural outliers. Published in 1931, Carl Becker's *Modern History* affirmed:

> While all history is our history in the sense that all history is the work of human beings like ourselves, modern history is our history in a special sense. Modern history is the history of our civilization, and of those recent centuries during which our civilization has taken on the form with which we are familiar.[2]

In the aftermath of the second great war, Becker's definition of the significant past seemed less adequate. Most Americans recognized that the global conflict, the ensuing Cold War, the multiplication of new nations, and the electronic revolution combined to make the world both a smaller place as a social sphere and a much larger place as a cultural construct in the collective consciousness of peoples everywhere. A bigger world worth understanding required a bigger world history. Leften Stavrianos, for example, enlarged his definition of world history in the textbooks he published in the 1960s and 1970s. He contended that "we cannot truly understand either Western or non-Western history unless we have a global overview that encompasses both. Then we can see how much interaction there is between all peoples in all times, and how important that interaction is in determining the course of human history."[3]

In the early 1990s, when the planet's geopolitics were drastically rearranging themselves and hi-tech warfare flared in the Persian Gulf, Stavrianos's definition of world history seemed both thoroughly vindicated and not quite large enough. The National Standards for World History, written in the mid-1990s at a time of rapid global change, urged a curriculum in which the primary social context for all inquiry would be humanity, not just nations and regions:

> These standards represent a forceful commitment to world-scale history. . . . The aim . . . is to encourage students to ask large and searching questions about the human past, to compare patterns of continuity and change in different parts of the world, and to examine the histories and achievements of particular peoples or civilizations with an eye to wider social, cultural, or economic contexts.[4]

That definitions of world history have changed over the years comes as no surprise to experienced history teachers. They know that all definitions of the past will inevitably be revised because each one is constructed using only cultural materials available to the living. One generation's "true" history is the next generation's nonsense, and no doubt the year 2050 will produce some new blueprint for the past that today we would think far-fetched. Good teachers also understand that historical redefinition is almost always contested. Because they teach their own students to deal skillfully with competing historical narratives, they know well that several conflicting proposals for the proper shape of world history are likely to be on the table at once. Scholars sort the significant from the insignificant in contradictory ways depending on their particular social and cultural precommitments.

Three Competing Models of World History

The American public in general probably has a rather blurry perception of world history in the school curriculum as the study of peoples and cultures in places other than the United States. Likewise, teachers and curriculum specialists who have had little or no opportunity to consider the subject as a distinct discipline may define it offhandedly as a residual category that includes all historical education other than what is American. Part of the reason for this vagueness is that universities and educational agencies have so far done an inadequate job of helping either prospective or veteran teachers come to grips with world history as a conceptually coherent subject. Even so, the educators who make decisions about the content of history curriculum, textbooks, competency standards, and assessments come to their tasks already equipped with assumptions about the structure and meaning of the human past. Just as students enter class not with blank historical minds but with a rich array of ideas and images about history learned from family, community, and the general culture, so educational decision makers draw on a large fund of prior knowledge, assumption, and ideology when they design curriculum.[5]

Professional and public debates over history in the schools have become quite intense in the past decade, as a result of both the national movement for rigorous standards of knowledge and skill in all basic subjects and the repeated flare-ups of "culture war" over the purposes of education. Amid these debates, three broad models of world history as a school subject compete for the attention of educators and the public. I call these the Western Heritage Model, the Different Cultures Model, and the Patterns of Change Model. All of them embody a general definition of world history intended to serve as a conceptual guide to what is significant or insignificant. None of them, on the other hand, is a metahistorical statement, that is, an explicit covering theory formulated to explain the *meaning* of the past as a totality. On the contrary, all three models emerged at different times in the past century out of a continuous, pragmatic conversation between scholars interested in the historiography and methodology of world history and teachers determined to find ways to help students make sense of the major civilizations as phenomena transcending the nation-state and of developments that have involved peoples of differing cultural traditions in shared experience. Often enough in this endeavor, scholars have been striving to be better world history teachers, and teachers have been pursuing world-historical research. In relation to all three models, the earliest discussions about world history research, teaching, and their interconnections took place mainly in universities. Soon, however, the conversation spread to the schools and subsequently affected curriculum, textbooks, standards, and pedagogical strategies.

The formulators and proponents of the Western Heritage Model declare that the central mission of history education is to transmit to the rising generation a shared heritage of values, institutions, and great ideas derived mainly from peoples of Europe and the ancient Mediterranean. Advocates of this model do not say, at least not today, that the West is the *only* historical civilization. But they do argue, at least implicitly, that it is the *most* historical in terms of its global impact and cultural contributions to humanity. World history, then, as the story of "our civilization" and its presumed antecedents is the framework that will commit young Americans to national unity and our cherished way of life.

In some measure the Western Heritage Model involves revitalization of the "Western Civ" course, which spread across the nation right after World War I. Though based on scholarly conceptions of the historical discipline as a project to discover the political and cultural origins of contemporary American society, the idea of Western civilization as the proper vessel of world history was from the start a teaching construct. Moreover, the rationale for the Western Heritage Model today is not so different from the justifications that educators of the interwar period offered for Western-Civ-as-world-history. These were to unify a demographically and socially changing society, protect the nation from rival foreign ideologies (then Bolshevism and Fascism, today fundamentalism and state terrorism), and encourage loyalty to values and institutions that made America great.[6]

The Western Heritage Model's dedication to democracy, freedom, and a shared system of cultural communication is valid and commendable. This model, however, also involves specific assumptions about the nature of world history. One is the essentialist view that Western civilization generated out of its own cultural ingredients exceptional seminal traits and that it continues to possess innate attributes, though these may at some periods be temporarily obscured. According to Samuel Huntington, for example, "the essential continuing core of Western civilization" notably includes "its Christianity, pluralism, individualism, and rule of law, which made it possible for the West to invent modernity, expand throughout the world, and become the envy of other societies. . . . The principal responsibility of Western leaders, consequently, is . . . to pre-serve, protect, and renew the unique qualities of Western civilization."[7] Following this view, world history in schools should aim to identify the inborn characteristics of the West, contrast them with the qualities of other civilizations, and demonstrate through lessons and narratives the importance of nourishing our civilization's "essential continuing core."

The Western Heritage Model also tends to anthropomorphize Western civilization, that is, to represent it as a tangible entity possessing powers of historical agency, particularly to act as animator of progressive change in the world during the past five or six centuries. Thus, the West "pro-duced the idea of freedom," "ended slavery," "created the Industrial Revo-lution," and "invented modernity." Teachers and students are thus en-couraged to explore the special personality of the West and to search for the ideals and institutions that Americans prize in its cultural genetics. The quest may lead at times to Asia and Africa but only to the extent that these places contributed formative elements to the making of the West or because thirst for knowledge of "other cultures" is itself one of the inher-ent traits of Western civilization that ought to be exercised. As historians generally know, however, expeditions to find origins usually take the ex-plorers where they want to go. Or, as Marshall Hodgson reminds us, "Most . . . possible facets of experience that are to be found in any major tradition can be found in corresponding traditions elsewhere. Accord-ingly, tradition can account for almost anything."[8] Despite his admoni-tion, however, the Western Heritage Model has numerous champions in college history departments, education agencies, and schools, particularly among committed humanists who want their students to share in the rich cultural and aesthetic legacy of Europe and the ancient Mediterranean and who may assume the validity of the notion that civilizations possess "natural" traits.[9]

I name the second framework for defining world history the Different Cultures Model. It emerged from the domestic social upheavals of the 1960s and 1970s and from the attendant broadening of the humanistic and social scientific disciplines to assimilate new faces, new questions, and new regions of the world that had previously been excluded. As a scholarly approach, multiculturalism may be linked to the new social his-tory, which took much fuller account of women, working people, and ethnoracial minorities, and to the federally funded area studies move-ment, which sent young researchers off to Africa, Asia, and Latin America to collect data that would presumably exceed in quantity and quality what the Soviets had. As educational theory, multiculturalism began as a much-needed critique of Eurocentrism in college and school curriculum and of the prevailing control that affluent, authoritative white males held over interpretations of culture and history.

The Different Cultures Model was elaborated, however, not so much by historians as by social science–oriented educators who insisted on curriculum that would be both internationally minded and respectful of all ethnoracial groups. Moreover, this approach did not for the most part challenge the Western Heritage Model's fundamental assumptions. Rather than disputing the idea that civilizations possess inherent attributes, a proposition that was at odds with the historical discipline's understanding of the dynamics of change, many multiculturalists insisted that world history courses amply represent other civilizations and ethnoracial groups besides the West and largely for essentialist reasons. Among the basic principles of multiculturalism, one educator includes the postulates that (1) "every culture has its own internal coherence, integrity, and logic" and (2) "no one culture is inherently better or worse than another."[10] The Different Cultures Model, then, mirrored on a world scale the emerging (though contested) definition of American history as the stories of diverse ethnoracial groups, each possessing "its own internal coherence, integrity, and logic." World history education, therefore, must give proper attention to the ancestral histories of all groups in America's "ethnoracial pentagon"—to the presumed forefathers of African-, Asian-, Hispano-, Native-, and European-Americans.[11]

Most multiculturalists have been far less determined than Western Heritage advocates have to catalog and celebrate timeless cultural qualities in the civilizations they want included in the school program. Even so, the Different Cultures Model does define world history largely in terms of autonomous histories, exceptional "contributions" of various civilizations, and stirring deeds or heroic personalities that exemplify positive characteristics of regions of the world other than Europe and North America. The model opposes the unicultural approach to world history that James Blaut calls the "European tunnel of time."[12] Then, however, it redefines the subject in terms of five or six additional tunnels, each representing a conventionally defined tradition or region. Each burrow contains a set of distinctive stories, achievements, contributions, and artifacts. Morever, each is quite short and narrow in the way it compresses change over time. To give one example, a published teaching activity used in California schools in grade six has students taking "a trip up the Nile" to visit famous sites such as the Pyramids, Karnack, and Abu Simbel. The activity does not, however, reveal that hundreds or even thousands of years separated the building of these monuments. Egypt, then, is not a place where important developments occurred in human history but an abstract, flattened representation of a grand and colorful culture that existed "long ago."

I call the third definition of world history for schools the Patterns of Change Model. Its early formulation may be associated with the scholarship of several world history pioneers who began writing in the 1950s or early 1960s, particularly William McNeill, Leften Stavrianos, Marshall Hodgson, and Philip Curtin. All of them shared a conviction that the nation-state was an inadequate framework for understanding the sweep of the human past and that scholars should venture courageously, if only metaphorically, to any part of the world to find answers to historical questions. These scholars believed that the ethnocentric presumption that some societies are more "historical" than others should not be permitted to limit the historian's range of inquiry. Moreover, they affirmed the scholar's privilege to seek explanations for change at any level of inquiry from the local to the global. Reliance on the rules and techniques of the discipline should not be less exacting just because the historical problem under investigation was of large dimensions in time and space.

While these early formulations of what became the Patterns of Change Model were being made, a constant interplay between research and teaching was also taking place. Indeed, that dynamic continues. For example, William McNeill wrote *The Rise of the West: A History of the Human Community* and at the same time taught his uniquely conceived world history course at the University of Chicago.[13] Philip Curtin based two of his well-known works in comparative world history, *Cross-Cultural Trade in World History* and *The Rise and Fall of the Plantation Complex*, on sets of lectures he wrote for his "World and the West" university course.[14] A look at the careers of leading expositors of the new, globe-encompassing world history—Janet Abu-Lughod, Michael Adas, Jerry Bentley, Edmund Burke, K. N. Chaudhuri, David Christian, Alfred Crosby, Andre Gunder Frank, Patrick Manning, Lynda Shaffer, Fred Spier, Peter Stearns, and several others—reveal a dual, mutually reinforcing commitment to both research and teaching in the field.[15]

Like the Different Cultures Model, the Patterns of Change Model calls for a socially inclusive curriculum. Unlike that framework, it is firmly based in the discipline of history, though drawing extensively on the social sciences, especially economics, sociology, and anthropology, for analytical constructs. In contrast to the Western Heritage Model, it shuns the search for cultural "origins" or the hypothesis that an actual chain of causation directly links paleolithic East Africa to Mesopotamia, Mesopotamia to Greece, and Greece to modern Europe. Like multiculturalism, it comes partly out of the social and ideological shifts of the 1960s and 1970s, the post-war knowledge explosion in history and the social sciences, and the critique of Western ethnocentrism. It is also a response to processes of globalization and the dawning realization that the complex relationship between *Homo sapiens sapiens* and the biosphere really does matter.

The model advances the idea that social and spatial fields of historical inquiry should be open and fluid, not predetermined by conventionally assumed cultural categories. Structuring world history curriculum, then, is not so much a matter of deciding how to juxtapose various cultures or how many days and pages to award each one but of framing historical questions children might ask unconstrained by the usual civilizational border lines. Patrick Manning characterizes world history as a field that examines "the interaction of the pieces (be they community, societal, or continental) in human history" and assesses "the experience of the whole of humanity through study of those interactions."[16] I add the corollary that school world history should devote itself to exploring concrete, time-and-place-specific problems always guided by the requirement that the inquiry embrace whatever geographical, social, or cultural field is appropriate.

The Patterns of Change Model by no means invalidates study that centers on a particular civilization or cultural tradition or on developments that occurred in Europe. Indeed, the model requires that students develop clear working definitions of and distinctions between such terms and phrases as "society," "nation," "culture," "cultural history," and "cultural difference." Systematic comparative study of cultural differences among civilizations or other groups contributes to a good world history education because inductive comparison of cases (contrasting systems of government, for example, or institutions of slavery in different periods and world regions) is a pedagogically effective way to discover large patterns of change and to formulate higher-order generalizations or narrative frameworks. Students are miseducated, however, if they are taught to believe that one group's cultural beliefs and practices today will certainly all be the same tomorrow, that all members of the group concur over which beliefs and practices ought to prevail, or that cultures are "solid, commonsensical, and agreed-upon" rather than "contested, uncertain, and in flux."[17]

Neither does this model replace autonomous civilizational stories simply with an array of nebulous historical "themes" such as empire, trade, belief systems, imperialism, gender, or nationalism. All these spheres of inquiry are important, but by themselves they are abstractions, not historical problems situated firmly in time and space. David Lowenthal is right when he argues (in this volume) that "topical themes may be the stuff of humanity but served up in isolation they obscure its history." In other words, world history teachers should beware of the dangers of disconnecting a particular type of phenomenon from the thick historical context of the times. The result may be interesting sociological speculation, but it is not a satisfying explanation of change. The better way in teaching a sequence of historical topics is to marry thematic selection or emphasis—which is pedagogically valid, even necessary—with investigation of specific, carefully delineated historical situations.

When teachers adopt a more elastic and situation-centered sense of historical space, they position themselves to probe the meaning of events more comprehensively, introduce data that reveal new patterns, and open up fresh lines of large-scale or comparative analysis. Teachers and students see interrelationships and meanings, perhaps of great importance, that they could not see before. Children range across the whole wide world, always on the lookout for explanations of *change*, not simply to describe "how things were" in Culture A, "what they had" in Culture B, or the "interesting things they achieved" in Culture C. For example, the emergence of European states as global maritime powers in the sixteenth and seventeenth centuries should not be presented as a cultural fact to be celebrated or condemned but as a world-scale historical problem (a big one to be sure) to be understood. The spatial context for investigating the question cannot possibly be Europe alone but must include a broader interregional terrain that involved at one moment or another North African Muslims, inhabitants of the Indian Ocean rim, American Indians, and many other people, all of whom should be represented as agents of change as much as were the Portuguese or French.

In short, the Patterns of Change Model offers in my estimation the best hope for enhancing students' ability to connect detailed knowledge of particular topics, events, and "facts" to larger frameworks of development and causation, a cognitive feat they must perform if the texts they read and materials they learn are to have any enduring intellectual or experiential significance. Elsewhere in this volume, Denis Shemilt writes of our need "to explore pupils' 'pictures of the past,' the narrative frameworks that they use to articulate past to past and past to present." History courses that follow the Western Heritage Model may effectively adopt and repeatedly reinforce for students an overarching narrative scheme of development to which much of the detailed, unit-by-unit learning may be connected. The trouble is that the narrative framework itself badly distorts world history by leaving the better part of humanity over the long run out of it altogether. The Different Cultures Model is theoretically inclusive of all peoples but usually waives any attempt to locate the experiences of different societies or cultural groups within some larger frame of meaning. The Patterns of Change Model by no means aims for a universalist, totalized world history. It does require, however, that teachers strive self-consciously to formulate world-scale schemata of chronology, progression, and historical meaning that will give shape to their entire course, rather than merely hoping students will somehow see large patterns and their significance to past and present by merely trudging, heads down, from topic to topic and unit to unit.

Whither the Three Models?

Which of these three models has the leading edge in American schools, at least in those where world history is taught? The answer is complicated because social studies curriculum is in flux and because the three models are not themselves pure conceptual constructs but penetrate and modify one another. In terms of the general precepts that inform world history education, the Different Cultures Model has led the pack for a couple of decades. This phenomenon is a facet of what David Hollinger calls "the triumph of basic multiculturalism." That is, "multiculturalism has proved to be a major preoccupation in American life as registered in the deliberations of local school boards and in the professional journals of the humanities and social sciences."[18] Thus, the multicultural tenets that world history courses should be culturally inclusive, attentive to diversity, moderately relativist, internationally minded, and hostile to the idea that any "one culture is inherently better or worse than another" have won acceptance, at least resigned acceptance, in virtually all state and large-city education agencies. All the world history textbooks currently enjoying success in the precollegiate market embody these tenets. The publishers vie for recognition that their product has the best "global coverage," and the latest crop of textbooks, despite pressures in some states from groups wanting more emphasis on Western and Christian themes, seems as inclusivist as ever.

However, if one looks at state standards documents, curriculum guides, and even the tables of contents of textbooks, the multiculturalist victory seems less complete. In educational practice, one finds a rather awkward and unstable blending of Different Cultures and Western Heritage history. This inconsistent mix is partly a reflection of politics: boards of education, curriculum officers, and publishers constantly grope for a safe road through mine fields laid on one side by multicultural or ethnoracial interest groups and on the other by organizations dedicated to advancing "Western values." This half-multicultural, half-West-centered curriculum also results from the fact that neither academic historians nor teachers well trained in history usually have a leading role in creating social studies curriculum. The specialists and civil servants who do generate curriculum operate on the whole, or so it seems to me, from a rather fuzzy ideological position that combines inclusivist and presentist ideas with a rather absent-minded assumption that after 1500 and up to 1945 European history can justifiably stand in for the world. As with the new American social history, which took a long time to penetrate the social studies curriculum, the fresh subject matter, angles of vision, and analytical constructs that characterize Patterns of Change history are only slowly penetrating curricula and teaching materials at the precollegiate level.

History educators made an important step in the right direction when they published the National Standards for World History. This comprehensive outline of subject matter that would constitute a "world-class" global history education appeared in 1994 and in revised edition in 1996. The stamp of current world-historical thinking and research is clearly on them, and their writing involved contributions from dozens of world history teachers and scholars. To be sure, the National Standards for History, for both the United States and the world, is a compromise document, the project involving as it did participants espousing Europe-centered, multicultural, world-historical, and two or three other points of view. The standards by no means describe the Patterns of Change Model, but they do encourage students not only to learn about major civilizations and key movements associated with the West but also "to draw comparisons across eras and regions in order to define enduring issues as well as large-scale or long-term developments that transcend regional and temporal boundaries."[19] Upon their publication, the standards were immediately sucked into the cyclone of cultural politics. Consequently, they have had less national influence than they might have, though they are more recently having a quiet and perhaps growing effect on curricular decision making.[20]

Apart from the national standards, almost all the leading world history textbooks and the more content-specific state standards documents that have been issued since 1996 exhibit a mix of the Western Heritage and the Different Cultures models.[21] The usual pattern is this: The first half of the text or standards guide presents major civilizations *ad seriatim*, each covered in a discrete unit encompassing several hundred to several thousand years. Diversity and internationalism thus honored, the scene shifts to Europe, whose internal history, together with the activities of Europeans abroad, dominates the second half of the document. The idea of the West as *entity*, whose "rise" may be ascribed almost entirely to internal mechanisms and foundational traits, remains largely unchallenged. No doubt, some multiculturalists rail at this unicultural structuring of the modern past, but they mostly defer to it, probably because they have nothing to offer in place of the West-and-the-rest metanarrative other than additional culture stories unconnected to one another or to world-scale realms of historical meaning.

Among recent documents that specify content for world history, the Massachusetts History and Social Science Curriculum Framework, the Virginia History and Social Science Standards of Learning, the California History/Social Science Content Standards, the Texas Essential Knowledge and Skills, and the National Council for History Education pamphlet titled *Building a World History Curriculum* all follow a generally similar mix of multiculturalism and Western Civ.[22] More troubling, none of these documents displays much awareness of the literature in cross-cultural, transnational, and comparative history that has been pouring forth during the past quarter century and that offers so many new and fascinating questions about how the world got to be the way it is.[23]

World History and Good Habits of Mind

Freed from the cage of what Andre Gunder Frank calls "culturology," that is, the preoccupation with culture-specific explanations of change in the world,[24] teachers will be encouraged to ground their courses more firmly in the historical discipline. First come the questions, whose investigation will require exercise of a variety of historical thinking skills. Then comes identification of what Philip Curtin calls the "universe of data" and Lewis Martin and Kären Wigen refer to as the "arena of human affinity" that is applicable to the problem at hand.[25] That universe of human action may be contiguous with medieval England or eighteenth-century France, but the appropriate area may also be the Atlantic basin, the Pacific rim, the Muslim region stretching from Morocco to Indonesia, or the entire globe. World history holds the possibility of becoming more relevant to students as they examine events within larger realms of meaning, investigate how developments occurring in different parts of the world affected one another, inductively compare developments across time and space, and recognize all the historical actors in a situation as human beings, not characters playing appointed roles in a culture drama. Students will also find analysis of conflicting accounts and interpretations of events more interesting when the relevant "universe of data" has multiregional or transnational scope.

High school graduates often come to college burdened with flawed conceptions of the nature of change. Several essays in this volume explore these problematic habits of historical thinking.[26] Two of these cognitive problems have particular, though not exclusive, application to world history. A fresh approach to designing curriculum might help to correct these misconceptions.

One problem is the tendency of students to perceive historical phenomena as exotic and remote. To one degree or another, all of us perceive events and peoples of the past as alien, obscure, and unconnected to our experience. Indeed, in large measure they are, partly because the multitude of variables that play upon a particular time and place are always unique and partly because most of the past can never be reconstructed at all. "The past was not only weirder than we realize," David Lowenthal reminds us in this volume; "it was weirder than we can imagine." No matter how deep into the past we probe, however, we discover that the beliefs and behavior of the human species are knowable to us to a degree that the ways of dolphins or chimpanzees could not possibly be. Chronicles, diaries, court records, prayer books, wall painting, and buried village trash heaps reveal much that rings familiar. The challenge in history education is to reduce to some extent the weirdness of the past and to build at least rickety bridges of empathy and comprehension between our students and the departed.

Surely, in teaching world history we should strive to divest students of the notion that peoples of "other cultures" were always drastically different from twentieth-century Americans but that seventeenth-century Virginians or fourteenth-century English peasants were not. Both the Western Heritage and the Different Cultures models of world history tend to fixate on cultural differences, particularities, and otherness. Thus, in the minds of students, Americans and their presumed European ancestors become more American, West Africans become more West African, and Japanese more Japanese. These approaches lead away from history as the study of human beings cooperating and competing in ever-changing circumstances and back toward the old-fashioned anthropological reification of each "culture group" as eternally homogeneous but utterly unlike any other group. By contrast, the Patterns of Change Model aims to be "culturally neutral," encouraging students to link developments of the past to their own experience as human beings rather than regarding peoples far away in time and space as comprehensible only if these people are their own presumed ethnoracial ancestors. The Africanist Joseph Miller has written:

> The historian's method of stimulating comprehension thus rests not just on relating events in chronological order but primarily on emphasizing how everything is continually becoming; how the present always exists in tension with a very different past even as it also trembles on the edge of dissolving into some still unknown future; . . . Another advantage of phrasing world historical processes as culturally neutral concepts is that they make everybody else's particular ways of getting on with things more teachable. By starting from functional equivalence, we show how other people accomplished tasks that are familiar, even if in fashions different from ours, thus rendering remote experiences and achievements intelligible to students who rightly want to learn about the world in terms that are meaningful to them.[27]

In Miller's sense, cultural neutrality does not mean practicing rigid relativism or being nonjudgmental. Rather, it encourages empathy and perspectivism through recognition that all human beings who occupy the "arena of human affinity" relevant to the historical issue at hand possess the potential of creative historical agency. The question of why the Atlantic slave trade occurred, for example, can be much more interesting if any crude culture-specific notion of there being an "African perspective" (their civilization) set against a "European perspective" (our civilization) is abandoned. The question will have more significance as an inquiry into why human beings, as individuals or in groups, behaved the way they did and how issues of power, economy, class, custom, gender, technology, and disease played into the process of creating an Atlantic economy that benefited so many people so little and some people so much.

There also seems to be a pervasive belief among college students that things happen in history because people possessed a clear idea of what was supposed to come next and performed acts of creative will to bring about the precognized results. British researchers have observed how young children believe that "things happen because people want them to" or that "the more agents want something, the more likely they are to achieve it."[28] Denis Shemilt's discussion (this volume) of young students' constructs about the past indicates that they may see history "as a one-way street that does not admit of multiple traditions or lines of development, of dead ends, false dawns, or might-have beens." Collegians, too, often hold such low-order conceptions of change. A student may write on an exam, for example, that ancient folk of the Middle East "decided" that agriculture was both a good idea and the next thing that ought to be done. Or textbooks may state that the Portuguese sailed down the western coast of Africa aiming from the start "to discover a route to Asia and open it up to trade," when we know that in fact they groped their way along seeking short-term objectives and profits with little idea of what the morrow would bring.

Living as we do in an utterly unpredictable world, why do such unsophisticated ideas of causality persist? Part of the reason may be our long tradition of teaching history as self-enclosed national or civilizational narratives in which historical actors (often, great men) play assigned parts to achieve what was going to happen. In world history textbooks, such standard non-Western characters as Ashoka, Mansa Musa, Cheng Ho, Lady Murasaki, and Mahatma Gandhi tend not to appear as human beings who felt their way through life with imagination and courage (or stubbornness and timidity) toward an unknown future. Rather, they come on stage mainly to exemplify particular features of their "culture." For example, in several textbooks the Mauryan emperor Ashoka is presented as an icon of a bounded, otherized India whose job in history was to do the clever things he did and show how worthy some ancient Indians could be. More realistically, he was a man embarked on a strange and remarkable experiment to rule, partly through moral suasion, in a world dominated by Hellenistic gangster-kings.

The Patterns of Change Model aims to help correct some of these ahistorical habits of mind. It values the dictum of Marshall Hodgson that "every generation makes its own decisions."[29] That is, change must invariably be understood as the consequence of the conditions and circumstances, usually a complex and contradictory array of them, that prevail at any particular moment. The "universe of data" that play upon a situation may of course include long-term cultural conditions, though custom usually has less explanatory power than students have been encouraged to think. "A generation is not bound by the attitudes of its ancestors," Hodgson writes, "though it must reckon with their consequences and may indeed find itself severely limited by those consequences in the range of choices among which it can decide."[30] Students living in the late twentieth century know this sort of thing by experience. Teaching them, therefore, that the Portuguese "decided" to sail to Asia because they had the right cultural attitudes or that Menelik II defeated the Italians at the Battle of Adowa to show that African cultures produce winners does not open for them a very clear window on the past.

Toward a New Definition of World History
in the School Curriculum

World history will not of course be taught the same way in every school and state. Indeed, the idea of a national curriculum for history, with which the American public flirted briefly in the early 1990s, is out of fashion today. World history curriculum across the country, however, might be more logical and coherent and more in tune with the "cognitive revolution" if history educators debated more self-consciously what we think we mean when we talk about this subject and what we think our students understand it to be. For example, the new state standards documents from California, Massachusetts, Texas, and Virginia include no clear declarations of the intellectual grounds on which particular topics were designated for study, no rationales for why students should know one thing rather than another, no discussion of why they should study specified topics in a particular order or grade level, no identification of the large patterns of change that might contribute to a more holistic "picture of the past."

All the social studies face tough competition with other subjects to get instructional space in the school day. Even so, we need to regard world history education as a particularly serious and critical business, not as a low-priority subject governed by fuzzy, contradictory ideas about inclusiveness, diversity, perspective, and the native qualities of the West. We need to ask lots of questions: How can we make explicit the ideological and cultural precommitments that underlie the different ways we define world history and justify its inclusion in the curriculum? Why do textbooks and standards directives show such obliviousness to the exciting world history scholarship of the past quarter century? At what developmental levels should we start teaching world history and why (third grade, for example, in Virginia)? If so many teachers teach world history these days, why don't public universities in their states offer courses that connect directly to the K-12 curriculum or that ask students to think about world history as a distinct and challenging field? Why, as Diane Ravitch has recently pointed out, are so many world history teachers so poorly trained in the discipline itself?[31] Why do teachers have a variety of avenues—workshops, institutes, published resources—for building their knowledge of particular parts of the world but so few opportunities to join together to develop coherent conceptions of world history that can underlie an entire year's work?

The key epistemological problem in history education is to figure out how students use their minds to connect their reality to the experience of human beings who are dead and gone. Where do students position themselves, if anywhere, in the stream of global time? How do they distinguish among the past as reality to be recovered, as social construction, and as literary fiction? How can teachers know when students cognize world history only as a page in a book, a fun activity, or a set of tasks to perform? These are big issues for world history educators. In my view, we should see what answers we get when we free the curriculum from identity politics, hunts for "our origins," and the telling of enclosed culture stories. The late world historian Marilyn Waldman advised, "I think we need to stop arguing over which books to read or which cultures to study and start talking about which questions to ask."[32]

NOTES

1. William Swinton, *Outlines of the World's History, Ancient, Mediaeval, and Modern* (New York, 1874), p. 2.

2. Carl L. Becker, *Modern History* (New York, 1931), p. 2.

3. L. S. Stavrianos, *A Global History from Prehistory to the Present*, 4th ed. (Englewood Cliffs, NJ, 1988), p. xi. The first edition was published in 1971.

4. *National Standards for History*, Basic Edition (Los Angeles, National Center for History in the Schools, University of California, Los Angeles, 1996), pp. 45–46.

5. On the relationship between prior historical knowledge and classroom learning, see Peter Seixas, "Historical Understanding among Adolescents in a Multicultural Setting," *Curriculum Inquiry*, 23, 3 (1993), pp. 301–327; and, in this volume, James V. Wertsch, "Is It Possible to Teaching Beliefs, as Well as Knowledge about History?"

6. On the origins and evolution of Western civilization as both an intellectual construct and a teaching project, see Gilbert Allardyce, "The Rise and Fall of the Western Civilization Course," *American Historical Review*, 87 (1982), pp. 695–725; and Lawrence W. Levine, *The Opening of the American Mind: Canons, Culture, and History* (Boston, 1996), pp. 54–68.

7. Samuel P. Huntington, *The Clash of Civilizations and the Remaking of World Order* (New York, 1998), pp. 72, 311.

8. Marshall G. S. Hodgson, *The Venture of Islam: Conscience and History in a World Civilization*, vol. 1 (Chicago, 1974), pp. 36–37.

9. For a recent reaffirmation of the Western Civ curriculum in colleges, see Michael F. Doyle, "'Hisperanto': Western Civilization in the Global Curriculum," *Perspectives* (American Historical Association), 36 (May 1998), pp. 1, 24–28. See also Edmund Burke III and Ross E. Dunn, "Western Civ in the Global Curriculum: A Response," *Perspectives* 36 (October 1998), pp. 31–33.

10. P. Adler, quoted in Rod Janzen, "The Social Studies Conceptual Dilemma: Six Contemporary Approaches," *Social Studies* (May/June 1995), pp. 136–137.

11. See David A. Hollinger, *Postethnic America: Beyond Multiculturalism* (New York, 1995).

12. J. M. Blaut, *The Colonizers Model of the World: Geographical Diffusionism and Eurocentric History* (New York, 1993), p. 6.

13. William H. McNeill, *The Rise of the West: A History of the Human Community* (Chicago, 1963).

14. Philip D. Curtin, *Cross-Cultural Trade in World History* (New York, 1984) and *The Rise and Fall of the Plantation Complex* (New York, 1990).

15. The main forums for discussing new developments in world history are the World History Association and its publications, the American Historical Association's periodicals and conferences, *The History Teacher*, and the H-World electronic list supervised by H-Net. In all these arenas, university scholars, community college instructors, and K-12 teachers exchange ideas equitably and shift easily between issues of scholarship and teaching.

16. Patrick Manning, "The Problems of Interaction in World History," *American Historical Review*, 101 (June 1996), p. 772.

17. Akhil Gupta and James Ferguson, "Beyond Cultures: Space, Identity, and the Politics of Difference," *Cultural Anthropology*, 7 (1992), p. 12.

18. Hollinger, *Postethnic America*, pp. 101.

19. *National Standards for History*, p. 66.

20. On the public controversy over the National Standards for History, see Gary B. Nash, Charlotte Crabtree, and Ross E. Dunn, *History on Trial: Culture Wars and the Teaching of the Past* (New York, 1997).

21. In my view, one recent text makes a partial break with the traditional structure. See Roger B. Beck, Linda Black, Phillip C. Naylor, and Dahia Ibo Shabaka, *World History: Patterns of Interaction* (Evanston, IL, 1999).

22. For quick access to virtually all the new state standards documents and projects, see the Putnam Valley College web site at www.putwest.boces.org/Standards.html, or the Thomas B. Fordham Foundation Report at the Educational Excellence Network site: www.edexcellence.net. See also *Building a World History Curriculum* (National Council for History Education, 1997).

23. For example, the Massachusetts content framework, titled "Core Knowledge: The World," presents twenty-three subject matter topics for periods up to 1450 C.E. Eleven of these topics designate Europe or its presumed Mediterranean antecedents for study in terms of ascribed cultural categories such as "literature," "philosophy," "religion," "practices," "legacies," and "components." The other thirteen topics list additional civilizations to be covered—China, India, Islam, and so on—largely in terms of static attributes, not historical developments. For the modern centuries, fully twenty-four of thirty standards specify study of Europe or North America. History and Social Science Curriculum Framework (Massachusetts Department of Education, 1997).

24. See Andre Gunder Frank, *ReOrient: Global Economy in the Asian Age* (Berkeley and Los Angeles, 1998).

25. See Philip D. Curtin, "Depth, Span, and Relevance," *American Historical Review*, 89 (February 1984), pp. 1–9; and Martin W. Lewis and Kären E. Wigen, *The Myth of Continents: A Critique of Metageography* (Berkeley and Los Angeles, 1997), p. 103.

26. Other literature on ways students construct historical meaning includes "Teaching History in a Changing World," special issue of *Social Education*, 61 (January 1997); and "Forces for Change in the Teaching and Learning of History," special issue of *Canadian Social Studies*, 32 (Winter 1998).

27. Joseph C. Miller, "The African Diaspora in World Historical Perspective," in Bryant P. Shaw, ed., *Africa in World History: A Teaching Conference* (Colorado Springs, 1987), pp. 103, 105.

28. See Rosalyn Ashby, Peter Lee, and Alaric Dickinson, "How Children Explain the 'Why' of History: The Chata Research Project on Teaching History," *Social Education*, 61 (January 1997), pp. 17–21.

29. See his discussion of "determinacy in traditions" in *Venture of Islam*, 1, pp. 34–39.

30. Hodgson, *Venture of Islam*, 1, p. 37.

31. Diane Ravitch, "Why Students Don't Know Much about History," *Education Week*, March 4, 1998.

32. Marilyn Robinson Waldman, "The Meandering Mainstream: Reimagining World History," inaugural address, College of Humanities, Ohio State University, March 2, 1988.

Part II

Changes Needed to Advance Good History Teaching

Needless to say, promoting good history education entails work beyond the kinds of explorations presented in Part I. It also involves improving professional development, teacher education, and the institutional and policy structures that support such improvements. Part II consists of three essays that address reform at this level.

In the first, Diane Ravitch investigates the educational backgrounds of history teachers across the United States and finds them lacking. Using data from the National Center for Education Statistics, she identifies a major problem in the numbers of "out-of-field" teachers, that is, teachers of history whose academic preparation lies elsewhere. She presents evidence for several linked hypotheses to explain this state of affairs, taking aim at state certification policies, the teacher education professoriate, and history's "submergence" in social studies. Finally, she calls for further research on these claims.

With G. Williamson McDiarmid and Peter Vinten-Johansen's chapter, we zoom in on teacher education, examining the work of one program that prepares history teachers. The structural innovation that lies at the center of their reform effort is the collaboration between departments of education and history (represented by the two authors, respectively). The program thus provides the history that Ravitch advocates but is also specifically tailored to the challenges of teaching that its students will soon face. While they point out the disincentives to engage in collaboration, McDiarmid and Vinten-Johansen also map the considerable promise that such efforts hold.

In the third chapter of the section, Shelly Weintraub explains history education reform in Oakland, California. As the district administrator responsible for the program, Weintraub placed professional development at the center of the district efforts but linked it closely to the development

of local curricular standards, materials, assessments, and teacher research. Collaboration, including teachers based in schools, as well as academics from university history and education departments, was, again,
important. The paths charted by McDiarmid, Vinten-Johansen, and
Weintraub should help to dispel any despondency felt by readers of Ravitch's analysis. Taken together, the chapters identify multiple levels at
which reforms might be addressed.

Chapter 8

The Educational Backgrounds of History Teachers

Diane Ravitch

Most youngsters who take a history course in junior high school or high school in the United States are studying with a teacher who has neither a major nor a minor nor a graduate degree in history. According to analysts for the U.S. Department of Education, 53.9 percent of the students in grades 7–12 who are studying history or world civilization are taught by teachers who lack at least a minor in the subject. That so many who teach history have not studied history must be disturbing; certainly, it undermines the current movement to set rigorous standards for students, for it is unlikely that teachers who are themselves unfamiliar with historical knowledge and controversies will be able to engage their students in high levels of historical thinking.[1]

What is the educational background of history teachers in the United States? What proportion of history teachers have a major or minor in history? What is the educational background of those history teachers who lack either a major or minor in history? How does teacher preparation in history compare to that for social studies as a whole? These are the questions that this essay will attempt to answer. To put the matter into context, it is important to observe that a mismatch between educational background and teaching assignment is not unusual in American schools. According to the U.S. Department of Education, those who teach a subject without so much as an undergraduate minor in the subject are teaching "out of field." Public attention tends to focus on the large numbers of out-of-field teachers in mathematics and science. The subject of history, however, suffers a higher rate of out-of-field teaching than either mathematics or science; indeed, only the "subfield" of physical sciences (physics and chemistry) has a higher incidence of out-of-field teaching than history.

The U.S. Department of Education's National Center for Education Statistics (NCES) reports on out-of-field teaching in two ways: first, by the proportion of children who are taught by teachers who lack at least a minor in the subject taught; second, by comparing teachers' classroom assignments to their educational background.

In 1996 NCES released a statistical analysis by Richard M. Ingersoll that showed the extent to which youngsters in public secondary schools (defined as grades 7–12) were taught academic subjects by teachers "without basic qualifications in those subjects." On the basis of data from NCES's Schools and Staffing Survey in 1990–91, the Ingersoll study found that the following proportions of students were enrolled in classes taught by a teacher without at least a minor in the field: 20.8 percent in English, 26.6 percent in mathematics, 16.5 percent in science, and 13.4 percent in social studies. When the same study examined what it called "particular subfields," the incidence of out-of-field teaching soared to 38.5 percent in life science (biology), 56.2 percent in physical science (physics, chemistry, earth science/geology), and 53.9 percent in history. The study accepted pedagogical studies in most fields as an academic major or minor, which lowered the out-of-field numbers. Thus, a major or minor in social studies education, science education, mathematics education, English education, or reading education was treated as equivalent to an academic major or minor in those fields. If these education courses had been excluded, the out-of-field numbers would have been far higher in science, mathematics, social studies, and English. In history and world civilization, it should be noted, only a major or minor in history was considered appropriate in-field training.[2]

For the other method used to calculate out-of-field teaching, the relation between teachers' assignments and their educational background, the data are equally disturbing. NCES reported in *America's Teachers: Profile of a Profession, 1993–94*, published in 1997, that 36 percent of public school teachers had neither a major nor a minor in their main assignment field; 39.5 percent of teachers of science, 34 percent in mathematics, 25 percent in English, 59 percent in social studies, and 13.4 percent in foreign language were teaching out-of-field. The most startling figure in this list, of course, is social studies; the figure of 59 percent was subsequently amended by NCES (in response to questions that I raised while researching the extent of out-of-field teaching in history) and reduced to

17.4 percent after NCES recognized an expanded definition of the fields that constitute social studies.[3]

The Ingersoll study offers important information about the distribution of out-of-field teachers. Contrary to what one might expect, out-of-field history teachers are not concentrated in schools where there are large numbers of poor and/or minority students, nor are qualified history teachers disproportionately assigned to affluent and socially advantaged students. As compared to 53.9 percent of history teachers who were out of field, 56.3 percent of history teachers were out-of-field in low-minority schools, 54.2 percent in high-minority schools, 54.3 percent in low-poverty schools and 55.0 percent in high-poverty schools. The lowest proportions of out-of-field history teachers were in medium-minority schools (49.9 percent) and medium-poverty schools (53.0 percent). For the field of history, none of these differences was statistically significant. This is a contrast to the situation in English, mathematics, and science, where students in high-poverty schools were far more likely to be taught by an out-of-field teacher; in history, students were equally likely to be taught by an out-of-field teacher regardless of the poverty enrollment of the school. In other words, affluent students stood a better chance of getting a well-educated teacher of English, mathematics, and science than did poor students, but when it came to history teachers, rich and poor students stood an equal chance of getting an out-of-field history teacher.[4]

Ingersoll asked whether students who were high achieving were likelier to get better-qualified teachers. This sorting, he found, was least likely to happen in history compared to other academic fields. Low-achieving classes were somewhat likelier to have an out-of-field history teacher than high-achieving classes (by 60.1 percent to 52.6 percent), but this gap was small compared to the those found in other academic subject areas (in science, for example, it was 26.6 percent to 9.2 percent). In other academic subjects, high-track students were more likely to have a well-educated teacher than low-track students, but in history there was little difference between those in low tracks (where 55.1 percent of students had an out-of-field teacher) and those in high-track classes (51.1 percent). Students in schools with low-minority enrollment were less likely to have out-of-field teachers of English, mathematics, and science, but the same students were slightly more likely to have an out-of-field history teacher than those in high-minority schools (by 55.6 percent to 51.4 percent). The highest incidence of out-of-field history teaching was in twelfth grade (62.4 percent), where history is seldom taught, the lowest in eleventh grade (47.0 percent), when American history is usually offered. Note, however, that the second-highest incidence of out-of-field history teaching occurs in the eighth grade (60.5 percent), which is the customary year for junior high school American history.[5]

There are large differences among the states in the incidence of out-of-field history teaching. Since each state sets its own entrance standards into teaching, it is clear that state policy makes a huge difference. In looking at disparities among states, one expects to find the poorest states at the bottom with the most out-of-field teachers, and the wealthiest states at the top, with the fewest. But this is not what happens when one examines the frequency of out-of-field history teaching. The states with the largest proportions of out-of-field history teachers are Louisiana (88 percent), Minnesota (83 percent), West Virginia (82 percent), Oklahoma (81 percent), Pennsylvania (73 percent), Kansas (72 percent), Maryland (72 percent), Arizona (71 percent), South Dakota (70 percent), and Mississippi (70 percent). The states with the lowest proportions are Wisconsin (32 percent), New York (32 percent), Illinois (37 percent), and Texas (39 percent). To keep matters in perspective, bear in mind that even in the "best" states, 32 to 39 percent of those teaching history are "out of field," figures far exceeding those in any other academic field except the physical sciences, where teachers are perennially in short supply.[6]

Delineating the educational backgrounds of the nation's teachers of history is a complicated matter, as I have discovered in working with the able and responsive staff at NCES in 1997 and 1998. After the publication of *America's Teachers* in July 1997, I contacted NCES to try to assemble data about history teachers in grades 7–12. This group is not identified in *America's Teachers*, which refers only to teachers of social studies. When I first worked on this subject, I was preparing a presentation for a meeting of the National Council of History Education. In September 1997, NCES released and reviewed data showing that:

- 18.5 percent of the nation's social studies teachers in grades 7–12 had a major or minor in history.
- 71 percent of the nation's social studies teachers in those grades had an undergraduate degree in education.
- 55 percent of all history teachers had neither a major nor minor in history.
- 53 percent of those who teach two or more history courses had neither a major or minor in history.

- 64 percent of those who teach one history course had neither a major nor a minor in history.[7]

To write the present essay, I turned again to the staff at NCES in the summer of 1998 to recheck the data, only to learn that NCES had redefined social studies, which changed the data. The numbers cited earlier referred only to those teachers who called themselves teachers of social studies. Left out of these calculations were those who described themselves as teachers of specific disciplines, that is, geography, civics, economics, political science/government, sociology/social organization, psychology, and other social sciences. When these teachers were factored in, the academic credentials of social studies teachers improved. The new data show that:

- *36.4 percent* of those who teach one or more social studies classes in grades 7–12 have a major or minor in history, and another 16.1 percent have a major or minor in another academic social science field. Thus, *52.5 percent* of social studies teachers in grades 7–12 have an academic major in history or a social science. An additional 24.5 percent of social studies teachers have a major or minor in "social studies education." So, in NCES's calculations, 23 percent of social studies teachers in grades 7–12 are teaching out of field.

- *40.9 percent* of those who teach social studies in grades 9–12 have a major or minor in history, and another 16.0 percent have a major in one of the social sciences. Thus, *56.9 percent* of high school social studies teachers have an academic major in history or a social science. An additional 25.2 percent have a major or minor in social studies education. Thus, NCES would say that 17.9 percent of social studies teachers in grades 9–12 are out of field.

In the case of those who teach courses in history and world civilization, NCES reports that:

- *45.5 percent* of those who teach one or more classes in history or world civilization in grades 7–12 have a major or minor in history.
- *48.1 percent* of those who teach one or more classes in history or world civilization in grades 9–12 have a major or minor in history.

NCES also finds that in grades 7–12:

- *59.9 percent* of those who teach two or more classes of social studies do not have a history major or minor.

- *64.2 percent* of those who teach one class of history or world civilization do not have a history major or minor.
- *52.6 percent* of those who teach two or more classes of history or world civilization do not have a history major or minor.

The data show that in grades 9–12:

- *55.6 percent* of those who teach two or more classes of social studies do not have a history major or minor.
- *63.6 percent* of those who teach only one class of history or world civilization do not have either a major or minor in history.
- *49.4 percent* of those who teach two or more classes of history or world civilization do not have a history major or minor.

The big change in the figures between 1997 and 1998 was the result of the addition of teachers who identify themselves with specific social science disciplines; these teachers have stronger academic credentials than those who are generic teachers of social studies. Even so, a majority of social studies teachers do not have either a major or minor in history. Among those who specifically teach history in grades 7–12, 52.6 percent do not have either a major or minor in history, nor do half of those who teach history and world civilization courses in high school.

Why So Much Out-of-Field Teaching?

Why should out-of-field teaching be nearly as prevalent in history as it is in physics and chemistry? We regularly hear that the schools have difficulty hiring people who majored in science because they receive far better pay in private industry. But it is doubtful that history majors are drawn away from public school teaching because of competition for their services by the private sector.

One reason for the high rate of out-of-field teaching in history is the popular view that anyone can teach history; this view supports the practice of assigning history classes to athletic coaches, without regard to their educational background. "How do you spell history teacher?" a teacher once asked me in a public forum, then answered her own question: "C-O-A-C-H." There appears to be a presumption that teaching history requires no special skills beyond the ability to stay a few pages ahead of the students in the textbook.

A second reason for the high levels of out of field teaching is state certification requirements, which favor pedagogical preparation and courses in social studies education rather than history degrees. State certification requirements are not especially demanding; despite the very high levels of out-of-field teaching in almost every academic field, more than 90 percent of the nation's teachers are certified. In Kansas, for example, 98.5 percent of the state's teachers are certified, but 21 percent of its English teachers are out-of-field, as are 12 percent of its math teachers, 42 percent of its teachers of life science, 74 percent of its teachers of physical sciences, and 72 percent of its history teachers. It is important to bear in mind, therefore, that certification offers no assurance that teachers for prepared for specific subject-matter assignments.[8]

Historians are permitted the use of anecdotes, so I will introduce here the story of Karen T. In response to an article that I had written on this subject, Ms. T. wrote in February 1998 about her inability to get a job teaching high school history because of her lack of pedagogical credentials. She has a bachelor's degree in literature and cinema studies; a master's degree in U.S. history with a specialization in African American protest and women's history; she is a doctoral candidate at a major university, concentrating on U.S. history and the history of the American family since 1945. She has worked as a substitute teacher and an SAT tutor; when a new public high school opened, she could not even gain an interview. She explained that "the state certification procedures continually threaten to derail my efforts to simply be a historian who teaches. The cost of becoming a certified teacher would not only strain my bank account, but would essentially require me to earn another Masters degree and make actually completing my doctoral work a faraway goal." Ms. T. offered to be a "poster child" for a campaign to allow people like herself—well educated in history but not in pedagogy—to teach history; she would, she wrote, "pose complete with academic regalia, outstanding teaching evaluations and file full of rejection letters." In Virginia, where Ms. T. lives, 68 percent of history teachers are out-of-field. Some states have established alternate routes into the teaching profession that allow well-educated men and women to enter teaching and to be judged by their ability to teach rather than by paper credentials; this, I believe, is a healthy trend.[9]

Another aspect to this puzzling situation was revealed in a letter from Professor S., who teaches social studies in a school of education in Missouri; he was concerned about the educational background of those who prepare future teachers of social studies. He explained that he was unusual in his department because he has master's degrees in history, from both Columbia University and the University of California at Berkeley; his colleagues, he wrote, "have 'social science' backgrounds which means they know next to nothing about history, but they are training future social studies teachers. If we want to raise social studies standards, we should insist anyone teaching social studies university courses must have at least a master's degree in history." The challenge, he claimed, was to integrate the "content knowledge" of history with the curriculum materials and methods of the regular classroom. But, if teachers of teachers do not appreciate the value of the "content knowledge" of history, this is not likely to happen.[10]

These problems are symptomatic of history's submergence in social studies. Social studies was invented in the early years of the twentieth century as part of an effort both to break the dominance of history in the curriculum and to teach contemporary social problems to students who presumably were not intelligent enough to study history. Thomas Jesse Jones is credited with teaching the first course in social studies at Hampton Institute, an industrial and trade school for African Americans and Indians in Virginia. Jones, a former social worker, served as chairman of the highly influential Committee on Social Studies of the National Education Association's Commission on Reorganization of Secondary Education. This commission, whose report is popularly known as the "cardinal principles of secondary education," had a large impact on American public education, pushing it in the direction of socially efficient studies. Jones' committee defined the new field of social studies, whose primary aim was social efficiency, good citizenship, and utilitarianism. Jones's committee assumed that students could not possibly be interested in history unless it was directly related to the present. The Committee on Social Studies decided that good citizenship would be the goal of social studies. Studies that did not contribute to that goal would have no claim to a place in the curriculum. This influential report cut the ground away from the study of dead civilizations and remote events, shifting the curriculum toward current events.[11]History was never part of the classical curriculum (the ancient languages and mathematics); like English, the sciences, and modern foreign languages, it found a regular place in the high school curriculum in the closing years of the nineteenth century. Nonetheless, the educators who believed that youngsters should concentrate only on studies that were relevant to their own lives and times were eager to restrict the study of history to college-bound students. A great divide opened in the 1920s and 1930s between proponents of a traditional liberal education for all students—like William Chandler Bagley and Isaac L. Kandel, both at Teachers College—and proponents of progressive education and social studies—like Harold Rugg and William Heard Kilpatrick, also at Teachers College. In this schism, history was treated as an elitist subject, not really appropriate for all students, because it dealt with events and issues too remote in time for average students to understand.

For many years, history was considered *primus inter pares* within social studies; as social studies became established, history remained the central, organizing study of the field. It provided depth to studies of government, civics, economics, sociology, and psychology; it was the balance wheel between the social sciences and the humanities. But, as the field shifted from "history and social studies" to simply "social studies," history lost its dominant role and became only one of many equal strands in social studies. This is certainly cause for concern for those who believe not only that history should be the central core of social studies but that knowledge of history is essential for the development of political intelligence.

Unfortunately, some social studies educators tend to deride concerns about the diminished status of history in the curriculum, with the following array of responses. First, they say that most courses taught in social studies are already history courses and that partisans of history are trying to squeeze out everything except history. Second, they say that historians who worry about such things are self-interested, eager to bolster enrollments in their own college courses. Third, they say that history is by nature a conservative field and that those who promote it share an insidious conservative agenda. Fourth, they say that history is too remote from the lives of students today, who can interest themselves only in what is relevant to their own lives.[12]

These themes are illustrated by an exchange that followed publication of Sean Wilentz's article, "The Past Is Not a Process," in *The New York Times*, April 20, 1997. Wilentz complained that leaders of social studies were opposing the adoption of history standards in the states and that social studies "has outlived its usefulness." The *OAH Newsletter* of August 1997 published a discussion of the article, beginning with criticism of Wilentz's views by Alan Singer, an education professor at Hofstra University. Singer claimed that historians like Wilentz, Eric Foner, Kenneth T. Jackson, and Gary B. Nash were wrong to seek "to replace secondary school social studies with a more in-depth study of history." He offered the usual arguments: History already dominates secondary social studies; history is not relevant to average students; a cabal of conservatives supports history, purposely diverting attention from racism, sexism, and inequality; supporters of history want only to teach facts, not critical thinking about the past; history neglects other disciplines, especially the social sciences.[13]

Responding to Singer, Kenneth Jackson pointed out that the two-year requirement of global studies in New York state was not history based and that teachers of social studies in that state could be certified without ever taking a single course in history; he cited a letter from a teacher who complained that "People who don't know any history are being asked to train others in historical methods and ideas, and it is not working. When I started teaching in 1964, every member of the department was a history major. Today I teach in a department of seven, and I'm the only one who majored in history."[14]

If the leaders of social studies are right and most social studies courses are history courses, it should be a matter of deep concern that so many social studies teachers have neither a major nor a minor in history. How will these teachers make history come to life for their students if they are relying almost exclusively on a textbook? How can these teachers enable their students to see the relevance of the past if they know very little of the past themselves? How can they offer alternatives to conventional interpretations when they have limited understanding of either conventional interpretations or alternatives to conventional interpretations? Why the animus against history, why the insistence that it consists of little more than regurgitating facts when a perusal of the historical work of the past generation shows the falsity of such a claim? Why the effort to portray history as indifferent to the social sciences when historians regularly rely on the social sciences to recapture choices and conditions in the past? Why the insistence that history is narrow when the field of history is vibrant with a rich palette of social, political, and ideological concerns? Why the repeated claims that anyone who promotes history must be a conservative or a dupe of conservatives?

Part of the animus toward history may be explained by the fact that many in the social studies field do not have degrees in history and therefore bridle at the suggestion that history should be treated as the core of social studies, a status that would make it more important than other parts of social studies. One would not expect the National Council for the Social Studies to be unduly concerned about the large numbers of teachers of history and social studies who do not have a major or minor in history. If the problem is to be addressed directly, it must be addressed by teachers and historians and by their fellow citizens who believe that a rich and comprehensive history education is a quintessential element in a liberal education for all children.

A Research Agenda for History Education

If we are serious in trying to find out why there are so many teachers of history who have neither a major nor a minor in history, there are several issues that require additional research.

First, researchers should analyze state policies that determine what is expected of future teachers of history and social studies (e.g., college courses, degrees, credentials, tests). We need to know which states grant certification to teachers of social studies who have neither a major nor minor in history and what qualifications they accept instead; we need to know which states certify teachers to teach social studies even though they have never taken any history courses in college. We also need to know which states have model standards for entry to social studies and history teaching.

Second, researchers should examine the educational backgrounds of those who teach social studies education and identify the extent to which these professors are themselves educated in history. Do the nation's professors of social studies have a major or minor in history? If, as the leaders of the social studies field say, most social studies courses are actually history courses, then all social studies teachers should be well-educated in history, as well as the professors who prepare them for the classroom.

History and social studies can and should coexist. But they should coexist in a context in which future teachers of history and social studies in the United States are expected to study American and world history, as well as the social sciences and the humanities. Parents have a right to expect that their children's teachers are well educated; this should be considered a solemn obligation on the part of state and local boards of education. This should be as true for their history teachers as it is for teachers of other school subjects.

Should we worry that half those now teaching history in high school do not have even a college minor in history? Perhaps this is not a very important issue after all compared to others in our society. Surely there are other, far more important issues. However, one reason to focus on this problem is that it can be solved. This is a problem that was created by state policy and that can be cured by state policy. States that refuse to certify future teachers of history and social studies who lack at least a minor in history will no longer be faced with embarrassing statistics on this score. Indeed, the states can end this problem within this generation if they confront it directly by requiring that every teacher—not only of history but of other major academic subjects as well—is well educated and well prepared.

NOTES

1. Richard M. Ingersoll, "Out-of-Field Teaching and Educational Equality" (Washington, DC, October 1996), p. 16.

2. Ibid., pp. 15–16.

3. National Center for Education Statistics, *America's Teachers: Profile of a Profession, 1993–94* (Washington, DC, 1997), p. 26; National Center for Education Statistics, "Errata for America's Teachers," October 27, 1997, revised Table A3.2.

4. Ingersoll, "Out-of-Field Teaching," pp. 16–18.

5. Ibid., pp. 15–23.

6. Ibid., p. 24.

7. Diane Ravitch, "Who Prepares Our History Teachers? Who Should Prepare Our History Teachers?" *The History Teacher*, 31(4) (August 1998), pp. 1–8; Diane Ravitch, "Why Students Don't Know Much About History," *Education Week*, March 4, 1998.

8. Ingersoll, "Out-of-Field Teaching," p. 24; *America's Teachers*, Table A3.13, pp. A63–A64.

9. Personal communication to author, February 25, 1998.

10. Personal communication to author, March 9, 1998.

11. Michael Bruce Lybarger, "Origins of the Social Studies Curriculum, 1865–1916," doctoral dissertation, University of Wisconsin–Madison, 1981, pp. 70–84; Edward A. Krug, *The Shaping of the American High School, 1880–1920* (Madison, WI, 1964), pp. 353–361; "Social Studies in Secondary Schools: Preliminary Recommendation by the Committee of the National Education Association," *History Teacher's Magazine* (December 1913), pp. 291–292. Originally printed by the U.S. Bureau of Education, 1913, Bulletin No. 41.

12. See, for example, Ron Evans, "Diane Ravitch and the Revival of History:

A Critique," *Social Studies*, 80 (May-June 1989), as well as my response in the same issue.

13. Sean Wilentz, "The Past Is Not a Process," *New York Times*, April 20, 1997; Alan Singer, Sean Wilentz, Gary B. Nash, and Kenneth T. Jackson, "Divisions, Real and Imagined," *OAH Newsletter*, August 1997, pp. 3–4, 12, 14.

14. Ibid., p. 414.

Chapter 9

A Catwalk across the Great Divide
Redesigning the History Teaching Methods Course

G. Williamson McDiarmid and Peter Vinten-Johansen

How best to prepare future history teachers remains a perennial puzzle. Since universities took over teacher preparation, history departments and departments of education have traditionally split the responsibility. Yet, faculty from these departments, especially at research universities, rarely appear to communicate, much less plan or teach collaboratively.

History faculty typically regard teacher education courses with mild contempt. Like Herodotus's Egyptian priest who, in response to the visiting Greek's boast of the reach of his lineage, disdainfully exhibited to his visitor ranks of sarcophagi representing his ancestors back several hundreds of generations, historians regard educationists not merely as academic arrivistes but as intellectual mountebanks, purveying watery nostrums and common sense as knowledge. For their part, educationists often view historians as pedantic fussbudgets, concerned more about their next book than about their students. Left to thrash about in the divide between these two camps are those who command the least experience and power and the fewest resources in the teacher education enterprise—prospective history teachers. As the two camps at best ignore and at worst snipe at each other, prospective teachers are usually left on their own to make connections between the substance of historical studies and how best to help others learn this substance.

What are the sources of this divide? One source is the cultural differences between history and education departments. Whatever their internecine disputes, historians share a long disciplinary tradition. They share the experience of initiation into a particular academic guild characterized by certain scholarly conventions and rites. And, although they may not share the specific rites and conventions of other disciplinary guilds, they recognize their legitimacy.

Teacher education does not constitute a discipline in the traditional sense but is a professional program dependent on various disciplines, such as psychology, sociology, philosophy, and history, for its intellectual and methodological moorings. In particular, teaching methods courses, common to all preservice programs, are typically informed, not by disciplinary scholarship but rather by professional practice. Hence, in the eyes of historians, teacher education faculty are not their scholarly peers, and teaching methods courses are most certainly not history seminars. In addition, many history faculty share with other citizens the perception that public schools are doing a lousy job and that teachers are largely to blame—and that, by extension, so is teacher education. For their part, few teacher educators are engaged in scholarly research in any discipline and may have little understanding of what historians and social scientists do as scholars.

Also contributing to the divide is the organization and culture of the university itself. Despite the lip service paid to teacher preparation as a "campus-wide" responsibility, administrators rarely provide either resources or incentives for disciplinary faculty and education faculty to collaborate. Coplanning and team teaching are time sumps that, at the very least, ought to be supported by faculty release time from other duties, arrangements chairpersons often find difficult to justify. In addition, work with education faculty is unlikely to be valued by departmental promotion and tenure committees in history, at least in research universities.

In short, the disincentives for education and history faculty to plan courses and teach together are legion. Rather than being surprised that such collaboration is not more common, we should be amazed when it does happen.

Research on the Learning of Future History Teachers

As Diane Ravitch notes in this volume, pedagogical courses for prospective history teachers are frequently taught by faculty who are themselves uneducated in history. Research that we have conducted at Michigan State University suggests that collaboration between history and education faculty is critical to preparing teachers who have both the substantive knowledge and the professional know-how to help all learners learn. In one project, we studied the learning of prospective history teachers in an introductory historiography seminar that was taught as a history workshop.[1] From their struggles with primary documents and conflicting secondary sources, the students appeared to learn a lot. For instance, we discovered that they learned about the foci of the seminar—the English-Spanish conflict at the end of the sixteenth century that culminated in the destruction of the Armada and the struggle between Parliament and James I of England that foreshadowed the bloodier and costlier conflicts to come in the middle of the seventeenth century. In learning about these conflicts, however, the students learned more than the facts; they also learned about the contentious nature of historical knowledge and the protracted and uncertain process of writing historical accounts. In the seminar, students not only read and analyzed competing accounts of the same event—the destruction of the Armada—but also wrote their own analyses of a 1604 controversy over a seat in Parliament, drawing on both primary and secondary sources.

Afterward, despite the fact that most students attested to the power of their experience in the seminar and evidenced considerable new knowledge, their views of how history is learned and should be taught appeared largely unchanged. Most continued to think that learning history consisted entirely of mastering mainly political information about the past and that teachers helped students do this through a combination of lectures, textbook assignments, and tests. Changing their views of history teaching was not, of course, explicitly a goal of the seminar. One might speculate, however, that learning history in a new way might have caused the students to rethink their assumptions about how the subject is best learned and, therefore, how it might be best taught.

In describing how they would teach, none of the students mentioned the workshop approach they experienced in the seminar. When asked directly about using the workshop, most claimed that such an approach could not work in high school. In the first place, "they"—an unspecified authority—would not allow teachers to use such an approach because it violated "their" notions about teaching history. Second, they assumed pupils either could not or, more likely, would not do the work and thinking that a workshop approach required. In other words, their conception of teachers' responsibilities did not include introducing students to new ways of learning.

Among those students who planned to teach, we found that even after they took their social studies methods course, they were inclined to conceive of their task as ensuring that their pupils learned what was in their textbooks. They seemed not to reference their experience in the historiography seminar at all.

In a subsequent study, we found that history majors in a required senior-level research-paper seminar, all of whom were planning to teach at either the secondary or the college level, had little understanding of how historical accounts are written.[2] As they wrote their historical essays, the students found it difficult to break with their past experience as students. Most made few substantive changes as they moved through three successive drafts, despite receiving both peer and instructor criticisms. Few demonstrated the ability to develop a thesis and substantiate its development with appropriate evidence. How well prepared are these future teachers of history to help their own pupils write competently?

Our analysis led us to question the assumption that taking history courses ensures that one learns the kind of inquiry-based history—using primary and secondary sources—that history faculty frequently expect to be taught in secondary schools. That is, history programs need to examine what they are doing for all undergraduate majors, including those who hope to enter teacher education programs and to become teachers.

Results from other studies also suggest the need for greater coordination between education and liberal arts faculty. Floden, McDiarmid, and Wiemers, in a study of mathematics methods instructors, found that these instructors, while recognizing that their students often lacked critical subject matter knowledge, felt that they lacked the time to go back and teach students this content. As it was, they felt they did not have enough time to cover what they were responsible for teaching, much less assume responsibility for teaching what they thought the students ought to have already learned.[3]

In short, leaving prospective teachers to their own devices in the difficult task of what Dewey termed "psychologizing" their subject matter seems to be an abrogation of the universities' responsibility. Many, if not most, history teachers arrive in their classrooms with a store of information about the past but with little sense of how to transform that knowledge for instruction. They are like people who have extensive passive vocabularies but can barely speak a language.

A Catwalk across the Great Divide: A Brief History

The authors of this essay have attempted, over the past seven years, to bridge the divide between departments of education and history. This effort is based on our conviction, supported by our research, that prospective teachers need opportunities to develop ideas about teaching grounded in specific historical concepts, information, and ways of thinking. We believe that the story of our attempts may be of some value to those contemplating a similar effort. As institutional support for such efforts is usually short-lived, we do suggest, however, that you not attempt this without a safety net.

In 1992 the College of Education at Michigan State University began the process of redesigning its teacher education program. Using the outline of a five-year program suggested by the Holmes Group, the College redesign rested on three core ideas about the kind of learning opportunities prospective teachers needed in order to learn to teach all pupils: opportunities to learn about their subject matters and about how to teach their subject matters, to consider how pupils' ethnicity and socioeconomic backgrounds affected their experiences in learning subject matter in school, and to try out their ideas and "moves" in classrooms with support from experienced teachers committed to reform.[4]

Another tenet of the Holmes Group reform was reaffirmation of teacher education as a campus-wide responsibility, not merely that of the college of education. Central administrative support for this idea was, at Michigan State, manifest in the form of funds provided by the Provost to support faculty in other departments as they worked with College of Education faculty on redesigning and teaching courses.

At that time, we had been collaborating on studies on student learning in Vinten-Johansen's introductory history seminar. The redesign of the teacher education program presented the opportunity, and the Provost's support provided the wherewithal and legitimacy, for us to collaborate on redesigning the methods course, a project we had often discussed.[5]

Consistent with the overall goal of the program as well as with our own convictions, we set out to design a course that would have considerations of the subject-matter—primarily history but also the social sciences—at its heart. Considerations of *how* to teach would grow out of an examination of the subject matter and a determination of what knowledge, understandings, and skills students should learn.

The course—TE 401/2—was taught for the first time in 1993. Because both of us were already committed to other courses, an advanced graduate student taught the course the first year under our joint supervision. Since then, we have team-taught the course, and McDiarmid has taught the course on his own. Vinten-Johansern has also team-taught the course with an advanced doctoral student in social studies education. In addition to teaching the course as part of the three-year undergraduate program, McDiarmid has taught TE 401/2 as part of an eighteen-month post-BA secondary certification program. The story of this course is the subject of this essay.

We brought different but complementary professional interests and experiences to the collaboration. Vinten-Johansen is an intellectual historian engaged in historical research as well as university teaching. McDiarmid, a former teacher of history in U.S. and European schools, is a teacher educator engaged in educational research. At the same time, Vinten-Johansen has focused much of his attention on improving his teaching, and McDiarmid has conducted historical inquiries as part of his research. Thus, we both brought knowledge of both the subject matter and methods for teaching the subject matter to the collaboration.

We initially collaborated in the studies of student learning of students described earlier. This collaboration produced four research papers.[6] In addition, we developed and taught a senior-level seminar in the history department at Michigan State University titled "Darwinism, Social Darwinism, and Public Policy." In the course, we explored the relationship between the intellectual movement known as Social Darwinism and, on the one hand, Darwin's actual writings and, on the other, U.S. public policy in the areas of immigration, intelligence testing, and tracking in schools. Beyond our shared interest in the topics, we also conceived the seminar to be a part of our larger plan: to establish a precedent for collaborative teaching in both the history and the teacher education departments.

First Attempt to Reinvent the Methods Course

For undergraduates, TE 401/2 is part of a three-year sequence of coursework, practica, and a year-long internship that leads to certification and half the credits required for a master's degree in education. During the first semester, students receive five credits for the course, which includes a practicum in the local schools of four hours per week. In the second semester, the practicum continues and another hour of contact time is added to make it a six-credit course. The course is expected to include state-mandated hours in "reading in the content area" as well as in special education.

On the basis of our research and our impressions of methods courses, we initially set out to marinate students in subject-matter knowledge, particularly inquiry. That is, we engaged students in each of the stages involved in historiographical research: formulating an historical problem from the secondary literature, choosing a topic and developing a prospectus, conducting research, and writing an interpretive essay. From our prior research, we knew that most history majors had not experienced this inquiry process. We had also learned that very few among our social science majors had done any social scientific or historical research. Consequently, we designed our course so that students would experience a truncated version of a history workshop approach.

The history workshop, as designed and taught by Vinten-Johansen, is designed to approximate what historians actually do.[7] The limitations imposed by time, resources, and students' background knowledge require that the teacher do much of the leg work and make many of the choices that practicing historians make. In this model, the teacher usually gathers primary source materials, thereby limiting both the range of questions and the extent of student research. The course we developed included not only history workshop activities but also mechanisms for drawing the students' attention explicitly to what we, the teachers, were doing to create such a workshop.

The primary problem with both our analysis and our approach was that we underestimated our students' anxieties about being ready to teach during their internship the following year and their preconceptions about methods courses. Our intention had been to turn the traditional methods course on its head: to start with specific historical topics; determine, through extensive reading and writing, what was problematic about the topics; and then determine how to engage learners in addressing the problem. We downplayed our students' complaints that the course was more like a history seminar than an education course. Bridling like frock-coated schoolmasters of an earlier era, we insisted that they eat their vegetables. Learning to do history and social science inquiry, like cold baths and broccoli, was good for them. Trust us, we asserted, the experience will make you a better teacher, even though the connection may seem tenuous.

Further exacerbating our students' anxieties was the well-documented disjunction between what they observed in their practicum classrooms and our objectives as they interpreted them.[8] Students believed we were force-feeding them history when what they—like their veteran counterparts in actual classrooms--thought they needed were practical answers. Scholarly debates about the frontier or the Constitution seemed irrelevant to their overriding concern: "What do I do on Monday?"

Revisiting our Assumptions

After reviewing the course, we reconsidered the sources of student resistance and redefined the goal of the course: to engage students in historical and social science inquiry in ways that would enable them to see the relevance of such inquiry to what they would do in their classrooms.

This change required us to nest our effort to get students to think about methods in relation to the specific subject matter in a context that the students would see as addressing the formidable problems they would face as interns and, subsequently, as beginning teachers. Their experiences in practicum classrooms had quickly disabused most of them of the idea that they already knew enough to teach. The task was to build both their repertoire of specific ideas for teaching, specific teacher "moves," and their confidence. But we had to do this in a way consistent with our emphasis on the critical connection between the specific content and opportunities for students to learn that content.

As we were puzzling over this problem, another issue was gaining in importance. While we were doing the initial design work on the course, the release of both national and state standards was imminent. While we were reconsidering the initial design, both actually arrived. We wanted to include them in our planning both because, in Michigan, high school graduation tests would be pegged to the standards and because we substantially agreed that the standards included knowledge and skills that were critical for teachers and pupils alike. The standards also provided welcome support for our argument that prospective teachers need to know how to conduct historical research and write in the historical genre and teach others to do the same. After examining the standards, the prospective teachers realize that they are responsible for helping their pupils learn to perform research-based inquiries and to write in the historical genre. They are, consequently, more motivated to learn how to do this themselves.

How one teaches the standards to teachers, much less to students, is not, however, self-evident. This is particularly true for standards such as "historical thinking."[9] If teachers are to help their pupils reach the standards, prospective teachers need opportunities to experience historical thinking for themselves and to learn ways to engage their pupils in such thinking. Merely reviewing the content of the standards does not constitute such an opportunity.

More than a Mere Device: Curriculum Unit Development

Redesign of the course focused, therefore, on two goals: to help prospective teachers see the relevance to their practice of a subject-matter-based methods course and to prepare them to help their pupils meet state and national standards. The solution at which we arrived—developing curriculum unit plans—was by no means new to teacher education. Typically, however, unit plans were developed as part of curriculum, not methods, courses.

Developing curriculum unit plans seemed to bring together most of the knowledge, skills, and dispositions we believed critical to good history teaching, including:

• *Knowledge of the subject matter.* Although our students sometimes arrived with either impressive knowledge of particular historical events and eras or information from social scientific fields, few were inclined to be reflective about what they knew. None had thought about their knowledge as a resource for teaching that needed to be reconfigured—or, in Dewey's term, "psychologized." More recently, researchers have reminded us that subject matter knowledge is but one ingredient in the development of "pedagogical content knowledge" that consists of both knowledge of the discipline and knowledge of how best to represent that knowledge to particular learners.[10]

Neither had our prospective teachers considered how they would address the inevitable gaps in their knowledge. This may have been an outgrowth of their assumption that textbooks would relieve them of the need to know all the information they would be expected to teach. Finally, they had rarely had the occasion to step back from their fields and consider the stability or certainty of knowledge, how it was created and tested, and by whom, much less what this implied for what and how they would teach. As a result, a primary goal of the course is to engage our students in inventorying their knowledge of history and the social sciences, transforming their knowledge into instructional activities, and supplementing their knowledge with the textbook and other sources.

(2)   • *Beliefs about the cognitive demands of various instructional activities.* Little in prospective teachers' experiences prompts them to consider the mental tasks—recognizing, defining, analyzing, synthesizing, memorizing, sequencing, relating, evaluating, and so on—that various instructional activities entail. For instance, although many prospective teachers assume that discussions are a good activity, they have not evaluated the specific mental tasks that such activities require of learners. Although they may be strong advocates of "critical" or "higher-order" thinking, they have rarely analyzed how such thinking is taught. Instead, they seem to assume that if they choose the "right" activities—discussion, not lecture; cooperative group tasks, not whole-class or individual tasks—critical thinking will automatically follow. Consequently, a primary goal of the course is to teach prospective teachers to determine the mental tasks that are appropriate for particular learning goals and then to select or develop activities that require those tasks.

(3)   • *Identification of goals and objectives for student learning as outlined in state and national standards.* We were aware that many teachers often start with activities, rather than learning objectives, in planning instruction. One of our goals in the course is to help our students learn to begin their planning process reflexively with their learning goals and objectives. We are not interested in their mastering the jargon and formulas associated with the "learning objectives" movement of the 1970s, although their experiences in prior education courses may lead them to expect that such mastery is the goal. Rather, we want them to become teachers who habitually think from ends to means, from their goals back to learning opportunities. Stating their goals and objectives for their unit also enables them and us to check to see that they are addressing the standards.

(4)   • *Acceptance of teachers' roles and responsibilities.* The goal is both to convince prospective history and social studies teachers to embrace their responsibilities to teach their pupils to read and write and to teach them

specific techniques for doing so. The rise in the number of specialists such as reading teachers has seemingly been accompanied by a decrease in subject-matter teachers' belief that they are responsible for improving the literacy skills of all their pupils.

• *Use of assessment strategies.* From their experiences as students, the prospective teachers bring with them a narrow concept of assessment—multiple-choice and short-answer tests, pop quizzes, and, for those who think of themselves as enlightened and demanding, essay tests that they administer at the end of a chapter or unit. We introduce two ideas that are new to our students: that instructional activities should be designed to provide continuous information on pupil learning, information to which the learners are privy[11] and that assessment should involve tasks that have some meaning beyond success in school.[12]

In short, by developing curriculum unit plans, the students engage in the thinking, historical research, writing, and other activities that are the goals for the class. In addition, at the end, they have in hand concrete products—curriculum unit plans—to use during their internship year. By requiring students to post their curriculum plans to their own Web sites created for the class, they also have access to other units with which they are already somewhat familiar. As part of the development process, the students are required to make frequent presentations on their units and to provide classmates with criticisms and suggestions on their evolving plans.

The Process of Curriculum Unit Planning

Descriptions of the course goals that the curriculum development assignment addresses give little sense of what the process is like for students. It is in the process that students must "psychologize" their subject-matter knowledge as well as develop new understandings. The process consists of a number of subtasks, each of which results in a product to enable us and the students themselves to closely monitor their progress:

- Identifying, researching, and writing about an issue of historical significance
- Creating a timeline for the issue
- Serving as a "critical colleague" to members of a development team
- Identifying a target group of learners

- Identifying instructional activities (including formative assessment activities) and assignments (particularly reading and writing assignments) and the mental tasks they entail
- Identifying alternative activities for special-needs students
- Teaching a portion of the unit
- Assessing effects, revising plans, posting to individual Web pages.

Identifying, Researching, and Writing about an Issue

Because they have experienced history and the social sciences only from a learner's perspective, the prospective teachers often take for granted the ubiquitous topical organization of history and social sciences. They plan, initially, to teach the Explorers, the Colonies, the American Revolution, the Constitution, Westward Expansion, and so on. Their history and social science classes do little to help them understand that the organization of information under topics is an end product of historical and social scientific interpretative work, stripped of the methodological and substantive arguments and debates by which academic fields progress. As commonplaces, topics paper over not merely the process of interpretation-challenge-reinterpretation but also the tenuousness of current accounts.

Consequently, we require, as a first step, that students choose historical problems or issues within assigned topics around which to build their curricula. This focus on problems and issues is a heuristic device. Since few teachers are blessed with the knowledge, skills, and time needed to make topical history appealing to all their pupils, issues offer a contemporary "hook" that is more likely to snare the interest of today's pupils than adherence to a purer ideal of historical study.

Across two semesters, students develop two curriculum unit plans. We choose the topic of the first unit that we develop together as a class. Both because of its ubiquity in our culture, the standards, and textbooks and because of the rich debate among historians, we develop class units around the frontier. Students examine representations of the frontier in popular culture—including excerpts from the film *Pocahontas*—and scholarly articles such as essays by historians Patricia Limerick and Richard White.[13] They also read Richard White's *The Middle Ground*, a book-length treatment of European-Indian relations in the Great Lakes region during the seventeenth and eighteenth centuries. As they read, they draft and revise an essay on the meaning of the frontier in U.S.

history and on what secondary pupils need to learn about the frontier, particularly in light of recent reinterpretations and representations in popular culture. Subsequently, in class, we work through the various steps of developing a curriculum unit plan on the frontier.

During the second semester, students choose historical problems, usually within the broad topic of the Constitution and the evolving definition of "citizen," that they could teach during their internship year. We encourage them to contact their supervising teacher-to-be to discuss their choice of problems. Before their issue is approved, they must show that it meets a set of criteria for "pedagogical fruitfulness," that it is:

• *Both significant and unresolved in the eyes of historians.* It must be an issue in which historians have recently taken a significant interest and for which multiple interpretations exist.

• *Connected to other key historical ideas, events, issues, and questions.* The issue has to have chronological "tendrils"—connections to other critical events that occurred before, during, and after the issue at hand. By following these tendrils, pupils can set their issue in its broader historical context as they also develop breadth of knowledge about the past. This is vital to addressing prospective teachers' concerns about "covering" the curriculum or textbook.

• *Included in the national and state standards, not merely a pet problem.* Like some of their experienced counterparts, if left to their own devices prospective teachers will select issues that interest them whether or not anyone else considers them worth investigating. They must therefore demonstrate which standards, both knowledge and skills, they are addressing.

• *Sufficiently interesting to engage secondary pupils.* The issue must bear on matters that pupils would agree are currently controversial. This is perhaps the trickiest of the criteria. The intent is to teach our students not to pander to pupils' fickle interests but rather to think hard about issues that bear on both their present and their future. We emphasize that part of the teachers' responsibility is to help their pupils see the connection between particular issues and their lives, which requires that they learn about their students' outside-of-school experiences.

• *Researchable.* Primary and secondary sources must be readily available and accessible. We also require the prospective teachers to think beyond conventional historical source materials and to identify unconventional materials and informants and experts whose knowledge could be tapped.[14]

We found that moving prospective teachers from thinking about topics to thinking about problems or issues is a major challenge. This is an indication of how little "psychologizing" of their subject-matter knowledge they have done. At this point, most have had no practice in transforming their knowledge into learning opportunities for their students. Many imagine that learning a few teaching techniques is all they need because they assume that teaching history consists solely of communicating information about the past.

Having to identify an issue as the focus of a unit also forces them to recognize the need to do more research—a shock for those who imagine their days of learning about history are behind them. Unable to identify an issue at first, many wake to the realization that they do not know enough *about history* to figure out an appropriate issue. They must read in the literature and talk to experts in order to focus their inquiry on a genuine issue. In a typical progression, one prospective teacher originally proposed a curriculum unit on the "social policies of the New Deal." Prompted to define a problem, he first posed an "informational" question ("What were the social policies of the New Deal?"). After reading more about the New Deal, talking to others, and investigating the current debate over welfare reform, he eventually identified a genuine problem: "To what extent, if at all, did New Deal social welfare policies undermine African American families?"

Supporting this progression from topic to specific problem were sustained discussions with classmates and instructors and multiple written revisions. We require students to write an essay about their issue in which they detail their research, justify their choice of issue, and specify how the issue meets each of the criteria we have described.

Creating a Timeline for the Issue

To help our students appreciate the importance of establishing the sequence of events, we require that they create a customized timeline specifically for their issue. The question we ask is: "What events are critical to addressing your issue, and what is the sequence of those events?" After drawing their timelines on newsprint, students present them to the class and offer rationales for the events they included. We also expect that, as part of their unit, they will require their students to create timelines. For a curriculum that is anchored by historical issues, opportunities for pupils to learn the chronology of critical events is particularly important. Emphasizing the importance of proper sequencing of events is also an occasion to discuss ideas about cause and effect and historical contingency.

Serving as a "Critical Colleague" to Members of a Development Team

Because history, social science, and teaching all occur within "discourse communities," we require students with related interests to organize themselves into groups. At each stage, group members provide reactions, criticism, and suggestions to one another. During class, students meet in groups to discuss their progress and ideas and to share resources. Given what we know about the isolation of teachers, we want our students to experience the value of working with colleagues on curriculum in the hope that they will be encouraged to try such an approach later in their own schools.[15]

Identifying Instructional Activities, Particularly Reading and Writing Activities and Assignments

We ask students to describe activities and assignments only after they have established what they want their pupils to know, understand, and be able to do. We provide multiple examples of various strategies, activities, and assignments. In preparation, they read case studies of accomplished teachers as well as texts with suggestions for activities. In addition, we demonstrate many of these strategies in our own teaching and through activities—particularly, literacy activities—and assignments in our class.

Given what we have learned about our students' lack of experience as writers in the historical genre, we devote a lot of time to teaching writing. We require our students to follow a particular staged approach to writing that involves developing a thesis statement, gathering data to support that thesis, and crafting an essay that argues the thesis.[16] At each stage in the process, students receive critical comments from both their classmates and us. In addition, they write successive drafts of their essay, revising adding all components—thesis, supporting evidence, conclusion—with each draft. Although we recognize that numerous writing process models exist, we use this approach because of Vinten-Johansen's past success with it and because it is tailored to a particular genre, historical writing.[17] In their own curriculum plans, students must identify writing activities and how they plan to help their pupils learn to write in the genre.

Similarly, we also attempt to focus our students' attention on their habits as readers and to provide a model process they can use with their pupils in reading different types of materials. In reading historical essays and accounts for the class, our students complete worksheets in which they identify and analyze each article's thesis, supporting evidence and arguments, and conclusions. Again, they must include, in their curriculum unit plans, strategies for helping their pupils become better readers of historical and social science material.

As noted earlier, we also require that our students identify what they expect their pupils will be "doing in their heads" (e.g., analyzing, memorizing, evaluating, synthesizing) while engaged in particular activities and assignments (e.g., reading, discussing, writing chapter outline). Making their assumptions explicit proved a challenge because our students had not thought about what they assumed learners "did in their heads" while engaged in common classroom activities. Our intent is to make them conscious of the fit between their goals for pupil learning and the kinds of activities they plan.

We also require that the students' proposed instructional activities and assessment tasks meet the criteria for "authenticity" that Newmann, Secada, and Wehlage propose on the basis of research from the Center on Organization and Restructuring Schools.[18] For instruction, these criteria include higher order thinking, deep knowledge of the subject matter, substantive conversation, and connections to the world beyond the classroom. For student performance, the criteria include analysis, disciplinary concepts, and elaborated written communication.

Identifying Alternative Activities for Special-Needs Students

Because of the movement to place special-needs pupils in regular classrooms whenever possible, we also require students to anticipate problems that might arise in implementing their planned activities. Their plans must include consideration of hearing- and seeing-impaired and physically handicapped pupils as well as non- or "emergent" readers. This is part of larger questions that we pose to them: What assumptions do you make about pupils' capabilities, and on what basis? And what accommodation do you make for learners whose forte is not verbal skills and who need opportunities to develop these skills? In developing this dimension of the course, we have drawn on the knowledge and experience of colleagues in special education, both in the schools and the university.

Teaching a Portion of the Unit

To ensure that our students have a chance to teach at least a part of the unit before they do so as interns, we have tried a number of variations, including bussing in secondary pupils from local schools and having our students teach other prospective teachers. Ideally, students would try out lessons in their practicum classrooms and then revise them. This is nearly impossible because the students' participation is frequently limited to observing. Moreover, timing the development of a lesson to fit the moving target that is the unfolding curriculum in most classrooms is difficult at best. After trying several variations, we have concluded that any teaching opportunity, no matter how unrepresentative of real classrooms, is better than none at all. We rationalize that the yearlong internship provides our students ample opportunity to, as they themselves say, fall on their faces, get off the floor, and learn to keep their balance.

Assessing Learning, Revising Plans, and Posting to Individual Web Pages

Because one of our goals is to help our students learn how to improve as they teach, we require that whoever serve as "pupils" for their test lesson provide criticism back to the "teacher." Specifically, the "pupils" comment on what they learned, the quality of the activities, and what they were actually doing in their heads during the activities and offer suggestions for improvement. On the basis of these comments and additional criticisms from the instructors, the students revise their plans and post them to the Web pages that each has constructed for the course. Thus, each plan becomes available to all the students.

The Need for Reassurance

Students need reassurance that, during their first year as classroom teachers, they should not expect to develop new, inquiry-based curriculum unit plans for every topic that they will be expected to teach. We point out that goals and objectives, however general, are provided by district, state, and national standards. Consequently, the curriculum is not as open-ended as it once was. We counsel our students, during their first year, to rely on their textbooks and to consider teaching one or at most two intensive curriculum units per semester. We show them how to use textbooks so that the textbook can serve as a resource in support of the curriculum rather than becoming the total curriculum, as it does in too many classes. In later years, we counsel, they can then gradually develop and introduce new units. In addition, we point out that "off-the-shelf" units are available on the Web, both on their classmates' sites and at other sites. They do not have to build everything from scratch.

Evidence on an Issue-Based Curriculum Unit Plan Development Approach

Unfortunately, we do not have systematic data on prospective teachers' experience in using the curriculum unit plans in their internship classrooms or, subsequently, in their own classrooms. This is not due, however, to lack of effort. We have invited our former students back to talk to us about their teaching experiences, and some have agreed to do so. In addition, we maintain contact with some of our former students via electronic mail. We do not know how representative are the experiences of these teachers who have reported back to us.

[handwritten margin note: lack of follow up research]

The evaluative comments offered here are based on information we have received from former students and from supervisors in the schools where our students were placed as interns. We are, of course, aware that our former students, despite our entreaties to the contrary, may be reluctant to criticize us, for a variety of reasons, including pity. Nevertheless, here is a sampling:

• During the internship, our students were not as well prepared to create daily lesson plans as were students in other sections of the course that devoted more attention to such plans. These lesson plans are intended to help the interns survive a single period, not teach an entire unit. Consequently, our students were much better prepared to plan for the longer term, whether a week, month, or year.

• The issue-based curriculum units may be no better than conventional textbook-driven approaches in helping pupils master information such as dates. At the same time, this approach may help pupils think more broadly and in greater depth about historical events and questions.

Here is an extended excerpt from an electronic-mail message we received from a former student:

> I created two large curriculum units last year: one on the Harlem Renaissance and the other on World War II. I found by posing a question concerning the unit (using a particular issue) made the students think over a larger area of time, make some different connections to issues over time, and increased their thinking skills. In opposition, I found that by creating curriculum units that dealt with issues and ideas increased their thinking skills but not necessarily the information that they gathered. For example, in my World War II unit the students thought long and hard about nationalistic ideals and wrote on the Holocaust, Japanese Internment, and Fascist. But when they were tested, most students could not tell me the date that Pearl Harbor was bombed on a multiple-choice section. I would argue that it is better for the students to analyze information and gain thinking skills and make connections other than memorizing data, but I am sure most traditionalists would not side with me.

• The issues-centered curriculum-unit approach may be too demanding for some prospective teachers. At least two students out of more than thirty about whom we have some information found that they were unable to carry off the approach in their internship classrooms. Perhaps not coincidentally, both lacked strong backgrounds in history or a related social science.

Conclusion: Benefits and Limitations

What, then, are the benefits of attempting to bridge the Great Divide? We believe we have developed a model for doing what accomplished teachers do in planning instruction: move from a deep understanding of issues and problems and an equally deep understanding of their learners to a plan for helping their pupils develop the knowledge and skills described in various standards. As a model for the preparation of history teachers, the issue-based curriculum unit plan appears infinitely adaptable—to the individual teacher, the subject matter, and learners in various settings. Anecdotal evidence suggests that at least some of the students who learn the process of inquiry and curriculum unit planning perform, during their internship year, more like accomplished teachers than those who have learned an array of methods and activities.

This approach keeps the prospective teachers' experience grounded in the subject matter while, at the same time, addressing their understandable anxieties about receiving adequate preparation for the classroom. They enter the classroom with curriculum units that they can use immediately and a process for curriculum development and instructional planning that starts with the subject matter rather than with a set of methods or activities.

A benefit of the collaboration for the history department was that it provided information on what history majors and minors could and could not do when asked to apply their training in history courses in a different setting. This information stimulated a major overhaul of the requirements for the teaching minor in history and for a second history–social studies major that adds coursework in the fundamentals of geography, political science, and economics to a slightly scaled-back array of history course work. The results of these changes will not be known for several years. Yet, as a response to new standards for historical knowledge, the changes seem more promising than the shrinking of content in favor of professional courses that Desmond Morton, in his chapter in this volume, described as occurring in several Canadian provinces.

The limitations of building such a catwalk are, however, considerable. Although the support of the university administration and departmental chairs was, in our case, critical, the collaboration between history and teacher education faculty members depended ultimately on the commitments of the individuals. We are skeptical that collaboration of this type can be mandated by the institution. A shared commitment to preparing teachers who are knowledgeable about the substance and methods of their subject matter and, at the same time, have learned to think like a teacher is at the heart of the collaboration.

At the same time, such collaboration is fragile and vulnerable precisely because it is not institutionalized. For example, when McDiarmid left Michigan State University, Vinten-Johansen faced opposition to the course from teacher educators and prospective history teachers who thought it was too focused on with subject matter. Without McDiarmid present to argue for the pedagogical benefits with his colleagues and to lend credibility in the classroom, the course was vulnerable. Such reactions in a teacher preparation program purportedly established to bridge the gulf between education and the arts and sciences is discouraging. In addition, when funding from the Provost to support cross-departmental planning and teaching expired, Vinten-Johansen had to justify to his department continued participation in a course for which his department receives no fiscal benefit or even student credit hours.

To build a catwalk, the teacher education faculty must be prepared to set the first girder. As noted earlier, not only are incentives for history faculty lacking but powerful disincentives operate to keep them away from such collaboration. Rare is the departmental promotion and tenure committee in the arts and sciences at a research university that values substantive collaboration with the teacher education department. In teacher education, on the other hand, faculty may well be rewarded for involving arts and sciences faculty in planning and teaching courses. At the same time, teacher educators who are unconvinced of the importance of subject-matter-based methods courses may view reaching out to academic departments as a waste of time.

Finally, we lack systematically collected and analyzed data needed to determine whether the anecdotal evidence is anything more than self-serving. Follow-up studies of prospective teachers are notoriously difficult to manage, especially at a university such as Michigan State where a high proportion of the graduates take jobs outside the state. Further, collecting data on graduates and what they do in their classrooms is not sufficient for many skeptics. They want to be able to compare assessment results for pupils of teachers trained in different approaches. However desirable, such research is not only difficult to carry out but also highly problematic.

In sum, the Great Divide is unlikely to be bridged on a large scale any time soon. We believe, however, that the little catwalk that we managed to construct holds some promise. We hope our efforts will encourage others to make and report on their own efforts. We also believe that the focus on the development of curriculum unit plans requires prospective teachers to ground their pedagogy in the subject matter of history. At the same time, such a focus reassures them that the work they do at the university truly prepares them to teach.

NOTES

1. G. W. McDiarmid, "Understanding History for Teaching: A Study of the Historical Understanding of Prospective Teachers," in M. Carretero and J. F. Voss, eds., *Cognitive and Instructional Processes in History and the Social Studies* (Hillsdale, NJ, 1994); G. W. McDiarmid, N. J. Wiemers, and L. Fertig, *Bounded by Their Pasts: Exploring the Relationship between Understandings of History and the Views of Teaching and Learning of History among Majors in a Historiography Seminar* (Chicago, 1991).

2. P. Vinten-Johansen and G. W. McDiarmid, *Stalking the Schoolwork Module: Teaching Prospective Teachers to Write Historical Narratives* (Anchorage, AK, 1999).

3. R. E. Floden, G. W. McDiarmid, and N. Wiemers, "Learning about Mathematics in Elementary Methods Course," in D. J. McIntyre and D. M. Byrd, eds., *Preparing Tomorrow's Teachers: The Field Experience* (Newbury Park, CA, 1996).

4. Holmes Group, *Tomorrow's Teachers: A Report of the Holmes Group* (East Lansing, MI, 1986) and *Tomorrow's Schools of Education: A Report of the Holmes Group* (East Lansing, MI, 1995).

5. G. W. McDiarmid and P. Vinten-Johansen, "Teaching and Learning History—from the Inside Out," special report (East Lansing, MI, 1994).

6. Ibid.; Vinten-Johansen and McDiarmid, *Stalking the Schoolwork Module*; McDiarmid, "Understanding History for Teaching" and "Challenging Prospective Teachers' Understandings of History: An Examination of a Historiography Seminar," in L. Schauble and R. Glaser, eds., *Innovations in Learning: New Environments for Education* (Mahwah, NJ, 1996).

7. Vinten-Johansen and McDiarmid, *Stalking the Schoolwork Module*.

8. S. Feiman-Nemser and M. Buchmann, "Pitfalls of Experience in Teacher Preparation," *Occasional Paper No. 65* (East Lansing, MI, 1983).

9. National Center for History in Schools, *National Standards for History* (Los Angeles, no date).

10. L. Shulman, "Knowledge and Teaching: Foundations of New Reform," *Harvard Educational Review*, 57(1) (1987), pp.1–22; S. M. Wilson, L. Shulman, and A. E. Richtert, "150 Different Ways of Knowing: Representations of Knowledge in Teaching," in J. Calderhead, ed., *Exploring Teachers' Thinking* (London, 1987), pp.104–124; P. Grossman, *The Making of a Teacher: Teacher Knowledge and Teacher Education* (New York, 1990).

11. P. Black and D. William, "Inside the Black Box: Raising Standards through Classroom Assessment," *Phi Delta Kappan* 80(2) (1998), pp. 139–148.

12. F. Newmann, W. Secada, and G. Wehlage, *A Guide to Authentic Instruction and Assessment: Vision, Standards and Scoring* (Madison, WI, 1995).

13. J. Grossman, ed., *The Frontier in American Culture: Essays by Richard White and Patricia Nelson Limerick* (Berkeley, 1994).

14. J. A. Percoco, *A Passion for the Past: Creative Teaching of U.S. History* (Portsmouth, NH, 1998).

15. P. W. Jackson, *Life in Classrooms* (New York, 1990); D. Lortie, *Schoolteacher: A Sociological Study* (Chicago, 1975).

16. Vinten-Johansen and McDiarmid, *Stalking the Schoolwork Module*.

17. J. A. Langer and A. N. Applebee, *How Writing Shapes Thinking* (Urbana, IL, 1987).

18. Newmann, Secada, and Wehlage, *A Guide to Authentic Instruction and Assessment*.

Chapter 10

"What's This New Crap? What's Wrong with the Old Crap?"

Changing History Teaching in Oakland, California

Shelly Weintraub

At a recent history standards committee meeting of the Oakland Unified School District in California, teachers were agonizing. Once we had finished the two-year process of putting these standards together, how were we going to explain them to anyone outside the group of teachers who developed them? We sat glumly looking at each other, thinking about the chasm between the committee and the rest of the teachers in the district, and one of the high school teachers predicted the response of her colleagues when they received the new document. "They'll say," she lamented, "'What's this new crap, what's wrong with the old crap?'"

Introduction

This volume has a few organizing questions; one of the central ones is "How can history teaching be improved in K–12 schools?" As is evident from the incident at the standards committee, Oakland Unified Schools are still grappling with an answer to this question. We have been engaged in a multiyear odyssey to try to improve history instruction. I hope that, by sharing a narrative account of parts of that journey, I can explain how we, as a district, seek to answer the question and give other districts ideas for what kinds of things might or might not work in their own communities.

Overview

What follows is a summary of the four major lessons we on the committee have learned, over the course of more than five years, that are critical to changing traditional history instruction. By traditional I mean an avoidance of history at the elementary level and, at the secondary level, instruction that consists of having students read the textbook, answer the questions at the end of chapter, listen to lectures, and take multiple choice tests:

1. *A strong staff development program.* In our district this staff development program was built around bringing historians from the University and members of the community together with teachers to discuss how historians approach the discipline of history, or historiography.

2. *The development of curriculum materials that model the kind of historical thinking that historians modeled for us in the staff development.*

3. *The creation of documents (standards) that give the stamp of district legitimacy to an approach that emphasizes historical thinking.*

4. *The creation of assessments linked to the standards that both model the kind of teaching expected and give power to the standards themselves.*

Background

These conclusions, printed on paper, seem arid, and yet the process by which they were reached elicited anger and contentiousness, as well as exhilaration and excitement, among the participants. It is helpful to use a narrative approach to explain.

1990 Textbook Adoption

Ours is a very large urban district in the San Francisco Bay Area. We have approximately 50,000 students. About 53 percent are African American. The next largest group is Latino, followed by different Asian groups and, finally, whites. While some elementary schools have large white populations, in all our six major high schools combined, there are only 400 white students. In addition to having a multiethnic mix, our district is also multilingual. At last count, students in our schools spoke at least fifty-four languages.

Controversy, especially over issues of race, is frequent. Thirty years ago, extensive protests against de facto segregation in Oakland schools led to many arrests, and, more recently, the district was in the national media spotlight over the Ebonics controversy.

In 1990 I was lured from fifteen years of classroom teaching to be in charge of curriculum and staff development for history–social studies in the Oakland public schools. That also happened to be the year the new history–social studies books were up for adoption in our district and all over the state. While I knew that it would be a logistical problem for teachers to choose a book, I never dreamed how controversial and bitter the debate around the textbooks would become.

Actually, "bitter" is a mild word to describe the year of textbook adoption. To help provide a picture of what I mean, a few specific examples will be useful. At one point our Board of Education invited Gary Nash, author of the Houghton Mifflin series that was up for adoption, to debate a professor at California State University–San Francisco, who opposed the textbooks. Before the meeting even started, posters calling the textbooks racist were hung on the wall. Once the meeting began, the tone was less than civil. As Nash was sipping a bottle of water he had brought, the professor complained that she hadn't been given equal treatment—she didn't have a glass herself. She insinuated that Nash didn't read Black authors and therefore the textbooks reflected racial bias against African Americans. She claimed that an excerpt in a sixth-grade textbook about early man eating the marrow of a bone was meant to show that Africans were cannibals. Comments from the audience were along the same lines. The African American community wasn't alone in its complaints. Jewish, Muslim, and American Indian speakers and others took to the floor to argue issues important to their communities.

While the "debate" seemed like a low point, the actual meeting when the board was to vote on whether to adopt the Houghton Mifflin texts (which had been recommended by the teachers) was even worse. In fact, the meeting had to be shut down twice and the police called to remove protesters. Teachers felt intimidated, some calling me in tears after the meeting. In the end, the board voted not to adopt the Houghton Mifflin textbooks, leaving grades 3–7 without a text.

A coalition of activists offered to write curriculum materials during the summer, but a group that started out as 100 people in June ended up with eleven people in September. They disagreed among themselves over what should and shouldn't be included in the curriculum. For example, the American Indian community didn't like the references in the new curriculum to the land bridge theory that explains population settlement in America. The NAACP objected to negative cartoons about Clarence Thomas in the seventh-grade curriculum. (Actually, these curriculum materials were supposed to be about medieval world history.)

As I mentioned earlier, I was taken by surprise by the anger and pain in the debate over the textbooks and have spent much time thinking about why the process was so fraught. There were some explanations that I would call logistical. For instance, usually the state offers districts a choice of four or five textbooks, and the argument focuses on which of those is the best. In this case, the State offered only one choice—which meant that any complaint anyone had was centered on that one text.

While I think that having only one choice helps explain some of the anger, I believe there were deeper causes. People opposed to the texts seemed to distrust teachers. They didn't believe that teachers could take a textbook as a starting point and then supplement or challenge it. They seemed to believe that the textbook did the teaching in the classroom. The unspoken message was that a predominantly white teaching force would not be sensitive to issues of racism in the textbooks. (One of the leaders against the textbook, a white professor, later, in a newspaper editorial, compared teachers to the Ku Klux Klan because they were on strike. She claimed that to strike against a school board and a school administration that was predominately African American was akin to what the Klan had done during Reconstruction.)

In addition to the distrust of teachers, there appeared to be a fundamental distrust of a traditional interpretation of American history: Those opposed to the book were afraid that this textbook would repeat that interpretation. The belief that history has been used as a tool against people of color is hardly new—and I found it pervasive when I was in the classroom. My students claimed to dislike history but, when pushed for an explanation, seemed to believe that history was an extended justification for the status quo. In other words, history held great power and fear for my students.

One short example—I was trying to teach a unit to eleventh-graders on slavery when I met much student resistance or ambivalence about the topic. When I asked them to write about how they felt about studying slavery, one student stated:

> I would like to know more of slavery but the past kind of hurts. When you think it's one way and it's another. I also feel that we should know our past

if it hurts or not. I would also like to know things, if blacks was the only ones in slavery. Also, I would want to know if we still in slavery or can we ever go back to slavery? I really will like to look back in the past, it could only affect your mind if you let it.

Another student wrote in response to the same question,

The way I feel about slavery is that I don't want to know any more about it. It's not the point that I don't care, it's just the fact that it's over with and I'm happy and my people are happy so why should I dwell on the subject? In conclusion, my feelings on this subject is leave all the sorrow and pain behind and look forward to the new opening.

Clearly, history is not a neutral, dry, academic topic; it can hurt. This experience relates to more systematic findings by Levstik and Wineburg, presented in the next section of this book.

After the Textbooks

While the lack of textbooks and the bitterness over the debate are probably unique to Oakland, the issues of distrust of a single narrative and distrust over the way history is taught in the public schools is probably not atypical of districts across the country. In addition, the issues of how to improve history instruction might have roused particular furor in our district, but all school districts have to grapple with teacher knowledge of their subject, materials students can use, and methods of evaluation.

With the dissolution of the community committee, I was left with one problem—what were we going to do to help teachers teach a history program without the use of texts?

Staff Development—Historiography

While I did several things at once to try to help teachers—some successful, some not—the most important was the development of a Historiography in-service series. Because this was so central to what followed, I'd like to describe it in a little more detail.

In the fall of 1991 I invited about thirty K–12 teachers to participate in an in-service series called Historiography. The purpose of the series was to link the teachers with the actual discipline of history. For example, I invited Candice Faulk, a historian who had written a biography on Emma Goldman, to discuss her process of writing biography. She discussed how she found her sources and the ambivalence she felt about using portions of Goldman's letters that Goldman clearly hoped would remain private. She talked about Goldman's reflection on her past work; Goldman looked back at what had interested her in her twenties and thirties when she wrote her book on sexual ethics and realized that this might not have been the center of her story if she had written it later.

Clay Carson, the editor of the Martin Luther King papers, invited us to see the King Papers at Stanford. He discussed such things as the ethics of historians' using FBI wiretaps as a source for their work as well as musing over the strangeness of eventually spending more time writing about a person's life than the person spent living it.

Patricia Limmerick discussed how, as a Westerner who traveled to the East, she came to a different interpretation of Western history and, through that, American history. Karen Cushman, a local writer who has won the Newbery Award for best children's fiction, discussed the kinds of liberties she takes in writing historical fiction and the kind of research she has to do before writing.

Larry Levine, Leon Litwack, and Ron Takaki, historians from the University of California, joined Connie Fields, a documentary film maker (*Rosie the Riveter*), and Robert Greenberg from the Conservatory of Music and more than twenty other speakers who, over the years, generously came to Oakland to talk to the teachers. All of them discussed what intrigued or drew them to their subject, how they used evidence, and new interpretations they had reached.

The series, which stretched over three years (with some new teachers coming in each year and some others leaving), was a huge hit. In addition to listening to the historians, participating teachers tried out new things in their own classrooms. For example, after they heard a historian who was a biographer, they would break down into grade-level groups to discuss how their students could write or read biography. What kinds of support would they need to give their students? If the students were too young to do original research, what would constitute reasonable expectations?

The series gave teachers, many of whom had had their last contact with history twenty years before in a college class, a different outlook on the teaching and learning of history. Even when they couldn't apply what the historians were saying directly to their classroom, they were thrilled to be stimulated, to think as adults. They began to understand that history was a flexible discipline, not a series of facts to be memorized.

Teachers talked to the interviewer Peter Seixas about the impact of the groups:

> I think that group gave me an opportunity to reshape and rethink the way I teach history. And it took me several years to do that. . . . But before those experiences with Shelly, I think I taught history the way a lot of people taught it or teach history now, which is reading the text, and discussion and maybe throw in a little research or maybe show a movie, bring in some current events, talk about things, give a test and then grade people on . . . what kind of content they retain.
>
> —Mel Stenger, seventh-grade teacher, November 7, 1997

> I've been a teacher now in a secondary school of oh well a long time, 17 years here. I take courses now and then. . . . But . . . it was a real shot in the arm to hear the different historians, and it just made me feel like an historian again. . . . And people would bring in their projects. . . . Their advanced students were writing these fabulous historical fiction and expository essays. And even though quite frankly my students can't quite do that—they will some day—I could at least take those ideas and then have my students do what they could do with them.
>
> —Anita Bowers, eleventh-grade teacher, November 7, 1997[1]

The Historiography series did many things for the participating teachers and the district. First, the series provided a different way of looking at teaching history. Teachers understood more deeply the importance of evidence, the varying interpretations of the past, and the possibility that history learning could be active rather than passive. Second, the series created a different kind of connection between teachers and historians. This was not the usual lecture of professors with teachers taking notes on content. Finally, unplanned, but ultimately most important, this series created a leadership group of teachers in the district. These were teachers who shared a common experience and had developed a common language. As one of them said in an interview with Seixas,

> We feel like we do have this sort of mission that many of the history teachers in Oakland, particularly at the secondary level, do not have. We feel like we've learned different way to teach history, to turn students into historians.
>
> —Judy Yeager, eleventh-grade teacher, November 7, 1994

Curriculum Development

Teachers without textbooks are not happy campers. The Oakland teachers wanted materials. While the district purchased some supplementary materials for the fifth and seventh grades, there were many teachers without anything. Working with Matthew Downey, a professor from the University of California (now at the University of Colorado-Boulder) we began to develop materials for the fourth grade (California history) and in so doing, create a model of what future curriculum development would look like. Downey believed that students should act as historians and had a concept of "layering." He believed that students should be given an artifact and asked to speculate about its uses, who created it, and why. Then, in the next layer, students would receive some visual evidence, such as a painting or photograph. Again, they would be asked to analyze it, but this time they would be asked what this new piece of evidence added to what the students already guessed from the artifact. Did it contradict any of their guesses? A third layer could be a primary account, a fourth layer a secondary source, and a fifth layer a piece of historical fiction. Each time students would revise and refine their understanding of a particular time in history.

Using this approach, we tried to create history kits. Each kit contained artifacts, music, visuals, and primary and secondary sources, as well as historical fiction. They also contained day-to-day lesson plans that helped teachers incorporate these materials into their teaching. Teachers are now using these materials to teach history in a way that is sharply different from the reliance on textbooks that characterized history teaching in the past.

If other districts are thinking of using this approach, they need to realize that there are some definite disadvantages that we have yet to work out. Specifically, we don't have enough resources to supply every teacher with a kit. Instead, we created one kit for every school. We have sixty elementary schools in our district, so this was a massive undertaking. But sharing one kit among many teachers is not an ideal solution. Artifacts get lost; literature is not put back in the kit; new teachers coming into the school are not even aware that the materials are available, and don't even know to ask for kinds of materials other than standard textbooks. Using this approach, because it is different, also calls for staff development. While our district did have in-service series that went along with the kits,

I know we were just touching the tip of the iceberg. For instance, there are more than 200 fourth-grade teachers in our schools. The in-service reached about eighty of them. Then, in a district like Oakland, which is very transient, the next year a third of those eighty might no longer be teaching fourth grade, or even be in the district.

Despite all these obstacles, the training and kits were received enthusiastically. Some teachers have told me that they're now happy that the Board decided not to adopt textbooks; they feel that the crisis created an opportunity for them to teach differently and that the kits offered a model of how this could be done.

Standards Development

Unconnected to any history staff development, our district, like many in the nation, felt the need to develop content and performance standards for key subject areas. In Oakland, I, along with my counterparts in math, science, language arts, and foreign language, was asked to develop district-wide standards for our subject area.

This assignment wasn't of my choosing, and, in fact, I had reservations. I had witnessed the argument over the national standards, and the last thing our district needed was another argument over the same issues that had come up in the textbook adoption. Additionally, if we were going to create a written document, I wanted it to be something that would be useful to teachers, not filed away on a shelf. Our district had last developed standards about twenty years earlier. These were called "Standards of Achievement," and in history they consisted of a list of very basic facts that students should know. Very few teachers even knew of their existence, much less used them.

I, along with a colleague, Stan Pesick, formed a Standards committee, made up of many people from the historiography series as well as some new members. We examined the California State Framework and the National Standards in history as well as in civics, geography, economics, and social studies. We looked at British standards, and we invited Peter Seixas to speak to us about historical thinking and to present his own categories. As a group, we were unified on the idea that we should use our State Framework as an outline of content to be covered each year. The Framework is accepted and used by teachers throughout our state, and to invent another scope and sequence seemed foolish and unnecessary. Briefly, the California History–Social Science Framework outlines which topics are taught at which grade levels (e.g., fourth grade, California history; sixth grade, ancient world history). The Framework is fairly prescriptive. For instance, in the sixth grade, teachers should cover six units, four of which are Early Humankind, Egypt and Kush, India, and Ancient China.

Since we had decided to accept the outline of the Framework, what additional contribution could we make? Teachers knew, after going through the historiography series and from their own experience in the classroom, that history was more than an outline. What we thought was important was to institutionalize an approach to the teaching of history.

While the National Standards include a section on historical thinking, and while we found this section extremely helpful, we felt that it was a definite add-on to the heart of the document—an outline of the content. We wanted to make the historical thinking standards the center of what we were doing in Oakland. We wanted to integrate the discipline of history with the specific content to be taught.

After several meetings devoted to looking at different models, we agreed on five areas of historical thinking that we felt all students K–12 should know. They are:

1. Chronological and spatial thinking
2. Use of evidence
3. Multiple perspectives and diversity
4. Interpretation
5. Significance

However, the important lesson for us and for other districts is less in the areas we chose and more in the attempt to institutionalize a different approach to the teaching of history. For example, we did not use a category in the National Standards entitled "Historical Comprehension," or one Seixas proposed, "Progress and Decline." Whether we made good choices is still to be seen, but we believe we made the fundamentally correct choice of emphasizing historical thinking.

Standards development, much to my delight and surprise, allowed time for teachers to organize what had been free-floating ideas and practices into something coherent. We were able to take some of the learning we had achieved collectively in the historiography sessions and create a form in which this could be shared with other teachers in the district.

Ultimately, what we were saying to teachers was the following: If you are an eighth-grade teacher, one of the units you have to teach is the Civil War. That is in the State Framework, and you, along with other teachers in the state, must teach it. However, we aren't telling you exactly what in the Civil War you have to cover. Rather, we are saying that, while students need to know what happened, and when and where it happened, they also need to use evidence (including primary sources) in the study of the Civil War and to examine that evidence critically. They need to understand the multiple perspectives of people who participated in that event; they need to understand that historians have interpreted the Civil War variously; and they need to make connections to today, to draw some conclusions about why the study of the Civil War is important.

While we used the topics prescribed in the California Framework topics, we divorced the Framework narrative from the topics in our standards document. For example, in the California Framework the tenth grade covers world history from approximately the 1700s to the present. Topics in the Framework include the Industrial Revolution, World War I, World War II, and so on. We used these broad topics but we didn't include the narrative except as a reference.

This raises the question, Why didn't we include the narrative from the Framework (or its more bulleted form in the recent State Standards) as part of our Oakland standards, and why did we include it as a reference? The answer to the first part of this question came from a discussion our committee had. As we looked at the Framework, we recognized that, for us, its strength was also its weakness. That is, the Framework is a compelling narrative. But, to adopt the Framework's narrative would mean undercutting our attempt to teach students that there is more than one interpretation of the past, that many narratives can be constructed on the basis of evidence.

For example, in the tenth-grade unit entitled "Nationalism in the Contemporary World," the Framework states:

> In this unit students have an opportunity to discuss differences among revolutions. What is a revolution? Why are some revolutions, such as the French Revolution and the Communist Revolution, followed by political purges and mass killings? Why are others, such as the American Revolution, followed by the establishment of democratic institutions and mechanisms for orderly change?[2]

Clearly, this is one interpretation.

The Framework also determines significance. Again, in the tenth grade, the Framework calls for case studies; for example, Israel and Syria are to be studied as one unit, Brazil and Mexico as another. The authors of the Framework have determined that Brazil and Mexico constitute a more significant comparison than, for example, Cuba and Mexico.

In some ways we saw an adoption of the Framework's interpretation of the past and its determination of significance as a contradiction of our historical thinking standards. Nevertheless, we included the Framework as a reference. Why? This is where reality meets ideology. We included the Framework for two reasons. First, it is a State document, and we felt that teachers needed to know the expectations of the State. Second, on a practical level, we understand that many teachers do not feel knowledgeable enough to create their own interpretations of the past. If a sixth-grade teacher has to teach a unit on India and has little knowledge of the content matter, she would probably welcome the State Framework's provision of a few paragraphs that highlight the major ideas to be covered. We felt it would be unfair to take this tool away from teachers. We, like many other people in our field, are learning to live with contradiction.

In addition to our concern about a framework or set of standards that implies the correctness of one interpretation, we were also concerned with the long list of facts to be covered (e.g., in the newly proposed California State Standards). This creates an impossible burden on teachers and a tension, if not an outright contradiction, with the emphasis on historical thinking. How can teachers use primary sources, look at different perspectives, provide students the opportunity to discuss, research, and write on topics, and cover all the content prescribed? This is particularly true in a district such as ours where low skills mean that much reading and writing occurs during class time. At best, the attempt to cover all the topics prescribed will lead to a weak pedagogical approach.

One of the major challenges facing our standards committee was how to look at historical thinking in a developmental way. The national standards made a stab at this, trying to figure out how a student's understanding of chronology, for example, changes as the student gets older. We wondered, "What should our expectations be of a high school student who examines evidence compared with a third grader?" We knew that sophistication should increase, but what exactly did that mean? For this portion of our standards, we relied heavily on Peter Seixas. He developed a possible developmental sequence. Teachers broke up into grade-level groups and relying on their own experience in the classroom, revised his list. Some things they thought were too difficult, others too easy. Peter warned us that we were stepping onto new ground, that there is no solid research base about how students develop a sense of history, as there is for language arts. Nevertheless, we plunged ahead, hoping to help develop that research base and to learn about what others had done as part of our continuing staff development.

Assessment

Finally, we reach the topic of assessment. District-wide and state assessment, unlike classroom assessment, is viewed negatively by teachers. I believe the reason for this is that assessment drives curriculum, and teachers want to have some control over the curriculum in their own classroom. Some assessment, like the recently adopted Stanford 9 state assessment system in history, will not drive our curriculum because it was essentially intended to be divorced from any content teachers actually cover. Instead, the test is a trivia contest of skills and facts that spans a range of subjects no teacher would teach in one year. (The czar in Russia, African political boundaries, map reading skills, supply and demand, FDR, First Amendment issues, and questions about the Ice Age all appear on one sample page for ninth-grade students.)

On the other hand, we could create a district assessment that would ask teachers to assess student work in meeting our historical thinking standards. We've taken the first steps in that direction for the middle grades, where we asked students to use historical evidence (provided in the test) to write essays tied to the content they were taught. This was our first attempt to put teeth into the Standards. As teachers see that students will be evaluated on how well they can use evidence, or their ability to understand different perspectives, the focus of teaching may change. Since this program is still in its infancy, it is too early to discuss the impact it will have.

Assessment, or at least the kind of assessment we're talking about, also requires tremendous commitment from the district. If students are asked to write, teachers need to be provided with the time both to score the papers and to discuss the implications of the assessment. They need time to think about how their instruction might change to get better results or how the assessment might be changed to reflect more accurately what we are trying to learn. Since time is money in the public schools, this is a substantial challenge.

Assessment also implies that we have a clear sense of how to distinguish good from weak historical thinking. Yet, as I have stated before, this is new territory for us. We're on scary ground that, like the state we live in, always seems to shift under our feet.

Next Steps

Ironically, as we come to a close on the creation of the standards document, a new textbook adoption is looming. How will things be different, and can the standards help? Our plan is to spend the next year training about 250 teachers (representatives from all the sites in the district) in the new standards. This will probably mean a minihistoriography series for all 250 teachers. At the end of the series we will ask teachers to create criteria for textbook adoption on the basis of the historical thinking standards. We hope that, with the standards, the criteria for curriculum materials will be deeper. In addition to asking questions of content and readability, teachers will ask, "Is more than one perspective shown? One interpretation? Are students given a chance to work with evidence to construct their own meaning? Are students given the opportunity to construct significance?"

Clearly, no textbook will do all of this. By its nature it can't, because the job of the text is to construct a narrative. However, ideally, teachers will see how texts can be used as a tool for teaching rather than as the entire curriculum.

Conclusion

Our district, sometimes deliberately and sometimes accidentally, has slowly, haltingly, and yet very definitely created a framework for a different kind of approach to the teaching of history. This is an approach that rests on historical thinking at its core. This approach has been built in stages. We began with staff development. Originally, the premise for strong staff development flowed from the belief that teachers should be treated with respect, both as learners and as professionals who engage in collegial discussions with other professionals. Because we wanted teachers to be treated with respect, we brought in historians and tried to link the work that historians do with the process of teaching history to K–12 teachers. Through this in-service opportunity, teachers came to see history in very different ways. They began to see that it wasn't static but rather a continuing conversation.

At the same time that the staff development was going on, curriculum was being created. Again, this curriculum flowed out of the belief that students could see that history wasn't a series of facts to be memorized but rather a past to be interpreted.

We also worked on assessment. Grant Wiggins, a proponent of alternative assessment, states that we value what we test. If this is the case, then the multiple-choice trivial-pursuit questions so prevalent in our classrooms, and more cruelly on our state exams, are doing the discipline a disservice. Our district's first steps to create an assessment that measures our Standards are a healthy beginning.

Finally, we created a document—our district's history standards—that embody the idea that historical thinking is at the heart of what we should be teaching. Once the document was written, we realized that we had pulled together many of the ideas that had only been implicit in the staff development, the curriculum development, and the assessments. Now that the implicit has been made explicit, we are ready to take on new challenges.

Final Thoughts

Will the work we're doing on historical thinking standards, staff development, and materials development change how history is taught in Oakland? There are many reasons that the answer to that question could be no. For one thing, it is difficult to reach a critical mass in a district as large as ours. For another, we have to depend on the district's capacity to provide the resources. Additionally, we have to cope with State assessments that contradict what we are trying to do.

Yet, at this point I reflect back on my childhood. My father was a college professor, union organizer, and lifelong socialist. I remember him telling me that if I decided to go into teaching I had to understand that the schools were set up to maintain capitalism. I know there is truth to this. There is truth to the fact that few of my students will be able to overcome the socioeconomic factors working against them, and yet every day in the classroom I made a leap of faith that I, along with my students, can make a difference. What choice did I have?

I ask the same question about our work in Oakland: What choice do we have? We have no assurance that all this work will change history teaching district-wide or that, if other schools try a similar approach, it will be successful. Yet, we have already begun to see changes in how some teachers approach teaching history, in their excitement at trying something new. We have to believe we can make a difference.

We want to help teachers articulate an answer to their question "What's wrong the old crap?" They need to understand that the old crap didn't help students understand that history was contested, that the past holds meaning for us today, or that the students have the power to both construct both history and the future. This is the goal of the new crap.

NOTES

1. Peter Seixas, "A School District Constructs Standards for Historical Thinking: History Education Reform in Oakland, California," paper presented at the meeting of the American Education Research Association, San Diego, 1998.

2. *History-Social Science Framework for California Public Schools* (Sacramento, 1987), p. 90.

Part III

Research on Teaching and Learning in History

This volume is predicated on the importance of research on history learning and on the need to take this research into account when thinking about history teaching and teacher training. Essays in this section reflect some of the newer types of learning research. The primary focus of this research is on how students cope with the demands of historical thinking—how they develop spontaneously, how their efforts may be improved upon—but also on how they disagree about what makes up history and historical thinking.

The purview of these essays goes beyond the classroom. School is just one of the venues in which we learn history in modern society. We become historical listening to discussions at our kitchen tables; when we watch TV or pop a video into the VCR; and, increasingly, when we design our own individualized history curriculum using the resources of the Internet. The chapters in this section examine the multiple venues in which history is learned, beginning with the classroom but expanding outward toward society. The formal history curriculum may be where we are introduced to certain historical topics, but our learning does not end there. These chapters reflect the fact that we continue to learn history across the age span.

In the first chapter, Peter Lee and Rosalyn Ashby present an overview of a focused program of research aimed at mapping children's growing sophistication in handling historical evidence. This work, which charts the craggy path along which intellectual development proceeds, provides the backdrop for designing educational interventions that reflect a keen attention to historical content with an equally keen attention to the thought processes, beliefs, and abilities of schoolchildren at different ages. Similarly, in the second chapter, Gaea Leinhardt focuses on how history is learned during one's final years in the American high school. By examining the progression of one student in an Advanced Placement U.S. history class, Leinhardt describes the unique aspects of historical literacy, such as learning how to frame arguments based on partial and conflicting evidence and how to marshal support for assertions using evidence of varying strengths and types. In doing so, she shows how the history curriculum affords unique opportunities for developing the forms of understanding essential to the conduct of civic life in a democracy.

The third chapter, by the German history researcher Bodo von Borries, introduces North American readers to the massive European study *Youth and History*. This pioneering undertaking surveyed more than 33,000 students and teachers from twenty-nine European and Middle Eastern countries in an attempt to understand the state of history teaching on the eve of the millennium. While von Borries's treatment focuses largely on school history, Roy Rosenzweig, in the fourth chapter, examines adults' engagement with the past. Asking a straightforward question—"How do Americans understand their pasts?"—Rosenzweig (in collaboration with David Thelen) undertook a phone survey of more than 1,500 Americans and found, contrary to the wisdom of op-ed page pundits, deep engagement with all forms of history in everyday life. Moreover, Rosenzweig's research was able to contrast perceptions of the past by White Americans with findings from a sample of African-Americans and Native Americans, allowing a crucial comparative aspect in historical sense making from people with different perspectives.

In the fifth chapter, Linda Levstik also focuses on contrasts, but in her case these contrasts compare history students to their teachers. Levstik found a willingness among students of color to engage issues of conflict and contention in the national story, while at the same time finding a reluctance on the part of teachers to address simmering conflicts. Instead, teachers chose silence over engagement, feeling ill equipped to deal with uncomfortable topics or fearful of the repercussions such topics might have among schoolchildren. In the final chapter of this section, Sam Wineburg begins with the learning of history in schools but shows that school is just one among many venues that teach individuals to be historical in modern society. In a longitudinal investigation of historical sense making, Wineburg followed a group of adolescents and their parents at a crucial time in development—the final years of high school. Wineburg's work offers a glimpse at some of the other venues—home, the media, and the larger culture—that inform modern historical consciousness.

Research on history learning is varied, as these essays demonstrate. It encompasses how students handle documents, how they relate classroom history to wider historical assumptions, and how their ideas about history vary in different national and social settings. While there is no single theme in the essays in this section, they reflect a consistent interest in the role of disagreement and divergent interpretation. The British project focuses strongly on studying how students learn to deal with historical debates. Work on adult ideas about history and about learning from outside the classroom suggests the need to deal more directly with divergent approaches than most teachers and textbooks now allow. The implications are by no means clear, for much of the research is ongoing, but the issues of acknowledging dispute and using it to advance historical understanding clearly demand attention, if and as learning research translates more fully into teaching practice.

Chapter 11

Progression in Historical Understanding among Students Ages 7–14

Peter Lee and Rosalyn Ashby

Introduction

History education in Britain has changed in complex ways over the past three decades, but one major shift in emphasis stands out. In the early 1960s reform of school history was almost entirely discussed in terms of historical content; by the early 1990s, although content issues figured large in public debate, the new National Curriculum focused on history as a discipline. While politicians, journalists, and some professional historians argued about the ideological implications of particular stories, for many teachers, textbook writers, and researchers the central concern was the development of students' ideas about the discipline of history itself.[1]

To make sense of these changes it is necessary to distinguish between *substantive* history on the one hand and *second-order* or *procedural* ideas about history on the other. Substantive history is the content of history, what history is "about." Concepts like *peasant, friar,* and *president,* particulars like *the Battle of Hastings, the French Revolution* and *the Civil Rights Movement,* and individuals like *Abraham Lincoln, Marie Curie* and *Mahatma Gandhi* are part of the substance of history. Concepts like historical *evidence, explanation, change,* and *accounts* are ideas that provide our understanding of history as a discipline or form of knowledge. They are not what history is "about," but they shape the way we go about doing history. The changes in English history education can therefore be described as a shift from the assumption that school history was only a matter of acquiring substantive history to a concern with students' second-order ideas.

It is important not to misunderstand this shift from substantive to second-order (structural, procedural, or disciplinary) interests. Despite popular polarities (usually portrayed as "skills" versus "knowledge"), there was no retreat from the importance of students acquiring historical knowledge. Instead, "knowledge" was treated seriously, as something that had to be understood and grounded. It is essential that students know something of the kind of claims made by historians and what those different kinds of claims rest on. "Something," because understanding is never all-or-nothing; the goal was not to produce miniature professional historians.

This shift of focus is well summarized in the claim that history is more important than any particular story it tells.[2] Such a claim tends only too easily to be distorted into something quite different: specifically, a claim that content does not matter. A misreading of this kind seems to offer support for a (perhaps postmodern) fragmentation and sectionalization of history, in which ownership is more important than validity or truth. But the point of saying that history is more important than any particular story is that it presupposes that history is a complex and sophisticated discipline, with its own procedures and standards designed to make true statements and valid claims about the past. Many stories are told, and they may contradict, compete with, or complement one another, but this means that students should be equipped to deal with such relationships, not that any old story will do.

Once learning history is thought of as coming to grips with a discipline, with its own procedures and standards for evaluating claims, it becomes easier to envisage progression in history, rather than just the aggregation of factual knowledge, whether the latter is construed as deepening or expanding.[3] As well as acquiring knowledge of the past, students develop more powerful understandings of the nature of the discipline, which in turn legitimate the claim that what they acquire is indeed knowledge. Hence, the acquisition of more powerful procedural or second-order ideas (about, for example, *evidence* or *change*) is one way—perhaps the best—of giving sense to the notion of progression in history.

What does it mean to say that students develop more powerful understandings of the discipline of history? We can exemplify what is meant through changes in students' conceptions of the basis of statements about the past. Students who understand sources as information are helpless when confronted by contradictory sources. No one from the past is alive now, so nothing can be known. History, construed as telling the truth about the past, becomes impossible. The problem is overcome by the recognition that people in the past may have left reports, which have survived. For students, thinking of sources as *testimony*, history can begin again, provided it is possible to find truthful reports. But, even where this conception carries with it new strategies for evaluating the trustworthiness of reports, this set of ideas is itself helpless in the absence of eyewitnesses upon whom the historian can call. Once again, history becomes impossible. It can recommence only when it is understood that historians can make inferences that do not depend on anyone telling the truth, because sources are relics of activities and transactions as well as reports. Sources as *evidence* allow history to proceed without true reports from eyewitnesses. The understanding that much of what historians talk about could not have been "eyewitnessed" (at least not under the descriptions used by historians) opens up still further possibilities.

Project Chata

Our study, Concepts of History and Teaching Approaches 7–14 (Chata) was funded by the Economic and Social Research Council. Its central task was to map changes in students' ideas about history between the ages of seven and fourteen years. (The second phase of the study, not reported here, developed instruments to elicit teacher constructs of history education.) The project focused on second-order procedural understandings like *evidence* or *cause*, not substantive concepts like *peasant* or *fyrd*, *revolution* or *ideology*.

Cross-sectional Study

In the main investigation, pencil-and-paper responses were collected from 320 children between the ages of seven and fourteen, across three task-sets, on three separate occasions. The task-sets were self-standing, providing children with the material necessary for the tasks. Each addressed different historical content from the English National Curriculum and included tasks on *evidence, accounts, cause,* and *rational understanding* (the latter meaning understanding of action in terms of reasons or of social practices in terms of beliefs and values).

Follow-up interviews were conducted with 122 students, including all those from the second grade, on all three task-sets. For the second grade,

TABLE 11.1
Phase 1 Schools

School	Phase and Type	Intake	Y3	Y6	Y7	Y9
School A	Primary	urban	17	29		
School B	Primary	small town	16	18		
School C	Primary	rural	22	28		
School D	Secondary comprehensive	urban			24	24
School E	Secondary comprehensive	suburban			24	25
School F	Secondary comprehensive	urban			23	
School G	Secondary comprehensive	small town				10
School H	Secondary selective (girls)	urban +			14	16
School I	Secondary selective (boys)	suburban +			15	15
Total in each year group			55	75	100	90

N = 320
Mean age of year groups[4]
Y3: 8 years 1 month; Y6: 11 years 2 months; Y7: 12 years 1 month; Y9: 14 years 1 month.

interviews were analyzed along with written responses; the remainder were used only to check that the written responses were not seriously misleading.

The written tasks took the form of four slim booklets and a color-printed clue sheet. The children were asked to complete these by writing, ticking boxes, ordering statements, or drawing arrows. The three task-sets were given over a period of three weeks for secondary school and a slightly longer period for primary school students. For the twelve- and fourteen-year-olds, about ninety minutes was available for a task-set, but the younger children had a full day: most eleven-year-olds finished within half a day. The eight-year-olds were read the background information and were then taken through the tasks by a research officer with considerable experience as a primary deputy head; they worked for short spells, alternating testing periods with time spent playing games in the playground.

Short Progression Study

The models and methods developed from the written tasks provided the basis for investigation of children's ideas in different teaching and curriculum contexts. Modified tasks and interview schedules were designed. A sample of ninety-two children drawn from three primary and four secondary schools (and taught by twelve teachers in all) was interviewed at the beginning of the spring and at the end of the summer term.

Longitudinal Study

The twenty-three second-grade children from the interview study formed the sample for a longitudinal extension of the project. They were interviewed in July of the third and fourth grades, using the same questions and interview schedule structure but different content. The sample fell to twenty by the fourth grade.

A METHODOLOGICAL NOTE

Second-order concepts of the kind investigated by Chata are likely to be tacit in the obvious sense that they are not generally made explicit, but also in the stronger sense that students may never have thought about their ideas. Direct questions to children about what they think about evidence or cause may produce responses that are hard to interpret. In any case, having a particular concept of *evidence* or *cause* does not entail being able to give an account of that concept.

For these reasons Chata took an indirect approach, attempting to infer tacit ideas from the way in which children tackled substantive historical tasks. Where the researchers had less experience of students' reactions to tasks in a particular area, the project tended to use a higher proportion of direct questions to supplement indirect ones. An indirect approach emphasizes the hypothetical and conditional nature of any claims about children's ideas. The best that research of this kind can achieve is an internally consistent system that is not disconfirmed by what children do. The expectation is that subjects will behave *as if it were true* that they believed certain ideas.[5] Moreover, while the aim is always to grasp the ideas of those under study, the researcher must be free to make sense of them in ways that go beyond the students' own framework. In this respect Chata's reading of students' ideas is similar to historians' reconstruction of the ideas of people in the past.

Research of this kind is partly descriptive, working with inductive categories in some sense "derived" from the data, but a notion of progression as the development of more powerful ideas carries an irreducibly normative element. It also involves decisions about how to partition students' ideas between broad conceptual strands. Although these decisions were not entirely a priori but were based on earlier (pre-Chata) work using video recordings of small groups, they were inevitably to some degree preemptive.[6] Any model of progression produced by the research should therefore be viewed as one among a range of possible ways of looking at students' ideas.

The Scope of the Present Chapter

Chata's initial mapping of changes in students' ideas suggests that it is possible to think in terms of broad patterns of progression within different strands. In the limited space available here, we will limit discussion of progression to one strand, historical accounts, which may have some (perhaps indirect) links with recent debates within history.[7] Our discussion will be based on data from the written tasks and interviews. Finally we turn to wider considerations for the way we think about school history.

The Development of Students' Ideas about Historical Accounts

We investigated ideas about historical accounts by presenting students with pairs of stories running vertically side by side down the page.[8] The stories took the same form on each task-set, but their content was different. On all three task-sets, we asked students questions about differences between the stories and why those differences existed.

Each pair of stories differed in theme, tone, and time-scale. In task-set one, dealing with the Romans in Britain, one story emphasized material life, and the other, culture and ideas. The first stressed the benefits to the Britons of improvements in material life and the peace brought by the Romans. The second emphasized British achievement before the conquest and the imposition of a Roman way of life. The first story ended with the (relatively) short-term deleterious consequences for material life in Britain of Roman withdrawal, but the second took the account through the beginnings of a unified kingdom to end with the survival of Roman ideas in the present. (Each "chapter" in the version for the second grade was slightly shortened.)

In addition to the questions common to all task-sets, we also asked students whether they agreed or disagreed with this claim: "If two historians read the same things and dig up the same things and do not lie, there will be no important differences between the stories they each write." We also asked why they thought as they did.

The stories in the second task-set dealt with the end of the Roman Empire.[9] Emphasis in the first was on barbarian incursions; it asserted that the "real end of the Roman Empire" was in 476, when the last western Emperor was overthrown. Its partner story focused on internal problems and claimed that the "real end" was in 1453, when Constantinople was captured by the Turks. The students were asked whether this meant that no one knows when the Roman Empire ended, or whether it is just a matter of opinion, or whether there was no single time when it ended, or whether one of the stories must be wrong about when it ended. Again, the students were to explain their views. They were also asked how we could decide when the Roman Empire ended and whether there were other possible times we could say it ended.

The stories in task-set three were about the Saxon settlement of Britain. The first concentrated on the details of the coming of the Saxons, and the second dealt with the longer period of settlement, through to the establishment of a unified English kingdom. In addition to the questions asked in all task-sets, students were asked to put in order of importance six sentences offering reasons why historians' stories might differ. They were also asked whether they agreed or disagreed with the statement "History really happened, and it only happened *one* way, so there can only be one proper story about the Saxons in Britain." They were then asked to explain their decision. (Appendix 11.1 gives the stories from task-set two.)

Students' ideas about what the difference in end dates for the Roman Empire in the stories from task-set two meant, and about how we could decide when the Empire ended, suggested an age-related progression. The following response excerpts indicate some key differences.

> One might be wrong. One of the stories was wrong. [*How could we decide when it ended?*] See what books or encyclopaedias say.
>
> —Kelly, fifth grade

> Nobody that we know is alive in history. [*How could we decide?*] Look it up in a history book. [*Would that help to decide?*] A bit. . . . [*How would that help?*] Well. . . it tells us about history. . . .
>
> —Lucinda, second grade. [Interview excerpt.]

> Nobody alive today was there so nobody knows when it ended. [*How could we decide?*] I do not think we could.
>
> —Claire, fifth grade

For all these students, the end of the Roman Empire was a factual problem. Kelly resorted to authoritative sources of information, but Claire thought the end is in principle unknowable because we have no direct contact with the past. Lucinda thought like Claire, and her strategy for deciding clearly lacked conviction.

Some students recognized the epistemological gap opened by the lack of direct access to the past but thought it might be bridged by reports.

> If two people put down two different dates then no one knows and they just guessed. [*How could we decide?*] I think no one knows unless someone wrote it on a bit of paper and someone found it.
>
> —Jenny, sixth grade

> You don't know, we wasn't there when it happened. It might have been passed down but it could have been changed or forgotten. [*How could we decide?*] Because there is no Romans now. It could have been passed down truthfully.
>
> —Tania, sixth grade

Jenny and Tania both shared Claire's and Lucinda's doubts but conceded that some sort of link with the past might be found. The problem is still factual, but the end of the Empire is contingently unknown, rather than unknowable. Surviving texts or truthful transmission at least open the possibility of reaching the correct answer.

For other students, such a move created new problems.

> One of the stories might of been lying about the ending. Somebody knows when it ended will be in books [*sic*] and people must of taken note and later recorded it in History books. [*How could we decide?*] Ask a teacher or look it up in a book.
>
> —Lynne, eighth grade

> Well I know there is a lot of difference but people could think they came and captured Rome but the Empire was still in power till 1453. [*How could we decide?*] I don't think we could find out definitely because there is only biased stories left.
>
> —Briony, eighth grade

Lynne's response had much in common with Tania's, and indeed Kelly's, but raised the issue of deliberate falsification of the record. The end of the Empire remains a factual question. Briony may have been implicitly making it a criterial matter but was more probably thinking that the writer of the first story failed to realize that the Empire had continued after the fall of Rome. The major problem for her was that reports from the past are corrupted by bias.

The next two responses accepted the possibility of knowledge of the past. For them it was the past's complexity that made deciding on the end of the Roman Empire difficult.

The barbarians might have smashed in half of the Empire then done the other half so someone might of put it down for the first half and another one for the second half. [*How could we decide?*] If you are really not sure just say it finished in the middle of the two times. Or look in loads of history books and the one which has the most of one in is the winner.

—Stephen, sixth grade

It could of started going wrong in A.D. 476 and actually fell apart in A.D. 1453. [It] started falling apart from A.D. 476 but totally went at A.D. 1453. [*How could we decide?*] To get more information and which comes up most or say about A.D. 921.

—Peter, sixth grade

Stephen and Peter still treated the end of the Empire as a factual question but did not think of it as a single moment. For Stephen it was divided into two packets, west and east, but for Peter it was a long, drawn-out process. They both dealt with the possibility of multiple endings by either averaging or counting opinions. (Although these two strategies are logically distinct, they often appear as equivalents in students' responses.) Examples of this kind suggest that students may have a sufficiently well-developed substantive concept of "empire" to know that it is not the kind of thing that ends at a specific date but still consider the problem to be a factual one.

The final three examples saw the end of the Roman Empire as a criterial matter. Stories are not just copies of the past, truthful or distorted. Authors construct stories and in doing so have to make decisions about what counts as an empire.

Because story one says that some sort of empire remained in the east, and it is a matter of opinion whether when the last emperor was overthrown the empire ended. [*How could we decide?*] You could see whether there was a proper empire in Constantinople from documents.

—Jeremy, sixth grade

There is no definite way of telling when it ended. Some think it is when its city was captured or when it was first invaded or some other time. [*How could we decide?*] By setting a fixed thing what happened for example when its capitals were taken, or when it was totally annihilated or something and then finding the date.

—Lara, eighth grade

People have different beliefs as to when the empire ended. Even after defeat some would say the Romans empire continued to survive but was not as great, as rich and as big as before. There was a period of time when it could have been deemed to have ended but this is probably somewhere in between the two dates. [*How could we decide?*] Assess when the empire stopped having an effect on the rest of the World. Beforehand it almost ruled the World now you could decide when it had decreased in size and riches and therefore when it ended. When the eastern half stopped being like the old Roman Empire.

—Simon, eighth grade

Jeremy, the son of a professional historian, offered the beginnings of a criterion ("a proper empire"). Lara made the formal point ("setting a fixed thing") and gave some examples. Simon still found the idea of an intermediate end attractive as a solution to the problem posed by a drawn-out process but probably saw it as indeterminate; in any case, he went on to suggest two alternative criteria.

Responses were analyzed using nine categories, but the overall picture is given by the conflated set in Figure 11.1.

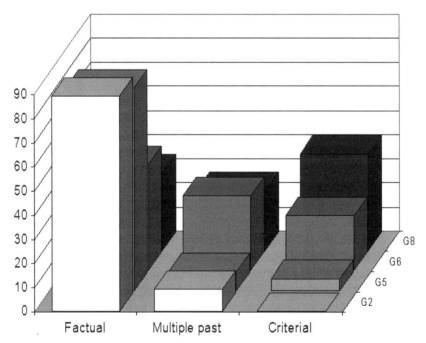

Figure 11.1. The end of the Roman Empire: What kind of problem is it? (conflated categories, percentages of grades)

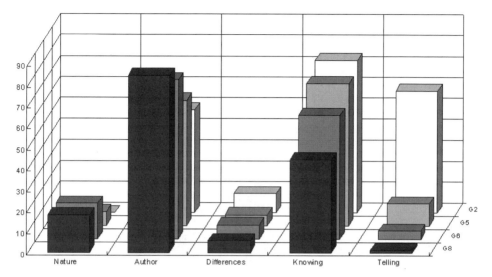

Figure 11.2. Ideas about differences in accounts (percentages of grades). Note that figures 11.2 to 11.4 register an idea only if it appeared on any given student's response on at least two of the three task-sets. For 3.75 percent of the sample, a total of twelve cases, no ideas appeared more than once, so single occurrences were used, at the risk of a reduction in reliability.

Categories in figure 11.2: *Nature:* It is in the nature of accounts to be different from one another. *Author:* Differences occur because accounts are written by different authors. *Differences:* The stories differ because they are about different things, times, or places. *Knowing:* Accounts differ because of problems in obtaining knowledge of the past. *Telling:* Any differences are only in how the stories are told; the accounts are the same.

A similar broad pattern emerges if we ask what students think about why there could be "two different stories about the same bit of history." Analysis of responses across all three task-sets indicates a broad shift with age from seeing history as stories ready-made and simply retold (perhaps in your own words), to stories told by historians who find, compile, and collate information, to stories told by historians who actively produce their stories, whether by distorting them for their own ends or legitimately selecting in response to a choice of theme (see Figure 11.2). A small proportion of (mainly) sixth- and eighth-grade students showed signs of understanding that it was in the nature of historical accounts to differ. They recognized that accounts could not be complete and had to fit parameters.

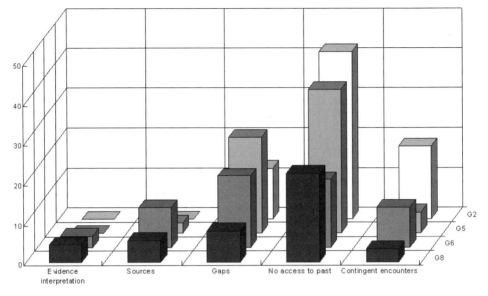

Figure 11.3. "Knowledge" by grade (percentages of grades)

A breakdown of the "knowledge" and "author" categories, in which most students responded, indicates the same sort of pattern within these categories as is visible in the overall picture, namely a shift from passive reception to active engagement. Figure 11.3 shows the distribution of ideas in the "knowledge" category.

A higher proportion of second-grade than fifth-grade students talked about different (contingent) encounters with books, objects, or stories, and problems of access to the past. Second-grade students were also more likely than fifth-grade students to refer to the impossibility of access to the past and were much more likely to do so than those in the sixth or eighth grade. For fifth-grade students, access problems were still the main issue, but they also mentioned gaps in knowledge.

Only a small proportion of students mentioned transmission errors, mistakes, and inaccuracies or intentional distortion (bias or lies) in the sources. Sixth-grade students (10 percent) were most likely to give explanations of this kind in which problems with sources lay behind differences in accounts. In the sixth and eighth grades (3 percent and 4.4 percent), students began to explain differences by pointing out that evidence needs interpretation. Here the role of the author of the account begins to be more important, even if the emphasis is still on the source.

Figure 11.4 shows the age-distribution of ideas about differences attributable to authors. In each of grades five, six, and eight, slightly more than 20 percent of students said that authors have different opinions, without further explanation, whereas in the second grade only about 13 percent responded in this way. The even distribution between age ten and age fourteen may conceal a differentiated structure; analysis of responses where "opinion" was further elucidated indicates the existence of a similar structure to the one suggested by Figure 11.2 (see Appendix 11.2).

When second-grade students mentioned author issues, they tended to explain differences in accounts in terms of the mistakes authors must have made (usually through inadequate knowledge). There was an increase with age in references to intentional distortion by authors (dogmatism, lies, and bias), but also to the importance of authors' viewpoints (without any intentional desire to mislead). A small number of students used sophisticated ideas about authors making interpretations and operating selection criteria or having theories and social standpoints. Surprisingly, although sixth- and particularly eighth-grade students were most likely to refer to these matters, two second-grade students gave responses that fell into this category.

Some older children recognized, explicitly or implicitly, that accounts cannot be complete or final and may have to meet different criteria. The very attempt to produce an account must impose selection of some sort

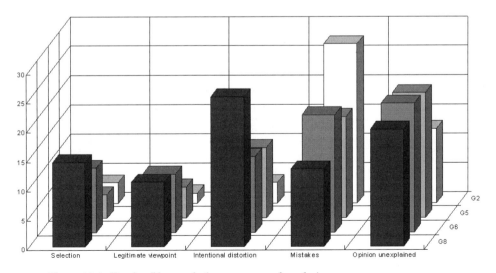

Figure 11.4. "Author" by grade (percentages of grades)

- **The past as given.** Stories are about the same thing: the story is equivalent to something "out there."

- **The past as inaccessible.** We can't know—we weren't there. Nothing can be known. Differences in accounts are a result of lack of direct access to the past.

- **The past as determining stories.** Stories are fixed by the information available; there is a one-to-one correspondence. Differences in accounts are a result of gaps in information and mistakes.

- **The past as reported in a more or less biased way.** Shift of focus from the story and reports to the author as active contributor. Differences in accounts are a result of distortion (in the form of lies, bias exaggeration, dogmatism); the problem is not just a lack of information.

- **The past as selected and organized from a viewpoint.** Stories are written (perhaps necessarily) from a legitimate position held by the author. Differences in accounts are a result of selection. Stories are not copies of the past.

- **The past as (re-)constructed in answer to questions in accordance with criteria.** Shift of focus from the author's position and choice, to the nature of accounts as such. It is the nature of accounts to differ.

Figure 11.5. Progression in students' ideas about accounts and their relation to the past.

on historians. Exactly 10 percent of students in the sample explicitly referred (on at least two task-sets) to accounts as answering different questions, fitting different criteria, or having a different range; or to accounts as being constructed, and not simply a conjunction of facts.

Figure 11.5 gives a summary of changes in students' ideas about historical accounts, but the relation between ideas about problems of knowledge and problems of authorship needs further work. Although the shift from authors as reporters and compilers to a more active role seems to go hand in hand with older students' increasing awareness of partisanship, individual students may treat knowledge and author problems as running parallel in explaining differences between stories. These students seem to be beginning to develop a more sophisticated and inclusive notion of "knowledge."

Some Wider Considerations

Using the data from the written tasks, Chata has produced models of progression in several strands of students' ideas about historical explanation and enquiry.[10] The project's findings on changes in student ideas, particularly about *evidence* and *rational understanding*, are close to those of earlier work by the Chata team and independent research elsewhere, notably that of Denis Shemilt.[11] Even in a fairly crude form, such models have considerable value for teachers in planning, teaching, and assessment, since they pick out major shifts in ideas and can be treated as general descriptors, allowing indicators to be written for specific tasks. Pervasive ideas can be addressed in teaching, and simplifications that might too easily be assimilated to those preexistent ideas avoided. For example, issues of what can and cannot be "eyewitnessed" can be tackled and the idea of a complete and perspectiveless account examined, perhaps initially in everyday contexts and then in passages of history that are relatively uncontroversial in contemporary terms. Such passages may be distant and still excite students: Mysteries and paradoxes arouse fierce interest without carrying the baggage of current concerns. Experience in the United Kingdom suggests that, as students become aware of the power of new ideas, history is increasingly valued as a difficult but worthwhile subject.[12]

Analysis of the richer Progression Study data has so far been confined to exploring changes in ideas about causal structure and rational understanding emerging in the space of two terms. Four points stand out.

1. At any given age students' ideas about historical explanation differ widely: some eight-year-olds have more sophisticated ideas than most twelve- or even fourteen-year-olds.

2. Individual students' ideas within the broad conceptual area of explanation are decoupled: They do not necessarily develop in parallel. A student may show progression in ideas of causal structure but not in rational understanding, or vice versa.

3. It is possible that development in different conceptual areas may occur at different times. The biggest gains on causal structure came in the fifth grade, and those on rational understanding in the third and sixth grade.

4. There was the least progression in the two schools (of seven investigated) where history was not a clearly identifiable subject in the curriculum arrangements.

Initial analysis of the Longitudinal Study data addressed the question "How did children's ideas change between second grade and fourth grade?"

1. Neither the component concepts for explanation (cause and rational understanding) nor those for inquiry (evidence and accounts) appeared to develop in parallel.

2. There were marked differences between children's ideas in the second grade, and by the fourth grade this spread had increased. One girl tried to reconstruct the situation, ideas, and values of Elizabeth I in order to explain her delay in ordering the execution of Mary, Queen of Scots, in a way not found in the responses of many eighth-grade children.

3. In some concepts, especially evidence, there were often changes in skills (e.g. cross-referencing a pair of sources) with no accompanying conceptual development.

4. Broad patterns of change were identifiable within the different concepts. For example, more than half the second-grade children made choices between claims without reference to the sources. By the fourth grade more than half the children were matching information in claims and sources to help them choose between claims. In the second grade three-quarters of the children treated accounts simply as "stories," but by the fourth grade many were insisting that it was essential that history stories be true. The greatest range of ideas occurred in rational understanding, where twelve children in the second grade had given explanations of action in personal terms, and six found the request for explanation itself baffling. By the fourth grade, two children remained baffled, but more than half had moved to or beyond explanations that appealed to agents' roles.

5. The three schools differed in the proportions of children making progress, in the highest and lowest categories for different concepts and in the category modes, at both second and fourth grade. Progression was clearest in the two schools where history was taught as an identifiable subject.

Progression in history is complex. A "mapping" exercise of the kind carried out by Chata can give the misleading impression that all that needs to be said about progression is that it is age related. While it is true that older students tend to have different ideas from younger ones, several caveats must be offered. First, it is not a reason for making assumptions about what students of any particular age cannot do.[13] Some ten- (and even eight-) year-olds will be operating with highly sophisticated ideas. Second, the Chata work does not support any claim that students' ideas simply mature of their own accord. Evidence from the Schools History Project clearly indicates that teaching changes pupil ideas.[14] Teaching and assessment must make distinctions between different strands of ideas and recognize that, as Chata indicates, students may be using pow-

erful concepts in some areas, but not in others. Such differences may be a
result of the fact that some ideas (e.g., evidence) are more widely taught
in an explicit way than others (e.g., cause or accounts), which may be less
securely understood by many teachers. Third, it seems likely, given what
we know about the impact of a wider culture on students' substantive beliefs about the past, that students' ideas about the discipline may also
change with shifts in the assumptions implicit in a culture.[15]

The changes picked out by Chata took place in a curriculum (partly)
designed to encourage the development of students' ideas and that came
at the end of a long period of development of techniques in teaching approaches, syllabus design, and assessment that attempted to achieve similar ends. Teaching that systematically builds on prior understandings and
assessment that rewards their development are both central to achieving
progression.[16] Of course, algorithmic approaches are possible in any form
of history teaching, and experience in the United Kingdom unsurpris-
ingly suggests that they are likely to be widespread where teachers do not
themselves have a good grasp of the ideas they are attempting to teach.
This may be the case even where entry standards for prospective history
teachers are high (a first or upper second class in a specialized history degree). Many British graduates leave university well able to summarize
current historians' views in particular content areas but ill equipped to
give a coherent account of historical evidence or of why there are alternative historical accounts. Hence, Ravitch's requirement that history teachers and their trainers be trained in history is extremely important but
needs to be unpacked.[17] She is right in arguing that generic pedagogy
cannot be substituted for a grasp of history, but wrong in assuming that
history graduates are automatically equipped to teach history (as distinct
from passing on particular accounts of the past).

Progression cannot be guaranteed. But, students may have more
chance of developing their ideas about history if their teachers have clear
ideas, can recognize their students' starting points, and have strategies for
building on them. The sine qua non is that history should have a clearly
identifiable place in the curriculum.

Some Practicalities

It is clear that some fourteen-year-olds have a better grasp of the nature
of historical accounts than some politicians and journalists. They will

hardly be satisfied with a diet of cultural icons masquerading as a common past when they already know that historical accounts are constructions, not just conjunctions of facts, and, in choosing themes, timelines, and questions, operate with appropriate criteria. These are powerful ideas, which do not leave their owners helpless in the face of alternative accounts, shrugging their shoulders at a multiplicity of opinions. Political commentators of different stripes, who insist on the one hand that stories are copies of the past or on the other that they are to be judged in terms of ownership rather than validity, are demanding that history education stop at preadolescent or young-adolescent conceptions.[18]

Understanding history means more than critiquing stories or encountering multiple perspectives. Students need to learn to question, but only if means are offered for making inroads into the problems they address. As students develop more powerful ideas about how we can make claims about the past and about the ways different kinds of claims may be substantiated or overturned, they acquire the best intellectual toolkit we have for thinking about the human world in time. This is not a set of generic "skills" that can be improved by practice but a complex of multitrack understandings. Nor is history second best to studies that "directly" address contemporary problems, because our concepts and the individuals that make up our present are past referenced; a large part of our thinking or knowing involves making at least tacit claims on the past.

Some caveats might be entered here. The point of studying history is to know something of the past, but what is learned in school is rapidly forgotten if it is not continually used. (Professional historians should ask themselves how much chemistry they remember.) Students may not come away from school with the picture of the past that any particular historian would like them to have. What they need is to develop frameworks of history that they *are* likely to use, frameworks that can assimilate new knowledge but are revisable and provisional. This demands assessment systems that measure students' achievement in terms of criteria like scope, resolution, dimensionality, explanatory "thickness," coherence, and validity, not the number of discrete facts students have memorized or whether their framework is accepted by particular social or political groups.[19]

It is naïve to think that history education will remove prejudices or make democratic citizens. There are causal factors at work here outside the control of history teachers. Moreover rethinking history in these terms cannot prevent algorithmic teaching that stultifies student ideas. Any approach to history education can be made pointless by poor teaching. But, if progression in ideas about history is not a sufficient condition of rational thinking about the past and present, it may nonetheless be part of a set of necessary conditions. Debates about the content of history must always end in compromise. What should not be compromised is students' right to be equipped with the tools for making sense of the past.

Appendix 11.1: Task-Set 2 Stories

FIRST STORY

Chapter 1

The Roman Empire got very big. It was hard to protect. Barbarians raided it, burning towns and farms and killing people. It cost a lot to keep up big Roman armies.

Chapter 2

After a time the Empire was split into two halves, east and west, to make it easier to run. But Emperors had trouble finding money to pay for the army. When lots of people were killed by disease, there were fewer people to be soldiers, especially in the western half of the Empire. Barbarians were allowed to join the army. Before long, even many army leaders were barbarians.

Chapter 3

An Emperor who lived in the eastern Empire allowed barbarians to settle in the western Empire. But still the western Empire couldn't protect itself. In 410 and again 455 the city of Rome was captured by barbarians. In 476 the last western Emperor in Rome was overthrown. That was the real end of the Roman Empire, even though in the east an Empire of some kind managed to last for a time.

SECOND STORY

Chapter 1

The Roman Empire got very big. That made it hard to look after and keep in order. It cost a lot to run the Empire. Emperors had trouble finding enough money.

Chapter 2

After a time, the Empire was split into two halves, east and west, to make it easier to run. Each half had its own capital city: Rome in the west and Constantinople in the east. Sometimes each half of the Empire had its own Emperor, sometimes one Emperor ran both halves. The east was richer than the west. Emperors often preferred to live in Constantinople in the east rather than Rome in the west.

Chapter 3

Barbarians attacked the Empire. The west was too poor to protect itself properly. The city of Rome was captured by barbarians. The eastern half managed to keep the barbarians out. It lasted a long time, but was soon very different from how the old Empire had been. The real end of the Roman Empire came nearly 1000 years later when Constantinople was captured by the Turks in 1453.

Appendix 11.2

Schematic pattern of progression in concepts of "opinion" used to explain differences in historical accounts, resting on qualitative analysis of different usage; quantitative analysis of distribution by age has not yet been performed.

Opinion as knowledge deficit

1. "Opinion" fills in for inevitable lack of knowledge (*qua* information), because of our lack of access to the past;
or
"Opinion" fills in for contingent lack of knowledge, because there are gaps in our information.
2. "Opinion" is a tentative substitute for properly established knowledge.

Opinion as point of view

3. "Opinion" is what we have when we take sides: it is a partisan viewpoint which distorts the past, and in that sense at least is illegitimate; but it is also inevitable (and it may be our duty to exercise it).
4. "Opinion" is a consequence of everyone thinking differently: it is a legitimate viewpoint.
5. "Opinion" is a judgment made on the basis of some sort of criteria, whether implicit or explicit, which in turn set the parameters necessary for the production of any story whatsoever.

NOTES

1. See P. J. Lee, "History and the national curriculum in England," in P. Gordon, A. K. Dickinson, P. J. Lee, and J. Slater, eds., *International Yearbook of History Education*, vol.1 (London, 1995), pp. 73–123, for a discussion of the basis of the history curriculum. R. Phillips follows the birth of the new curriculum in *History Teaching, Nationhood and the State: A Study in Educational Politics* (London, 1998).

2. See D. Shemilt's review of L. Kramer, D. Reid, and W. L. Barney, eds., "Learning History in America: Schools, Cultures and Politics," *History and Theory*, 35(2) (1996), pp. 252–275.

3. "Easier," not just "possible," because it was always to some degree possible to specify progression in terms of deeper understanding of substantive concepts and processes. There were two serious difficulties. First, the practical specifica-

tion of progression was made difficult by the vast range of interlinked paths followed by students as their substantive concepts developed. J. Coltham's unpublished Ph.D. thesis, *Junior School Children's Understanding of Historical Terms*, University of Manchester (1960), for example, grappled informatively with pupils' substantive ideas, but this whole research programme almost completely ground to a halt in the United Kingdom in the mid-1970s. It is now beginning to be revived: H. Cooper's unpublished Ph.D. thesis, *Young Children's Understanding in History*, University of London (1991), for example, investigated primary children's understandings of substantive concepts. Second, substantive understandings were closely related to the stories that framed them, which, as well as complicating the research task, set limits on their effectiveness in helping students to come to terms with the multiple versions of the past they were likely to encounter in later life.

4. For the rest of this chapter the English "year group" will be converted to the equivalent U.S. grades. Hence, "year 3" children, made up of children between the ages of seven and eight, will be described as "second grade." The difference between the U.S. "second" and English "3" appears innocently to represent the difference in the age at which formal schooling begins, but a moment's thought about "formal schooling" will indicate that the differences lurking here are more complicated. The translation is not straightforward.

5. This follows the strategy employed by MacIntyre in defining "intention": "the meaning of 'intention' is elucidated by a categorical reference to behaviour supplemented by a hypothetical reference to avowals." See A. MacIntyre, *The Unconscious, A Conceptual Analysis* (London, 1958), p. 57.

6. This kind of approach to progression in the United Kingdom is based on three kinds of work. First, there is a considerable body of small-scale research. See, for example, R. Ashby and P. J. Lee, "Children's Concepts of Empathy and Understanding in History," in C. Portal, ed., *The History Curriculum for Teachers* (Lewes, 1987), pp. 62–88; R. Ashby and P. J. Lee, "Discussing the Evidence," *Teaching History*, 48 (1987), pp. 13–17; M. B. Booth, "Inductive Thinking in History: The 14–16 Age Group," in G. Jones and L. Ward, eds., *New History, Old Problems* (Swansea, 1978), pp. 104–121; M. B. Booth, "Cognition in History, a British Perspective," *Educational Psychologist*, 29(2) (1994), pp. 61–69; Cooper, *Young Children's Understanding*; P. Knight, "A Study of Teaching and Children's Understanding of People in the Past," *Research in Education*, 44 (1990), pp. 39–53; D. Thompson, "Understanding the Past: Procedures and Content," in A. K. Dickinson, P. J. Lee, and P. J. Rogers, eds., *Learning History* (London, 1984), pp. 168–186.

Second, there has been much discussion of the conceptual basis of history education. Examples include A. K. Dickinson and P. J. Lee, eds., *History Teaching and Historical Understanding* (London, 1978); Dickinson, Lee, and Rogers, eds., *Learning History*; C. Husbands, *What Is History Teaching? Language, Ideas and*

Meaning in Learning about the Past (Buckingham, 1996); Portal, *History Curriculum*; P. J. Rogers, *The New History: Theory into Practice*, Historical Association Teaching of History Series 44 (London, 1978).

Third, there was wide practical experience in curriculum development of the kind found in the Schools History Project and its follow-up for sixteen- to eighteen-year-olds, the Cambridge History Project. H. G. Macintosh, *Testing Skills in History*, in Portal, ed., *History Curriculum*, pp. 183–219, discusses parallel innovations in assessment, and J. Slater, *The Politics of History Teaching: A Humanity Dehumanized?* (London, 1989) sums up the changing picture in teaching.

Research in North America and Spain in the past decade has begun to touch on similar issues and to influence thinking in the United Kingdom. The American research is discussed in S. Wineburg, "The Psychology of Learning and Teaching History," in D. C. Berliner and R. C. Calfee, eds., *Handbook of Educational Psychology* (New York, 1996), pp. 423–437. The recent work of, for example, Carretero, Barton, Beck, Boix-Mansilla, Dominguez, McKeown, Kuhn, Levstik, Leinhardt, Limon, McDiarmid, Perfetti, Pozo, Rouet, Seixas, Voss, Wertsch, and Wineburg has been especially influential in the United Kingdom, partly because some of it has become easily available in four collections: M. Carretero and J. E. Voss, eds., *Cognitive and Instructional Processes in History and the Social Sciences* (Hillsdale, NJ, 1994); G. Leinhardt, I. L. Beck, and C. Stainton, eds., *Teaching and Learning in History* (Hillsdale, NJ, 1994); J. Brophy, ed., *Advances in Research on Teaching: Teaching and Learning History* (Greenwich, CT, and London, England, 1996); and J. E. Voss and M. Carretero, eds, *International Review of History Education*, vol. 2: *Learning and Reasoning in History* (London, England, and Portland, OR, 1998). Nevertheless, U.S. research in particular exhibits a wider range of approaches than the British and perhaps places more emphasis on students' substantive understanding.

7. Historical narrative is at the center of debates about the nature of history. See, for example, F. R. Ankersmit, *Narrative Logic: A Semantic Analysis of the Historian's Language* (The Hague, 1983); P. Novick, *That Noble Dream: The "Objectivity Question" and the American Historical Profession* (Cambridge, 1988); H. V. White, *The Content of the Form: Narrative Discourse and Historical Representation* (Baltimore, 1987), especially pp. 26–57; H. V. White, "Historical Emplotment and the Problem of Truth," in S. Friedlander, ed., *Probing the Limits of Representation: Nazism and the "Final Solution"* (Cambridge, MA, 1992), pp. 37–53. The frightening intensity with which the debate can spill over into what should be taught is documented in G. Nash, C. Crabtree, and R. Dunn, *History on Trial: Culture Wars and the Teaching of the Past* (New York, 1997). Narratives have also become an issue for *how* history should be taught in schools and universities, as in K. Jenkins's two polemical books, *Rethinking History* (London, 1991) and *On "What Is History": From Carr and Elton to Rorty and White* (London, 1995).

8. "Accounts" is used in this chapter to cover both narratives and develop-

mental accounts of change, and is intended to avoid dichotomies between "mere narrative" and "explanatory narrative." "Story" will be used interchangeably with "account" because, when talking with young children, "story" is the nearest available intelligible equivalent.

9. The status of colligations like "the Fall of the Roman Empire" is of course much discussed in recent philosophy of history. Examples include F. Ankersmit, *Narrative Logic*, especially ch. 6, and C. B. McCullough, *The Truth of History* (London, 1998), particularly ch. 2. We hope that, despite our use of a concretized simplification, "the end of the Roman Empire," none of the central issues were closed down for students. (None of them was heard to claim that the end of Empire was a nonreferential narrative substance.)

10. R. Ashby, P. J. Lee, and A. K. Dickinson, "How Children Explain the 'Why' of History: the Chata Research Project on Teaching History," *Social Education* 61(1) (1997), pp. 17–21; P. J. Lee, "'None of Us Was There': Children's Ideas about Why Historical Accounts Differ," in S. Ahonen et al., eds., *Historiedidaktik, Norden 6, Nordisk Konferens om Historiedidaktik, Tampere 1996* (Copenhagen, 1997), pp. 23–58; P. J. Lee, R. Ashby and A. K. Dickinson, "Progression in Children's Ideas about History," in M. Hughes, ed., *Progression in Learning* (Clevedon, Bristol, PA, and Adelaide, 1996), pp. 50–81; P. J. Lee, R. Ashby, and A. K. Dickinson, "Children Making Sense of History," *Education 3–13*, 24(1) (1996), pp. 13–19; P. J. Lee, A. K. Dickinson and R. Ashby, "Just Another Emperor: Understanding Action in the Past," *International Journal of Educational Research*, 27(3) (1997), pp. 233–244.

11. Shemilt's work has had enormous influence. See in particular his *History 13-16 Evaluation Study* (Edinburgh, 1980); "The Devil's Locomotive," *History and Theory* 22(4) (1983), pp. 1–18; "Beauty and the Philosopher: Empathy in History and Classroom," in Dickinson, Lee, and Rogers, eds., *Learning History*, pp. 39–84, and "Adolescent Ideas about Evidence and Methodology in History," in Portal, ed., *History Curriculum*, pp. 39–61.

12. Shemilt, *Evaluation Study*.

13. See S. Wineburg, "A Partial History" (essay review of *Teaching and Learning History in Elementary School* by Jere Brophy and Bruce VanSledright), *Teaching and Teacher Education*, 14 (1998), pp. 233–243.

14. Shemilt, *Evaluation Study* and unpublished follow-up studies.

15. K. Barton, "'My Mom Taught Me': The Situated Nature of Historical Understanding," paper presented at the annual meeting of the American Educational Research Association, San Francisco (1995); V. Boix Mansilla, this volume; R. Rosenzweig, this volume; P. Seixas, "Popular Film and Young People's Understanding of the History of Native-White Relations," *History Teacher*, 26(3) (1993); J. Wertsch, this volume; S. Wineburg, this volume.

16. P. Stearns, this volume.

17. D. Ravitch, this volume.

18. There are signs in some sixth-grade and eighth-grade responses of a belief in the right or the duty to give an opinion in history, which transcends any obligation to validity or truth. This seems to be partly a consequence of the belief that nothing can ultimately be known for certain about a past that is no longer open to direct inspection. See R. Ashby and P. J. Lee, "Information, Opinion and Beyond," paper presented at the annual meeting of the American Educational Research Association, San Diego (1998), for examples, and Appendix 11.2 of this essay for "opinion" categories.) Some students seem to operate with a notion of "relativism" (at least in history "topics") very similar to the one that Rorty claims is not in fact held by anyone: "'Relativism' is the view that every belief on a certain topic, or perhaps about *any* topic, is as good as every other. No one holds this view. Except for the occasional cooperative freshman, one cannot find anybody who says that two incompatible opinions on an important topic are equally good." (R. Rorty, "Pragmatism, Relativism and Irrationalism," *Proceedings and Addresses of the American Philosophical Association*, 53 [1980], pp. 719–738, quoted in R. J. Bernstein, *Beyond Objectivism and Relativism* [Oxford, 1983], p. 201.)

If teaching stresses distinctions between "fact" and "opinion" without making distinctions within the latter, or if it makes no attempt to differentiate provisionality from skepticism, it is likely to push adolescent views about differences in historical accounts into a potentially vicious relativism, or at least a shoulder-shrugging helplessness. Since some students have already moved beyond such positions, it would be unfortunate if teaching, in trying to offer helpful simplifications, appeared to justify them.

19. P. J. Lee, "Historical Knowledge and the National Curriculum," in R. Aldrich, ed., *History in the National Curriculum* (London, 1991), pp. 39–65, esp. pp. 58–62; D. Shemilt, this volume.

Chapter 12

Lessons on Teaching and Learning in History from Paul's Pen

Gaea Leinhardt

It is an auspicious time to have a discussion of how we might proceed in the systematic study of the teaching and learning of history. It is auspicious because we have both a solid corpus of research that spans a variety of instructional settings and geographical locations and a generous array of questions to ask and tools with which to answer them. It is auspicious also because we have a vital new set of challenges and occasions for study. We can concern ourselves with the content of history instruction. We can concern ourselves with the historical stance to be taken by texts, teachers, and students. We can concern ourselves with the kind of historical knowledge we expect from our teachers and desire for our students. We can also begin to concern ourselves with the potential for learning that exists in the media and in places such as museums and historical sites. In this essay I use an example from my own work to explore the ways in which we can look at one line of questions that might be fruitfully asked, one set of tools that might be effectively employed, and one location that might be usefully explored in studying history teaching and learning.

My own research asks these questions: What is the nature of highly effective educational practice in history, and what is the nature of the history learning that results from such practices?[1] These questions belong to a family of questions about effective educational practices. I focus on these questions because as an educator I am interested in the specifics of what particular subject matters can contribute to the life and learning of students. I am also interested in the general ways in which specific subjects can contribute to the overall growth and development of a literate populace. Thus, one core question behind the research program is the following: What are the essential opportunities that teaching and learning in history provide? Opportunity here implies both the "chance to" and what is essential. What are the critical or most important things that the learning or teaching of history affords—or what essential thing do we lose when students do not study history?

To get a feeling for what I am thinking about, consider the following: Imagine a student who is in the tenth grade or maybe a student in the second year of college (generally they are age 15 or 19). This student is a C-minus student. He is taking the last formal history course of his life. This student might grow up to be a heartbeat away from the presidency or might someday sit in judgment on the presidency. Or, imagine instead a young woman in her third year of college who is an education major. Filled with idealism and caring, she, too, finds herself to be a less-than-stellar student, but she will likely teach for forty years and potentially influence over a thousand students. What should these students remember and understand, twenty-five years later, from this last history class? What powerful and unique opportunity does the content and disposition of history provide the teacher and the learner?

Further, consider that while our hypothetical students have taken their last history class, they have not been exposed to their last bit of history. No, they will go on to hear Rush Limbaugh declare that history is just the facts, see Tom Hanks convey the entire Vietnam era in *Forrest Gump*, and witness various incarnations of John Wayne present World War II, or maybe it will be Steven Spielberg's version that captures their attention. They will be awash in history, they will live in it, but they will have no more history from the academy.

This question of educational opportunity leads to issues of content, processes, and ownership. What might be taught and learned—and who decides—and how might that instruction best be accomplished? Instructionally, what are the richest mixes of educational processes, such as physical experiences (field trips, films), textual analysis and integration (reading and writing from historical sources), and performance (debates, theater) in which students should engage? What sorts of content emphasis seem to be of greatest, or at least of great, value: a clear, singular, historical chronicle; an understanding of multiple perspectives; an understanding of source and its import; a process of reasoning; or a corpus of integrated and annotated knowledge? And how should we decide?

As work by Peter Seixas, Sam Wineburg, Jim Wertsch, and Terrie Epstein—and my hypothetical students—have all shown, students learn history outside of school.[2] They learn history from their parents. They learn history from television. They learn history from movies. They learn history in museums. The voice of the academy is not privileged in the development of historical memory or in the historical constructions of students, their parents, or even teachers. If, in reality, the academy is not privileged in the memories of individuals, then who actually owns the historical agenda? And if there is not a single owner, what again is most essential for us to offer and try to ensure is learned (both mastered and appreciated) by students in the classroom specifically?

Learners and teachers come to their classes with a sense of history. What is their sense of history, what are their historical understandings, and how do they develop them? As Levstik and, more recently, Gregg have shown, both teachers and learners have a priori understandings and content knowledge about and of history.[3] Some of that understanding may be quite sophisticated and subtle; some other understandings might be quite simplistic and deeply flawed. Substantial research in fields such as physics has shown us that we cannot hope to provide a meaningful educational experience for teachers or students unless we have some sense of these other understandings.

What information does answering these sorts of questions provide? In general, the answers help us to gain a clearer picture of students as learners and of teachers as both practitioners and historical consumers; they also give us a better feel for the relationships among the academic sense of history, the popular-cultural sense of history, and the local and personal sense of history. In my work on classrooms, I have examined common, very good practice. This research provides a baseline for what constitutes good history teaching and learning. I can describe what a solid, thoughtful history teacher can and does accomplish with minimal intervention or support. I can show, I think, how teachers with quite different perspectives on teaching history can accomplish enormous amounts in terms of student learning. I can also describe what highly committed and thoughtful students can gain with little intervention or support beyond being lucky enough to have an excellent teacher. That information helps us to set goals that most can aim for, and it suggests the ways in which more carefully designed interventions can be built.

A Case Study of History Teaching and Learning

Let me turn to the specifics of the program of research that I have engaged in over the past decade. The program has examined in detail the instructional practices and learning consequences of several talented teachers.[4] One teacher in particular, Sterling (pseudonym), has been the focus of much of my work on exemplary practices and their outcomes. Sterling was among the several teachers selected for study; she was chosen on the basis of the excellent scores achieved by her students on the Advance Placement exam, as well as of recommendations from parents across the city in which she taught and from fellow teachers and supervisors. Sterling was a content-based teacher. By that I mean she was passionate about her subject, had been formally educated in it, and was a voracious reader of it. She was also a child of Western Pennsylvania, steeped in the traditions of labor unions and labor conflicts, aware as well of the extreme wealth and power of the industrial barons whose names are on our parks, avenues, and museums.

Briefly, our database for Sterling spans two years and two courses (A.P. U.S. history and A.P. modern European history).[5] The data include audio- or videotape records of an entire first semester and portions of the second semester of a U.S. history course (slightly over 100 lessons) plus sixteen audiotaped lessons in European history, as well as the complete written productions of six students in U.S. history (including their notebooks) and a series of interviews with the teacher. This corpus of data has allowed us to ask a variety of questions about the fundamental models of history that this teacher holds, the ways in which history is explained by teachers and students over time, and the way in which historical reasoning develops over time.[6]

My current project involves tracing one student, Paul (pseudonym), and analyzing the way in which he gradually learned both to write with greater command of historical ideas and to speak in more historically sophisticated ways while retaining a rather narrow view of the discipline of history. Paul was observed during the course of one semester of A.P. U.S. history. Tape recordings of every day of class were annotated with identifications of every time Paul spoke. We collected copies of every piece of written material that he turned in to his teacher, as well as copies of all the pages in his notebook. The observations also included audiotapes or detailed notes from weekly discussions we held with his teacher, Sterling, and the collection of similar student data (except for annotating all their talk) from other members in the class. We transcribed all the data and now can analyze every phrase that Paul uttered in class for the entire semester as well as every sentence that he wrote.

In another essay, I have described what we have learned about the development of understanding and thinking on the part of other students.[7] Paul, however, needs his own investigation; he is unique. Paul was an unusually articulate student who expressed a strong desire to "master" history; he was personally both ambitious and willing to put an enormous amount of effort into learning history. He wanted to be able to "talk the talk" and "walk the walk"—to both *appear* knowledgeable and *be* knowledgeable. I did not initially intend to study Paul. Paul was a white, middle-class, male student; he was politically conservative, socially amiable, and totally goal driven. He had no particular demographic characteristic to recommend him as a subject for study. But Paul had so many intriguing aspects to his learning and his goals that he demanded to be studied. For example, although he was technically ineligible for the A.P. history class, Paul talked his way in.[8] His glossy, pompous, and often amusingly misapplied manner of speaking seemed jarring at first, but the frequency of his speech drew our attention to him. Over the course of the semester he learned to refine his speech and to focus it on increasingly complex historical issues. Paul never reached a tolerance for historical ambiguity, but he did apply a lawyerly take on evidence and the support of arguments. He had an automatic, procedurally driven way of writing, but he struggled with it and forged it into a more reasonable and clearly serviceable style.

I will not go through the entire story of Paul, but I will use him as a way of showing how certain analytic tools might contribute to deepening our understanding of the complexity and subtlety of learning or perhaps contribute to our appreciating what it is a student has to come to grips with in order to learn. Here, I focus on those tools that when used over substantial lengths of time—months, for example—can help us to see the development of a student's ability to engage in historical analysis. The two powerful data resources for seeing this happen over time are acts of semiformal speaking in class and acts of semiformal writing in and out of class.

Why "semi"? or why "formal"? Formal acts of writing and speaking are ones in which there is considerable amount of prior thought and rehearsal—or revision—before they are publicly shared. For example, a speech or debate presentation, a term paper, or a final project are what I would call formal in the school context. Informal speech is purely conversational and completely unrehearsed. Informal speaking can careen from the specific and subject-focused to the highly personal and non–discipline based; informal writing is free or stream-of-consciousness writing; it does not try to mimic a particular academic style, nor is it edited for clarity or accuracy.

In our work we have seen considerable growth in the "semi" range of speaking, in which students respond to the teacher's or their own questions in class in a thoughtful and elaborated way.[9] It is in these semiformal discussions that students display their accountability to the discipline in terms of content and form, to the general level of the discussion to date, and to the purposes of discussion at hand. It is under these circumstances that students muster evidence and refer to sources as well as to the arguments and explanations already given within that community. Likewise, in writing, when students are given substantial time—an hour or two—to produce essays in answer to specific questions, they begin to develop a more sophisticated form of presentation and more well composed content. The advantage of the semiformal situation for researchers is that it is a naturally occurring event of some frequency; it is a situation that reveals what students are learning; and, in most high school and college-level classes, it occurs at least three to five times a term for each student.

Thus, the use of core questions about highly effective instructional practice has led us to examine the results of those practices and their impact on one student's development. In examining Paul, I focus on both the way that he learned to write and the way in which he developed his competence in speaking about historical ideas and "facts." I am taking as a given that the course itself was a legitimate one, in the sense of being a reasonable set of materials to share with young high school students, and I am taking as a given that it was reasonable for Paul to make intense efforts to learn the material and the ideas. That the course could have been dramatically improved is also true, but if we focus on that, we will never get to what Paul did accomplish.

Analyzing the Writing: Paul's Pen

Because of space constraints, I focus here on how Paul developed in his historical writing, reserving the analysis of his talk for another venue.

One advantage of analyzing students' textual productions is that it is easier than analyzing their spoken productions. Writing is also more straightforward to explain. We can closely examine the demands of the task itself, including the question posed; we can consider the understandings of rhetorical forms that are used; and we can consider how evidence is mustered in support of an idea. The ambiguities that flood almost any act of speech are less prevalent in written text, and thus the complexity of analyzing text is greatly reduced. But, there is an additional reason for examining the development of a student's textual competence. As an educator, I study history learning for two reasons: first, because it is enormously important for people to know and feel the content and questions of history and, second, because in the process of learning history and the tools of history, students have the opportunity to learn specific kinds of thinking and reasoning, one of which is a form of writing.

Paul was asked to write four essays during the first semester. Three of these essays made use of retired items from the A.P. exam, specifically the Document Based Question (DBQ). The DBQ follows a standard format: A general question is posed to the student and is accompanied by eight to eleven "documents." These supporting documents do not include textbook summaries; they are only partially overlapping in content; and they provide a mosaic of the time and issue of focus rather than a cleanly specified set of pro and con arguments. The set of materials often includes one or two speeches on the topic from notable historical figures; one or two diagrammatic presentations, such as an editorial cartoon, a chart, or a map; and newspaper accounts or interviews. These are oblique moments rather than continuous texts portrayed in various forms. The design of the DBQ requires that the student transform his or her knowledge by manipulating the different sources, using background understanding, and peeling through the multiple layers present in the documents (the authors, the dates, the stance, the critical points within them).

The DBQ asks students to write a short essay in which they respond to the question by using the evidence in the documents and any relevant general knowledge that they have about the time or events. There are various dimensions along which the students might be seen to make progress. One dimension is the historical sense of the piece, including its accuracy and general rhetorical and temporal organization. In addition to the overall historical sense, my colleague and student Kathleen Young and I examined two other dimensions that helped us to see how the student was developing skill in handling the demands of the task.[10]

One dimension we called the Organizational Pattern, and the other we called Document Use. It is in the organizational pattern and the document uses that we can see the development and growth of students' competence in historical writing as opposed to the development of more general reasoning.

Organizational pattern refers to the specific construction of the essay. In examining some thirty essays, we identified three commonly used organizational patterns—*list, specified list,* and *causal list*—that reflect the way the essay demonstrated its content coherence. A list is simply that— an arbitrary series of facts or units that are somewhat elaborated upon. The list could be organized in a number of different ways without changing the meaning of the essay. A list pattern is indicative of a rich, perhaps overwhelming collection of information that drives the essay. A specified list provides advanced organizers that may be specified by number (e.g., "There are three major factors") or, in a more sophisticated manner, by category (e.g., "There are economic, political, and social factors"). Having a specified list in an essay suggests a rhetorical sensibility, and it provides a structural frame within which the student can work. A specified-list pattern suggests the student is in control of the "story" and is accessing information for it. A causal list, as its name suggests, uses the inherent causal relationships among the elements to structure the essay. In a causal list arrangement, the essay could not be rearranged arbitrarily because the linkages among elements are directional and sequential. This pattern suggests that the student has a fairly strong sense of the counterplay of forces that occurred.

In addition to the overall type of organization employed for an essay, our analysis of organizational pattern included the types of connectors that were used between idea units within an essay. These connectors were often reflective of the type of underlying organization employed by the student in the essay. We identified the following types of connectors: list, exemplar, equivalence, place-holder, causal, and qualifier. These connections are highly local and link two or more ideas within the essay. Interestingly, students, in both their speech and their writing, take some time to develop a repertoire of connecting statements. It is the employment of various patterns of connections—different ones suitable for different idea relationships—that turns out to be worth monitoring. One might well ask why? After all, students in an A.P. class surely know the words, "and," "for example," "similarly," "first," "because," and "however." They do indeed, but they are less certain of the underlying relationships between specific concepts—of how they wish to express those relationships.

Beyond issues of organizational pattern, however, the DBQ places greater demands on the student writer than does a direct essay question. These increased demands stem from the availability of, and the charge to make use of, the multiple nonoverlapping documents. The use of documents is complex not only because of the inherent interpretation and meaning of the documents themselves but also because of the specific issues of referencing. Should documents be identified by title (the cartoon, the speech, the chart) or by code (A, B, C)? Should they be grouped by position on an issue or by some content value? Should they themselves be analyzed and should parts be brought in to support an argument? Our analysis of students' document use identified the ways in which students made use of the documents in their essay, by either mentioning them, restating them, or integrating and interpreting them. We analyze this aspect of the essays because using documents is both the task of and the reasoning tool for the DBQ.

Using these analytic tools for examining writing, we can get a sense of Paul's development as a writer by comparing his first DBQ essay of the semester, written in October, to a later one, written in January. For the analysis of each essay, I present the DBQ question, describe briefly the supporting documents provided, describe the overall historical stance Paul adopted, present a schematic diagram of the entire essay response, describe specific organizational and document-use features, and then examine in some depth the concluding paragraph.

Question 1

From 1781 to 1789 the Articles of Confederation provided the United States with an effective government. Using the documents and your knowledge of the period evaluate this statement.

This DBQ question included eight documents: a letter from the Rhode Island Assembly to Congress (1782); a chart with three columns (one with a list of years from 1770 to 1792, another with the corresponding market value of exports to Great Britain, and a third with the estimated U.S. population in thousands) but with no identifying sources; a letter from Joseph Jones to George Washington (1783); John Jay's instructions to the U.S. minister to Great Britain (1785); a map of western lands ceded by the states 1781–1802; a segment of John Jay's speech to Congress on negotiations with Spain (August 1786); a letter from John Jay to George Washington (June 1786); and Rawlin Lowndes' speech to the South Carolina House of Representatives as it debated the adoption of the federal constitution (January 1788).

Paul took on the DBQ question as if it could have a factually correct answer and stated in his first sentence, "The statement that the Confederation provided the United States with an effective form of government during the Critical Period in American history is false." He undoubtedly took such a strong stance because he heard Sterling emphasize the importance of making a point and backing it up rather than being wishy-washy about the question. In his essay his most repeated point was that no one respected the United States in its early years. Paul identified the areas of agreed-upon weaknesses in the Confederation: foreign relations and domestic policy. He elaborated with evidence the lack of functionality in conducting foreign affairs but continuously used the personalized stance that the United States was unable to gain the respect of foreign nations and "The Articles were a laughing stock to the British and spanish [*sic*]." Paul, however, was a student only three weeks into the term and he had done an acceptable job of presenting the canonical historical issues. In terms of answering the DBQ for an A.P. exam, he had a way to go.

In reading Paul's essay, one gets the sense that he searched for a single unifying idea around which he could group the document bits. The unifying idea was that the United States (personified) was not respected while it employed the Articles of Confederation—almost as if Uncle Sam needed to switch from driving a Buick to driving a BMW to gain the respect of friends and colleagues. For Paul, answering the question "Was the government effective?" and uniting the essay were two separate tasks. He wrote an essay about respect and about why and how it could be seen that Uncle Sam did not receive any.

Paul began this course with a fairly good mastery of the generic five-paragraph essay (theme) form. In this form, the first paragraph presents the main argument and the structure that will be followed, the next three (or eight) paragraphs elaborate each of the core ideas identified, and the final paragraph recapitulates. Figure 12.1 shows a diagram of the structure of Paul's ten-paragraph, 766-word essay. In this diagram, the small black nodes represent idea units or multiword phrases that express a central concept, and line links show the connections between ideas as stated in the essay. Ideas that are adjacent in the essay but have an unstated relationship are also shown as connected. However, when ideas are separated

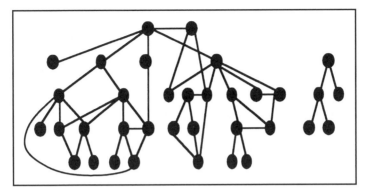

Figure 12.1. Node-link diagram of DBQ essay 1—Articles of Confederation

by other ideas and there is no specific statement that links them, the nodes are shown as unconnected. The concluding paragraph is shown as a separate cluster of nodes to the far right. The diagram can be "read" from top to bottom, with more or less smaller details appearing lower in the system than major ideas. In Paul's essay, two sets of ideas were developed: the ideas surrounding foreign policy (shown by the cluster of nodes to the center right of the diagram), and ideas surrounding domestic policy (shown by the cluster of nodes to the left). As one can see just from the diagram, however, ideas literally crisscross each other. Nodes high up in the diagram are connected strangely to rather minute points lower down in the system.

The overall pattern of the essay was a specified-list pattern as determined by Paul's presentation of the main ideas in the form of a collection of concepts with a descriptive connecting structure. For example, he used constructor links ("first," "second") as organizers. The beginning of the second paragraph reads, "First of all, under the Articles of Confederation the United States received very little respect from foreign nations and was unable to effectively negotiate foreign policy." Two paragraphs later, the opening sentence reads, "Secondly, the Spanish also refused to respect the American states while they were bound by this loose Confederation." (Note the reversal of the causal structure that is implied in this essay; Paul seems to be suggesting that the Spanish knew that the U.S. government was going to get stronger and that it was when the governmental structure was loose that they did not respect it—an odd form of presentism.)

The essay made use of time-based, place-based, and some causal-list organization. As was the case with many students, Paul, once inside a structure, showed some evidence of difficulty in climbing out of it. An example of this difficulty can be seen in the essay's fourth paragraph:

> Secondly, the Spanish also refused to respect the American states while they were bound by this loose Confederation. During this period in American history, Spain closed off the mouth of the mississippi [*sic*] to the Americans and refused to budge or compromise on this matter. John Jay's speech to Congress on the negotiations with Spain's Don Diego de Gardoqui shows that the Spanish refused to allow the United States to navigate the mississippi [*sic*]. It also illustrates Spain's lack of respect for American negotiators because this Treaty was never signed. As Gardoqui alluded to in Jay's speech, the states were too divided on issues in the west to sign the treaty. As a result, the vote needed was never acquired to ratify the treaty. The Articles were a laughing stock to the British and spanish [*sic*].

In this rather lengthy paragraph, Paul made a short excursion into the issue of domestic affairs—the inability to obtain ratification—as a means of supporting his interpretation of the international problems. He then used this mentioning of domestic issues in the following paragraph ("this leads to another ineffective aspect of the Articles . . .") to bring up domestic policy, rather than realizing that there were two core ideas—foreign and domestic—and that he needed organizational language to bring him back up to the top of the organizational structure.

The specific connection language used by Paul throughout the essay helps to illustrate the way the essay itself was structured. Paul used causal links ("although," "however," "thus," "as a result," "because," "in order to"); he used some constructor links ("first of all," "secondly," "during," "next," and "finally"); and he used exemplar connections ("for example," "as G alluded to," "as illustrated"). Although there is a lack of an overall logical argument in this essay, the presence of these kinds of connections does not in and of itself mean that Paul could not have made a causal argument with them; rather, his connection language is consistent with the general sense that he is using a less than powerful essay structure to make his point. When Paul did use causal connections, they were not placed between assertions and evidence. Evidence was used to exemplify, not to explain. The essay is apparently being driven by the essay form with which Paul is most familiar rather than by the content of the ideas. In this essay Paul did not make use of traditional historical specified-list categories—such as social, economic, and political factors—as organizing devices.

The DBQ requires that students construct a coherent account, respond to the question posed, and use the documents provided. Students need not use all of the documents, but they are expected to find ways to make use of most. Paul's essay shows signs that he was moderately well along in his ability to incorporate documents. He specifically mentioned four of the documents by identifying a feature within them and then listed three other documents in a set. On the sheet with the essay question, he placed a check mark next to each "used" document. He was unable to "see" or perhaps to "use" the information in the chart (a document that helped to show a pattern of steady growth in population and productivity before the revolution and a less steady pattern afterward). Paul did not integrate or transform the documents; rather, he used them in conjunction with his initial organizing structure to support or flesh out the concept. Yet, he was more sophisticated than other students who simply listed the documents by letter or number ("the third document and fourth document prove X").

In examining the written productions of students, there are several locations that prove revealing. One location is the first paragraph, which is important because it is hard for a student to escape the inherent structure or lack of it that is set up there. The middle paragraphs are revealing because it is there that students are most likely to produce statements backed up by evidence. The final paragraph is particularly telling because it is there that the student can clean up the less-than-perfect structure and enhance the initial argument; yet, it is most commonly written under time pressure. The final paragraph of Paul's first essay follows:

> As a result of inability to effectively negotiate foreign policy, maintain and establish domestic policy, and enforce decisions, the central government under the Articles of Confederation did not provide America with an effective government between 1781 and 1789. The documents and events of the period illustrate this point.

What can we see here? Paul had at least part of the canonical list of weaknesses of the Articles. He had a causal connection, "as a result of," and he had a time-based summary. He left out any discussion of what the Articles provided for and he treated them as an unanalyzed unit. He was less than articulate about the documents themselves and how to use them in this last paragraph. Essentially, he wrote as though the documents were

well known speakers who proved his point. He did not unpack them
or integrate their content into his content. He knew the "answer" to the
essay question without the documents, and so he wrote that answer
and summarized it in his last paragraph, but he never appropriated the
contents of the documents for use within the confines of the essay. In his
first attempt for the year, Paul made substantial use of a variant of the
five-paragraph essay with a structure built around foreign and domestic
policy. Three months later Paul had considerably greater mastery of the
essay form.

In January Paul wrote his last DBQ essay of the term in response to the
following question:

Question 3

Documents A–H reveal some of the problems that many farmers in the
late nineteenth century (1880–1900) saw as threats to their way of life.
Using the documents and your knowledge of the period, (a) explain the
reasons for agrarian discontent *and* (b) evaluate the validity of the farmers' complaints.

The DBQ contained eight documents: the platform from the People's
(Populist) party (1892); William McKinley's acceptance speech (August
1896); a three-column chart of dates, population, and money in circulation (1865–1895); a political cartoon titled "The Eastern Master and His
Western Slaves," from the late 1880s or early 1890s; a section of an article from "Causes of Agricultural Unrest" by J. Laurence Laughlin, taken
from the *Atlantic Monthly* (1892); *A Call to Action*, by James B. Weaver
(1892); testimony before the U.S. Senate by George W. Parker of the
Cairo Short Line Railroad (1885); and a section from Frank Norris' *The
Octopus* (1901).

In his nine-paragraph, 1,346-word essay, Paul started by restating the
question and locating it in time both by date and setting: "Between 1880
and 1910, the average American farmer faced several problems as the nation and its government moved towards an industrial trend heading into
the twentieth century." Within the confines of the first paragraph Paul
laid out a highly usable and effective structure for the rest of the essay. He
identified three reasons for farmers' discontent, elaborating upon each
one. He ended the paragraph with the evaluation that some of the reasons were not valid and then proceeded. Each subsequent paragraph explicated a grievance, using the documentary evidence, and then analyzed
its validity, also using the documents. Paul tended to express a view sym-

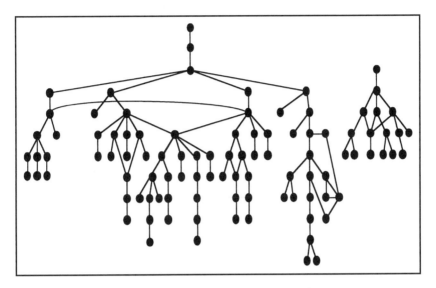

Figure 12.2. Node-link diagram of DBQ essay 3—Farmers' Discontent.

pathetic toward the farmers' condition and disagreeing with the farmers' explanations.

In this last DBQ essay, Paul showed that he had managed to integrate the skeleton of the five-paragraph essay form with the substantive content of the history. In contrast to the first essay, Paul here combined his knowledge of the form of the essay together with the information provided in the documents and his own knowledge about the topic. What was in an awkward collision before is now mutually supportive. For example, when Paul argued against the validity of the farmers' free silver position, he wrote, "If one looks at the population and money in circulation . . . it is easy to see that inflating the economy. . . . " When Paul argued that the railroads discriminated against the farmers but did not conspire to do so, he cut a particularly fine-grained distinction. Absent from his account, however, is any sourcing of who the documents' authors were and why their particular voice as historical actors was important.

Figure 12.2 shows the node-and-link diagram of this third DBQ essay. The structure appears more detailed (more nodes) and more evenly balanced in terms of depth than does the first. The diagram helps us to "see" how Paul made a series of central points and then elaborated on them, generally returning to the higher structure when it was rhetorically appropriate.

The organizational pattern of the essay remained a specified list rather than a causal list, although Paul included many causal statements inside the essay itself. Consider the first two sentences of the first paragraph: "Between 1880 and 1900 [note date anchoring], the average American farmer faced several [note unspecified organizer] problems as the nation and its government moved towards an industrial trend heading into the twentieth century [note accurate placement of the temporal setting—industrial trend—but awkwardness of phrasing]. Correspondingly, [note weak connect when causal connect is available], these problems led [causal link] the farmers to harbor many grievances against the American government and American industry." The main sections of Paul's essay used a numerated, specified-list organizational system ("the first reason," "the second reason," "in conclusion"), but within the sections Paul incorporated causal language.

In examining still another part of the organizational features of Paul's last DBQ essay of the semester—the specific use of connections—we can see that there was a great deal of growth since the first essay in October. Paul used more and a greater variety of causal links inside the essay ("i.e.," "this is evident from," "because," "however," "reason can be seen," "it stemmed," "instead of stemming," "as a result," "would result," "while," "in spite of," "due to the fact," "due in part," "although," "causing," "only reason," "due to"). There are also constructor links and exemplar links inside the essay. The point here is not to suggest that Paul should have been drilled on the use of various types of linking phrases but rather to see exactly how Paul struggled to merge his prior knowledge of a particular writing system with his current knowledge of the specific historical issues and with the task of writing a coherent and carefully specified essay.

A final area of growth in Paul's writing is reflected in the way he learned to incorporate documentary evidence in his citational system. In his first essay, Paul, apparently running out of time, was forced to say things like "illustrated in documents C, G, and H." In his last essay, we have two kinds of evidence of his increased document use. First, on the DBQ examination sheet itself, Paul wrote comments next to each of the documents—"farmers and currency," "conspiracy," "money," "shows invalid problem." In many cases, more than one point was summarized on a document. Why is that so important? One of the difficulties that students face is not only mentioning the documents but making use of them— chewing them up, so to speak, and transforming them. If each document is used only once, then it is likely that the use is more list-like than transformative. By making multiple notations, Paul was laying the ground-work for using documents to serve his arguments rather than simply to annotate a list. Second, Paul used the documents themselves multiple times and used multiple documents to support a single point. His own coding for that was to place stars on the areas inside the document that made points he would use and to make a sweeping check mark when the document had been used.

The specific attachment language—that is, the language that was used to insert the document—was still awkward ("In fact, an editorial cartoon in . . ."). At other points in his essay Paul showed greater facility—for example, when he wrote, "This is evident from the testimony of George W. Parker, vice president of Cairo Short Line Railroad . . . in which he said that discriminating rates were used." Here, Paul not only made use of a reasonable lead-in but also identified both the speaker and his role. Such sourcing, as Wineburg has shown, is rare.[11] From the node-link diagram of Paul's third DBQ essay (see far right portion of Figure 12.2) and from the text itself, we can see that this essay's closing paragraph showed con-siderable improvement over the one in his first essay. Here, he has care-fully recapitulated both the core question and his response.

> In conclusion, the farmers' discontent between 1880 and 1900 stemmed from four factors. First, farmers believed that the railroads and industry were conspiring against them. Although the railroads did charge farmers discriminatory rates, the idea of a mass conspiracy against the farmer goes unproven and is more attributed to the frustration of the farmer instead of factual data. Second, farmers were angry because the government did not advocate free coinage of silver and cheap money. This also was an invalid complaint because had inflated currency arisen, depression and panic would result causing the farmer more injury than prosperity. Finally, farm-ers were upset that they had to sell their products in a fierce unprotected market while industry could sell their goods in a protected market. This complaint was valid and it could be listed as a contributing factor to the decline in prices of cotton and wheat, which were the major crops in America at the time. Thus, although there was some substance to the com-plaints and reasons of discontent of the farmers, many of their grievances were partially or completely invalid and more attributed to the severity of their circumstances instead of factual information and reasoning.

What can we see here? First and most striking is Paul's own personal stance: A child of the urban rust belt felt no sympathy for farmers from a century ago. His own views in favor of protectionist markets surfaced when he supported the farmers' complaint about that issue, but, generally, he assumed that totally external factors caused the farmers' plight and that their (the farmers') attributions were sadly misguided. In putting forth his conclusions, Paul wrote an eight-sentence, temporally situated conclusion that fit tightly with the question that was asked. He made use of causal connections between major ideas. His mastery of the use of documents was substantial. The documents are no longer thrown in as an added bonus but are integrated throughout the essay and then summarized seamlessly in the conclusion. Paul also managed to keep a steady hand on the voice in his essay, using an at times artificial, almost condescending third person. (Note: I am not arguing for using such a voice as historically appropriate, only noting that learning how to use one is not trivial.)

Learning to write history—or English, for that matter—is really very hard. Paul is engaged in a type of mimicry, but not a thoughtless or mindless kind. He is truly trying to understand how to make an argument that functions, and in his conclusion he pointed out somewhat reflexively that the "argument" of the farmers did not work ("the idea of a mass conspiracy against the farmer goes unproven"). His struggle with and growing mastery over a particular rhetorical form is worth acknowledging, and the nuances of exactly how brilliantly he positioned himself politically—he was, after all, sixteen years old—should not detract from his accomplishment.

In analyzing these essays, I am not suggesting we grade for or teach the use of connectors or node-link diagrams; nor am I suggesting that such increasing competence just develops. I am suggesting that by studying these features of essays, we can gain an appreciation of how hard the task of writing such essays truly is. We will realize that we need to go beyond telling students to "be coherent," "take a stance," or show their "personal voice."

A question that emerges after considering Paul's gradual mastery of the genre of writing DBQ essays is: How did he do that? If we reject simple development, we need to consider what role instruction played, if any. What might he have learned differently? How could he have been even more fruitfully supported? The data do not directly support answers to the follow-up questions but there are some hints.

One of the activities that was going on concurrently with Paul's writing activity was his responses in class to the discussion of historical facts and ideas. The talking and writing activities seem to have been mutually constitutive rather than directionally supportive. In some ways Paul made more rapid advancement in his speaking, while in other ways his writing improved more dramatically. Analyzing talk is more complex than analyzing writing. Where should a unit of speech be declared to start or end? (It is arbitrary, for example, where one inserts punctuation in a transcript, since we do not speak in punctuated forms.) Often the object of one incomplete sentence becomes the subject of the adjoining one. Modifiers float over a list, selectively enhancing some portions and not others; the listeners rarely have difficulty distinguishing, but transcribers and readers may flounder. The voices of other participants are literally and figuratively present, making the task of interpreting the talk more difficult. It is important to trace the development of talk because it is an indicator of disciplinary engagement. Talk appears more frequently than writing and is corrected more immediately. Although we do not address that point here because of space limitations, the development of spoken reasoning has been explored somewhat elsewhere.[12]

Over the course of the term Paul learned to balance the constraints of the ongoing class discussion, the new "facts" to be added, and the development of a causal story that made use of his knowledge and understanding. The development of this type of language skill is partly learned but partly constructed anew for each class. The teacher prompts and prods the students in each incoming group to reach the level of detail, exposition, and coordinated group conversation that he or she feels is appropriate. The constant rehearsal of pulling together ideas, supporting assertions with data, and presenting a coherent view to other students supports the mastery of similar activities in writing, but it is not directly instructional.

Paul learned to write history better both because of his own diligence and effort and because of the design efforts of and feedback from his teacher Sterling. The feedback on spoken explanations was ongoing and regular. However, Sterling gave more modest feedback on the written work. For the written work, she set increasingly complex goals. In the beginning of the year Sterling emphasized the issues of voice and thesis; as the year progressed she set goals of increasing the sophistication with which the documents in the various essays were incorporated. Further, in class discussions she became relentless in her insistence that students source their oral arguments and weave into their discourse not only their own voices but also those of the authors of textual positions. Paul was listening, and he seemed amazingly capable of responding to these cajolings by integrating others' arguments into his spoken and written efforts.

Paul learned a content of history, a manner of writing history, and a manner of discussing history. He learned that there were multiple perspectives and positions, and he learned how to express his own. His educational experiences flooded him with resources and opportunities. He had little time, however, to reconsider, recraft, and rebuild a case or position. Once considered, an idea was left, and he moved on to the next one. Instruction might have been even more effective if it had permitted or required a return to and a reexamination of both written and oral arguments.

Expanding the Questions and Locations for Study

The story of Paul's development in explanatory and narrative sophistication is interesting and goes on to a substantial level of proficiency. But, that is not the only point. Another point is that we have at our disposal a battery of tools for textual analysis that can help us learn how students and teachers gain command of and control over the rich details of history as well as the intricacies of building and developing a case within it. These tools allow us to consider very small local developments, such as the appropriate use of causal connections between concepts, or larger more global developments, such as the core structure of an argument and its use of supporting evidence. These analytic tools also allow us to consider those issues in the context of elements of accuracy and completion, not simply as uninterpreted indicators.

My research emphasizes the textual nature of history because I think that one of the gifts of history is its powerful use of language, in addition to its support for the development of one kind of understanding of who we are and why. The research also focuses on the classroom, on the practices of teaching, and on the consequences of teaching. I think it is critical to advance a program of research that continues to examine in detail how classroom activity works, thus developing a corpus of instructional cases. But, there are other venues where more informal learning of history occurs, such as museums and the media, which we need to start to explore in systematic ways. As I mentioned at the beginning of this chapter, history provides many opportunities, and we should come to understand those opportunities in the school setting, but exposure to historical ideas goes on beyond the academy and we should know more about how those opportunities contribute to historical understanding as well.

One function of history instruction is to lead students to the awareness of the "pastness" of things—to problematize the present. We live in a world of crises, successes, and patterns that do not spring forth unattached. Yet, students, and many adults, not only do not know the specific routes and roots of current circumstances; they also do not know that they could and should look for them. I am arguing for an increased awareness that the question of the past should be raised. To return to our hypothetical students at the beginning of this chapter, I would want them to know there is a past and to go looking for it when they confront important issues of the present. I want them to search out support for and opposition to their own dearly held positions. History requires a rigor of thought and behavior that may be even greater than its gift of helping us to understand who we are and how we got here. It presses on a flexibility of thinking and uses of evidence that can make us more mindful human beings. Our instruction must help to support people's search for themselves and their contexts while providing tools for distinguishing truth from fantasy.

I close with an anecdote that illustrates this issue of truth and fantasy. Part of my research in museums has led me to observe informally the behavior of visitors to our local natural history museum, particularly in Egypt Hall. One Sunday, I noticed a group of four middle-aged visitors clustered around a small, triangular, display case. They attracted my attention in part because they were so absorbed in the display and in part because they did not exactly seem to be typical museumgoers. From their broad Western Pennsylvanian accents, their clothing, and their interactions, I presumed they were retired blue-collar workers, a group not normally seen in Egypt Hall. This group appeared to be fascinated by a collection of small, metal objects that might have been hair ornaments but were labeled as "unknown." The men exclaimed repeatedly to the women that the metalwork was unbelievable and amazing, given that it was more than 3,000 years old. Their appreciation of the metalwork led me to further presume that the men might be retired steelworkers. Yet, I was still puzzled, since it was not obvious exactly what about the items in the display case was so intriguing. Finally, I heard one man say clearly, "See, that's what I'm telling you. It's impossible for them to have done that

3,000 years ago." Ah, thought I, historical skepticism. "They had to come from outer space—that's what they showed on T.V." Leonard Nimoy had defeated Flinders Petrie.[13]

Our move.[14]

NOTES

1. Suzanne Wilson has pointed out that there are some weaknesses in the particular chain of reasoning that has been followed in this and other work. In my work I identify highly effective teachers (through examining the performance of their students, through peer nomination, through supervisor nomination, and from personal visits—a selection process that can take up to two years). Identified teachers are then observed and their lessons recorded daily for a period of up to two years. The resulting data are analyzed and the effective practices described. What is missing from this process is an experimental manipulation that introduces the identified behaviors into a setting in which they are not present to see if they produce improved or excellent student performance.

2. See Terri Epstein, "Deconstructing Differences in African American and European American Adolescents' Perspectives on United States History," *Curriculum Inquiry* (in press); Peter Seixas, "Popular Film and Young People's Understanding of the History of Native American-White Relations," *The History Teacher* 26, no. 3 (1993), pp. 351-370; Peter Seixas, "Confronting the Moral Frames of Popular Film: Young People Respond to Historical Revisionism," *American Journal of Education,* 102 (1994), pp. 261-285; Peter Seixas, "Towards a Conception of Prior Historical Understanding," in A. Pace, ed., *Beyond Prior Knowledge: Issues in Text Processing and Conceptual Change* (Norwood, NJ, 1994); James V. Wertsch and Mark Rozin, "The Russian Revolution: Official and Unofficial Accounts," in James F. Voss and Mario Carretero, eds., *Learning and Reasoning in History,* International Review of History Education, vol. 2 (London, 1998), pp. 23–38; and Samuel Wineburg and Susan Mosborg, "Historical Thinking and Other Unnatural Acts," paper presented at the annnual meeting of the American Educational Research Association, San Diego, CA, April 1998, www.pdkintl.org/kappan/kwin9903.htm

3. See Madeleine Gregg, "The Impact of Museum Visits on Student Teachers' Understanding of Civil Rights and Racism," manuscript in preparation, University of Alabama, Tuscaloosa (1999); and Linda S. Levstik, "Articulating the Silences: Teachers' and Adolescents' Conceptions of Historical Significance," this volume.

4. These observations consist of more than 200 audio- and/or videotaped history lessons in middle- and high-school classrooms in different states as well as pre- and postinterviews with teachers and students, copies of all classroom handouts, and photocopies of student work.

5. A.P. (Advanced Placement) courses are offered in high school as college equivalency courses. They are considered challenging and are used to prepare students to take a national exam. A high score on the exam may allow a student entering college to be excused from a course or to be placed at a higher level in a sequence of courses.

6. For a discussion of this teacher's conceptualization of history, see Gaea Leinhardt, Catherine Stainton, and Salim Virgi, "A Sense of History," *Educational Psychologist*, 29(2) (1994), pp. 79–88. For a description of students' and teachers' historical explanations over time, see Gaea Leinhardt, "Weaving Instructional Explanations in History," *British Journal of Educational Psychology*, 63 (1993), pp. 46–74. For an analysis of historical reasoning, see Gaea Leinhardt, "History: A Time to be Mindful," in Gaea Leinhardt, Isabel L. Beck, and Catherine Stainton, eds., *Teaching and Learning in History* (Hillsdale, NJ, 1994), pp. 209–255.

7. See Kathleen McCarthy Young and Gaea Leinhardt, "Writing from Primary Documents: A Way of Knowing in History," *Written Communication*, 15(1) (1998), pp. 25–86.

8. In the complex ways of the school systems, schools receive additional funds for educating special students if and only if those students receive something different. Gifted students are considered special students; therefore, if A.P. classes are reserved for them alone, the school can get extra money for the courses.

9. See Gaea Leinhardt, "Paul's Voice, Paul's Pen: Learning to Reason in History," manuscript in progress, University of Pittsburgh, Learning Research and Development Center, Pittsburgh, PA; and note 7.

10. See note 7.

11. See Samuel Wineburg, "Historical Problem Solving: A Study of the Cognitive Processes Used in the Evaluation of Documentary and Pictorial Evidence," *Journal of Educational Psychology*, 83(1) (1991), pp. 73–87.

12. See Gaea Leinhardt, "Weaving Instructional Explanations in History," *British Journal of Educational Psychology*, 63 (1992), pp. 46–74.

13. Leonard Nimoy is an actor who played the original role of the Vulcan Mr. Spock in *Star Trek* and who has gone on to become a television commentator and host of programs about the paranormal and fantastic. Flinders Petrie (1853–1942) was a renowned archeologist and Egyptologist "who made valuable contributions to the techniques and methods of field excavation and invented a sequence dating method that made possible the reconstruction of history from the remains of ancient cultures." ("Petrie, Sir [William Matthew] Flinders," *Encyclopedia Britannica Online*, http://www.eb.com:180/bol/topic?eu=60991&sctn=1).

14. I am grateful to Sam Wineburg for his helpful comments and enthusiastic encouragement as I prepared this chapter. I also wish to thank the anonymous teacher and student who were the focus of my research for allowing me to observe them in action and Joyce Fienberg and Mary Abu-Shumays for their thoughtful assistance.

Chapter 13

Methods and Aims of Teaching History in Europe

A Report on Youth and History

Bodo von Borries

In this chapter I report the findings of two major studies conducted in Europe:

• In 1992 a survey was administered in East and West Germany, which had recently been united. About 6,500 sixth-, ninth-, and twelfth-grade history students were surveyed concerning their motivation to learn history, their knowledge and understanding of the subject, the use of media as a teaching tool, types of instruction, and the students' ability to interpret historical events and political decision-making. The goal was to probe historical consciousness, not simply the learning of school history. Students' teachers were surveyed as well. They responded to a shorter questionnaire about teaching, as well as to some questions that also appeared on the students' survey. This allowed researchers to make explicit comparisons between students and teachers.[1]

• In 1995 a similar study, *Youth and History*, was conducted,[2] but on a much larger scale. More than 30,000 students from twenty-seven different countries (and some ethnic minorities within these countries) were surveyed. The developmental perspective of the German study was replaced by a cultural comparison. Reasonably representative samples were collected of ninth-grade students in twenty-seven countries.[3] Again, a teachers' questionaire was administered.[4]

In this chapter I shall restrict myself to the cross-cultural study, *Youth and History*. In particular, I will focus on student and teacher responses in respect to questions about:

a. Methods of learning/strategies of teaching history
b. Aims of learning/teaching history
c. Problems of teaching history
d. Preferences concerning media used in history teaching
e. Interests in historical topics
f. Theoretical benefits/achievements of dealing with history

Strategies of Teaching History

Students' descriptions of two of the most frequent activities during history lessons[5] were "We use the textbook and/or worksheets" (M_{Europe} = 3.65) and "We listen to teacher's stories about the past" (M_{Europe} = 3.43) (see Table 13.1). Two other activities were more rare: "We use a range of activities, e.g. role plays, local projects or visiting museums/sites" (M_{Europe} = 1.57) and "We listen to radio programs or tapes or look at historical films and videos" (M_{Europe} = 1.87). The differentiation (Diff. > 1.50 and < 2.10) between "old" teacher-centered methods and "new" student-centered ones highlights the predominance of a rather traditional or old-fashioned form of history instruction. Other items, which described a moderately reformed or problem-centered teaching, were situated in the middle: "We discuss different

TABLE 13.1
Strategies of Teaching and Methods of Learning in Students' and Teachers' Perceptions
(means on scales from 1 to 5)

Methods of Learning	Means of the European history sample		
	Students	Teachers	Diff.
use the textbook and/or worksheets	3.65	3.91	+.26
listen to teacher's stories about the past	3.43	3.49	+.06
are informed of what was good or bad, right or wrong in history	3.00	3.06	+.06
discuss different explanations of what happened in the past	3.10	3.39	+.29
study historical sources, e.g., documents, pictures, or maps	2.69	3.36	+.67
use a range of activities, e.g., role plays, local projects, or visits to museums/sites	1.59	2.23	+.64
listen to radio programs or tapes or look at historical films and videos	1.87	2.46	+.59
retell and reinterpret history our/themselves	2.32	2.61	+.29

explanations of what happened in the past" ($M_{Europe} = 3.10$) and "We study historical sources, e.g., documents, pictures, or maps" ($M_{Europe} = 2.69$).

Students' reports in some respects agreed with those of teachers. Teachers tended to stress the "modern" or "open" methods more than students; yet they produced estimates of the frequency of traditional strategies as high as those of the students.[6] Thus, the rank order was nearly the same for both groups. If we assume the existence of some "socially desired answers" among the teachers and some "typically juvenile protest" among the students, truth (or reality) may be situated in the middle.

There are dramatic differences in the mean values from country to country. To give an example, "teachers' stories" are clearly more common in the postsocialist world of Eastern Europe and the Mediterranean world of Southern Europe than in the Nordic and Atlantic countries of Northwestern Europe (as well as Israel). Of course, this is not a geographical but a social phenomenon, closely connected to "modernization," "secularization," "individualization" (used in a strictly neutral and nonnormative sense!), and simply "wealth." "Students' activities" (e.g., projects) are much less common in Lithuania and Hungary, Israel, and even France than in Denmark, Britain, Portugal, and Palestine (West Bank and Gaza). Sometimes the reasons for a nation's score are obvious (e.g., the new national curriculum in Britain and the lack of marks for history in Denmark). Apparently, there are also specific national traditions and habits of instruction. We may call them cultures of learning and cultures of history.[7]

There are also cases in which students' and teachers' responses more or less paralleled each other. "Study of historical sources" is a good example. In six countries (Spain, Portugal, Belgium, France, England/Wales, and Scotland), all of them situated in Western Europe, students' as well as teachers' ratings have the highest means. In four countries (Iceland, Sweden, Russia, and Poland) where teachers' ratings had negative means, the estimates were noticeably low among the students as well. Thus, we find a rather high correlation between student and teacher ratings on the national level ($r = .82$, $N = 29$).

The case of "being informed about good and bad, right and wrong" is very similar ($r = .80$). The practice of transmitting authoritative (or even authoritarian) judgments and interpretations about history from teachers to students is much more common in traditional, collective, religious, and poor Eastern and Southeastern Europe than in Western and Northern Europe.

Aims of Teaching History

Teachers were asked to rate the importance of nine aims of teaching history; students were asked about eight of these aims. Defining goals is part of the professional work of teachers; students' observations and impressions are important as well. A comparison between teachers' ratings and students' impressions provides a measure of the transparency of the lessons, which likely has a large impact on the effectiveness of learning.

Generally, teachers did not drastically distinguish among the various goals (see Table 13.2); they estimated nearly all aims at nearly the same level of importance ($M_{Europe} \approx 3.95$). Nevertheless, "explanation of the situation in the world today and finding out of the tendencies of change" ($M_{Europe} = 4.20$) and "internalization of basic democratic values" ($M_{Europe} = 4.18$)[8] were rated highest; "understanding of the behavior of past persons by reconstructing the special situations and contemporary thoughts of the period" ($M_{Europe} = 3.75$) and "valuing of the preservation of historical relics and old buildings" ($M_{Europe} = 3.77$) rated lowest. There are in general only minuscule differences in the weight given to the major dimensions: collection of facts ($M_{Europe} = 3.99$), understanding

TABLE 13.2

Aims of Historical Instruction in Teachers' and Students' Perspective
(means on scales from 1 to 5)

Focus on	Means of the European history sample		
	Teachers	Students	Diff.
seek knowledge about the main facts in history	3.99	3.61	−.38
morally judge historical events according to the standards of human and civil rights	3.86	2.92	−.94
imagine what it felt like in the past, taking account of all viewpoints	3.83	3.12	−.71
understand . . . past persons by reconstructing the special situations and contemporary thoughts of the period when they lived	3.75	2.91	−.84
explain the situation in the world today and find out the tendencies of change	4.20	2.93	−1.27
acknowledge the traditions, characteristics, values, and tasks of our nation and society	3.96	3.21	−.75
value the preservation of historical relics and old buildings	3.77	3.04	−.73
be fascinated by and have fun dealing with history	4.00	2.78	−1.22
internalize basic democratic values	4.18	—	—

by reconstruction and empathy ($M_{Europe} \approx 3.80$), moral judgment and decision making ($M_{Europe} \approx 4.00$), aesthetic enjoyment and fascination ($M_{Europe} = 4.00$), preservation of the traditions ($M_{Europe} \approx 3.85$), and understanding of the present ($M_{Europe} = 4.20$).

Students' ratings differed greatly. The average for all goals was lower by nearly a full scale point ($M_{TeachersEurope} = 3.95$, $M_{StudentsEurope} = 3.07$). This may result from the fact that aims appear less important to students than to teachers, which is an expected result. Nevertheless, there were significant differences in the rankings given by the two groups. For students, "knowledge about the main facts in history" ($M_{Europe} = 3.61$) had clearly the highest level of importance, followed by "acknowledgment of the traditions, characteristics, values and tasks of our nation and society" ($M_{Europe} = 3.21$). All other goals had only neutral means; the lowest rank was given to "fun and fascination" during instruction ($M_{Europe} = 2.78$). This implies the existence of different sets of priorities among students and teachers. Confirmed by low correlations on class level, there seems to be insufficient transparency of the goals of history instruction. When students cannot discern the aims of their teachers, learning is obviously impeded.

There are significant national differences on the one hand and significant contrasts between teachers and students on the other. Let us begin with "knowledge of historical facts." Generally, teachers assigned a moderately higher rank to this aim than did students; but in some Eastern European (Lithuania, Russia, and the Czech Republic) and some Western European states (Portugal, Spain, and the Netherlands) the opposite was true. Several other countries showed large differences in teacher and student rankings of aims: Denmark, Sweden, Slovenia, Israel, and Palestine. The group of countries with the lowest means (including also Italy and the Netherlands) may suggest the influence of national crises in which teaching history is seen as imparting "mere knowledge." But this conclusion should be viewed cautiously, for the correlation between students' and teachers' estimations (on the national level) is a low one ($r = .31$, n.s.).

This poses a remarkable contrast to the aim "transmission of historical traditions," where national contrasts run parallel ($r = .66$), although teachers and students differ. Southeastern samples have the highest means by far; and Eastern ("postsocialist") adolescents apparently score higher than their Northern and Western counterparts. But there is another important trend: "Postsocialist" teachers (and those in Iceland and Israel as well) rank "tradition" as highly as their Middle Eastern counterparts do, but their responses are not echoed in students' responses. Perhaps this is a result of teachers offering "socially desired answers"; they may feel guilty about not having used the history classroom to transmit traditions.

Effects of Teaching Strategies

To push toward more complex relationships, two basic dimensions can be identified: "conventional strategies of teaching" and "innovative strategies of teaching."[9] It is worthwhile to examine some correlations for students and nations between teaching strategy and key concepts (see Table 13.3).[10]

TABLE 13.3
*Impacts of Teaching Strategies on Student and Country Level
(correlation coefficients)*

Constructs	Level of students (N > 31.000)		Level of countries (N = 30)	
	Conventional teaching strategies	Innovative teaching strategies	Conventional teaching strategies	Innovative teaching strategies
Correct chronological concepts	.10	−.11	.09	−.51
General historical motivation	.52	.23	.75	.07
Hitler as a monstrous criminal	.03	−.06	−.47	−.24
Hitler as a great politician	.03	.07	−.30	.21
1985 as a process of liberation	.15	.04	−.08	−.07
1985 as a defeat of socialism	.05	.11	.11	.59
Past influence of important events and mighty persons	.28	.07	.32	−.18
Past influence of scientific and technological progresses	.22	−.06	.05	−.14
Past influence of ecological and demographic processes	.17	.08	.11	.18
Negative associations to epochs	.14	−.00	−.22	−.19
Positive associations to epochs	.23	.07	.47	.11
Skeptical distance from collective identities	−.02	.08	.11	.47
Conventional affirmation of collective identities	.31	.04	.51	−.33
Conventional pragmatism	.29	−.02	.40	−.41
Fundamental altruism	.02	.13	.11	.46
Materialistic privatism	.11	−.02	−.30	−.08
Authoritarian traditionalism	.22	.16	.49	.20

The correlation coefficients on the student level and on the national level are often (but not always) parallel. Of course, the national level is confounded by the national particularities of learning and historical cultures, which cross-cultural research can help to reveal. Additionally, it must be remembered that correlation does not mean causation. There are, nonetheless, relatively high connections between conventional teaching strategies on the one hand and motivation, conventionalism, and traditionalism on the other. Conversely, innovative teaching strategies do not seem to correlate strongly with anything on the student level. Does this really indicate the irrelevance of concepts vis-à-vis innovative teaching?[11]

On the national level, the results are more clearly structured. The relation between conventional teaching on the one hand and strategies, motivation, traditionalism, and conventionalism on the other becomes even stronger, that is, conventional strategies are observed and followed more intensively in the countries that are relatively traditional, collective, religious, and poor. But, a relatively close relationship between innovative strategies on the one hand and a lack of historical knowledge, a lack of transmitted convention, skeptical distance from collective identities, and fundamental altruism on the other is obvious, also.[12] Autonomous, open-minded, unconventional thinking on the part of students has been an explicit demand in many European countries.[13] No wonder that conventional teaching strategies are so heavily criticized and leave adolescent students so unmotivated.

A measurement of the effectiveness of different teaching strategies was not the main aim of the *Youth and History* study. Other methods of investigation may be more adequate for this purpose, but the number of applicable studies is small. Despite the many problems of using surveys to tap student learning, the findings are not favorable with respect to "innovative teaching." The newer teaching strategies do not seem to promote students' motivation, acquisition of knowledge, methodological abilities, or moral judgments. These results are a bit dissatisfying,[14] but this is not the first time they have surfaced.[15] The picture of the effects of "conventional teaching" is more complex. This type of teaching may help to motivate students, but it does not seem to affect their knowledge; it may foster not only their pragmatism and conventionalism but also their traditionalism and even their authoritarianism. Apart from the finding on knowledge acquisition, this is by no means unexpected. Nevertheless, despite these limitations on our understanding these factors, any discussion about improvements in historical instruction must take into account the pattern of these findings.

Logical Levels of Forming Historical Meaning

Joern Ruesen has proposed a theory that suggests there are four types of meanings that can be derived from history and applied to the present.[16] Although this theory promises to be important for everyday instruction, it turned out to be rather difficult to use (and verify!) in empirical studies. First, an example: If you teach the American Civil War (1861–1865), there are various ways to apply its lessons to the present;[17] these are not necessarily mutually exclusive, but they should be distinguished clearly. You may interpret the Civil War:

1. As the starting point of a binding tradition of maintaining national unity and supporting "human and civil rights" at any cost (reverence for ancestors)
2. As an example of an escalating conflict that follows certain common patterns that have characterized earlier wars and that can be applied to situations in the present and in the future (applicable examples resulting from regularities in history)
3. As the object of criticism and rejection as some people reject "official" versions in favor of traditional interpretations, traditions, or historical generalizations (adversarial stance and critical perspective)
4. As an early stage in an ongoing process of national transformation and development, in which the war may be seen as a cause of feelings of historical identity among Americans today (Ruesen calls this the genetic type; the most mature stage, it emphasizes tension between continuity and change in a constant process of historical development).

Previous attempts to make empirical use of this theory had more or less failed. This time, we investigated the normative or programmatic convictions of students about what meanings historical study should produce. Of course, these theories are not identical with their practical application to concrete historical phenomena. Fortunately (but contrary to our skeptical point of view), a factor analysis with ten items[18] produced a very clear and internationally stable result with just four dimensions exactly representing the four logical levels of Ruesen's scheme.

Table 13.4 presents data on some nations' modes of forming historical meaning or extracting significance from the past. There appears to be a simple pattern for the differences between "traditional" and "critical" use of history. Scandinavian (except Icelandic) and Northwestern European adolescents are less "traditional" and more "critical" than the average. These students come from the most modernized, secularized, individualized, and wealthy countries. Just the opposite is true in several Eastern (Croatia and Bulgaria) and some Mediterranean (Portugal, Spain, Greece, and Turkey) countries, along with the remote Iceland, which scored above average in "traditional interpretation" and below average in "critical interpretation" of history. There is much evidence that these are more traditional, religious, collective, and poor societies (again in a completely descriptive sense).

Predictably, many countries did not fit into this simple scheme. In the Near East, the answers of Arab Israelis and of Palestinians from the West Bank and Gaza are at the same time more "traditional" and more "critical." This is easy to understand. Although highly "traditional" and collective as societies, Arab Israelis and Palestinians don't accept (mostly European) history because of their Muslim religion and their unenviable political fate in recent history. This situation undergirds their "critical," rather than the expected "uncritical," mode of interpreting history. This explanation becomes even more convincing when the views of Middle Eastern Arabs are compared to those of the Jewish Israeli majority with its simultaneously "antitraditional" and "anticritical" bias, perhaps suggesting that they feel "modernized" and yet "satisfied by history," too (the survey was administered 1995, the year of the Oslo Accord).

For the majority of "postsocialist" societies, the situation is even more complicated. Some nations (e.g., the Westernized Czech Republic, Hungary, but also Russia) are "nontraditional" and "noncritical" at the same time; they may have different reasons for this juxtaposition, as is suggested by the "genetic" interpretation. Others, like Poland and Ukraine, but also Estonia and Slovenia, have above average-ratings on both "traditionalism" and "criticism" in their attitude toward history. Are there long-term cultural traditions that lead to similar uses of history in different situations and to different uses in similar situations?

The distribution of means for the "regularities" type and the "genetic" type is less clear, and the contrasts are less marked. Great Britain, Norway, and Bulgaria express the greatest preference for historical examples or regularities, while Belgium, the Netherlands, and Israel express the

TABLE 13.4
Logical patterns of making historical meaning
(factor-scores on four orthogonal dimensions)

Participants	Traditional	Exemplary	Critical	Genetic
Iceland	.16	−.09	−.08	.02
Norway	−.29	.33	.22	−.01
Denmark	−.36	.05	.32	−.16
Sweden	−.48	.22	.25	−.01
Finland	−.15	−.04	.23	.21
Estonia	.14	.05	.11	−.28
Lithuania	−.01	−.13	.29	.81
Russia	−.20	−.06	−.26	.64
Ukraine	.35	−.04	.05	−.03
Poland	.29	−.22	.11	.06
Hungary	−.31	−.19	−.06	−.06
Czech Republic	−.44	.12	−.54	−.19
Slovenia	.14	−.18	.27	−.28
Croatia	.12	.13	−.16	.04
Bulgaria	.02	.33	−.18	−.15
Greece	.81	−.12	−.28	−.60
Turkey	.63	.21	−.47	.19
Israel (Jewish majority)	−.33	−.34	−.24	−.32
Israel (Arab minority)	.52	.13	.33	−.06
Palestine	.69	.03	.24	−.01
Portugal	.38	−.07	−.23	.06
Spain	.17	−.17	−.06	.02
Italy (national sample)	−.11	.07	−.28	−.03
South Tyrol (three language groups)	−.12	.13	.05	−.05
Germany	−.24	−.07	.38	−.16
Netherlands (delayed delivery)	−.55	−.27	.27	−.06
Belgium (Flemish)	−.57	−.34	.14	.08
Great Britain (England and Wales)	−.45	.38	.30	−.12
Great Britain (Scotland)	−.21	.26	.18	−.10
France	−.44	.19	.00	.35
Total	.00	.00	.00	.00

least.[19] This finding seems to reflect mainly a struggle inside the modernized countries. Surprisingly enough, the genetic interpretation does not generate distinctive reactions in the most "developed," most "modern" participants. This Northern and Western group of countries (which excludes France) is more or less neutral (< 22 percent of the standard deviation from the European average). Therefore, this approach mainly divides the group of postsocialist and Near Eastern samples: Students in Lithuania and Russia definitely claim to think genetically, but those in Estonia and Slovenia reject this mode; while Greece and Israel seem to abhor genetic interpretations Turkey tends to accept them.

We have to keep in mind that this is a normative expression of what history generally should mean.[20] These theoretical concepts may simply reflect distinctive national cultures and conventions, and they should not be confused with the real intellectual achievements, activities, and applications of the students. Nevertheless, it is obvious that history is most commonly used to reinforce traditions and provide examples.[21] Real genetic thinking has a complicated and elaborated structure; it may be a lofty goal for schools to strive for. It goes without saying, however, that different types of interpretations should be made more explicit to students during history instruction.

Although Ruesen stresses the exhaustive character of the taxonomy of logic patterns, this is mainly related to the cognitive domain. Looking to the affective and the moral domains, we may distinguish a series of different mental approaches to history as well. Four basic types exist: "antiquarian collection," "empathetic reconstruction," "moral judgment," and "aesthetic projection."[22] Fortunately, a factor analysis of eight items clearly confirms the distinction among these four dimensions.[23] Thus, we can also produce a "profile of mental approaches" for every national culture of history, though space limitations prevent detailed discussions here.

Some Preliminary Conclusions

It is possible to conclude from our findings that "open," "innovative," "modern," "student-centered," and "autonomous" strategies of teaching history are not as common as we might expect after twenty-five years of school reform. Teachers in many countries confess their ignorance of these approaches, as do students. On the other hand, "open," "innovative," "modern," "student-centered," and "autonomous" strategies of teaching history cannot be shown empirically to be superior to more traditional ones. At present, the opposite is perilously close to the truth. It is not easy to reconcile these two empirical trends. Of course, the search for effective methods of student-centered teaching cannot and should not be stopped. But, the theoretical and normative legitimation should be carefully reexamined.[24] There are at least six important arguments for this, supported by the European and German empirical studies.

1. At least in Europe, history teaching and its results are poorer than current theory or policy assume. Syllabi and textbooks are often documents of illusions.[25] Of course, this is not a problem particular to history, for it extends to the whole enterprise of schooling itself. It could easily be shown for geography, mathematics, or foreign languages, as well. The goal of empirical research is not to discourage teachers (as often is suggested) but—modestly—to provide a down-to-earth diagnosis that leads to better teaching (compare Ravitch and Morton, this volume).[26]

2. Teachers have real leeway in making instructional decisions, a flexibility they should take advantage of. The cultural comparisons presented here show that there is no single main street but rather many alternative paths in history instruction. This applies not only to the interpretation of special topics like the medieval period, colonialism, industrialization, or Hitler but also to more conceptual forms of historical sense making (see Table 13.4). National traditions have a strong influence on teachers' behavior. Nevertheless, teachers may discuss, reflect, and decide more openly what history is really about and why it is fruitful for students to study it (see Gutierrez and Weintraub, this volume).

3. Teachers' goals and decisions have to be communicated to the students more explicitly than they have in the past. Teachers should review their earlier choices of instructional method and should evaluate and generalize from these choices at the end of a teaching unit. The same is true for the choice of media. Teachers often refuse to adapt to students' media preferences (e.g., films instead of textbooks). Of course, giving way to some youthful fashion is not the king's way of education. But, if teachers do decide to go against students' wishes, they must justify their decisions with more cogent "transparency" (see Leinhardt and Rosenzweig, this volume).

4. Historical instruction cannot succeed in making students store an abridged, canonical version of world history in their minds, and it should not try. Rather, it should strive to enable them to study and judge history

responsibly and correctly. The reason is very simple: Most adolescents will experience at least sixty years of very important history over the course of rest of their lives—history that the teacher cannot know, because it has not yet happened.[27] It is unclear which parts of history will be necessary for identity and orientation in 2020 or 2040. Thirty years ago, few people anticipated the impact of the women's movement or of the environmental movement, or of the Baltic nations and the Eastern Central African nations that are now riven by murderous conflict (compare Dunn and Lowenthal, this volume).

5. History teaching should follow a "method-centered" and a "problem-centered" structure.[28] The hope is that carefully researched methods of problem solving can be transfered to new (and as yet unknown) cases. This autonomous studying and judging of history is the aim of the whole process of historical education, not a precondition or a self-evident ability at the beginning. The operations of historical thinking have to be introduced step by step, taking into account the fact that children differ from adults.[29] It is difficult to produce the systematic learning of the structure of history, and this cannot be replaced by the teaching of mere chronology (compare Lee and Ashby and Shemilt, this volume).

6. During the process of developing historical thinking, teachers cannot restrict themselves to a textbook and cover it chapter by chapter. Textbooks necessarily reflect "school" rather than "life," "results" rather than "problems." They strongly promote the illusion that historiography is a perfected and preconceived product, not an ongoing process of debate and disputation.[30] Therefore, historical instruction must go beyond school and textbook to embrace films, television, newspapers, museums, archives, citizens' initiatives and other evidence of life lived in a contentious historical culture (compare Levstik, Seixas, and Wineburg, this volume).

NOTES

1. The study is published as Bodo von Borries, *Das Geschichtsbewußtsein Jugendlicher* (Weinheim/München, 1995), and, in English, as Bodo von Borries, "Concepts of Historical Thinking and Historical Learning in the Perspective of German Students and Teachers," *International Journal of Educational Research* 27 (1997), pp. 211–220.

2. In the German case, it even served as a replication of the 1992 investigation.

3. The European project is also published as Magne Angvik and Bodo von

Borries, eds., *Youth and History: A Comparative European Survey on Historical Consciousness and Political Attitudes among Adolescents* (Hamburg, 1997).

4. Nevertheless, comparisons between students and teachers of only one nation have to be handled carefully because of the low number of teachers per nation (about thirty to fifty).

5. Nearly all questions used a five-point Likert-scale from "totally disagree" to "totally agree." Thus, group means above 3.25 indicate grades of acceptance, and those below 2.75 reflect a pattern of rejection. Means about 3.00 are neutral or undecided.

6. In Germany, teachers clearly don't report using traditional methods. They seem to feel uncomfortable about using these techniques; this is likely the result of long-standing debates about student-centered teaching.

7. Additionally, the frequency of use of various media in historical instruction may be compared to students' preferences. All over Europe, the empirical result is striking, although not unexpected: Students report the frequent use of those media they don't like (e.g., textbooks) and yearn for those they do like (e.g., museum visits, fictional films, and TV documentaries).

8. Because of a technical mistake, this item was omitted from the questionnaires given to students.

9. This is the result of a second-level factor analysis with four first-level constructs and two remaining single items. The structure is internationally and interculturally stable. "Instruction as verbal information and communication" and "concentration on knowledge of historical facts" constitute the "conventional strategies," while "instruction as manifold media and activities" and "instruction as retelling and reinterpreting" make up the "innovative strategies." The two most important constructs of the aims "concentration on fun with historical traditions" and "concentration on operations of historical thinking" show loadings on both factors (a bit higher on the first).

10. For the analysis on the national level, the data are aggregated. The sample size ($N = 30$) is very low, near the minimum for correlations. Thus, the threshold of confidence is rather high ($r \approx .37$). Nevertheless, many of the coefficients are significant or highly significant.

11. Of course, self-report data are inferior to data obtained by observing instruction. In Germany there is no research tradition of observational classroom research.

12. It is worthwhile to mention a distinctly strange phenomenon: "Conventional teaching strategies" go along with lower scoring in both Hitler concepts ("monstrous criminal" and "great politician"), and "innovative teaching strategies" is correlated with higher scoring in "Eastern Europe since 1985 as a defeat of socialism."

13. Nevertheless, "innovative teaching strategies" are not always a sign of "modernity"; both Arab samples score very high.

14. Of course, many detailed analyses were conducted; the outcomes were compared not only to students' reports about teaching but to the teachers' own reports of their methods, goals, and topics as well. Additionally, the calculations were made for special items (instead of constructs) and for single countries (instead of Europe overall). The findings vary a bit but don't generally change the basic results.

15. Only one study shall be mentioned here: Sabine Gruehn, "Vereinbarkeit kognitiver und nichtkognitiver Ziele im Unterricht," *Zeitschrift für Pädagogik* 41 (1995), pp. 531–553. The problem is discussed in more detail in Bodo von Borries, "Historische projektarbeit im vergleich der methodenkonzepte: Empirische befunde und normative überlegungen," in B. Schönemann et al., eds., *Geschichtsbewußtsein und Methoden historischen Lernens* (Weinheim, 1998), pp. 276–306

16. See Joern Ruesen, *Studies in Metahistory*, edited by Pieter Duvenge (Pretoria, South Africa, and Providence, RI, 1993); *Historische orientierung über die arbeit des geschichtsbewußtseins, sich in der zeit zurechtzufinden* (Köln/Weimar/Wien, 1994); and *Historisches lernen: Grundlagen und paradigmen* (Köln/Weimar/Wien, 1994). See also B. von Borries, "Linking time levels in historical consciousness" in J. Létourneau, ed., *Le lieu identitaire de la jeunesse d'aujourd'hui: Études de cas* (Paris/Montréal, 1997), pp. 139–174.

17. These applications may be done consciously or unconsciously, explicitly or implicitly. It is impossible to avoid them but necessary to admit and discuss them frankly.

18. Eight characteristic "meanings of dealing with history" were combined with two "traditionalist" goals of historical instruction. Some others were excluded in order to improve the intercultural stability. The respective loadings are always high (> .66) and usually very high (> .80). There is only one double loading: "background of present way of life" is more "genetic" and less "exemplary."

19. All others are less than 25 percent of the standard deviation from the international mean.

20. The normative and general character is obvious, although the questions literally read: "What does history mean to you?" and "What do you concentrate on in your history lessons?"

21. To a high degree, criticism is confounded with lack of motivation or even disgust in dealing with history. Fifteen-year-old students seem to begrudge the fact that they have to invest even more time in studying history if they want to deny "false" obligations and conclusions from the past.

22. This is a surprising result, because many examples in the previous empirical studies show that students are not really able or willing to distinguish between "empathetic reconstruction" and "moral judgment." This is an important point because both aspects are necessary for historical thinking.

23. The analysis was done with six "methods of learning" and two "meanings

of dealing with history" ("importance of knowledge about the past" and "source of adventure and excitement"). The solution with four factors is sufficiently stable for nearly all national samples.

24. Instead of producing preliminary (or premature) advice for more effective teaching, there is another (perhaps a more important) task: to provide a better description of the theoretical and practical problems ("causes of disappointing results") and to undertake a long-term research program. But to do so requires more time and space, as well as more careful articulation of what we mean when we say "student-centered" or "open."

25. In the German empirical studies, it was found that many students are not able to understand their history textbooks because of the students' inadequate reading skills.

26. Conservatives often fear that catastrophes will occur if changes are made in methods of teaching history. But there has never been a "good old epoch" before the liberal reform, a period when students truly learned history well (see Wineburg, this volume). If there is any catastrophe, it is as old as compulsory historical instruction itself. Progressives always hope for a "brave new world" caused by radical reforms in the teaching of history. Although earnest attempts at change persist in the late twentieth century, they have for the most part not been fully successful at effecting improvements in the average school.

27. In the debate about teaching reform, this argument is often forgotten, but its importance can be easily calculated. If you are older than fifty, as I am, you have only to remember explicitly which periods you could not have learned about in high school: everything since the start of the Cold War in 1948. This insight has another implication: All the history up to 1948 has had to be seriously abridged in order to make time to teach the postwar epoch. What parts of your own school syllabus in history have been shrunk or eliminated?

28. *Youth and History* presents many empirical hints for moving in this direction, such as students' specific interest in contemporary history and family history, students' contempt for textbooks and preference for museums and films, the contrast between students' theoretical acknowledgement of the importance of understanding foreign or strange behavior and their practical incapacity to do so, and students' strong feeling for changes in descriptive phenomena and their weak feeling for changes in causes or determinants. But this is another article.

29. At least in Germany, theories of historical learning have yet to sufficiently engage Piagetian and post-Piagetian debates.

30. Our empirical studies have shown that students identify history with important facts and sources with objectivity. Even those textbooks that explicitly want to foster students' autonomous thinking are often misunderstood as a source of stored facts.

Chapter 14

How Americans Use and Think about the Past

Implications from a National Survey for the Teaching of History

Roy Rosenzweig

In the late 1980s, Lynne Cheney, then chairwoman of the National Endowment for the Humanities, began a widely circulated pamphlet that she called *American Memory* with the declaration that "a refusal to remember . . . is a primary characteristic of our nation."[1] Although Cheney wrote from a conservative position, the recent sense of alarm about "American memory" has not been confined to cultural conservatives. Commentators on the political left have also raised concerns about the overall level of historical knowledge and interest. "Most Americans," the historian Michael Wallace wrote in a 1987 essay, "The Politics of Public History," "do not have a high regard for history. We tend to focus on today and tomorrow, not yesterday. This may be because our culture undercuts our capacity to make connections in time." "Ours is," he concluded, "a *historicidal* culture." Writing in the *Radical History Review* in 1981, Michael Frisch similarly described "our public culture" as "characterized by a broad and seemingly willful disengagement from the past."[2]

Laments about students and a public uniformed or uninterested in the past have also become a staple of mainstream professional historical discourse. In innumerable variations, such laments are repeated wherever college professors, high school teachers, museum curators, and other history professionals gather in faculty lounges, at department meetings, and at formal professional meetings. Speaking to the members of the American Historical Association in his 1989 Presidential Address, the distinguished historian Louis R. Harlan deplored the "present public ignorance of our cultural heritage." "This ignorance and indifference," he argued, "has alarming implications for the future of our nation and our historical profession."[3] Across the ideological spectrum of historians, there is a remarkably wide agreement that Americans are disengaged from the past.

This general dismay about public disregard of the past has infected popular commentators as well as worried historians. A column by the *Washington Post* writer Jonathan Yardley is illustrative precisely because it puts the matter in such clichéd terms: "By and large we Americans don't know history because we are indifferent to it, except on those rare occasions when it bumps up against our real or fancied self-interest. We are an impatient people, ever on the go, so the notion of taking the time to devote careful study to the past has never sat well with us." You do not have to go far in the media or in professional circles to find broad agreement that the public cares little and knows less about the past.[4]

For all this widespread anxiety about historical indifference and ignorance, we have had surprisingly little investigation of what Americans do know and think. To be sure, there is considerable evidence on the factual historical knowledge of students, although there is also much debate about the meaning of that evidence.[5] But, regardless of where one stands in those debates, they do not address the actual content of popular historical consciousness—the ways that Americans use and think about the past and whether or not Americans are, in fact, disengaged from or indifferent toward the past.

In 1994 Dave Thelen and I set out to investigate the seemingly simple but largely unstudied question of how Americans use and understand the past. With the help of the Center for Survey Research at Indiana University, we undertook a telephone survey of 808 Americans, a representative cross-section of the nation. Such a sample size allows for comparisons based on age, gender, income, and education but is less good at capturing subgroups based on race and ethnicity. As a result, we also included three "minority" samples of African Americans, Mexican Americans, and Sioux Indians, about 200 people in each group.[6] Although we asked a number of quantifiable, closed-ended questions, we confined those questions to about ten minutes of interviews that lasted an average of forty minutes. Thus, the results of our survey are embodied not only in four thick volumes of tables but even more in 850,000 words of transcribed phone conversations that lasted about 1,000 hours. Despite this qualitative emphasis, the survey was far from a full-scale ethnography, and it shares the

limitations and biases of most phone surveys. Still, it offers the only existing systematic evidence on what a cross-section of Americans think
about the past.

What did we find? Contrary to the conventional wisdom, our survey
documents the widespread nature of American engagement with the
past. We can get an overview of the extent of this historical activity from
Table 14.1, which summarizes the percentage of Americans pursuing
each of the ten past-related activities we inquired about. More than half
of the people in the national sample had pursued at least five of the activities on our ten-item checklist in the past year; almost no one reported
that he or she had done none of the ten activities.

To find out more than the simple frequency of activities, we asked our
respondents to use a 10-point scale to describe the intensity of their engagement with the past. Most had no trouble assigning a number between 1 and 10 to describe how "connected to the past" they felt when
they celebrated holidays, gathered with their families, studied history in
school, read history books, visited history museums and historic sites,
and watched historical films and television programs (see Table 14.2). If
we decide that a choice of 8, 9, or 10 indicates a close association with the
past, then more than half our respondents felt very strongly connected to
the past on holidays, at family gatherings, and in museums.

A thirty-two-year-old physical therapist reported feeling most connected to the past in the three contexts most often given by our respondents. Asked to explain why he felt connected to the past at holiday celebrations, he answered, "Usually when you celebrate holidays, you have
your ancestors there—your grandmothers and great-grandmothers.
They're bringing a part of their traditions and so forth into the celebration." For him, all family events evoked the past:

> Because when you gather with your family, everyone has stories about the
> way things used to be. It's always story time. We don't gather for that par-
> ticular purpose, but we always end up telling stories, and it inevitably ends
> up being about what life was like when they were kids.

Although respondents described the past as being with them in many
settings, they shared the sense that the familial and intimate past, along
with intimate uses of other pasts, mattered most. More than two-thirds
said that they felt very strongly connected to the past when gathering
with their families; more than half said the same about visiting museums
and historic sites and celebrating holidays, activities they usually did with

TABLE 14.1

Percentage of Americans Who Have Done the Following in the Past 12 Months

Looked at photographs with family or friends?	91.1%
Taken any photographs or videos to preserve memories?	83.3
Watched any movies or television programs about the past?	81.3
Attended a family reunion or a reunion of some other group of people with whom you have shared a common experience?	64.2
Visited any history museums or historic sites?	57.2
Read any books about the past?	53.2
Participated in any hobbies or worked on any collections related to the past?	39.6
Looked into the history of your family or worked on your family tree?	35.8
Written in a journal or diary?	29.3
Taken part in a group devoted to studying, preserving, or presenting the past?	20.2

TABLE 14.2

How connected to the past do you feel (1–10 scale)?

		Percent choosing	
	Mean	8–10	1–3
Gathering with your family	7.9	67.7%	6.7%
Visiting a history museum or historic site	7.3	56.0	8.6
Celebrating a holiday	7.0	52.7	13.8
Reading a book about past	6.5	39.5	12.0
Watching a movie or TV program about the past	6.0	27.4	14.0
Studying history in school	5.7	27.8	20.8

family members. Only sixteen people in the national sample gave gathering with their family the lowest possible "connectedness" score of 1.

Respondents felt most unconnected to the past when they encountered it in books, movies, or classrooms. They felt most connected when they encountered the past with the people who mattered the most to them, and they often pursued the past in ways that drew in family and friends. Five-sixths of those surveyed took pictures to preserve memories of their experiences; more than nine-tenths looked at photographs with family and friends; more than one-third worked on their family trees or investigated the history of their families; almost two-thirds attended reunions, three-quarters of them family reunions. More than half of the respondents who pursued hobbies or collections related to the past said that family members had initially interested them in that hobby or that the hobby preserved a family tradition. Typically, a twenty-five-year-old student from Massachusetts described refinishing a small chest and dollhouse from her grandmother that she wants "to pass down as an heirloom . . . if I have a daughter someday."

Whatever questions we asked, respondents emphasized the importance they attached to the intimate past and intimate uses of the past. Asked to "name a person, either a historic figure or someone from your personal past, who has particularly affected you," 52 percent named family members—29 percent parents, 14 percent grandparents, 9 percent other family members—while 36 percent named public or historical figures. Reminded that the past includes "everything from the very recent past to the very distant past, from your personal and family past to the past of the United States and other nations," respondents were asked, "What event or period in the past has most affected you?" Again, the largest number (nearly two-fifths) mentioned a purely personal event such as the birth, death, marriage, or divorce of a loved one.

For many respondents, the line blurred between "personal" and "national" pasts. Some turned national events into settings for personal stories. For example, more than a tenth reported a public event in which they participated (most often by fighting in a war); more than a quarter chose a public event that had personal significance. Rather than abstractly discussing the significance of World War II or the assassination of John F. Kennedy, they talked about how such an event had figured in their personal development or the setting in which they heard about it. Only one in five chose a public event without also indicating some personal association with that event.

We tried to get at how people thought about the past when we asked which past was most important to them: that of their family, their ethnic or racial group, their community, or the United States. Sixty-six percent named the past of their family. Twenty-two percent named the United States, 8 percent chose their racial or ethnic group, and 4 percent chose their community. Ethnic and racial groups varied in how they responded to this question (see Table 14.3), but every subgroup of the population—men and women; young and old; rich and poor; white, black, and Indian—listed family history first. To put the statistical findings of our study in a single sentence: Almost every American deeply engages the past, and the past that engages them most deeply is that of their family.

Harder to quantify but still evident in the answers offered are the "uses" that Americans make of the past. Most fundamentally, Americans make what we could call "intimate" uses of the past; they turn to the past to live their lives in the present. Through the past, they find ways to understand and build relationships to those close to them and to answer basic questions about identity, morality, mortality, and agency. Individu-

TABLE 14.3
Most Important Pasts

We asked our respondents: "Knowing about the past of which of the following is most important to you—the past of your family, the past of your racial or ethnic group, the past of the
community in which you now live, or the past of the United States?"

Group	White	National	Black	Mexican-American	Oglala Sioux
Family	69%	66%	59%	61%	50%
Race/Ethnic	4	7	26	10	38
Locality	3	4	4	7	7
U.S.	23	22	11	22	5

als turn to their past experiences to grapple with questions about where
they come from and where they are heading, who they are and how they
want to be remembered, and whether and how they can make a difference
in the world. A young woman from Ohio spoke of giving birth to her first
child, which caused her to reflect upon her parents and the ways that
their example would help her to become a good mother. An African
American from Georgia told how he and his wife were drawn to each
other by their shared experiences and lessons learned from growing up in
the South in the 1950s. A Massachusetts woman traced much of her
guarded attitude toward life to her witnessing the assassination of John F.
Kennedy on television when she was a child.

Interestingly, these patterns often cut across standard sociodemo-
graphic categories like age, income, and race that often divide people. We
spent considerable time with computers and statistical programs looking
for variations in patterns of responses only to discover that, to a surprising degree, participation in historical activities and a sense of "connectedness" to the past are not for the most part tied to particular social
groups or backgrounds. Our survey, for example, offers little support for
the claim that an interest in the past or in formal history is the property
of "elites." Income, for example, significantly affects participation in only
one activity: taking photographs or videos, which requires money to pur-
chase the equipment.

Nevertheless, gender and education do affect the statistical patterns to
some degree. Women, for instance, reported higher levels of participation
in seven of the ten historical activities we asked about (for example, looking into the past of their families or participating in reunions); they also
told us they felt more connected to the past in two of the six settings we
described. More women than men said they felt strongly connected to the

past at holiday celebrations (with a mean score of 7.6 for women and 6.3 for men) and family gatherings (a mean score of 8.3 for women and 7.4 for men).[7] For women, as for men, the intimate and familial past matters most, but for women it is even more important. Still, the difference is a matter of degree rather than a sharp divergence. Similarly, even when education most clearly affects the pursuit of a particular activity, many people with limited education still participate. More than twice as many college graduates as non–high school graduates had read a history book or visited a history museum or historic site in the past year. Yet, about one-third of those without a high school diploma had done both.

Probably the question that showed the most substantial demographic variations was the one that asked which area of the past people thought was most important. (See Tables 14.3 and 14.4.) Seventy-three percent of the women, for example, selected family history, compared to 58 percent of the men. An even larger difference emerged along racial lines. Black Americans were more than six times as likely as whites to choose the history of their ethnic or racial group as most important to them, and Oglala Sioux Indians from Pine Ridge Reservation were almost ten times as likely to make the same choice. At the same time, however, both African Americans and Sioux Indians, like white Americans, still chose family history as most important. Thus, what is particularly interesting— and this finding is much more pronounced in the open-ended responses than in the quantitative answers—is the way that members of these groups connect the past of their family to the past of their racial group.

Whereas when most white Americans talked about "we" or "our" they referred to their own family, African Americans meant, as one interviewee put it, "*our* race, *our* people." Similarly, Sioux Indians talked regularly about "our history," "our heritage," "our culture," "our tribe," "our language," and "our traditions"—phrases that would be hard to find in the interviews with white Americans. Explaining her family's participation in the Wounded Knee Pine Ridge Survivors Association, one woman commented: "That is our identity, part of our culture. A way of life that we have to teach our children. . . . If we lose our culture then we cease to be Indians." For the Oglala Sioux, a strong sense of group identity both drew upon and reinforced a distinctive sense of the past—a shared set of historical references to particular events, places, and people that they repeatedly invoked and used, albeit not always in the same ways. Asked about an event or period in the past that "has most affected you," the Sioux drew their answers from a specifically Indian historical chronology. Almost

TABLE 14.4
Percentage of Selected Groups Listing U.S. History as Most Important

Men 65 or over	42%
Household income over $75,000 per year	31
White Americans without high school diploma	31
All men	29
People 65 or over	28
White Americans	23
Postcollege education	22
All Americans	22
Mexican Americans	22 (minority sample)
Women	16
18–29-year-olds	13
Household income under $15,000 per year	12
African Americans	13 (national sample)
African Americans	11 (minority sample)
African Americans without high school diploma	7 (minority sample)
African Americans under thirty years of age	6 (minority sample)
Pine Ridge Sioux Indians	5
Pine Ridge Sioux Indian men	1

two-thirds cited events from American Indian history, with most of them talking about the 1973 occupation of Wounded Knee, the 1890 massacre at Wounded Knee, the confinement of American Indians to reservations, the signing and violation of various treaties between American Indians and the U.S. government, and Columbus's arrival in the New World. Not a single white respondent cited any of these events.

The Sioux described a historical landscape just as distinct as their timeline. Sioux Indians (about two-thirds of our sample), more than any other ethnic or racial group, reported that they had visited a museum or historic site during the previous year. They almost always chose such places as the Wounded Knee massacre site, Crazy Horse Mountain, Little Bighorn Battlefield National Monument, and the Sioux Indian Museum in Rapid City, South Dakota. At least twenty-six Oglala Sioux noted that they had visited the giant sculpture of Chief Crazy Horse that is being carved in the Black Hills. Only fifteen mentioned visiting nearby Mount Rushmore, and most of them did so only in the context of a visit to the Crazy Horse monument.

African Americans also constructed distinctive historical narratives. These respondents talked about distinctive historical holidays (e.g., Martin Luther King's birthday), distinctive historical sites (the civil rights museums in Birmingham and Atlanta, the Frederick Douglass House in the Anacostia), and distinctive historical sources (especially

Roots and *The Autobiography of Malcolm X*, both, in effect, written by Alex Haley). But, what was most distinctive of all was not so much the obvious racial cast to these responses but the structure of the larger narrative often told in the interviews. To a startling degree, black Americans constructed a story of progress when they looked at the past, a rather traditional story that was hard to find among white Americans. When they named public events that had affected them, about one-third of the African-American respondents talked about change for the better or worse, and of that third, almost three-quarters described change for the better. By contrast, more than four-fifths of white respondents described change for the worse.

Black respondents often used metaphors of distance or travel when they drew lessons from past events, talking about "how far Martin Luther King brought us" or "where we came from to how we struggled to where we are today." Black respondents most often found a story of progress in the civil rights struggle. A Detroit woman spoke about "freedom" and then defined it by saying, "Thank God we're able to drink from the same fountains as other races, we're able to vote, and we're able to go places." For a sixty-five-year-old Detroit woman, the changes could be summarized in two incidents separated by six decades. The first was from her Arkansas childhood: She and her father were run off the road and threatened by a white man who was angry because he'd been turned away at a country store that had given her father credit. "We didn't deal with white people too much," she said of those days. The second was a recent shopping trip: "When we got groceries, a young [white] man took our groceries to the car. . . . I think it's so nice. It's just so different now."[8]

This tendency to construct collective narratives about the past and to use materials from those collective narratives to understand their lives in the present, which is so evident among African Americans and Sioux Indians, is much less marked among most white Americans. To be sure, there are times and places in which white Americans draw upon narratives about the past of particular communities, regions, or ethnic groups. And, all Americans sometimes make use of our national history. Yet among the 624 white Americans we called, we heard people making profound use of the intimate pasts of their families. What we didn't hear—or didn't hear very loudly or very often—was people using other narratives and historical materials in the same ways. For most white Americans, then, the "usable past" was largely the story of their own families. Or, when they used bits and pieces of the national past, they did so in intimate ways that privatized the public past and used it to answer more personal questions about identity, morality, or mortality.

Equally significant, we did not hear many of the conventional, textbook narratives of linear progress that are often associated with capital "H" history. Respondents rarely mentioned the triumphal national narrative favored by those who write textbooks or advocate history as a means of teaching patriotism and civics. Instead, they placed national events within their familial stories or made national personages into familiar figures in personal narratives. Or they talked about national events as disconnected incidents not linked to a larger narrative, and about national figures and events in distant and attenuated terms, rather than the rich terms they used for describing moments in their personal and family histories. Or they did all of these.[9]

Ironically, it is particularly among Sioux Indians and African Americans that American history as a progressive narrative is kept alive, albeit not in its most easily recognizable forms. They offer something much more like a national narrative—but with a bitter twist. In this counternarrative, the arrival of Columbus, the westward movement of European settlers, slavery, and emancipation add up to an American history in which blacks and Indians have been oppressed and betrayed by whites, who then depict their actions in movies and textbooks that lie about Indians and exclude African Americans. A thirty-seven-year-old Pine Ridge Sioux Indian summarized this perspective when he described his own sense of the past as "pretty much opposite" that of "most of the Americans." "Well," he pointed out, "when they were fighting the Civil War, we were fighting the Cavalry and when they were homesteading the West, we were stuck on the reservations. . . . Whereas they gained their freedom, we lost ours."

Meanwhile, there is some evidence that traditional textbook narratives focused on the American national story are losing their appeal for many white Americans. Significantly, Americans over age sixty-five in our survey were more than twice as likely as those under age thirty to describe the history of the United States as most important to them. While some might be inclined to blame an insufficiently nationalist school curriculum, I believe that the fading of the power of the national story is rooted in much deeper changes than shifts in school curriculum—for example, the suspicion of traditional nationalism fostered by American misadventures in Vietnam and the globalization of the economy. Some will regard the apparent waning of nationalism as a threat; others will see it as an opportunity. But, regardless of your view of either ethnic or civic nationalism, there is no reason to automatically equate History with the Nation State even though that equation has long been at the heart of professional historical practice. "Historians," as Eric Hobsbawm has observed, "are to nationalism what poppy growers in Pakistan are to heroin addicts: We supply the essential raw material for the market." But, history and historians can supply other markets beyond those organized by nation and nationalism, and, in any case, popular history-making is not governed by that market structure. The past, our survey respondents suggest, has many mansions, and in America at least, the past is very much alive, even if traditional textbook narratives of the national past seem to be gasping for life.

What are the implications of such findings, particularly for the teaching of history in the schools in the United States? Here I should begin by offering some cautions. First, we need to keep in mind the well-known limitations of all surveys and this one in particular. Although we asked a number of questions that bear on history in the schools, that was not the primary focus of this study. Moreover, because we wanted to get a cross-section of the entire population, our interviewees ranged in age from eighteen to ninety-one and were located throughout the continental United States. As a result, their reports on encounters with school-based history reflect experiences widely scattered in time and place. A more focused (and considerably more costly) inquiry would look at specific cohorts of people who studied history in particular schools at particular times. Second, my analysis reflects the perspective of someone whose own experience is with teaching history at the college level.

Despite the limitations of the data and my own expertise, I think it is useful to speculate on what this survey, which is after all the first one ever done on this subject, might tell us about teaching history in the schools. In so doing, we need to confront the one apparent exception to the ubiquitous sense of connectedness with the past that I reported. Ironically, our survey finds people most detached from the past in the place that they most systematically encountered it—the schools. Asked to identify how connected to the past they felt in seven different situations, they ranked classrooms dead last with an average score of 5.7 on a 10-point scale (as compared, say, with 7.9 when they gathered with their families). Whereas one-fifth of respondents reported feeling very connected to the past in school (by giving those experiences a rank of 8 or higher), more

TABLE 14.5
Trustworthiness of Sources of Information about the Past—by Racial/Ethnic Group

	National	White	African American	Mexican American	Pine Ridge Sioux
Museums	8.4	8.5	8.1	8.6	7.1
Personal accounts	8.0	8.0	8.4	8.3	8.8
Conversation with someone who was there	7.8	7.8	7.9	8.2	8.0
College history professors	7.3	7.4	7.0	8.3	7.1
High school history teachers	6.6	6.7	6.2	7.5	5.9
Nonfiction books	6.4	6.4	5.6	6.6	5.4
Movies or TV	5.0	4.9	5.2	6.0	4.2

than two-thirds felt very connected with the past when they gathered with their families. When we asked some respondents "to pick one word or phrase to describe your experiences with history classes in elementary or high school," negative descriptions significantly outweighed positive ones. "Boring" was the single most common word offered. In the entire study, the words "boring" or "boredom" almost never appeared in connection with the pursuit of the past, with the significant exception of when respondents talked about studying history in school—where it comes up repeatedly.[10]

To be sure, the comparison that our survey posed between schools on the one hand and family, holidays, films, museums, and books on the other hand is not an entirely fair one. Schools are the one compulsory activity that we asked about; the others are largely voluntary (though some might disagree about family gatherings). The interesting comparison—though not one we asked about, unfortunately—would evaluate how students feel about history classes compared to other subjects that they study in school. Is history viewed as more or less "boring" than, say, math or English?

In addition, these negative comments about classroom-based history were not always reflected in remarks about specific teachers. Some of this can be seen in a question about sources that people "trust" for information about the past (see Table 14.5). To be sure, respondents were most likely to trust people close to them, such as grandparents and eyewitnesses, but they still found teachers a more trustworthy source than books or films.

An even more positive assessment of some teachers comes in the qualitative comments that many offered. Respondents valued teachers for some of the same reasons they valued family members: They brought experience to supplement books. Their authority came from having lived things as well as having studied them. A forty-year-old African American from Park Forest, Illinois, recalled that, when her high school class reached the subject of civil rights, her teacher "had marched and had been there and he knew what was true because he had been there and talked with those people." Like relatives, teachers "have lived through things . . . more than I have been through," reported an eighteen-year-old Hispanic from Houston. And teachers were honest. Whereas books and movies "tend to glamorize things," believed a secretary in her late forties from Portsmouth, Ohio, teachers "really try to teach the truth." In contrast to books and television programs that distorted the past, many respondents agreed with the assessment of the forty-year-old trucking company manager from Beverly, Massachusetts, of his high school history teachers: "I just saw them as very honest people."

Respondents likewise praised teachers for their dedication to the personal growth of students. They were individuals who took responsibility, instead of faceless purveyors of the past. "TV and movies . . . are based on a producer I don't know, and in a book I don't know the individual" author and "I wouldn't have a personal feeling," began a mechanical engineer from Royal Oak, Michigan. But, "with a teacher you'd at least have some personality. It'd be a one-to-one relationship versus a removed, an unknown person writing the book." Many viewed history teachers as agents through whom the community passed on to young people the formative stories of where their community values had come from, the framing experiences they needed to know. Like parents, teachers were role models who assisted the development of young people. Since "kids need someone to look up to," explained a thirty-nine-year-old property manager from Pocatello, Idaho, "most of them will look up to teachers as someone who is truthful and honest."

Respondents remembered how history teachers had assisted their development. They talked of teachers who treated them like members of their family, who engaged them with the past in the same spirit that family members did. "Teachers were more like a family in school," recalled a forty-eight-year-old police dispatcher from Piscataway, New Jersey. "When you did wrong you got punished. There was respect." Some teachers passed on stories about their families as well as their nation: An African-American day care provider from Little Rock reported that "usually high school teachers have helped someone in the family in

TABLE 14.6
Connectedness to the Past on Six Occasions by Age—National Sample

	Total	Age				Significance test
		18–29	30–44	45–64	65+	
Family	7.9	7.6	7.8	8.2	8.0	NS
Historic Site	7.3	7.1	7.3	7.2	7.5	NS
Holiday	7.0	6.4	7.0	7.3	7.4	.01
Reading a book	6.5	6.2	6.4	6.6	7.0	NS
Watching movie	6.0	5.9	6.0	5.9	6.3	NS
School	5.7	5.5	5.6	5.6	6.5	.00

the past. My teachers knew me and someone in my family. And I think they would be able to know something about someone in your family that maybe you didn't know." They appreciated teachers who cared about them. "Right now I'm a senior in high school," explained a nineteen-year-old Virginian, who had "a lot of confidence" in a particular teacher because "he's the only one that took time to make sure that we understand what's going on."

Although teachers could make history classrooms resemble the settings in which, and the ways that, respondents liked to engage the past, most Americans reported that history classrooms more often seemed to them to be shaped by remote bureaucrats, to include a content that was removed from their interests, and to feature memorization and regurgitation of senseless details. They often pictured themselves as conscripts and even prisoners and their teachers as drill sergeants or even wardens who simply did as they were ordered. "A lot of schools are forced to follow certain procedures, taken from certain books," observed a fifty-nine-year-old man from Palmyra, Wisconsin, whose imagery was echoed by a forty-seven-year-old businessman from Conway, Arkansas, who talked of "force-fed subjects" and by a thirty-eight-year-old man from Durant, Oklahoma, who noted that teachers "have to teach the material that they have to deal with."

Respondents recalled with great vehemence how teachers had required them to memorize and regurgitate names, dates, and details that had no connection to them. They often added that they forgot the details as soon as the exam had ended. "The teacher would call out a certain date and then we would have to stand at attention and say what the date was. I hated it," recalled a sixty-four-year-old Floridian. "It was just a giant data dump that we were supposed to memorize . . . just numbers and names and to this day I still can't remember them," declared a thirty-six-year-old financial analyst from Palo Alto, California. "I remember one of my history teachers who was so old and had been a teacher for so long that you could tell that she had memorized what she said," reported a fifty-four-year-old self-employed Mexican American from Whittier, California. A fifty-year-old man from Mobile, Alabama, had the most vivid complaint: "My teacher was seventy years old, and she carried a blackjack."

Although fashions in teaching history have seemingly changed over the course of the century, our respondents offer a relatively unchanging portrait of fact- and textbook-driven instruction. The sense that classrooms provide less of a connection to the past than other arenas appears to be shared across different generations. (See Table 14.6.) The one exception is among people over age sixty-five who gave "studying history in school" a higher "connectedness" score of 6.5, compared to the 5.5 or 5.6 rating assigned by other age cohorts. It seems possible that this difference stems from the fact that older people give higher connectedness scores to all settings we asked about, rather than from some different schooling experience. Even people over age sixty-five put schools close to the bottom of their list.

In general, then, respondents found particular fault with a school-based history organized around the memorization of facts and locked into a prescribed textbook curriculum. Thus, while the history wars have often focused on content—what should be taught in classes or presented in exhibits—our respondents were more interested in talking about the experience and process of engaging the past.[11] They preferred to make their own histories. When they confronted historical accounts constructed by others, they sought to examine them critically and to connect them to their own experiences or those of people close to them. At the same time, they pointed out, historical presentations that did not give them credit for their critical abilities—commercialized histories on television or textbook-driven high school classes—failed to engage or influence them.[12]

What respondents told us runs counter to the narrative of declension that says Americans are disengaged from history because cultural radicals have captured the schools (and museums) and are teaching gloomy stories about our nation—stories about McCarthyism rather than America's triumph in the Cold War, about Harriet Tubman rather than the Founding Fathers, about destroying Indians rather than taming the West.[13] If only we would get back to the good old facts of American triumph (and the old-fashioned methods of teaching those facts), they maintain, then Americans would be reengaged. The people we interviewed said that they are already quite involved with the past—through activities like going to museums. They like history in museums and didn't like history in schools—not because Harriet Tubman has been added but because the schools require recitation of facts instead of inspiring direct engagement with the "real" stuff of the past and its self-evident relationship to the present.

One of the deepest ironies to emerge from this survey is that some of those who are alarmed by a supposed lack of historical knowledge have prescribed a revival of the most traditional forms of history teaching, particularly a focus on memorizing a canon of historical facts. Yet, our survey strongly suggests that people who grew up under that system found it boring and irrelevant. Even if one shares the goal of promoting a program of historical literacy, nationalism, and patriotism, this survey suggests that the current methods are not the way to do it.

A more plausible strategy for capturing the interest of high school students, our survey suggests, is to look at some of the bases of deep engagement with the past that so many Americans reported even while they talked of their alienation from school-based history. Moreover, our respondents indicate, that at least some creative teachers are engaging students in the study of the past through active learning and making connections with more intimate pasts. A North Carolina man in his mid-twenties, for example, praised a teacher who "got us very involved" because she "took us on various trips and we got hands-on" history. A Bronx woman similarly talked enthusiastically about the "realism" of a class project's engagement with an incident in Puerto Rican history: "Everybody had different information about it, and everyone was giving different things about the same thing, so it made it very exciting."

Those teachers who have most effectively embraced new technology are, in fact, those who are using approaches most compatible with what our respondents praised. The Internet has opened up vast new possibilities for students to work directly with primary-source materials (massive collections of photographs and manuscripts from the Library of Congress, for instance) that are not readily available at a rural high school in Oklahoma or an inner-city high school in Baltimore. By putting "the novice in the archive," in Randy Bass's nice phrase, teachers have enabled students to make themselves into historians. The World Wide Web also fosters constructive projects in which students both model the work of historians and create an archive of student work, because the Web so readily makes student work publicly available.[14]

I mention the Internet partly because it is the focus of my own current work and partly because it is sometimes perceived as antithetical to first-hand engagement with learning. One could cite numerous other types of examples.[15] Anyone who has judged History Day, for example, knows quite well what excites students about the past. Phil Bigler, a Virginia history teacher recently named national teacher of the year, is known for his historical simulations in which students stage presidential elections, debate great issues confronting the Greeks, prepare Islamic/Mideastern festival projects, and recreate the trial of John Brown. Asked recently what he wanted students to take away from his classes, Bigler answered, "I want students to leave my class with the sense that they have been through something significant and relevant to their lives—that they can take away lessons from history and apply them to their own lives."[16]

There is nothing very surprising about the efforts by creative teachers to tap into the most powerful patterns in popular history-making by allowing and encouraging students to revisit, reenact, and get close to the past through encounters with primary documents and living historical sources, to connect the past and the present, and to link personal and intimate pasts with wider narratives. What is surprising is that such efforts have come under attack in recent years from advocates of traditional curricula who regard even "critical thinking" as an insidious threat.[17] Recently, I wrote to a fifth-grade teacher in Northern Virginia to praise her student-developed Web site on world cultures. She wrote back to say that, yes, the project had been very successful but that "burdens" imposed by the new Virginia Standards of Learning made it unlikely that she would be able to repeat it: "We are torn between in-depth study with fantastic results like the museum artifacts versus preparing seriously for the exams which rely heavily on lower levels of thinking."[18]

The success of this project on cultures that are temporally and spatially distant is important because, in arguing for a historical practice that draws upon the popular interest in intimate pasts and intimate uses of the past, I do not mean to suggest that school-based history should be purely local or personal. An emphasis on the firsthand, the experiential, the intimate, and the familial can be confining as well as illuminating. A privatized version of the past can reinforce rather than break down barriers between people, resist rather than promote change.

The understanding of the past that the white Americans with whom we talked get from their families is an enormously potent resource for living in the present, a way of coming to terms with personal identity and of gaining personal autonomy. But white Americans, it seems to me, less often use the past to reach beyond their families and to recognize their connections to wider groups of neighbors and fellow citizens. Just as Americans seem to be bowling alone, as the political scientist Robert Putnam argues in his commentary on the decline of civic society, they also seem to be writing their histories alone—or at least in small familial groups.[19] Many white Americans understand and use the past in ways that make them suspicious of outsiders.

Nevertheless, when people do let down their guard, the common patterns of history-making that we observed can allow individuals to identify and empathize with others. Moreover, the past can provide a safe, because distant, arena in which people can imagine alternative identities and explore different points of view. We need to marry experience with imagination and enable people to connect with "imagined communities" beyond the ones that they have learned in family circles.[20]

Here, in particular, is a key role for history teachers. Teachers can help to enrich popular uses of the past by providing context and comparison, by offering structural explanations, and by introducing students to different voices and experiences. They can help to counter false nostalgia about earlier eras, caution against simply projecting the present onto the past, and suggest some of the differences (as well as the similarities) between memory and history.[21] They can make students aware of possibilities for transforming the status quo. Recognizing how the civil rights movement broke the fetters of a stable and racist social order or how the CIO challenged entrenched notions of management "rights" can inspire people to work for social change in the present.

Interestingly, Linda Levstik's study (this volume) of fifth- to eighth-grade students and teacher and teacher candidates suggests that a history that challenges preconceptions may actually be *more* engaging to students. "Students," she writes, "expressed interest in exactly those aspects of the past that teacher and teacher candidates found profoundly disturbing." They find school-based history "meaningless, inaccurate, and irrelevant" precisely because it avoids subjects of controversy like "race, cultural conflict, social inequities, and oppression."[22] And, they are (rightly) suspicious of a history that simply celebrates a pregiven national narrative of progress and avoids the coercion and pain hidden in that national narrative. We need a history teaching that is somehow simultaneously more local and intimate and more global and cosmopolitan, more shaped by popular concerns and more enriched by insights based on systematic and detailed study of the past.[23] Like people in our survey, I suspect, students want history to engage fundamental questions about identity, morality, immortality, and agency, and there are multiple ways that teachers can mobilize that engagement.

The results of this survey, then, suggest some encouraging news as well as some important challenges for historians and history teachers. On the one hand, there is some evidence that conventional and celebratory narratives of the nation state—the ones that have generally organized our basic courses—are losing some of their appeal. On the other hand and contrary to the conventional wisdom, people of all types demonstrate a widespread engagement with the past, particularly if they can do it first-hand, confronting direct historical evidence and constructing their own historical narratives. Moreover, their interests are far from antiquarian. In our interviews, the most powerful meanings of the past come out of the dialogue between the past and the present, out of the ways the past can be used to answer pressing current questions about relationships, identity, mortality, and agency. Indeed, this was a point that Carl Becker recognized back in 1931 when he wrote his famous essay "Everyman His Own Historian" and used the example of popular historical practice to argue that historians need to "adapt our knowledge" to "the necessities" of the present rather than "cultivate a species of dry professional arrogance growing out of the thin soil of antiquarian research." Our interviewees implicitly join Becker in insisting on something that professional historians can too easily forget—"our proper function is not to repeat the past but to make use of it."[24] For our respondents, the past is not only present; it is part of the present. That powerful sense of connectedness to the past (and between the past and the present) that we find in everyday life must also be infused into our classrooms.

NOTES

1. Lynne V. Cheney, *American Memory: A Report on Humanities in the Nation's Public Schools* (National Endowment for the Humanities, undated but published in September 1987), p. 5. (Cheney is approvingly quoting the poet Czelaw Milosz.)

2. Michael Wallace, "The Politics of Public History," in Jo Blatti, ed., *Past Meets Present: Essays about Historic Interpretation and Public Audiences* (Washington, DC, 1987), p. 38; Michael Frisch, "The Memory of History," *Radical History Review*, 25 (October 1981), p. 14.

3. Louis R. Harlan, "The Future of the American Historical Association," *American Historical Review*, 95 (February 1990), p. 3. See similarly Robert Dallek, "Perspective on History," *Los Angeles Times*, April 22, 1994, Metro, Part B, p. 7.

4. Jonathan Yardley, "Bad History: Some Textbook Examples," *Washington Post*, March 28, 1994, p. D2.

5. The most influential study is Diane Ravitch and Chester Finn Jr., *What Do Our 17-Year-Olds Know? A Report on the First National Assessment of History and Literature* (New York, 1987). There is a large literature debating the work of Ravitch and Finn. See, for example, William Ayers, "What Do 17-Year-Olds Know? A Critique of Recent Research," *Education Digest,* 53 (April 1988), pp. 37–39; Dale Whittington, "What Have 17-Year-Olds Known in the Past?" *American Educational Research Journal*, 28 (Winter 1991), pp. 759–780; Deborah Meier and Florence Miller, "The Book of Lists," *Nation*, 245 (January 9, 1988), pp. 25–27; Terry Teachout, "Why Johnny Is Ignorant," *Commentary* (March 1988), pp. 69–71. There have been two more recent studies by the National Assessment of Education Progress (NAEP). For brief reports on these, see Michael Mehle, "History Basics Stump U.S. Kids, Study Finds," *Bergen Record*, April 3, 1990, p. A1; Carol Innerst, "History Test Results Aren't Encouraging; US Teens Flop on 'Basic' Quiz," *Washington Times*, November 2, 1995, A2.

6. The results of the survey are reported in Roy Rosenzweig and David Thelen, *The Presence of the Past: Popular Uses of History in American Life* (New York, 1998), which includes a detailed discussion of methodological issues. The research reported in this article draws from that book and my joint work with Thelen and, in particular, the sections on the classroom draw directly from chapters that were Thelen's primary responsibility within the book. Nevertheless, I am solely responsible for the interpretations offered here. The Sioux Indian sample was gathered from calls to Pine Ridge reservation; the methodological appendix and introduction from the book as well as a detailed set of tables are available at http://chnm.gmu.edu/survey.

7. Though just as many men as women had hobbies or collections related to the past, women undertook them for quite distinct reasons. Thirty-six respondents described their hobbies or collections as ways to maintain family ties or traditions; thirty of them were women. The results from this survey suggest the words "past" and "history" (understood as the world of presidents and treaties) may have gendered associations in American society. Men occupy most seats around Civil War roundtables, for example, and three times as many men as women join the History Book Club, which emphasizes military and political history. For an empirical study of gender-based framing assumptions about history,

see Janice E. Fournier and Samuel S. Wineburg, "Picturing the Past: Gender Differences in the Depiction of Historical Figures," *American Journal of Education*, 105 (February 1997), pp. 160–185. Based on a study of fifth- and eighth-graders, they conclude: "In girls' minds, women in history are blurry figures; in boys' minds, they are virtually invisible."

8. In a very revealing study of the historical perspectives of adolescents (a group not included in our survey), Terrie Epstein found major differences in the perspectives of African Americans and European Americans that, in part, parallel what we saw in our survey. Her study does, however, seem to suggest a greater acceptance of nationalist frameworks and stories by white Americans than we found, but it is difficult to compare directly because the methods, settings, questions, and groups are different. See "Deconstructing Differences in African American and European American Adolescents' Perspectives on United States History," in *Curriculum Inquiry* (forthcoming).

9. Telephone interviews of this sort, it should be noted, are probably not the best way to gauge views of something as complicated as nationalism and the American national story. I would hope that further research—using ethnographic methods, for example—will give us a fuller (and perhaps more complex) picture.

10. We asked seventy-six respondents to give a single word to describe their high school experience with history. (We had intended to ask this question of a larger percentage of respondents but stopped asking when their answers turned out to be very similar.) The results: boring, irrelevant—26; incomplete, biased, ignorant—15; interesting—14; educational and useful—6; vaguely favorable—9; vaguely unfavorable—3; average or okay—3.

11. The National History Standards, for example, included an excellent set of standards in "historical thinking." But, as far as I know, they were largely ignored in the content-centered debate over the standards. Charles Krauthammer did, however, complain that there was not enough emphasis on "dates, facts, places, and events," and Elizabeth Fox-Genovese and Albert Shanker argued that children needed to learn facts first and analyze meaning only later. Gary B. Nash, Charlotte Crabtree, and Ross E. Dunn, *History on Trial: Culture Wars and the Teaching of the Past* (New York, 1997), pp. 175–178, 191, 229–230.

12. There is, of course, a problem in relying on survey data to draw conclusions about the influence of mass media. Given popular distrust of the media, people surveyed may be more likely to emphasize their own critical perspective on versions of the past that they encounter in movies and on television. Sam Wineburg's study of history students and their parents, reported in this volume ("Making Historical Sense"), offers a very powerful example of how a film—in this case *Forrest Gump*—can shape popular historical consciousness.

13. For an example of this narrative, see Myron Magnet, "How to Smarten up the Schools," *Fortune* (February 1, 1988), pp. 86ff.

14. Randy Bass, "The Garden in the Machine: The Impact of American Studies on New Technologies," available at *http://www.georgetown.edu/bassr/garden.html*. For examples of on-line student work, see the section on "The Student as Historian" in "History Matters: The U.S. Survey Course on the Web," at *http://historymatters .gmu.edu*. On constructive projects on line, see also Randy Bass, "Five Areas of Application & Integration: Working Synthesis I" at *http://www.georgetown.edu/ crossroads/conversations/synth_1.html*. See also Bass's essays in the very useful guide from the Crossroads Project, *Engines of Inquiry: A Practical Guide for Using Technology in Teaching American Culture* (Washington, DC, 1997), which can be ordered from *http://www.georgetown.edu/crossroads*.

15. For one compendium, now somewhat out of date, see Stephen Botein, Warren Leon, Michael Novak, Roy Rosenzweig, and G. B. Warden, eds., *Experiments in History Teaching* (Cambridge, 1978).

16. Interview with Roy Rosenzweig for "History Matters: The U.S. Survey Course on the Web." See *http://historymatters.gmu.edu/teachers.html*.

17. "Critical thinking" was apparently one target of supporters of Virginia Governor George Allen's plan for "back-to-basics" state standards, which emphasized rote memorization. See, for example, Spencer S. Hsu and Robert O'Harrow Jr., "Allen's Back-to-Basics Plan For Schools Draws Outcry; Changes Would Reverse Progress, Critics Say," *Washington Post*, March 29, 1995, p. A1; Nash, *History*, p. 262.

18. See "Virginia Run Fifth Grade Virtual Museum of World Cultures" at *http://www.fcps.k12.va.us/VirginiaRunES/museum/museum.htm*.

19. Robert D. Putnam, "Bowling Alone: America's Declining Social Capital," *Journal of Democracy*, 6 (January 1995), pp. 65–78. Putnam's work raises a host of complex questions that go well beyond this discussion. For some perceptive critiques, see, for example, Michael Schudson, "What If Civic Life Didn't Die?" and Theda Skocpol, "Unraveling from Above," both in *American Prospect*, 25 (March/April 1996), pp. 17–25.

20. I borrow this phrase from Benedict Anderson, *Imagined Communities: Reflections on the Origins and Spread of Nationalism* (London, 1991).

21. Richard White's *Remembering Ahanagran: Storytelling in a Family's Past* (New York, 1998) provides some very thoughtful reflections on the tensions between "memory" and "history."

22. Linda Levstik, this volume.

23. Harvey Kaye offers some thoughtful comments on the ways that "the powers of the past" can break "the tyranny of the present" in chapter 5 of *The Powers of the Past: Reflections on the Crisis and the Promise of History* (Minneapolis, 1992).

24. Carl Becker, "Everyman His Own Historian," *American Historical Review*, 37 (January 1932), pp. 253–255.

Chapter 15

Articulating the Silences
Teachers' and Adolescents' Conceptions of Historical Significance

Linda S. Levstik

At the level of mythology, emancipation—from kings, lords, tyrants, slavery, caste, tribes, superstition, poverty, patriarchy, even heterosexuality—is the very essence of "America." . . . America has held out the promise of a freedom greater than any [immigrants] had known before. But . . . becoming American cannot be understood in "emancipationist" terms alone, for immigrants invariably encountered structures of class, race, gender, and national power that constrained, and sometimes defeated, their efforts to be free. Coercion, as much as liberty, has been intrinsic to our history and to the process of becoming American.

—Gary Gerstle[1]

Ideas of historical significance are cultural constructs transmitted to members of a society in a variety of ways.[2] This is especially the case for national history. In an era of fragile nation-states, it is instructive to watch the ways in which, in the hands of nationalists, history becomes the "raw material to be recycled to produce daily myths . . . an enemy that must be dealt with in a radical, bloody way."[3] Even in countries that aspire to a more democratic and civic rather than ethnic principle of nationality, decisions about what is historically significant have as much to do with what is repressed as with what is recollected.[4] As Gerstle notes, "nationalism demands that boundaries against outsiders be drawn, that a dominant national culture be created or reinvigorated, and that internal and external opponents of the national project be subdued, nationalized, vanquished, and even excluded or repelled."[5] Even under the most repressive forms of nationalism, however, alternative histories develop beneath the surface and on the margins of official history. In a multicultural democracy such as the United States, alternative histories also develop, but they are more overtly disseminated through family and cultural and religious associations as well as through such public channels as museums and print and visual media. Because of the potential disparity between the version of history encountered in these contexts and that disseminated in school—a site where some form of overarching national history is explicitly introduced—students in multicultural societies may be faced with reconciling widely varied accounts of the past. In Hollinger's view, such nations should aspire to a history "'thick' enough to sustain collective action yet 'thin' enough to provide room for the cultures of a variety of descent groups."[6] Individuals develop and express group identities but also take part in "an ongoing collective debate about the character and direction of the nation."[7] Thus, according to Hollinger, teaching and learning national history should include study of the different systems of ethnoracial classification used in the nation, including consideration of the various constituencies empowered or disempowered by these classifications. This approach to studying history, Hollinger argues, would demystify ethnoracial categories and "challenge the authority that [U.S.] society has traditionally allowed skin color and the shape of the face to exercise over culture."[8]

There is little evidence that U.S. teachers (or any substantial part of the American public) are prepared to help students participate in the type of debate described by Hollinger.[9] Indeed, the ways in which knowledge is created, transmitted, distorted, politicized, and used for specific purposes is rarely made evident in teacher training programs.[10] Without such challenges to the status quo, prospective teachers may uncritically accept existing curriculum content as well as the social arrangements reflected in and supported by that content. Students, in turn, are unlikely to expect different ways of teaching or demonstrate different patterns of learning history if they have never seen them modeled.[11] Indeed, in several studies, students from diverse racial and ethnic backgrounds experienced difficulty fitting their own perspectives on historical significance with those presented in the school curriculum.[12] Some stood in active resistance to what they encountered in school, drawing instead on forms of history presented in what they perceived as more culturally relevant sites, such as neighborhoods and families.

Students', Teachers', and Teacher Candidates' Views of Historical Significance

Developing a history that can sustain collective action while embracing the cultures of a variety of descent groups is more than a theoretical nicety; it is a practical necessity. Whether in workplaces or schools, Americans are linked to the world in complex and interesting ways, not least of which is through an influx of immigration that rivals numbers at the turn of the century.[13] Meanwhile, the teaching force remains largely white, with relatively little experience teaching about diverse ethnoracial groups.[14]

In this chapter I consider the implications of this disparity between who American students are—and will be in the near future—and who their teachers understand Americans to be in the context of national history. I will focus on the results of two studies: first, an investigation of early adolescents' understanding of historical significance and, second, a similar study with teachers and teacher candidates. In the first study, in open-ended interviews, forty-eight students in grades 5 through 8 were presented with a set of captioned historical pictures and asked to choose the ones important enough to include on a timeline of the past five hundred years and to explain their choices (see Appendix).[15] In the second study, twenty teacher candidates (preservice teachers at the beginning of their social studies methods course) and twelve teachers (inservice teachers with one or more years of experience) were asked to complete the same task with a nearly identical set of captioned historical pictures (see Appendix).[16]

Both studies used semistructured interviews and included a task that required participants to choose from among a set of twenty (for students) or twenty-five (for teachers and teacher candidates) captioned historical pictures and to respond to a set of broader questions and probes designed to explore their understanding of historical significance.[17] In the teacher and teacher candidate interviews, groups worked simultaneously, though separately.[18] The teachers and teacher candidates also worked with five pictures that were not used in the student study. These were selected to better represent the diversity of the U.S. historical experience as well as the "rights" issues that were prominent in student discussions of historical significance.

After interviewing participants and identifying a set of thematic strands in their responses, we subjected the interview transcripts to a systematic content analysis; coding included a systematic search for negative or discrepant evidence. The coded data were then analyzed using cross-case analysis (grouping the answers of students responding to the same items in the selection task and interview) and constant comparison (comparing students' responses across different portions of the task and interview). This resulted in a set of descriptive generalizations that forms the basis for this chapter.

In both studies, participants' choices focused primarily on the origin and development of the political and social structure of the United States, and the explanations pointed to steadily expanding rights and opportunities as the central theme in American history. At the same time, students had difficulty incorporating some historical patterns and events into their image of progress, and their discussion of these issues indicated a familiarity with a "vernacular" view of history separate from "official" views that justify the contemporary social structure.[19] Teachers and teacher candidates, on the other hand, rarely focused on any form of vernacular history. Instead, most of the adult participants explicitly selected pictures that showed a positive image of nation-building, identifying their selections as "the main story," "what formed us," what made America "our family," what "made us a world power."

First Person Plural

The first person plural came naturally to these students, teachers, and teacher candidates as they talked about an American past. "We" fought the revolution, "we" discovered a cure for polio, "we" pushed the Taino, the Cherokee, or the Nez Perce off their land. From the respondents' perspective, historical events took on significance when they "formed us," "changed us," or "made us a nation." At first, this seems barely worth noting; after all, almost all of the student respondents and all but one of the adult respondents were American citizens, and they *were* sorting through images of U.S. history. But pronouns are shape-shifters, and it is useful to pay attention, particularly when antecedents shift around. Who are "we," and what is "ours"?

Regardless of their own ethnic background, their gender, or the re-
cency of their families' immigration to the United States, students, teachers, and teacher candidates consistently used the pronouns "we" and
"our" in talking about the events related to the settlement and creation of
the United States. Their explanations suggest that they considered these
events important because they defined a collective community. Beginning with a Thanksgiving picture that showed "the start of the United
States, when we all became possible, because we all came from over there,
and a bunch of immigrants came over here, and that's basically how we
started our nation," students depicted the United States as a nation of immigrants. Teachers and teacher candidates also described immigration as
one of the most distinctive aspects of American history. "This is why we
got America. Why we are here," explained Celia, a teacher candidate.
"This is where a large chunk of us are from, and this is like the basis for a
lot of our cities, our development, our society." Her classmate Parker
agreed: "When you think about it, we're all immigrants." Geri, a veteran
teacher, said that the picture of immigrants was "*our* family."

Along with immigration, the Bill of Rights and the American Revolution
elicited comments from adults about the establishment of "our country,"
"our fundamental rights," and "guidelines for working together." This emphasis on the origins of the United States—both its settlement and its creation as a political unit—reflects the importance of the past in defining a
community of identification. While previous research indicates that children's understanding of the colonial period and the American Revolution is
often vague and riddled with misconceptions, students had internalized one
element that contemporary society considers important—that this is where
"we" began.[20] Additionally, students and adults identified immigration as a
key component in establishing the boundaries of national identity. For
most of these students and adults, their community began with European
settlement and expanded over time to include an unspecified array of European immigrants. Students and adults distinguished their historical community from that of Native Americans, explaining that "we"—European
settlers—pushed "them"—the original inhabitants of the Americas—off
"their" land.[21] As one teacher candidate explained, the exploration of the
Americas was "a white man's event . . . it doesn't include any African Americans, any Indians because we were pushing Indians off their land . . . and
the African Americans [pictured among the explorers] were probably [the
Europeans'] slaves."

Just as consistently, students and adults distinguished between "us"—those historically possessing rights and freedoms—and "them"—those historically disenfranchised or discriminated against on the basis of ethnoracial categories or gender. Thus, at Thanksgiving "it was kind of like the beginning of us becoming friends," said one student. "We was making a bond with Native Americans; that's good because that's a tradition that goes on forever." In similar terms, another student noted that the civil rights movement was important because it gave African Americans "a lot of opportunity to get jobs and stuff because [before] they weren't really recognized as people." Similarly, Ryan explained that the civil rights movement was important "because African Americans were not treated equally." His interview partner, Juan, agreed that "they need just as much rights as we do." Students also recognized that there were problems in uniting historically segregated people. As Lincoln explained, "although [African Americans] got to be free we still kinda pushed 'em . . . we still gave them the cheap neighborhoods so they didn't live with us. . . . Kind of like the Indians . . . and the voting thing for women." Byron nodded, adding, "We said hey, they're here, pfft," gesturing as if brushing them out of the way. Teacher candidates (but no teachers) also used an us-and-them dichotomy in discussing the significance of civil rights. Without civil rights, several said, "They [African Americans] would still be slaves"—just as earlier they had said that without the American Revolution "we would be ruled by England."[22]

Veteran teachers spent considerably less time discussing civil rights than did either of the other two groups. They almost unanimously placed civil rights on the timeline, sometimes distinguishing between "our overall rights," guaranteed in the Bill of Rights but not extended to all of "them," and civil rights and women's rights that had to be wrested from a resistant society, generally identified as "us." Once gender was raised as an issue, however, students shifted from generic identification with European Americans to identification by gender. In the case of women's suffrage, girls identified with women in the early twentieth century, explaining that "we [females] came along . . . and got the vote." Boys, on the other hand, identified with the men from the period, arguing that "we [males] already had the vote."[23] This pattern was not as prominent among the adults, most of whom were women. While some adults strongly identified with women in the women's movement, others were just as adamant in not doing so.

The emphasis by students, teachers and teacher candidates on the expansion of rights and opportunities and the steady improvement of social relations indicates concern with establishing the United States as a country in which historic hardships and injustices are corrected and overcome. This should not be surprising. In societies in which contemporary groups experience wide differences in their economic or social status, emancipatory historical stories serve to establish the legitimacy of the status quo and dissipate concern about the persistence of disparities in circumstance.[24] But, as Gerstle notes in the opening quote, "becoming American cannot be understood in 'emancipationist' terms alone. . . . Coercion, as much as liberty, has been intrinsic to our history and to the process of becoming American."[25]

Ignoring the complexity of the American experience may serve to maintain existing economic and social structures, but it certainly confuses students and teachers about a good deal of American history. When the history curriculum "emphasizes the obvious, cheerful, and stereotypical," students and teachers are deprived of an important mechanism whereby they might understand their own lives as having historical context(s), and they are given no help in understanding the continuation of inequities and injustice in their (or others') society.[26] Instead, they are faced with a history long on myth, short on intellectual rigor, and extraordinarily slow to incorporate the wide range of behavior that has characterized American history.

Challenging the Obvious, Cheerful, and Stereotypical

Some participants—particularly among the adolescent students—were aware of and sometimes disturbed by anomalies in the historical record. For European American students, the continuation of racism was one such puzzle. African Americans "have rights," Rhiannon said, pondering the problem; Sonja agreed but noted that "we still have prejudice." "Yeah," Rhiannon acknowledged, "there's still prejudice . . . and there are even like other religious groups and other different countries that . . . have prejudice, too. Even if everybody has the right, doesn't change people's emotions." She and Sonja continued to turn the idea around, suggesting that recent immigrants seemed to be treated most badly. Rhiannon said, "Illegal—not illegal, but aliens—that have just come here like Puerto Ricans and Mexicans . . . they came here but they're legally allowed to be here, but people think they're like taking our taxes and taking all our government stuff that would go to them." Another group of girls also mentioned hostility towards recent immigrants, noting that California was involved in "making laws" about immigration. As they discussed this disjuncture between progress and prejudice, Rachel mentioned that "people think of America as the land of opportunities but I don't think they think of racism." Saara also pointed out that "[s]ome places are going back to segregation. I think it's sad. It took such a long time to get it the way it is now." Rachel nodded and commented, "It's not perfect, not where we want to be."

African American students framed the past as a story of learning from mistakes, as had European American students, but they sometimes introduced a more complex analysis of progress in extending rights to marginalized people. They, too, argued that the Bill of Rights was, as Isabella said, "only for rich white men who could vote and you had to pay taxes . . . so the Bill of Rights just protected wealthy, white, male landowners, but that [civil rights] applied to everyone and gave everyone a chance." They also mentioned the lack of attention to civil rights in school. "You don't really learn about [civil rights] in school," Isabella commented. "You know I've read books about it. My parents have books and I've gone to the library and I've seen movies and stuff and I mean at this school and at my other school I didn't learn too much about it 'cause like you celebrate Martin Luther King but you don't hear about it . . . you just hear that he helped."

Sometimes, too, when a European American student argued that "we're all equal now," a student of color would drop out of the conversation, at least temporarily. In one instance, Robert, a European American, remarked that one of the results of racism was that "most black people are poor and on free or reduced lunches like 93 percent or so." Derek, his African American classmate, looked at him in surprise, pointing a finger at his own chest and shaking his head. He stayed silent, however, until the conversation shifted to Native Americans. When Robert said that Columbus discovered America, Derek leaned forward and asked, "How did *he* discover America? There were already people here!" Oliver, a European American, intervened, saying "they didn't know where the U.S. was; since they didn't know it, it was a discovery [for them], but not for the Indians." Again, Derek withdrew, shaking his head in disagreement. Similarly, when the eighth-grade girls discussed recent immigration from "Puerto Rico and Mexico," Patricia, whose father was Mexican American, remained silent during the discussion of legal and illegal immigration, re–entering the conversation at a later point to discuss ethnic contributions—food—to American culture. In contrast, her classmate Saara, an immigrant from Poland, intervened forcefully when Rhiannon joked that Saara was an "illegal alien." Saara declared that she was legal and had a green card—"actually, a *pink* green card."

Teachers and teacher candidates spent much less time discussing the continuation of racism. Instead, they stressed the continued need for inclusion, folding racism and ethnicity into one "issue of culture" where "we still have problems." One teacher candidate, Jerrie, suggested that these problems were so crucial that her group should focus on "a social perspective, *like what made things better*" (emphasis mine). Another group of teachers discussed continuing discrimination against immigrants, and a third group argued about whether to include the Depression picture because "it was at this time that we established all the social programs . . . all the things we're trying to change now." This last group of teachers also kept the immigration picture on the timeline because, Bonnie explained, "you wouldn't get to civil rights without that." While the adults' brief attention to ethnoracial history stands in contrast to the students' lengthier discussion of racism and discrimination, the topic arose most often among students in schools with the greatest degree of ethnoracial diversity.[27] Similarly, adults who worked in more diverse school settings were more likely to address race as an issue separate from ethnicity.

Just as ethnoracial history provoked discussion among participants in the study, so did the Vietnam War. For students, Vietnam raised question about American exceptionality. They thought that Americans were different in that they did not fight wars of aggression, and fought only to "help people . . . we were fighting . . . for other people." They could not reconcile what they knew about Vietnam with this view. They weren't sure whom Americans were helping in Vietnam. Rhiannon struggled to explain with whom America was fighting. "The Vietnamese people," she finally declared. When asked *which* Vietnamese people, she hesitated. "North or south?" she asked, laughing. Sonja volunteered that she thought "it was like a civil war between like Vietnam, I think." Lewis speculated that the war "helped Vietnam be different. Well, it helped the north and south or something." His classmate Peter shrugged and said, "I don't really know much about the Vietnam War." After listening to his peers struggle for awhile, Jared commented that "they're trying to make excuses for a war we lost."

Teachers and teacher candidates also had difficulty reconciling what they knew of Vietnam with their ideas about why Americans enter wars. While they were not as convinced as the students that Americans went to war solely for altruistic purposes, they did think that Americans were supposed to get something out of the war—access to oil or some other economic advantage, for instance. They were unsure what Americans intended to "get out of [Vietnam]," knowing only that "we lost that war." Lisa, a teacher candidate, described the loss as "a change for the worse . . . it was being pushed out," and compared the American experience to the way in which Native Americans were "pushed out of their land." Younger teacher candidates said they didn't know much about Vietnam, claiming they never studied it, either in precollegiate or collegiate history classes. Teachers and older teacher candidates evidenced some first and secondhand information about the war, usually gathered from having lived through the time period, or from family or acquaintances who served in Vietnam. This information did not help them understand why America was involved, only that the war precipitated protests at home and bad treatment for returning soldiers. Stacie, a teacher, said, "it may have been the longest war, but we weren't even fighting for our country. I mean, I know it's significant, but. . . ." Celia nodded, saying, "See, I think, my Dad [a Vietnam veteran] would kill me, but I don't think we should take it [on the timeline]." Mason agreed, arguing that "it certainly had an era of its own, but as far as forming who we are, I don't know."

In part, these ideas reflect the development of a wider public mythology "in which the U.S. government disappears as a devastating force, the Vietnamese people cease to be victims, and the principal focus of concern becomes psychic stress for those veterans who survived."[28] This interpretation of the Vietnam era makes the antiwar movement especially confusing. Such protests challenged students' and adults' schema of cooperation and reconciliation. Why, they wondered, did people object to helping another country? Isabella, a student, wanted to know "how [the war] was started and why some of the best people were against it. I mean to me, I want to know why they were against the Vietnamese people." Another student, Lincoln, offered the conclusion that "people were going mad." Three students, Oliver, Jacob, and Robert, thought that more people died in Vietnam because "you have all these shootings because people in the U.S. were arguing over something," but they were unclear as to what the argument was about. They had no inkling that war resistance was a regular feature of America's history; so far as they knew, Vietnam was a singular incident of dissent.

Though students expressed interest in the Vietnam era, teachers and teacher candidates worried about including it on their timeline because "it was a negative thing." In one group of teacher candidates, discussion centered on when "negative things like protests" should be introduced. "You wouldn't talk about it in elementary school," Jana claimed. They also worried about discussing Vietnam because they connected anti-Vietnam protest to more general social unrest. As Tara, a teacher candidate, explained it, "the whole value system or beliefs changed in the country, maybe not as a direct result of the war, maybe just the times, but there was the sexual revolution." Others argued that, despite the social upheaval of the period, Vietnam didn't "form us." When Mason, a teacher, asked, "what did [the war] do?" his peers had difficulty formulating a response. "Well," Celine said, "it's a huge deal . . . a huge controversy on whether or not this was even an important thing at the time." Susan added that "it caused us to have dissent and we started to become critical of government." Celine frowned, adding, "Weren't we already critical in some ways?" "Not as overly," Susan explained.

In all the adult discussion of Vietnam, only Celine's remark indicated any awareness that protest or criticism of government might predate the Vietnam era. Yet her peers dismissed her reservations; they had a vague sense that something was different about the kind of protest and criticism leveled at the government during and after the Vietnam years, though they had trouble articulating that difference. Later in the discussion, for instance, Susan returned to the idea that Vietnam marked a critical turning point in how Americans viewed their government. Vietnam, she argued, represented "our conscience. Even though it was kind of a negative thing, I think it gave us a conscience." Her peers remained unconvinced. Vietnam had been "a problem at the time," not something with long-term consequences, and certainly not something that explained "who we are"—their bottom line for determining historical significance.

 This tendency to see history as a series of separate and singular events showed up in several other discussions among teachers and teacher candidates. Only one adult, for instance, remarked that the United States had suffered economic depressions prior to 1929. Not unlike the students who treated the Depression as a one-time event when "everyone was poor" and America "realized that they weren't the god of all countries," some adults saw the effects of the Depression as limited to a single generation. At most, they thought the experience of economic depression explained some of their parents' or grandparents' attitudes toward work and money, but they perceived little effect for subsequent generation of Americans. As Abby, a teacher candidate, noted, "the Depression [is] a big part of our *history*, but as far as how *we* are. . . ." She shrugged. Abby and her peers tended to describe history as a series of time-bound problems recognized, debated, and resolved (or just forgotten)—a depression in the 1930s, a civil rights movement in the 1960s, the invention of a technology or medical cure at a particular moment in time. When individuals did mention the long-term or world-wide effects of events or eras, they were greeted with surprise by some of their peers. In two groups of teacher candidates, for instance, a member of each group connected economic depression in the United States to current social welfare systems. Nila explained that "the Depression sets up all that stuff that FDR does, like welfare. Without all that, the welfare system as we know it wouldn't exist. Like we still have the TVA in 1998, you know, sixty years later." Moira raised her eyebrows, turned to Nila, and asked, "Were you some kind of history major?" "No," Nila responded. "I had a really good history teacher in high school." In another group of teacher candidates, Hanna argued that the Depression had "world-wide impact," but her peers disagreed, countering that its significance was confined to changing things "for our grandparents."

In other instances, adults relied on fragmentary or conflated pieces of historical information to argue for or against the significance of an event or era. Susan, a teacher, was probably conflating information about instances of women's suffrage prior to 1920 with early restrictions on male suffrage when she argued that the Nineteenth Amendment was not important because women could already vote. "See, women voted in the 1700s! It just was who owned land," she told her group. "So some men didn't vote, but some women could, it just depended on who owned land." Fragmentary information also led Bonnie, another teacher, to make law-like statements about historical cause-and-effect relationships. She recalled that World War II helped lift the United States out of economic depression and concluded that the Depression was significant because "war usually grows out of [depression] and produces prosperity."

The Code of Silence

When a student, Jaclyn, noted in regard to antiwar protests that "disagreement can lead to such a big conflict that could have been solved a lot easier," she inadvertently characterized a basic tension in teaching and learning national history. As White characterizes it:

> Even more important than transmitting public scholarly knowledge, elementary and secondary schools serve as institutions that enculturate the young of our nation with the core values, beliefs, and practices of the contemporary mainstream American culture. . . . Therefore, historical, geographic, economic, or political events that do not reflect the United States and its inhabitants at their finest hour, embodying the ideas for which we stand, tend to be ruthlessly edited out when "what is or was" meets the filter of "what should be."[29]

While students, teachers, and teacher candidates all ascribed significance to aspects of the past that promoted social unity and consensus, they did not all respond in the same ways to more divisive aspects of American history.[30] Instead, students expressed interest in exactly those aspects of the past that teachers and teacher candidates found profoundly disturbing. Given the adults' desire to identify with and introduce children to a community at once stable and emancipatory, the coercive and divisive elements in national development presented teachers and teacher candidates with a dilemma. First, they worried that introducing "negative" history was developmentally inappropriate; perhaps children in elementary and middle school were not mature enough to handle an ambiguous past. Next, they suggested that these aspects of the past were aberrations rather than patterns in American history. Finally, not only did they argue that knowing about coercive and divisive parts of America's past were not fundamental to the formation of children's national identity; they suggested that such knowledge threatened to undermine that identity. In building these arguments, teachers and teacher candidates circumscribed a national identity that was inclusive but not plural, civic but rarely social. Thus, civil rights movements that sought to include more people in joint civic life with European Americans were significant, but instances of ethnoracial repression (Indian removal, Japanese internment) or resistance (Vietnam) or movements that challenged Americans to alter basic social or economic conditions (labor movements, economic depression) rarely were. As examples of coercion and resistance in nation-building dropped off the adults' timelines, there was silence at exactly the points where students expressed confusion about and interest in the past.

Safety in Silence

The teachers and teacher candidates in this study were not unaware of the dilemma presented by the contrast between their desire for a beneficent national history and students' desire to know more about exactly those aspects of the past with which teachers felt most uncertain. They argued that their own experience as students of history had failed to prepare them to understand national history in sophisticated ways or to make sense out of the persistent problems of a diverse nation or an increasingly interdependent world. They said, for instance, that history "should be multicultural," but they also wanted to look past differences and establish some sort of common identity. Several declared that they didn't see color in their classrooms and couldn't imagine discussing with their students how color was used to construct racial categories in the United States.[31] They were aware that injustices had happened in the past but were terrified of what they might unleash by speaking about them in the present. In response, they chose silence. These silences in the history curriculum are reflections of silences in the larger culture—codes of politeness that constrain what adults think it is appropriate to discuss in public or with children, a desire to enculturate children into what teachers perceive as mainstream American culture.

As the products of schools that were often silent on cultural differences, these teachers extend the silence into their own classrooms. They avoid topics that make them uncomfortable or that they think will disturb their students.[32] When faced with accommodating a more diverse student population, their tendency is to celebrate relatively minor, nonthreatening differences—clothing, holidays, food—and avoid overt discussion of race, cultural conflict, social inequities, and oppression.[33] In so doing, they inadvertently present students with stereotypes and misrepresent past and current circumstances. Not surprisingly, individuals whose history is so often misrepresented in the curriculum are likely to reject history as meaningless, inaccurate, and irrelevant. In consequence, they are more likely to understand themselves and others in local and presentist terms.[34] Of course, we can always argue that what these students and teachers really need is more history. The students in this study will get just that. They are embarked on a course of study that will provide them with perhaps the most concentrated attention to history in their schooling. Between fifth and eleventh grade they are likely to take at least five history courses.

The teachers and teacher candidates also took history at both precollegiate and collegiate levels.[35] They recalled that their history instructors introduced all of the topics pictured in the timeline task, with the exception of Vietnam. They expressed embarrassment and frustration over the gaps in their recollection. Despite their foggy memories for some parts of the past, however, they recalled the main point of the mainstream story—emancipation, progress, and exceptionality—even as they acknowledged its silences. In this they were much like the African American adults surveyed by Rosenzweig (this volume), who also perceived American history as a story of progress over time. A national story of progressive emancipation without attention to the coercive elements of nation building, however, fails to provide teachers or students with a framework for making sense out of much of history and leaves them vulnerable to myth and manipulation.[36] Engaging students in in-depth study of the coercive as well as emancipatory potential in the American experience, on the other hand, can be challenging for teachers. As I analyzed the comments of the teachers and teacher candidates engaged in the timeline task, three specific challenges emerged:

• *Narrow conceptions of American polity.* As the teachers discussed what was or was not historically significant, they built a dichotomous picture of American history. "Our" story focused on the construction of a European American polity that was a single culture in a multicultural world. While other cultural groups appeared at various points in the story, their activities were generally sidebars to the main events. Few of the teachers or teacher candidates knew enough about individuals and groups they perceived as "other" to discuss them in a sensitive, reasonably accurate way, even when they were sympathetic to their inclusion on the timeline. While they knew brief immigration and civil rights stories that emphasized the emancipatory pull of America, they knew almost nothing about the factors that pushed people to emigrate or about the varied circumstances that constrained their participation in American society. As Gerstle notes, a nation is itself a structure of power that, like class, gender, and race, limits the array of options available to its citizens.[37] With no information about the ways in which national power is brought to bear in the process of nation building, teachers have little hope of helping students analyze either emancipation or coercion in the making of Americans.

Changing this requires more than increasing the required doses of national history. Rather, it suggests that historical study might benefit from anthropological perspective that would encourage teachers "to reflect on cultural variation . . . combat . . . ethnocentrism . . . and see other people's points of view more clearly."[38] Focusing on questions about human actions and thoughts in a range of "strange" settings might also "expose taken for granted substantive values to scrutiny," while raising a new set of questions to frame national history: What constituencies have various social, political, and economic systems apparently served? To what uses have these systems been put by various empowered and disempowered agents? Which ethnoracial categories have been introduced when and by whom, and who, if anyone, resisted their application and in what context? To concentrate on telling such a story could demystify and historicize the categories, without denying their ordinance, for good or ill, over specific people at specific times and places.[39]

• *Little experience with historical inquiry.* Shifting history instruction from the transmission of cultural verities to their investigation highlights another problem. Neither teachers nor students report experience with historical inquiry.[40] As a result, both need *different*, not necessarily *more*, history—history that engages them in inquiry into the kinds of questions suggested earlier.[41] Perhaps collegiate level history classes could more systematically involve students in such inquiry (see, for example, McDiarmid, this volume). In turn, methods courses and professional development activities could focus on developing forms of historical inquiry appropriate for K–12 students.[42]

• *Fear of repercussions from administrators and public.* There is a wonderful scene in the movie *Lonestar* in which contending community delegations meet with two social studies teachers to discuss their approach to Texas history. When one of the teachers says that she is simply trying to show her students the complex ways in which different individuals and groups came together in Texas, a parent retorts that she doesn't want complexities for her child and suggests that the teachers stick to food and celebrations. When I show that scene to my graduate classes, it always elicits a groan. It is exactly what they are afraid of—irate parents who want a sanitized version of history and will fight to keep it. The teachers and teacher candidates in this study share that anxiety. They want to smooth over differences, not hold them up for examination.

Not surprisingly, they prefer that parents support rather than attack their programs. Traditionally, Americans have looked to history to provide a justification for the current way of things, and they are likely to resist instruction that questions the foundations of the status quo. Teachers, then, need to learn how to garner support for change and how to respond to challenges.[43] It is not enough to educate students for democratic citizenship; teachers, too must learn to take part in meaningful and productive discussion with people of diverse viewpoints.[44]

Conclusion

The ways in which the students, teachers, and teacher candidates in these two studies talked about history and historical significance in relation to national history are both encouraging and frustrating. While both groups expressed faith in the mainstream American story of gradual emancipation and progress, students were more likely to maintain an alternative story in which private prejudices and, sometimes, public policy worked against inclusion and thwarted what they perceived as the promise of the Bill of Rights. Teachers and teacher candidates, on the other hand, often rejected "negative" images as having little to do with the formation of national identity, especially as it applied to children and adolescents. Their reluctance to include divisive or coercive—or simply alternative—elements from the past contrasted sharply with students' interest in those areas.

Of course, once these historical topics enter the curriculum, they, too, may be sanitized and lose their appeal to students. While this is possible—even probable—it is not necessary. If race, dissent, gender, and class become questions for inquiry rather than topics for study, perhaps they can maintain their power for students.[45] To this end, teachers' notions of freedom, expanding rights, and the dangers of conflict, as well as their ideas about discrimination and oppression, need to be examined, "drawn on and pushed against . . . [so that] the history usually reserved for the few . . . is the history that . . . belong[s] to all."[46] Then the challenge for teachers will be to help children build a framework for making critical sense out of legitimating stories as well as alternative, vernacular histories (see Lee and Ashby, this volume). Lacking such a framework, students may simply replace nationalist self-satisfaction with cynicism.[47] Neither prepares students to understand national history. Indeed, not only are both likely to leave students uninterested in history, but they are probably equally likely to lead students away from active civic participation.

NOTES

1. Gary Gerstle, "Liberty, Coercion, and the Making of Americans," *Journal of American History*, 84(2) (1997), pp. 524–558.

2. K. Anthony Appiah and Amy Gutmann, *Color Conscious: The Political Morality of Race* (Princeton, 1996); David W. Cohen, *The Combing of History* (Chicago, 1994); Michael Kammen, *Mystic Chords of Memory: The Transformation of Tradition in American Culture* (New York, 1991); Samuel Shama, *Dead Certainties: Unwarranted Speculations* (New York, 1992).

3. Slavenka Drakulic, *Cafe Europá* (New York, 1996), p. 187.

4. Cohen, *Combing of History.*

5. Gerstle, "Liberty, Coercion, and the Making of Americans," p. 555.

6. David A. Hollinger, "National Solidarity at the End of the Twentieth Century: Reflections on the United States and Liberal Nationalism," *Journal of American History*, 84(2) (1997), pp. 559–569, 565.

7. Ibid.

8. Ibid., p. 569.

9. Gloria Ladson-Billings, "Coping with Multicultural Illiteracy: A Teacher Education Response," *Social Education*, 55 (1991), pp. 186–187, 194; Bruce A. VanSledright, "'I Don't Remember—the Ideas Are All Jumbled in My Head': 8th Graders' Reconstructions of Colonial American History," *Journal of Curriculum and Supervision*, 10 (1996), pp. 317–345.

10. JoBeth Allen, ed., *Class Actions: Teaching for Social Justice in Elementary and Middle School* (New York, 1998); Etta R. Hollins, *Culture in School Learning: Revealing the Deep Meaning* (Mahwah, NJ, 1996); Ladson-Billings, "Multicultural Illiteracy"; Theresa Mickey McCormick, *Creating the Nonsexist Classroom: A Multicultural Approach* (New York, 1994).

11. VanSledright, "I Don't Remember."

12. Keith C. Barton and Linda S. Levstik, "'It Wasn't a Good Part of History': National Identity and Students' Explanations of Historical Significance," *Teachers College Record*, 99(3) (1998), pp. 478–513; Terrie L. Epstein, "Makes No Difference If You're Black or White? African American and European American Adolescents' Perspectives on Historical Significance and Historical Sources," paper presented at the American Educational Research Association, New Orleans, April 1994; Terrie L. Epstein, "Sociocultural Approaches to Young People's Historical Understanding," *Social Education*, 61 (1997), pp. 28–31; Peter Seixas, "Mapping the Terrain of Historical Significance," *Social Education*, 61 (1997), pp. 22–28.

13. Jane J. White, "Teaching Anthropology to Precollegiate Teachers and

Students," in C. P. Kottak et al., eds., *The Teaching of Anthropology: Problems, Issues, and Decisions* (Mountain View, CA, 1997), pp. 289–298.

14. Ibid.

15. Linda S. Levstik and Keith C. Barton, *Doing History: Investigating with Children in Elementary and Middle Schools* (Mahwah, NJ, 1997); Linda S. Levstik, "The Boys We Know; the Girls in this School," *International Journal of Social Studies* (in press).

16. Group rather than individual interviews were used in order to promote discussion and elaboration among participants. We used single-sex groups in the student study in order to provide more easily analyzed data on gender differences. This was not possible with the teachers and teacher candidates, as there were only three men in the participant pool. Ethnic identification of students was based on teachers' judgments and students' self-identification; adults self-identified.

17. See, for instance, Barton and Levstik, "National Identity."

18. All the teachers and teacher candidates were enrolled in undergraduate (teacher candidates) or graduate (teachers) courses and were familiar with small-group work during which instructors moved among groups. Questions that arose were most often procedural ("Can we really only pick eight?"), though sometimes participants asked for more specific historical information ("When did women get the vote in England?"), and I briefly answered these questions.

19. John Bodnar, *Remaking America: Public Memory, Commemoration, and Patriotism in the Twentieth Century* (Princeton, 1992).

20. Margaret G. Mckeown and Isabel L. Beck, "The Assessment and Characterization of Young Learners' Knowledge of a Topic in History," *American Educational Research Journal*, 27 (1990), pp. 688–726; VanSledright, "I Don't Remember."

21. Interestingly, whenever the name of Christopher Columbus arose, students were quick to point out either that Native Americans already lived in North America or that the Vikings had explored here and that Columbus could not therefore be considered to have discovered the continent.

22. Keith C. Barton, ""Bossed Around by the Queen": Elementary Students Understanding of Individuals and Institutions in History," *Journal of Curriculum and Supervision* (in press).

23. See also Levstik, "The Boys We Know"; Barton and Levstik, *Doing History.*

24. Gerstle, "Liberty, Coercion, and the Making of Americans"; John R. Gillis, "Memory and Identity: The History of a Relationship," in R. Gillis, ed., *Commemorations: The Politics of National Identity* (Princeton, 1994), pp. 3–24; Bronislaw Malinowski, *Magic, Science, and Religion and Other Essays* (Glencoe, IL, 1948); Edward Shils, "Tradition," *Comparative Studies in Society and History*, 13 (1971), pp. 122–159; Robert Williams, *Marxism and Literature* (New York, 1977).

25. Gerstle, "Liberty, Coercion, and the Making of Americans."

26. Anne Martin, "Social Studies in Kindergarten: A Case Study," *Elementary School Journal*, 90(3) (1990), pp. 305–317.

27. The students interviewed included children who identified themselves as African American, as being of European extraction, or as a mixture of these. In one of the schools, about one-fourth of the students interviewed were first- or second-generation residents of the United States.

28. Kammen, *Mystic Chords*.

29. White, "Teaching Anthropology," p. 291.

30. Joyce Appleby, Lynn Hunt, and Margaret Jacob, *Telling the Truth about History* (New York, 1994); Bodnar, *Remaking America;* Henry S. Commager, "The Search for a Usable Past," *American Heritage Magazine* (1965), pp. 4–9; M. Douglas, *How Institutions Think* (Syracuse, 1986); Patricia H. Hinchey, *Finding Freedom in the Classroom: A Practical Introduction to Critical Theory* (New York, 1998); Malinowski, *Magic, Science, and Religion*; Shils, "Tradition"; Williams, *Marxism and Literature*.

31. Appiah and Gutman, *Color Conscious*.

32. White, "Teaching Anthropology."

33. Allen, *Class Actions*; Ladson-Billings, "Multicultural Illiteracy."

34. Linda Mcneil, "Empowering Students: Beyond Defensive Teaching in Social Studies," in C. Emihovich, ed., *Locating Learning: Ethnographic Perspectives on Classroom Research* (Norwood, NJ, 1989), pp. 117–139; White, "Teaching Anthropology."

35. Not all teachers and teacher candidates identified specific courses in responding to the question about where they had learned about history. All of them reported studying American history at the precollegiate and collegiate level. The teacher candidates generally take a two-semester sequence in American history (some students took Advanced Placement American history in high school instead). There are insufficient data to describe the specific courses taken by the teachers.

36. Jere Brophy and Bruce VanSledright, *Teaching and Learning History in Elementary Schools* (New York, 1997); Tom Holt, *Thinking Historically: Narrative, Imagination, and Understanding* (New York, 1990); Levstik and Barton, *Doing History*.

37. Gerstle, "Liberty, Coercion, and the Making of Americans."

38. Jane J. White, "Teaching about Cultural Diversity," in C. Kottak, J. White, R. Furlow, and P. Rice, eds., *The Teaching of Anthropology: Problems, Issues, and Decisions* (Mountain View, CA, 1997), pp. 70–76, 71–72.

39. Gerstle, "Liberty, Coercion, and the Making of Americans."

40. Fred M. Newmann, Walter G. Secada, and Gary G. Wehlage, *A Guide to Authentic Instruction and Assessment: Vision, Standards and Scoring* (Madison, WI, 1995).

41. Holt, *Thinking Historically*; Levstik and Barton, *Doing History*.

42. See, for instance, ibid.

43. Linda S. Levstik, "'Any History Is Someone's History': Listening to Multiple Voices from the Past," *Social Education*, 61(1) (1997), pp. 48–51.

44. Allen, *Class Actions*; Carole L. Hahn, *Becoming Political* (Albany, 1998); Levstik, "Any History"; Levstik and Barton, *Doing History*; James Loewen, *Lies My Teacher Told Me* (New York, 1995).

45. Holt, *Thinking Historically*; Levstik and Barton, *Doing History*.

46. Dennie P. Wolf and Robert Orrill, "Editors' Introduction," in Tom Holt, *Thinking Historically: Narrative, Imagination, and Understanding* (New York, 1990), pp. xi–xiv.

47. Barton and Levstik, "National Identity."

Appendix

Pictures

Adolescent Study	*Additional Pictures: Adult Study*
Hernando de Soto	Triangle Shirtwaist factory fire
The First Thanksgiving	Indian Removal Bill/Trail of Tears
The American Revolution	Induction ceremony for U.S. citizenship
The Bill of Rights	Executive Order No. 9066
Emancipation Proclamation	United Farmworkers demonstration
Western frontier	
Electric light bulb	
Public education	
Immigration	
First successful airplane	
Women's suffrage	
Development of the car	
Depression	
World War	
Polio vaccine	
Civil rights movement	
Rock 'n' roll/Elvis Presley	
Vietnam War	
Computer	
O. J. Simpson Trial	

Interview Questions

Adolescent Study

1. Why did you choose this one [point to each]?
2. Which pictures do you think other people might have picked, and why?
3. Are there any pictures that you don't think anyone would pick? Why?
4. [Point to any pictures not mentioned] Can you think of any reason someone might have included this one?
5. Is there anything in history that's not on any of these pictures that you think should have been included?
6. If a group of [opposite sex: girls/boys] were doing this, do you think they would make any choices different than you did?
7. If little kids, like third or fourth graders, were doing this, what do you think might be different about their choices?
8. If older people, like your parents' or grandparents' ages, were doing this, what do you think might be different about their choices?
9. What are the most important things about history that you've learned in school, and why do you think they're important? What are the least important things you've learned about history in school, and why don't you think they're as important?
10. What are the most important things about history you've learned outside of school?

Adult Study

1. Which pictures do you think other people might have picked, and why?
2. Are there any pictures that you don't think anyone would pick? Why?
3. Is there anything in history that's not represented in any of these pictures that you think should have been included?
4. If a group of your students were doing this, do you think they would make any choices different than you did?
5. If students younger or older than yours were doing this, what do you think might be different about their choices?
6. What are the most important things about history that you've learned in school (including college/university), and why do you think they're important? What are the least important things you've learned about history in school (including college/university), and why don't you think they're as important?
7. What are the most important things about history you've learned outside of school?

Chapter 16

Making Historical Sense

Sam Wineburg

Imagine the following test question:[1]

> Identify the source of this statement:
> *Surely a grade of 33 in 100 on the* simplest *and* most obvious facts *of*
> *American history is not a record in which any high school can take pride.*

This characterization of the knowledge of high school students comes
from:

a. Ravitch and Finn's report of the 1987 National Assessment of Educational Progress in history, in which they argued that students' test
   scores indicate they are "at risk of being gravely handicapped by . . .
   ignorance upon entry into adulthood, citizenship, and parent-
   hood."

b. The 1976 *New York Times* test of American youth, published under
   the banner headline *"Times* Test Shows Knowledge of American
   History Limited."

c. Reports of the 1942 *New York Times* history exam that prompted
   Allan Nevins to write that high school students are "all too ignorant
   of American history."

d. None of the above.

The correct answer is (d), none of the above.[2] The source of this quotation comes neither from the recent National Assessment nor from any of
these earlier reports. We would have to go back all the way to 1917 to find
the source of this quotation, a time long before TV, the social studies
lobby, the teaching of "thinking skills," the breakup of the family, or any
of the other explanations used to explain today's low test scores. Yet, the
conclusions of Professors J. Carleton Bell and David McCollum, who in

1917 tested 668 Texas high school students and published their findings in the fledging *Journal of Educational Psychology*, differ little from those based on any subsequent test of historical knowledge. Bell and McCollum found that more than a third of Texas teenagers could not identify 1776 as the date of the Declaration of Independence, and more than half could not name Jefferson Davis as president of the confederacy—this only fifty years after the end of the Civil War. Considering differences between who attended high school in 1917 and the near-universal enrollments today, the stability of students' ignorance is puzzling. The whole world has turned upside down in the past eighty years but one thing has seemingly remained the same: Kids don't know history.

Is there another way to understand this phenomenon? Is it possible that we have spent so much time discovering (only to rediscover and rediscover) what students *don't* know that we have neglected more basic and more useful questions about young people's historical knowledge? For example, what is it that students actually *do* know about the past? What sources beyond teachers and textbooks contribute to their understanding? How do young people navigate between images of the past learned in the home and those encountered in school? How do they situate their own personal histories in the context of national and world history?

I write these words at a time when the scent of blood rises from the fields of Kosovo. When sixteen- and seventeen-year-old adversaries lay waste to each other's villages and shell each other into oblivion, they do so as *historical* beings, as representatives of struggles each side has inherited and made its own. We know little about how images of the contemporary self come to be formed by collective images of the past— whether in Bosnia-Herzegovina, Ramallah or Jerusalem, the barrio of East Los Angeles or the markets of Koreatown. Indeed, some clues suggest that the images students carry with them come from places quite distant from the classroom—from the media, from popular culture, from the church and the home.[3] Rather than lamenting the inaccuracy of these images (e.g., the ubiquitous Betsy Ross apocryphally piecing together the first stars and stripes[4]), we might ask instead how these images come to be formed in the first place and why they, rather than the content of school history courses, become lodged in the national consciousness. National assessments may tell us what students don't know. But, we remain woefully ignorant of what they *do* know and how they come to know it.

The Legacy of Behaviorism

A good part of our ignorance as history educators is the direct legacy of behaviorism. Simple as it may seem, the act of listening carefully to what adolescents say about history is a form of inquiry that rests on an image of mind profoundly different from the one that has guided nearly a century of educational and psychological research.[5] From Bell and McCollum's 1917 survey to the 1987 National Assessment, the method for understanding children's knowledge has followed a well-beaten path: Adults come together to figure out the facts kids should know. They write a test. When the results come back showing that students did poorly, adults rarely ask what youngsters might have been thinking or how students might have interpreted the task they were given. Test writers rarely consider that youngsters might have known something important that the test did not measure or might think about history in ways very different from those used by adults. In these cases, deliberations about children's minds resemble, as David Olson[6] has wryly observed, those of an entomologist peering at an ant: The ant is viewed as a species not only smaller but vastly inferior to ourselves. We look at it from the outside, measure it, and assign it a label. With reference to young people, we easily forget the inferential chasm between the statement that they don't know what we want them to know and the conclusion that they don't know anything at all.

The strategy of concentrating on students' historical deficits has led to arid discussions of pedagogy. Students would know more history, according to one common (and ahistorical) explanation, if teachers taught content rather than "skills." For commentators such as Arthur Bestor, writing in 1953, or Sean Wilentz, writing in 1996, the bogeyman is the "social studies lobby" (one has to wonder what kind of lobby was at work in Dallas and Houston in 1917, something neither Bestor and Wilentz happened to mention).[7] Other aspects of the discussion focus on how to periodize the U.S. history course or how to assign the proper sequence to topics in the curriculum. The recent Bradley Commission, mostly mute on issues of pedagogy, noted that, as with life, "variety is the spice of learning" and encouraged teachers to select from a mix of teaching methods and techniques.[8] But, skilled history teaching is no more a case of selecting the right mix of methods than is historical interpretation a case of selecting the right mix of documents. The common thread in all of these discussions is a blurry and indistinct image of the learner and the kinds of ideas this learner brings to instruction. We know precious little about how adolescents create historical contexts for their existence. It's no wonder that recommendations about enlivening history instruction so often ring hollow.

History trails behind other subjects in the school curriculum in this regard. In many history education circles there is still the presumption that if children blacken the appropriate circle with a No. 2 pencil they "know" history. Such thinking is another curious holdover from behaviorist models that dominated educational thinking. For the behaviorist, assessing learning was straightforward. If the proper behavior was "emitted," the child "knew." But in the past twenty or thirty years, we have become more astute about what the "correct answer" really means and how the beliefs, conceptions, and assumptions students bring to instruction shape what they take from it. The "cognitive revolution," as Howard Gardner has called it, has provided us with a new lens for understanding what students actually learn in our classrooms.[9]

One of the earliest studies representing the cognitive approach was conducted by the physicist-turned-cognitive scientist Andrea diSessa, who studied what MIT students learned from their introductory classes.[10] DiSessa gave college students a test in which they had to calculate problems that reflected the Newtonian principles of motion they had studied. Students calculated flawlessly—something that would typically lead to the conclusion that students had learned the appropriate course material. DiSessa, however, went one step further: using a computer game, he created qualitative versions of these same problems. Most of these highly able MIT students, when asked to solve different versions of the same problems, reverted to common-sense Aristotelian notions of movement and force, abandoning the Newtonian principles they supposedly had mastered. In other words, their "new" learning came on top of a teetering cognitive structure that went virtually unchanged from the start of the course to its finish.

Dozens of similar examples abound.[11] The great majority of these studies take up issues in the math or science curriculum; many have received funding from the National Science Foundation (NSF). Since the debacle of the 1960s curriculum reform project, *Man: A Course of Study* (MACOS), NSF has retreated almost entirely from supporting projects that have a social science or history slant.[12] Because research follows funding, this retreat created a major imbalance between what we know about children's thinking in a discipline like mathematics and what we know about their thinking in history. While math textbooks and curriculum now reflect research on children's misconceptions and naive beliefs about fractions (and how teachers can take these beliefs into account when planning instruction), materials in history are designed using the same criteria used forty years ago. To be sure, there has been a major shift in the historical topics covered and greater attention to the histories of traditionally underrepresented peoples (see Dunn, Nash, this volume). But, the image of the "end user" of these texts and materials—the student—is still a blur. If there is any presumption on the part of text designers, it is that students don't know *any* history. The situation is not unlike that of a surgeon skilled in the use of laser technology but utterly lacking in knowledge of the patient's anatomy.

One thing *is* certain. American children are by no means "blank slates" when it comes to ideas and beliefs about the past. By adolescence, young people have been exposed to a wide variety of sources for learning about the past. Most have encountered U.S. history twice in the curriculum, once in fifth grade and again during middle school, and will get it again during the year-long eleventh-grade U.S. history course. But the classroom is only one source—and not necessarily the most important one—for learning about the past.

Each of us grows up in a home with a distinct history and a distinct perspective on the meaning of larger historical events. Our parents' stories shape our historical consciousness, as do the stories of the ethnic, racial, and religious groups that number us as members. We attend churches, clubs, and neighborhood associations that further mold both our collective and our individual historical senses. We visit museums and travel to national landmarks in the summer (see Rosenzweig, this volume). We camp out in front of the TV and absorb, often unknowingly, an unending barrage of historical images. Indeed, by the time children have celebrated a decade of Thanksgivings and Martin Luther King Days, they are already seasoned students of American culture and history. But, the notion that these sources of historical information form a coherent whole mocks the complexity of social life. Historical consciousness does not emanate like neat concentric circles from the individual to the family to the nation and to the world. Lessons learned at home contravene those learned at school. What we hear at school conflicts with what we hear at church or synagogue—if not in the pews, then certainly in the bathrooms. If we pay attention to the lyrics of grunge rock or tune our dials to Rush Limbaugh or Howard Stern, we confront more disjunctures. To make historical sense, we must navigate the shoals of the competing narratives that vie for our allegiance. As Carl Becker noted long ago,[13] each day we awake to the morning news—whether by unfolding the paper or by pointing our browsers to *www.cnn.com*—calls us to be a historian.

Or maybe we aren't called. Maybe the only thing that accompanies the cacophony of modernity is the call to choose those messages that make us feel good about ourselves, our group, our faith, or our race. Perhaps this is the sole imperative of contemporary society, where the past emerges as a treasure trove available to us in building our identity. Heritage, like history, uses the past, but it makes no pretense of being self-critical: It makes no apologies for pursuing its work with the predetermined goals of making us feel proud of our past, whether or not we ought to feel proud (see Lowenthal, this volume).[14] In the everyday language of public discourse, history and heritage (or history and memory) tend to get conflated, an unfortunate turn of events that draws inspiration from the postmodern reflex to blur any distinction. However, the normative issue of whether these categories should be kept separate is a different question from how history, memory, heritage, and an amorphous collection of widely held social beliefs converge in people's thinking about the past. If we want to understand the nature of modern historical consciousness, we must examine how young people *become historical* in modern society. Knowledge of the past, as Michael Schudson felicitously put it, "seeps into the cultural pores," even if such knowledge is not "readily retrievable by seventeen-year-olds answering a quiz." Such tests play a role in understanding historical knowledge, but to assume that they constitute the essence of historical knowledge "short-circuits real analysis of the American sense of the past."[15]

Thinking about the Past

In 1996, with a grant from the Spencer Foundation, I embarked on a longitudinal study of how ordinary people conceptualize their lives as historical beings. I focused on the lives of fifteen different adolescents who attended three different high schools in the Seattle area. One school was a meandering inner-city complex, with a tracked and differentiated curriculum, large classes, and students who spoke twenty-three different native languages. A second school was at the opposite extreme: with tuition set at $10,000/year, this private preparatory academy had classes of ten to twelve students who would sit around a table with their history teacher, who held a Ph.D., to discuss the day's assignment. The third school, also private, had as its motto "strengthening students' commitment to serving Lord Jesus Christ." Students attending this school were mostly white and middle-class, from a range of Evangelical and Pentecostal denominations.

In each of the three schools, I selected five students as they embarked on their state-mandated eleventh-grade U.S. history course. I wanted to understand how these young people thought of themselves as historical beings prior to starting eleventh grade, their last formal exposure to U.S. history in high school. I wanted to know what the experience of learning U.S. history meant to them during the year and how the content of instruction was remembered a year later, as students completed high school and prepared for the future. For a year, I, along with my team of graduate students,[16] spent countless hours in these three schools, watching history classes, audiotaping lectures, touching base with our fifteen participants, all the while collecting, cataloging, and sorting their assignments, tests, class notes, and term papers.

Our interests went beyond the classroom. We wanted to understand how these fifteen teenagers understood their *own* pasts, including the histories of their own families and communities. This meant interviewing them in the context of their own homes, typically in their living rooms, and asking them to tell us the stories of their own births (an event that they had heard about entirely from others) and to narrate the most important events in their lives. From here, we asked students to "draw a map"[17] of the most significant important events in the life of the nation, offering a look at how a diverse cross-section of adolescents conceptualized history from their own perspective. This initial interview, which in some cases ran as long as three hours, was one of eight formal interviews over the course of two and a half years.[18]

Each of these students grew up in a family, and we wanted to capture this aspect of their experience as well. The educational literature is filled with claims about the "family as educator," but the meaning of this term is anything but clear. To better understand students' contexts for developing a historical self, we subjected parents to the same grueling life history interviews that students engaged in, and over the course of the study interviewed or surveyed parents twice more.[19] Finally, each of the three teachers participated in the same life history interview, along with several other interviews similar to those completed by students.

The Vietnam Interview

Space limitations prevent me from doing more than conveying a flavor of the findings that have emerged from our nearly 150 formal interviews with students, parents, and teachers; 130 hours of direct classroom observation; and our analyses of more than 2,000 pages of written documents. In the spirit of economy I focus here on what was the richest and certainly the most memorable data gathering activity across the two years of data collection: our joint parent-child interview about the Vietnam War and the meaning of the sixties.

In studying Vietnam, we wanted to examine a historical event that was experienced by parents in their own lifetimes but had already become "history" for their children—the difference, if you will, between lived memory and learned memory. We were faced with the question of how to examine this issue, for the last thing we wanted to create was a setting that seemed test-like when our primary goal was to get one generation to talk to the other about an issue of historical significance. To reduce the pressure and to try to create a somewhat natural setting, we decided to focus on pictures and song.

We built our interview around a series of six iconic pictures and a two-minute presentation of a song. The pictures included the *Life* magazine picture of nine-year-old Kim Phoc running naked after a napalm bomb attack; an ambiguous picture in which a GI, holding two Vietnamese children under his arm, appears to be fleeing a battlefield; construction workers at pro-war rally in front of Manhattan's City Hall in May 1970; a flower child placing a daisy into the gun barrel of a National Guardsman in the march on the Pentagon in October 1967; a Vietnam vet, chalk in hand, tracing the name of a fallen comrade at the Vietnam War Memorial; and a cartoon from 1968 in which the Angel of Death, standing against a background of tombstones, asks Uncle Sam, "What should I put down as the reason for dying?" The song we played was "Woodstock," by Joni Mitchell and performed by Crosby, Stills, Nash, and Young. ("Who are they?" wondered nearly half of the teens.) The interview took the form of free response: Parents and children first wrote down their reactions to the pictures and song (without revealing their responses to each other) and then shared these responses with us in discussion.

After the first few interviews, it became clear that we had stumbled upon a format more powerful than we had imagined. Tissue paper joined the list of required supplies in the interview room. For many parents,

Vietnam was something that inhabited and continues to inhabit their present, and does so with an intensity that spills over with little provocation. Parent responses to this interview captured the contemporary political spectrum in microcosm, from those people who mark Vietnam as the beginning of the fall, the event that launched America into its current abyss of crime, sex, and lawlessness, to those parents who were more in tune with one mother, who wistfully turned to her sixteen-year-old and sighed, "It's not like now, where everybody is out for himself. Back then we had a *purpose*."

The interview with the Delaney family, sixteen-year-old John and his mother, Karen, and his father, Ken, reveals the potential of this approach to shed light on the larger questions of historical consciousness that motivated our work. The Delaneys are white, middle class, and devoutly Christian. John attends the Christian high school described earlier. He is an intelligent, outgoing student, active in the school drama society, articulate in his responses, and well-spoken about his beliefs. In his history class of twenty-two students, he was consistently among the most vocal participants. The Delaneys live in a modern two-story house in a picturesque suburb of Seattle, with quiet cul-de-sacs, well-tended lawns, and children riding their bikes on the sidewalks.

Ken and Karen are in their mid-forties. Both parents were in high school during the last years of the draft, and neither had siblings or close relatives who served in Vietnam. But this fact did not dull the emotion displayed by both mother and father. Like many respondents in our sample, the Delaneys regarded the Vietnam experience not as a distant event that brushed against their lives but as a core moment that continues to shape their present. Indeed, it was the intensity of the emotion displayed by Ken and Karen that provided a point of contrast with sixteen-year-old John. On viewing the Pulitzer-prize-winning picture of Kim Phuc running naked after a napalm attack, Karen, sobbing, turned to John (who did not recognize the picture) and explained its origin. Her husband, Ken, his voice shaking as well, picked up her sentence, using language that blurred past and present: "What are we accomplishing, why are we doing this? And who's profiting by all this show of force? That doesn't look like a very substantial army they're fighting there."

After a period of silence during which the parents regained their composure, I turned to John and asked if there was anything he wanted to ask his parents, anything that aroused his curiosity as he watched the emotion this picture evoked. In response, John offered ideas about the role of emotion in understanding history. Because of his distance from Vietnam, John claimed that he was "more objective" than either parent and, consequently, could offer a better historical account.

> *John:* I think I have more of an objective view because I didn't live through it, I don't know people who went to Vietnam and didn't come back, or anything. . . . I didn't live through it, I never had to look at our government and go, "Why are they in there?" I can look back more than, I think, than [my parents] can. . . .
>
> *Int.:* Do you think the fact that you have less emotion with it helps or hinders you in understanding what went on?
>
> *John:* [Having less emotion] helps, but I think if I was dealing with someone who'd gone through it, [having less emotion] wouldn't [help] at all. I think it would dampen me because I wouldn't be able to relate as much if I was talking to someone who'd gone through it and all of a sudden was just kind of feeling sad about what went on, I would be like—I wouldn't have much response for them. But I think in a logical scholarly way—I'm not a scholar or anything—but I guess in a logical Vulcan kind of response (laughs)—I can go, "Well, this is what happened, these things happened and these things happened and this is the"—I think I can probably weigh the pros and the cons more objectively.

Here, then, is a rough epistemology of historical understanding, according to a bright sixteen-year-old participant in American culture. For John, emotion threatens historical objectivity, yet it is the very ingredient that would help him if he had to "deal with someone" who had experienced the trauma of war. However, this emotion, which John viewed as the foundation for empathy, remained outside the purview of legitimate historical understanding. For John, historical understanding is best captured by Mr. Spock, the character from *Star Trek*, whose most salient characteristic (besides pointed ears) is the inability to feel.

John's views need to be taken seriously, for they were not unique among our participants, and surely there is a grain of truth to them. Unbridled passion poses a threat to historical understanding, especially when the forces of emotion cause the historian to skew or suppress data or to hold on to cherished beliefs in the face of disconfirmatory evidence. Yet, it is also hard to imagine serious historical work in which emotion plays no role—if not in the historians' passion for the subject (which allows scholars to spend endless hours slogging through documents, often in dark and poorly heated archives), then at least in historians' ability to empathize with the people they seek to understand. John, a serious and intelligent high school junior, has an image of historical scholarship carried out by emotionless drones alienated from their human origins. At the base of this epistemology is a contradictory implicit logic: Historians are most objective when they are not personally connected to their subject; however, it is precisely one's personal connection that generates interest and passion. Oddly, for John, those best suited to carry out historical work are those least interested and motivated to do it.

John's response is consistent with the instruction we observed at Revelations High School,[20] where his history teacher marched a straight line through the U.S. history curriculum. His class was characterized by a heavy dose of minute and copious historical facts, with weekly objective tests intended to help prepare students for the Advanced Placement exam. We noted a wide chasm between the biblical posters lining the room (the largest in neatly printed letters read: "What would Jesus have done?") and the generic "anywhere anyplace" quality of instruction. If any factor gave shape to this history curriculum, it was not the testaments of Mark and Matthew but the policy decisions of the Educational Testing Service in New Jersey.

In light of what we observed in John's classroom, it's tempting to connect his views to the kind of history to which he had been exposed. There is surely a connection, but we believe that John's beliefs cannot be explained by his experience with a single teacher plowing determinedly through the curriculum. Indeed, his views about what makes good history were shared, for the most part, by his parents. History, for John's dad, was about "analysis," and he even expressed concern that the emotion he displayed in our interview might introduce unwanted "bias" into our study. In this regard, father and son were of like mind.

At work here, we believe, are powerful and relatively stable ideas about everyday criteria for sound historical judgment and about the day-to-day work of the historian. To some extent, the Delaneys' views reflect notions prevalent in the early days of history's arrival at the modern research university. By the 1930s, however, such views were being questioned by AHA presidents Becker and Beard. It is also important to note the chasm between these ideas and those expressed by contemporary historians about their work. One might even claim that in our postmodern age, historical works that abjure emotion are themselves suspect, viewed as tools that mask, through rhetorical means, the underlying polemical nature of their arguments. As the profession celebrates subjectivity and positionality, two cardinal virtues of postmodernity, notions of objectivity and its attainability live on in the Delaney household.

John may feel that he is more objective and less emotional about Vietnam than his parents. However, there were points in the interview when he displayed clear and strong reactions and looked to bolster his claims by appealing to sources that were hardly dispassionate or objective. One of these instances came when John responded to the picture of the GI leaving a battle scene with two young boys tucked under each arm. The picture is itself ambiguous and was variously interpreted by our respondents. Some viewed the GI as a kidnapper, while others (including John and his parents) viewed the soldier as a rescuer. Indeed, it was John's interpretation of the picture, of a soldier saving young lives in the midst of the horrors of war, that led to the following response:

> Here's this guy running, and maybe that's not what he was doing, but it looks like he's running out and he's got these two kids under his arms, kind of ironic that we think of Vietnam, you always hear someone say, "Oh, baby killers." So here's this guy running out, and he's got these two kids, it's like he's saving them from the disaster that's going on behind him. I thought it was a well-taken photo.

John's language merits attention. First, it was a rare moment in our interviews when an adolescent so clearly reported an instance of the past intruding into the present. John reports that he has heard the epithet "baby killer" aimed at Vietnam vets not once or twice but "always." Where might John have heard this? From our observations and documentation in his classroom, we know that Vietnam hardly figured at all into the school curriculum, that it was restricted to a single sixty-minute discussion in this U.S. history course. Nor was this the type of thing, given our understanding of his mother and father, that either would likely say. Moreover, according to the work of historians and sociologists, the actual historical basis for the "spat-upon" veteran is weak, to say the least, hardly documented to the point that would warrant, some thirty years later, the strength of John's everyday recollection.[21] In fact, as Eric Dean notes in *Shook over Hell: Post-traumatic Stress, Vietnam, and the Civil War,* the first American troops withdrawn from Vietnam were greeted in John's backyard, downtown Seattle, by a crowd that cheered its thanks: "Flags waved, ticker tape showered down on the troopers, and pretty girls pressed red roses into the men's hands."[22]

Where, then, might John have heard such epithets? Or, more generally, what sources of information have contributed to John's understanding of Vietnam? In the course of this interview, John mentioned several sources and events that contributed to his understanding. One was a report he completed on Richard Nixon in which he set out to prove that "Nixon was a good president based on his accomplishments in foreign affairs." In researching this report, John read "some biographies and autobiographies," but he did not note the actual names of any. (Nor did we have the presence of mind to probe for them.) Indeed, the only places in the interview where John provided a specific reference to a historical claim came in response to his statement that "war was good for the economy."

> *Int.:* Okay, so help me get a little bit better understanding for a second. One person might say that the war was a very costly effort. We are expending all of these armaments and we're losing our planes and we're losing young people and it's the sheer cost of transporting [troops] there, so, how does, from your understanding, how does profit enter into it?
>
> *John:* Oh, because you—any point in history you look at, war builds up an economy. It's like in *Schindler's List*—Schindler said, I tried all these businesses and they never worked because I never had one thing. What changed his luck? War. And it's, because with war there's a higher demand for metal works because you're losing your planes and your equipment and your helicopters and tanks and what not, you need to make those, and you have to have someone back in the U.S. to make those things.

Asked to elaborate on a claim about the benefits of war, John turned neither to something learned in school nor to formal knowledge about economics. His proof text came from Steven Spielberg's *Schlindler's List*, a movie based not on a piece of history but on a piece of historical fiction by Thomas Keneally. John's claim about the relationship between war and profit may have some basis, but this is surely beside the point. Important here is the specificity of his reference compared to his earlier vague statements about "some books and autobiographies" for his report on Nixon. His language in this instance was direct and came with no introduction, qualification, or preface such as, "It's like, I saw in the movie *Schindler's List.*" John worked on the assumption that he and the interviewer shared cultural knowledge (in this case, a correct assumption), and that he could draw on a facet of this shared knowledge using shorthand. In making his claim about war, John called upon the past, but it is a filmic past that he remembered, a past that blurs fact and fiction and that ultimately, in John's reasoning, provides the basis for a historical claim.

This was not an isolated instance, either in the rest of John's interview or, for that matter, in our other interviews. Indeed, another movie played an even greater role in John's understanding—in this case, a movie that integrated actual historical footage into the visual flow of fictional events. *Forrest Gump* served, and apparently continues to serve, as an occasion for the Delaney family to sit together and discuss the past.[23] The family owns the tape and has watched it together repeatedly. John: "We talk about Vietnam and I guess the family, *Forrest Gump* always brings up something along those lines. You know, they always mention the money and the greed and I understand where they're coming from." The movie also served as the meeting point between the Delaneys and close family friends, for example, with Don Waverly, a Vietnam vet. John: "Don, doesn't talk about Vietnam. Doesn't really say anything about it. . . . Don watched [*Forrest Gump*] with us once and he was real quiet during the Vietnam scenes."

Forrest Gump served as the starting point in the Delaney's discussions of the sixties. Unlike other families in our sample, who made pilgrimages to the Vietnam War Memorial, the Delaneys' point of reference was a videocassette. In terms of specificity of information about Vietnam, the only source of information that John quoted verbatim came not from parents, teachers, ministers, or any of the books he had read. In John's case it was a snippet of dialogue from *Forrest Gump*.

> *Int.:* You mentioned *Forrest Gump* in the beginning of the interview.
> *John:* Good movie.
> *Int.:* And you mentioned it in reference to what?
> *John:* Oh, that movie really just centers around the sixties. It's a story of the baby boomer generation, from 1950-something to 1980-something. It's their life. My parents I think related to it in a totally different way than I did. I have friends who say it was one of the most boring movies they've ever seen. Now I disagree with that statement, I thought it was a really good movie. That it had a lot to say, could learn a lot from it—attitudes. But you watch Vietnam and the guy says to Forrest Gump, one of the hippies looks at Forrest Gump in his military uniform, and he goes, "Who's the baby killer?"

Recall that it was this very scenario, in which civilians taunt returning Vietnam veterans by calling them "baby killers," that John claimed to "always hear" in his daily life. It is, in fact, the clearest and sharpest recollection John had of the entire Vietnam era.

It is tempting to characterize John's comments here as just another instance of how contemporary film influences our understanding of the past, a phenomenon that has become a cottage industry for scholars in cultural studies.[24] Obviously, John is influenced by a film, several films to be exact. But, to leave it at that only scratches the surface. A film, or, in this case, a home video, has become an occasion for the Delaney family to revisit the past. They convene in their living room, take a cassette from their shelves, and insert it into a VCR. Unlike a pilgrimage to a historical site or a trip to a history museum, the videos in our home entertainment centers speak to the American imperative of convenience. While we may "go out" to the movies to see the past, in the video age the past becomes something we possess. The usable past on video is, above all, the *always available past.*

Like our other possessions, the videocassette is available to us when the need arises. In this interview alone there were three specific references to watching *Forrest Gump* as a family activity, including one time when the Delaneys watched with their friend, the Vietnam vet Don Waverly. We can even imagine that there were other times the Delaneys watched the tape. Through this repeated viewing, the video came to take on a role not unlike that played by cherished writings and sacred texts in earlier times. Snippets of video dialogue offer convenient metonymies—their invocation calls up a flood of feelings, values, and associations. Because the human mind remembers detail far better than its provenance, the detail remains, but its source falls away.[25] So, John is correct when he says that he always hears "baby killers," but it's likely that he hears it most often from a character whose lines were written by the screenwriter Robert Zemeckis. In other words, the fictionalized past, not the historical event, becomes John's frame of reference for the present.

The Delaneys' viewing habits give a new twist to the notion of the family as educator. The family still educates, to be sure, but not in a stylized, Norman Rockwell way. It's not around the kitchen table where stories are transmitted from generation to generation but on the living room couch, once the VCR starts on play. The family serves as the context for this video history lesson by mediating the larger cultural narrative provided by Hollywood. Whereas in traditional societies the family would travel to sites of memory—battlefields, shrines of saints, or other commemorative locales—here the "lieux de mémorie," to invoke Pierre Nora, is not a site per se but an object.[26] The videocassette obviates the need for pilgrimage and conforms to the imperatives of modernity. It permits ritual without pilgrimage by putting the past at the touch of a button.

Conclusion

We have embarked on an empirical journey into the colliding worlds of history and memory, of knowing the past through the ordinary sense-making capacities we use to know most things about the world, and knowing it as the result of disciplined habits of mind. In analyzing our data, we are less concerned with whether people's historical understanding corresponds to some canonical body of information than we are with trying to generate topographies of historical memory, rough maps of how ordinary people think about the past and use it to understand the present. An investigation related to ours was recently completed by Roy Rosenzweig and David Thelan (see Rosenzweig, this volume), who undertook a telephone survey of more than 1,000 Americans to understand how the past is used in everyday life. Such an approach allows these researchers to generate a broad image of the incidence of everyday activities related to the past (and the meanings people attach to these activities), such as pursuing family genealogies or visiting historical museums. But, as valuable as such information may be, it does not allow us to locate individual responses in the context of the family, the school, the church and the community. Nor does it provide the kind of detailed portraits of understanding that would allow educators access to the nooks and crannies of students' cognitive landscapes. Our study is much more narrow in sample size, and, in that sense, our generalizations are, by necessity, more modest. Such "generalizations" point us toward an emerging theory of everyday historical understanding rather than to any direct statement of incidence and frequency beyond the participants in our study. Nonetheless, commonalties across our different participants, with different educational backgrounds, religious views, and ways of seeing the world, give us confidence that the trends we see in this sample are more than idiosyncratic.

As the interview with the Delaneys illustrates, historical memory is highly selective: It is not just that the details of historical events become less acute as time goes on. Rather, what is remembered or forgotten from the past is constantly being shaped by contemporary social processes, acts of state that commemorate certain events and not others, decisions by novelists and film makers to tell one kind of story and not another, and an amorphous set of collective social needs that draws on some elements from the past while leaving others dormant.

Indeed, it was this last aspect—the demands that the present places on the past—that led the French sociologist Maurice Halbwachs to claim that collective memory was not about the past at all but was entirely a reflection of contemporary social needs and the contemporary social condition. With the onset of modernity and the rapidity of social change, Halbwachs saw an abyss between the present and the past, akin to "two tree stumps that touch at their extremities but do not form one plant because they are not otherwise connected."[27]

The neo-Halbwachians, the sociologists Barry Schwartz and Yael Zerubavel, take a less extreme stance and see a dialectic between historical memory and the historical record (as represented in the work of historians).[28] Like Pierre Nora, these scholars focus their attention on sites of memory—battlefields, monuments, and museums—as well as on the production of cultural materials related to the past: novels, popular books, films, and essays. But, to date, there have been few if any attempts to track how the processes of historical memory play out in the lives of ordinary people, how it is that the proverbial person on the street embodies (or doesn't embody) the broad social processes posited by the theorists of collective memory. Without this perspective, we open ourselves to the criticism noted by Wertsch (this volume) of conflating the production of cultural products with their consumption. Individuals are influenced by, as well as act upon, the products of elites. Attempts to arrive at a conception of collective memory that bypasses the individual (a collective memory, if you will, held by no one in particular)[29] will run aground on the banks of reductionism and essentialism. To understand how societies remember, we need both macro and micro analyses of cultural transmission, adaptation, and reformulation.

We are clearly in the earliest stages of trying to understand our data. Our hope, ultimately, is that, by shedding light on how adolescents make sense of the past, we can learn how to better engage their historical beliefs, stretch them, and call them into question when necessary. In that sense, our investigation is more than a foray into cultural studies. As a cognitive scientist (in the 1970s sense of that term—an interdisciplinary field that mixes anthropology, sociology, and psychology in arriving at an empirical understanding of the phenomena of consciousness[30]), I am also a meliorist: Given these findings and continued support for them in other studies, what direction should new curricula take? How would we design effective education for new teachers of history? What software might we design, and what on-line questions would we ask on the basis of these and similar findings? As we design new educational interventions, who, exactly, are we designing them for? And, what do we actually know about the existing understandings and beliefs of the "end users" of our educational innovations?

I recently described these findings to a friend, a longtime veteran of the high school history classroom. He was chagrined and pointed out that too many history teachers depend on videos and should remove them from the classroom. This, I believe, won't help. The calculus classroom may be the site where we learn advanced mathematics, but we learn history everywhere—school hardly possesses a monopoly. Removing videos from the classroom leaves them intact in the home, on the DVD, on cable and DirecTV, and practically everywhere else. Rather than pretending that we can do away with popular culture—confiscate videos, banish grunge rock and rap music, magnetize Nintendo games, and unplug MTV and the Movie Channel—we might well try to understand how these forces shape historical consciousness and how they might be used, rather than spurned or simply ignored, to advance students' historical understanding.

NOTES

1. This work was supported by a grant from the Spencer Foundation, but the views expressed are those of the author. In all phases I have been ably assisted by Susan Mosborg, without whom this work could not have been completed.

2. See Diane Ravitch and Chester Finn Jr., *What Do Our 17-Year-Olds Know? A Report on the First National Assessment of History and Literature* (New York, 1987) p. 201; Allan Nevins, "American History for Americans." *New York Times Magazine*, 95 (May 3, 1943), pp. 6, 28–29; J. Carleton Bell and David F. McCollum, "A Study of the Attainments of Pupils in United States History," *Journal of Educational Psychology*, 8 (1917), pp. 257–274; *New York Times*, May 2, 1976, p. 1.

3. Maurice Halbwachs, *The Collective Memory* (New York, 1980); Jacques LeGoff, *History and Memory* (New York, 1992).

4. Michael Frisch, "American History and the Structure of Collective Memory: A Modest Exercise in Empirical Iconography," *Journal of American History*, 75 (1989), pp. 1130–1155.

5. One major exception to this statement in an English-speaking country is the work of the School's Council History Project (see Lee and Ashby, Shemilt, this volume). British researchers, led by the pioneering work of Peter Lee, Alaric Dickinson, Peter Rogers, Denis Shemilt, and others, had a head start on their American counterparts, since the writings of Jean Piaget (a major impetus behind taking children's thinking seriously) were discussed in Europe a good ten years before they were popularized in North America. Since the late 1980s, a small but vigorous group of North American researchers has been exploring aspects of historical cognition. For reviews, see Mario Carretero and James F. Voss, *Cognitive and Instructional Processes in History and the Social Sciences* (Hillsdale, NJ, 1994), or the special issue of the journal *Educational Psychology,* "The Psychology of Teaching and Learning History" (Spring 1994).

6. David R. Olson and Nancy Torrance, *Handbook of Education and Development* (Cambridge, MA, 1996).

7. Arthur Bestor, *Educational Wastelands: The Retreat from Learning in Public Schools* (Urbana, IL, 1953); Sean Wilentz, "The Past Is Not a Process," *New York Times,* April 20, 1996, p. E-15. Wilentz predicted that the "historical illiteracy of today's student will only worsen in the generation to come." No reference was made to similar baleful predictions from 1917, 1942, or 1987.

8. Bradley Commission on History in the Schools. *Building a History Curriculum* (New York, 1988).

9. Howard Gardner, *The Mind's New Science* (New York, 1985).

10. Andrea diSessa, "Unlearning Aristotelian Physics: A Study of Knowledge-based Learning," *Cognitive Science,* 6 (1982), pp. 37–75.

11. See the final report of the Committee on the Developments in the Science of Learning of the National Research Council, *How People Learn: Brain, Mind, Experience, and School* (Washington, DC, 1999). See also Howard Gardner, *The Unschooled Mind* (New York, 1995).

12. Peter Dow, *Schoolhouse Politics: Lessons from the Sputnik Era* (Cambridge, MA, 1991).

13. Carl Becker, "Everyman His Own Historian," *American Historical Review,* 37, pp. 221–236.

14. See Lowenthal's extensive treatment of the topic in *Possessed by the Past: The Heritage Crusade and the Spoils of History* (New York, 1996).

15. Michael Schudson, *Watergate in American Memory: How We Remember, Forget, and Reconstruct the Past* (New York, 1992), p. 64.

16. These interviews were conducted by me, as well as by Alex Shih, Diana Hess, and Susan Mosborg.

17. I was inspired by Peter Seixas's development of this task. See his "Mapping the Terrain of Historical Significance," *Social Education,* 61 (1997) pp. 22–27.

18. Space limitations do not allow a description of all of our other research tasks and interviews. Suffice it to say that they ranged from an interview in which students read the daily newspaper (to see how they connected past and present) to an interview in which they were asked to narrate the struggle for civil rights in American history, to another interview in which they explained to us what they thought their teachers meant by written comments on their term papers.

19. One of the things we asked parents to do was to take a multiple-choice test on historical facts, which allowed us to compare their scores with those earned by their children on the same test.

20. The name, like all other proper names used here, is a pseudonym.

21. See Jerry Lembcke, *The Spitting Image: Myth, Memory, and the Legacy of Vietnam* (New York, 1998).

22. Eric Dean, *Shook over Hell: Post-traumatic Stress, Vietnam, and the Civil War* (Cambridge, MA, 1997). Dean's source is *Time*, "Joy in Seattle; Troops Withdrawn from Viet Nam," July 18, 1969, p. 5.

23. *Forrest Gump* played a major role in adolescents' reconstructions of the Vietnam era, more so than any other single source, including parents, teachers, and textbooks. Other movies spontaneously discussed by adolescents included *Rambo, Dazed and Confused, Platoon,* and *Apocalypse Now.*

24. See, for example, William Adams, "War Stories: Movies, Memory, and the Vietnam War," *Comparative Social Research*, 11 (1989), pp. 165–183.

25. Colleen M. Seifert, Robert B. Abelson, and Gail McKoon, "The Role of Thematic Knowledge Structures," in John A. Galambos, Robert B. Abelson, and John B. Black, eds., *Knowledge Structures* (Hillsdale, NJ, 1986).

26. Pierre Nora, "Between History and Memory: *Les Lieux de Mémoire*," *Representations*, 26 (1989), pp. 1–15.

27. This source of this citation from Halbwachs is Barry Schwartz, "The Reconstruction of Abraham Lincoln," in David Middleton and Derek Edwards, eds., *Collective Remembering* (London, 1991), p. 104.

28. See ibid.; and Yael Zerubavel, "New Beginning, Old Past: The Collective Memory of Pioneering in Israeli Culture," in Laurence J. Silberstein, ed., *New Perspectives on Israeli History: The Early Years of the State* (New York, 1990).

29. For a related point, see James Fentress and Chris Wickham, *Social Memory* (Cambridge, MA, 1992).

30. On the difference between current fashions in cognitive science and its earlier interdisciplinary roots, see Jerome Bruner, *Acts of Meaning* (Cambridge, MA, 1990). For examples of a cognitive approach to the interpretation of historical texts, see Sam Wineburg, "Reading Abraham Lincoln: An Expert/Expert Study in the Interpretation of Historical Texts," *Cognitive Science*, 22 (1999), pp. 319–346, and Sam Wineburg, "Historical Thinking and Other Unnatural Acts," *Phi Delta Kappan*, 80 (1999), pp. 488–499, www.pdkintl.org/kappan/kwin9903.htm.

Part IV

Models for Teaching

Ultimately, the goals of research on history learning, as they blend with methods used by history teachers, must focus on improving learning outcomes. The essays in this section, though diverse in many respects, join in examining ways to develop historical skills and understandings more successfully, at the school and the college level alike. They join also in defining successful teaching in terms other than of maximum factual memorization. All the essays are seeking ways to create students who can gain and transfer historical habits of mind, and most of them also sketch assessment mechanisms by which such achievements can be measured.

History teachers author three of the essays, learning researchers the other three. Two of the essays by the researchers focus heavily on studying the learning process itself, moving toward interventions as part of the research results. The essay by Voss and Wiley discusses measurements of historical understanding that result from different teaching procedures, particularly multiple sources and analytical essay assignments, but in the process it implicitly addresses successful teaching and learning strategies as well. Veronica Boix-Mansilla works on students' capacity to analogize between a historical episode and a more recent, somewhat similar event. The result is a research piece that probes what students are able to do and how this can be evaluated but also moves toward the creation of procedures that might improve capacities not only to draw but also to qualify analogies. The two essays that refer to secondary school classrooms strongly emphasize the importance of good, sensitive teaching, beyond any particular methodologies. Christine Gutierrez sees historical understanding in terms of students' personal development and their capacity to participate effectively in democratic communities. She describes the approaches and some of the exercises that work toward this goal in her classroom, while referring also to more familiar historical habits of mind such as using documents and dealing with multiple interpretations. Robert Bain, also as a classroom teacher, has goals that are somewhat differently defined. Bain's essay is directly concerned with applying cognitive lessons, particularly in helping students to understand how historical knowledge is constructed. His goal is to develop students' abilities to handle historical or contemporary issues in cases where dealing with change and understanding diverse interpretations are involved, whether in or outside the classroom. The last two essays describe more specific interventions. The essay by Britt, Perfetti, Van Dyke, and Gabrys builds particularly on history learning research, utilizing computer-aided lesson and practice design in dealing with sources. The Stearns essay utilizes cognitive principles somewhat more generally in relationship to learning goals developed through experience in world history teaching.

Collectively, the articles relate closely to issues raised in earlier sections of this book, particularly the section on learning research. Considerable attention is paid in these chapters to improving student ability to handle sources (both primary and secondary), including identification of bias, and to deal with diverse interpretations—topics discussed in other ways in earlier essays. Voss and Wiley's assessment of student use of multiple viewpoints, for example, should be juxtaposed with the procedures used in the United Kingdom described in chapter 5. None of the articles fully tackles the issue, raised in earlier discussions by Wineburg and Levstik, of recognizing and using student versions of history, though Gutierrez works hard to elicit students' preconceptions and feelings. Clearly, there are gaps still to be closed between research and the foci of imaginative teaching practice. On the other hand, the essays collectively highlight additional, possibly more complex skills areas—particularly those involving change, causation, and comparison—that have received less learning research attention, and they argue that here, too, use of cognitive research and principles can accelerate student mastery. The Boix-Mansilla essay, while dealing with change, ventures still further, sketching one of the most common uses of history—analogy—that is rarely studied explicitly or assessed in the classroom.

Collectively, also, the essays argue for a mix of good teaching practice and explicit innovation. Not only Gutierrez, writing as a working teacher, but also Voss and Wiley rely heavily on things good teachers have long attempted, such as the use of essay assignments and multiple materials. These two articles add a somewhat more explicit appreciation of why these approaches work, producing students who become more tolerant or who are better able to make connections or to venture reasonable explanations. But self-conscious drills and techniques designed to improve students' analytical capacity factor in as well, suggesting that even good teachers can move students along more rapidly than is commonly now the case.

The essays, again collectively, inevitably raise some additional issues. None fully assesses the trade-offs between expanded coverage and the extra time it takes to deal with diverse sources and viewpoints or to utilize the desired analytical techniques. Questions about the use of time crop up, as the Bain essay, for example, demonstrates. The essays uniformly argue, or at least assume, that the extra time will be well spent: Students will emerge with more useful and transferrable historical understandings than they would have had the sessions been devoted strictly to covering additional chapters of the textbook. The essay by Britt, Perfetti, Van Dyke, and Gabrys goes so far as to urge the use of formal history laboratory sessions in alternation with more standard class meetings. The practical concerns of such a setup are potentially resolvable, but we're not yet to that point in history teaching.

All of the essays offer evidence that good teaching, including new practices, will pay off in measurable student achievements. Again, however, there is work to be done in extending the assessments beyond a single year to see what skills are retained and what habits of mind continue to be transferrable to other encounters with the human social experience. The essays uniformly seek this transferability as the chief teaching goal, but at the same time they invite additional experimentation and outcomes research. Furthermore, most of the experiments, tests, and methods discussed in this section have been used for single years or single semesters of a history curriculum, rather than with a more extensive course sequence; their long-term value needs to be studied.

It remains important to celebrate what the essays do accomplish. They suggest refinements in our ability to identify what good teaching is and what historical understanding is all about. They point to direct connections between learning research and particular interventions that seem capable of moving understandings along more rapidly than has traditionally been the case. In a field beset by serious problems and uncertainties, they suggest new ways to argue about why history counts and how the real contributions of history learning can be evaluated. They suggest, in fact, a certain degree of . . . optimism.

Chapter 17

Into the Breach

Using Research and Theory to Shape History Instruction

Robert B. Bain

For years I lived like Bruce Wayne or Clark Kent, with separate yet connected dual-identities. By day I was a high school history teacher, and at night I was a graduate student pursuing advanced degrees in history. The difference was greater than merely day and night, greater than simply shifting roles from teacher to student. I switched worlds.

During the evenings, I interacted with others who defined historical study as a way of thinking, a manner of conducting research, and a style of writing. We participated in a professional community to improve the quality of our historical work. History at the university was a discipline, a unique way of knowing the world that professionals shared. In the high school, history was a subject students took and teachers taught, differing from other subjects only in the facts covered. Students claimed that they did in history exactly what they did in other courses—used texts, memorized facts, did homework, and took tests. In the minds of adolescents, there is little unique about history.

Early in my teaching career, it became clear that making these two worlds less dichotomous would be valuable for my students and for me. Actually, my research goals and teaching goals were not so different. As a historian, I tried to develop and use my critical intelligence to build an understanding of the past; as a teacher, I wanted to help others develop their critical faculties and deepen their understanding of the world. The discipline of history, filled with lively debate and thoughtful interactions, held great promise for my high school students. With an analytical stance deeply embedded in the discipline, history did not want for higher level thinking or need any special, decontextualized add-ons to promote critical thought.

Though this point is not widely acknowledged in schools or schools of education, history is more than a discrete subject matter; it is an epistemic activity.[1] The discipline of history depends upon historians reconstructing the past, for doing history is more than merely uncovering facts. Likewise, learning history is more than memorizing facts. Students of history actively construct the past in their own minds. As the discipline of history has unique problems, practices and habits of mind, so learning history involves distinctive problems and cognitive characteristics. History as a discipline and a course of study demands "meaning over memory."[2] Historians work to give meaning to historical facts, while students must work to give meaning to their historical experiences.

This chapter supports a cognitive approach toward learning history, demanding that teachers understand the nature of historical knowledge, student thinking about history, and the context within which learning history occurs. It urges teachers to consider their classes within disciplinary frames, to design activities consistent with the generalizations, concepts, methods, and cognitive processes of the discipline of history itself.[3]

How to do this? The problem for history teachers begins with trying to understand what defines meaning-making in history. What makes it distinctive? How do historians construct meaning?

History teachers, of course, must have subject-matter knowledge to teach history. I share the concerns of those who point to the alarming numbers of teachers who are teaching out of their areas of academic preparation.[4] However, teachers must go beyond merely knowing the subject. They also must consider how students typically learn history. How do students build meaning as they study the past? How can teachers help students move from surface or scholastic understanding to "deep" understanding? Little in my training prepared me for these pedagogical questions.

As a high school history teacher for more than twenty-five years, I found great value in history-specific research on cognition. A chance reading of an article by Samuel Wineburg introduced me to research by Wineburg, Leinhardt, Voss, Seixas, and Beck, among others.[5] These scholars shared my historian-educator's belief that, as Seixas wrote, "there is something distinctive about the teaching and learning of history, which cannot be known by simply applying general principles of teaching and learning to issues of history education."[6] Unfortunately, little of this work seems to have found its way into national conversations about teaching history.

This essay demonstrates the value of research for practitioners. It argues that emerging research can assist history teachers in designing and implementing instruction. To illustrate these points, I provide examples from my own practice in a ninth-grade world history course.

Research as Teaching Tool

Stimulating students' critical thinking is a cherished goal. It has provided an island of relative agreement in the contentious storm surrounding United States national history standards. Discussions of history's habits of mind or standards for thinking have been central to all the major reform reports.[7] While admirable in the attempt to articulate historical cognition or link thinking skills to content, these reports represented historical thinking as decontextualized lists with discrete sets of objectives. For teachers, these lists flattened out a complex process.[8]

The literature in history-specific cognition offers exciting possibilities because it yields thicker descriptions, showing historians and history students thinking while engaged in disciplinary activities. Too often, history students and history teachers work with the end products of historical thinking—textbooks and monographs. Like all skilled artisans, historians polish these final products, intentionally removing signs of the struggles and strategies along the way. Ironically, such polish complicates the instructional problem for teachers and students. It is very difficult to model or practice forms of historical thinking that are not immediately evident. Therefore, by making visible the "invisible" cognitive work of historians, scholarship in history-specific cognition creates a richer, more nuanced picture of cognition than linear lists of skills or general taxonomies of thought.

For example, Wineburg's study of expert-novice approaches to reading documents demonstrates a "breach between the school and the academy." Wineburg revealed the multiple strategies—corroboration, sourcing, and contextualizing—historians employ as they read documents, strategies that are absent from students' reading. These descriptions of situated historical thinking fill in the cognitive details of such classroom activities as "working with documents" or "analyzing primary sources." They help the teacher construct a more complex and, ultimately, more satisfying understanding of historical thinking, yielding richer goals for our courses.[9]

Further, the studies describe ways children understand history, how they approach text, and their underlying epistemological beliefs. The work points out specific ideas that students bring to their study of history, including ideas about the nature of history itself. It reminds us that students are not tabulae rasae, that they pass their classroom experiences through their own presupposed webs of meaning.[10] It encourages teachers to consider students' assumptions and beliefs, for these may undermine the most engaging classroom activity.

This research, then, clarifies the context within which experts and novices reconstruct the past, define historical problems, work with evidence, and build plausible arguments. It enables practitioners to begin instructional design with a deeper, more robust understanding of historical thinking.

However, this only begins the teacher's task. Unlike the researchers who reveal these hidden elements of historical thought, teachers must design activities that engage students in using such thinking in the classroom. How can we help students move from surface or scholastic understanding to "deep" understanding? How do students learn to contextualize, corroborate, hear voice in text, and assess significance?

To put it bluntly, does any of this research, theory, or scholarship really matter when a teacher teaches history?

To be sure, this complicated picture of the discipline does not fit a transmission model of learning. Though storytelling may help students develop models of historical narratives, lectures and textbooks do not seem to develop in them the historian's thinking skills. The widely proposed alternative is active learning, engaging students in the "authentic" tasks of the historian. Developing an analogy to on-the-job training—indeed, the creed is "student as worker"—many researchers urge teachers to require students to do what historians do by working with documents or artifacts to construct arguments.

While I share the spirit, I fear adopting the active stance may beg the instructional question. In embracing the sensible strategy of having students do history to learn history, teachers focus on the trappings of the activities—the behaviors—without considering the thought processes that underlie all disciplinary action. Clearly, history students can mimic behavior. They can read a document set without engaging in the thinking that characterizes the behavior.

Is an authentic disciplinary activity itself transformative? Seixas cautions that activities taken from a community of experts may not automatically be transplanted to a body of novices.[11] Disciplinary tasks embedded within the epistemic community draws meaning from the community's frames, scripts, and schemas. However, students learning history do not yet share the assumptions of historians. They think differently about text, sources, argument, and the structure of historical knowledge.[12] The frames of meaning that sustain the disciplinary task within the community of historians may not exist within the classroom. Hence, the students may reject the transplanted activity. Or, the culture of the classroom will assimilate the "authentic" activity, using it to sustain novices' naive or scholastic views. Engaging students in some legitimate disciplinary activity without restructuring the social interaction or challenging students' presuppositions may yield only ritualistic understanding. The problem for practitioners is to design activities that engage students in historical cognition without yielding to the tempting assumption that disciplinary tasks mechanically develop students' higher functions.

Teaching history is more complicated than either transmitting historical facts or engaging students in history projects. Seeing it as an epistemic activity challenges teachers to merge a substantive understanding of the discipline with an equally sophisticated understanding of learning.

To this end, cultural psychology helps me use the history-specific research in the classroom. Cultural psychology—here I refer to the work of Vygotsky, Bruner, Cole, Shweder, Lave, Rogoff, and Wertsch—has deepened my picture of learning, broadening my focus from the individual to locate the learner within the context of both the classroom and the discipline.[13] Two useful mediating principles emerged to help me translate history as a form of knowledge to teaching that form of knowledge: (1) externalize all thinking in the classroom, and (2) create cultural supports for disciplinary thinking.

Effective cognitive apprenticeship demands that we make thinking explicit.[14] Teachers and students must try to "see" all the thinking in the history classroom. This is particularly complicated in history instruction as four "types" of thinkers hide within the activities of history classes—students, historical actors, expert historian, and the history teacher. Certainly, this idea of the multiple minds present in the history classroom merits further exploration, which this discussion can only suggest. Suffice it to say that, by exteriorizing the thinking of students, past actors, disciplinary experts, and teachers, we create and shape a disciplinary specific zone of development with beginning points (student thinking), historical content, and process goals (historical actors/event and historians' habits of mind), while encouraging pedagogical reflection.

The second principle that emerges from cultural psychology helps teachers confront the paradoxical problem of trying to engage novices in expert thinking. Here Vygotsky's famous rule of cognitive development provides a wonderful guide:

> Any function in the child's cultural development appears twice, or on two planes. First it appears on the social plane, and then on the psychological plane. First it appears between people as an interpsychological category, and then within the child as an intrapsychological category. . . . Social relations or relations among people genetically underlie all higher functions and their relationships.[15]

With social assistance, learners can perform many more competencies than they could independently; *through* social assistance the higher functions emerge and are subsequently internalized. Tharp and Gallimore remind that "until internalization occurs, *performance must be assisted*."[16] Therefore, by embedding historians' disciplinary thinking into classroom artifacts and interactions (demonstrated later), we transform a class of novices into a community with shared disciplinary expertise. Participation in such a community creates opportunities for students to internalize the discipline's higher functions or expertise.[17]

These bodies of scholarship place the teacher between the novice and the expert, within the breach between the school and the academy. With an emerging picture of historical cognition and a mediated view of learning, this research and theory refocus teachers' attention, redefine educational problems, and assist in instructional design and implementation. The examples that follow, taken from my high school world history course, display these ideas in action.

Into the Breach: Constructing a Dynamic Picture of the Discipline

Where to begin with high school students? Since students' underlying assumptions impact instruction, I began with their beliefs about history itself. My students entered class with a clear conception of history, its purposes and processes. In describing their initial understanding, students mixed homilies about history's value with almost Gradgrindian images of the subject matter. For my students, history consisted almost entirely of past facts that are "always true" (SS, 8/29/95). World history is "the study of different cultures . . . [having] to do with the study of maps" (MA, 8/29/95). It is a "written record of events that happened in chronological order" (SK, 8/29/95). For one student, history entailed objects drawn from the past, that is, "if you got a pencil two days ago, you use it today, so now you are using history" (RP, 8/29/95). History's value rests in its ability to inoculate us against errors; one student wrote, "History repeats itself because we do not learn from our mistakes" (SK, 8/29/95). When giving proof of these repetitive patterns, students give broad examples; one said, "There is always war" (XX, 8/29/95). One student advises, "You cannot change history, but you can make history" (SS, 8/29/95).

These journal entries reveal a static, formulaic vision of history. The past is filled with facts, historians retrieve those facts, students memorize the facts, and all this somehow improves the present. After reading these opening journal entries, I realized that this sea of assumptions about the discipline threatened to engulf our exploration of world history. Therefore, we began with an epistemological introduction to history itself. This was not a "get-them-settled-accustomed-or-acquainted" activity. Rather, we began with a minicourse on the nature of historical knowledge, designed to construct a different, more complex view of the structure of the discipline.

Certainly, I am not alone in beginning this way. University programs require historiography for history majors. It remains one of the most important courses in my own training, revealing the secrets of the craft while challenging me to consider the underpinnings of the discipline. McDiarmid reports that a solid course in historiography altered ways college students thought about history.[18] The English Schools Council began their 9–13 history with a historiographic introduction.[19] The International Baccalaureate program devotes an entire section of its required "Theory of Knowledge" course to the study of history as a way of knowing the world. The cultural psychologist Michael Cole provides an even more compelling rationale through his discussion of prolepsis, the "cultural mechanism that brings 'the end into the beginning.'"[20] In this sense, Cole suggests that we "presuppose that the children understand what it is that [we are] . . . trying to teach as a precondition for creating that understanding."[21]

How to teach something as abstract as the structure of the discipline? Should we try to "deal with the contradictory and complex nature of history by teaching them to use the strategies and heuristics exhibited by historians? Or do these cognitive processes make sense only when under-girded by a broader set of beliefs about historical inquiry?"[22] In this opening unit, I tried to do both by nesting the "strategies and heuristics exhibited by historians" within the "broader set of beliefs about historical inquiry." Through a series of activities, we developed a picture of the discipline that entailed both broad beliefs and the specific cognitive strategies that would inform all our activities for the remainder of the year.

The crucial first step is to problematize the concept "history" and to challenge students' "merely-facts-beamed-through-time" view of the discipline. We began by differentiating between history as a past event and history as an interpretive account. Students wrote a history of the first day of school that they read aloud on the second day. The great variance in their choice of facts, details, stories, and perspectives revealed differences between the event under study (the first day of school) and the accounts of the event. I listened carefully for opportunities in the discussion to point out the two different ways students used the word "history"—(1) as a past occurrence ("that happened in history") or (2) as an account of past occurrences (" I wrote in my history").

After naming the two concepts History-As-Event (Hev) and History-as-Account (Hac), students engaged in activities to explore these ideas. For example, they compared their own experience of an event with other accounts of the event. In one exercise involving a baseball game, students not only compared multiple accounts of the game (a typical activity) but also compared these accounts to the event itself. How were the accounts related to the event? Did the accounts capture the full event? Is it possible for accounts to capture events fully? How did the accounts differ? Did they use different facts? Different sources? Different pictures? Different language? Did the accounts identify different turning points or significant events in the game? Were the accounts connected to each together? Are there other possible accounts of the event? Did the accounts serve different purposes? What explains the fact that people studying the same event create differing accounts? Can one account be better than another? How can we assess competing truth claims?

The entire first unit challenges students' fact-based suppositions of history by creating epistemological problems out of their own experiences. For example, after asking students to create an account of an event they did not experience, we ask, "How is it possible to reconstruct a past event that no longer exists in the present?" Students grapple with these

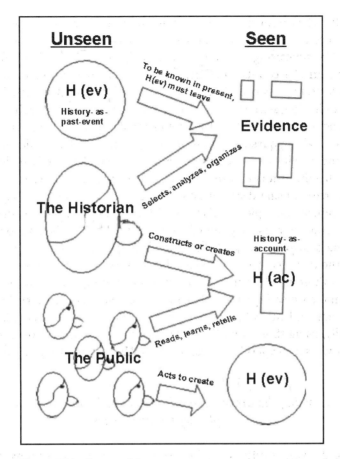

Figure 17.1. Concept Map

problems through journal writing, substantive conversation with others, and evidence from the thinking of expert historians. Throughout, we confront and complicate students' understanding by raising issues of evidence, significance, validity, organization, chronology, spheres of human life, forms of historical accounts, the public's relationship to accounts, and the role historical accounts themselves play in shaping decisions and events. Slowly, students develop a graphic record of their understanding of the discipline. The graphic grows over weeks with students modifying it until we have a complex, dynamic view of the discipline.

The graphic shown in Figure 17.1 hangs prominently in my classroom, guiding disciplinary self-reflection, assessment, analysis, synthesis, and evaluation. Before, during, and after a unit of study, the students use the picture as a concept map to locate classroom activities within the disciplinary frame. Creating, using, and modifying this picture of the discipline demystifies historical accounts for students. It constantly reminds them that historical texts, broadly conceived, are products of a cognitive process involving investigation, selection, evaluation, interpretation, and thought.

On occasion, we use the structure of the discipline to think about instruction, raising questions about my perspective in selecting documents, designing activities, or determining a unit's length. This activity demonstrates that the history classroom itself is a construction of the past that can be understood using disciplinary standards. This opening unit helps students connect the typical artifacts of history instruction, such as the textbook, lecture, movies, maps and facts, to a world beyond the classroom.

Using a map to locate our position, though, does not mean we can travel the territory. The skills needed to traverse a landscape are not the same as those involved in using or even in creating a map. In the classroom, merely creating a more dynamic understanding of history does not mean that students will use the intellectual processes represented. Paradoxically, using those cognitive skills fosters their growth. How can student novices use expert historical thinking? We turn to this question later.

Crossing the Breach: Assisting Student Performance of Disciplinary Competencies

During the year, students use historical thinking processes long before they have mastered them. Such performance before individual competence requires assistance. The examples that follow demonstrate three forms of assistance: (1) externalizing thought through informal journals, (2) mediating thought through classroom artifacts, and (3) embedding thought in structured interactions.

Externalizing Thought Through Informal Journals

One of the most important tools for teaching and learning history epistemically is informal writing.[23] Informal writing or thinking on paper allows students to explore connections, speculate about historical phenomena, and develop understandings of the past. Informal writing captures thinking in process. Hence, it is tentative; neither the writing nor the thinking is polished or complete. We do not expect it to meet formal standards of grammar, punctuation, spelling, or tight, logical coherence. Nor do we use informal writing to test or evaluate students. Instead, informal writing stimulates students' historical thinking.

To employ informal writing, students keep a journal or learning log exclusively for world history. They do not combine class notes and the informal journals because each serves a different purpose. Whereas class or reading notes captures others' thinking, students use journals to capture their own thinking. Students make their ideas overt, revealing that which is difficult for students to see—the changes in their own thinking. Teachers and classmates also gain access to a student's prior knowledge and emerging conceptions and misconceptions. When public, informal writing lays the foundation for a community of inquiry.

The writing strategies I describe in this section stimulate students' historical imaginations while assisting their thinking. In many ways, the strategies capture the activities of working historians.

• *Externalizing understanding through freewriting.* Students use journals to begin thinking about a historical topic, reading or problem. They capture their initial thoughts through freewriting, responding to questions such as "What do you know about . . . ? What do you think about . . . ? What attitudes do you bring to this subject? What questions do you have? How would you respond in a similar situation? What difficulties do you have with the subject? What do you suspect is most significant about the issue? What is most memorable?"

These questions encourage students to explore a given problem or issue on their own before studying it in class. It requires students to consider their own thinking about the topic. Most important, such writing identifies existing ideas, attitudes, questions, and values. Depositing current thinking on the pages of the journal makes it easier to consider and to avoid presentism later.

• *Creating narratives through story writing.* Story writing invites students to create a narrative from the facts or events in a unit of study. Too often, texts appear to students as a string of disconnected facts, without a coherent beginning, middle, or end.[24] Story writing encourages students to create a narrative structure. It enables teachers and students to explore the voice of the storyteller and to retell a story from multiple perspectives.

Often students create narratives without referring to notes, stressing the coherence of the story line over names and dates. Then, of course, students return to their notes and the facts to rework the story more accurately. With this activity, teachers can raise important historical questions. What changed in the telling of the story? Did any particular facts alter the story? Did your understanding change? Such procedures allow students to participate in the trials and tribulations of assembling and creating historical narratives.

• *Reading through writing.* Students use the journals to read historical texts. Journal writing urges students to think about what they are reading, to discover what they understand about the material, and to identify its significance. Writing-to-read is different from merely taking reading notes. In the journal, students capture their own thinking about the text, initially guided by teacher-posed questions; the questions engage students in expert thinking as they read. Sample questions include "What were your first thoughts as you read? What questions occurred to you? Does this text remind you of anything else? What passage was most important for you? What passage was important for the author? Is there a difference between what you think is important and what you think the author thinks is important? What questions does the text answer? What is the author's perspective? How does this connect to other sources?"

Often we use a double-entry method in the journal. Students take quotes or paraphrase the text in one column and then respond to the text on a facing column or page. This establishes a dialogue between the reader and the text, a dialogue similar to what expert readers construct in their minds as they engage text.[25]

• *Developing dialogues through interactive writing.* Dialectical, interactive writing engages students in an informal, written conversation with others around a historical problem. Working historians participate in a variety of such conversations through conferences, publications, collegial exchanges, and, increasingly, e-mail. Interactive journal writing creates an opportunity for similar exchanges among students. Students read and respond to classmates' thoughts on a topic or issue under study. To generate conversation, teachers might divide the class into groups of three. Then students exchange journals within the group and write their reactions to their classmates' entries. Finally, students read and respond to their classmates' comments. As skills develop in giving and getting comments, we assign roles before students read and respond to classmates, such as "defender of the text," "doubter," "believer," or "friendly critic."

• *Self-reflection through meta-cognitive writing.* Journal writing also helps students to think about their own thinking. For example, by asking students to consider and reconsider the same question at regular intervals, teachers can help students monitor the changes in their ideas. Informal writing can also help students see how newly acquired information alters their understanding. I ask students, while they are working on term papers, to write weekly descriptions of what they know and think about their topic. Such regular writing prompts students to work out meaning in their sources and note cards as they research, rather than waiting until they have collected all their data. Such writing enables us to raise questions about how to determine the "end" of data collection or the dynamic relationship between evidence and thought.

• *Community building through public readings.* Journal writing actively involves all students in making sense of the material they are studying. An important step in this process requires students to read journal entries aloud in class. Analogous to historians who talk to colleagues or present tentative conclusions at conferences or in their teaching, students publicly share their formative thoughts. In class, students often read short entries consecutively, withholding comment until all students have read. Such quick sharing frees students to listen to their classmates, rather than concentrating upon what they are going to say. It allows timid students to say what is on their minds without the "Oh-I-was-just-going-to-say-that" disappointment of being called upon later in a discussion. All students read what they have written, even if someone else has already read a similar response. This also allows the class to look for patterns in collective responses and points to variations in ideas and perspectives.

Teacher participation in this process is important, though risky. Like the students, teachers should write in a journal, read aloud in class, and participate in journal exchange groups. This models for students that teachers work on historical problems in the same tentative manner—adjusting, modifying, testing, and revising. Joining in the informal writing activities places the teacher within a community of inquiry.

Mediating Thought through Classroom Artifacts

Students also rely on tools and artifacts to support their use of expert thinking before they have internalized historical skills. A good example is found in fostering students' thinking around issues of significance.

Determining significance is a fundamental element of historical thinking. Assumptions about significance shape the way historians select, organize, and periodize their studies. It is central to the historical enterprise. The failure to determine significance turns history into "one damn thing after another." In our age of abundant information, discriminating between the significant and the insignificant is a vital intellectual skill.

How can we engage students in using strategies for determining significance? Early in the course, my ninth-grade students build a virtual time capsule, with each student deciding items to include and exclude. This is certainly a well-worn activity that does "hook" students. After a very short discussion of their items, though, we go "meta" by turning from the objects they have chosen to a consideration of the thinking they used to make their choices. We externalize students' criteria and construct a set of statements that the class agrees shaped their decisions. We call these our "Tools for Determining Significance" and place these statements on colorful posters around the classroom. One typical poster reads, "Period 3's Tools for Determining Significance: (1) Rare, first-time, or last-time events, (2) Impacts many people in many places, (3) Impacts many areas of human life, (4) Effect lasts across time."

Through the year, students use the posters to make cases for events' importance or to argue for a turning point that signified the end of an event or an era. The posters help students assess historical accounts and decide whether a historian has made a strong case for the importance of an event or interpretation. At times, students discover fundamental interpretive conflicts among historians by applying their charts.

In fact, this classroom artifact often presents intellectual conflict during the year. At first, students used the different criteria in a rigid algorithmic procedure. However, gradually they blurred the lines and overlapped criteria. This raised questions about relative and comparative significance. Students wondered whether and how significance could change over time. We posted these questions as we confronted them, thus visually recording our own epistemological dilemma.

The students created many charts or posters to capture expert thinking in history. Analogous to the way they used the periodic table hanging in the chemistry class, students used these visual tools of history to read, write, take tests, discuss an issue, or make journal entries. They depended upon these aids, regularly referring to them until they internalized the procedures. One student wrote, "I find that I am often using the institutions and rules of significance on a daily basis, without even thinking" (PG, 6/7/96).

Embedding Expert Thought in Classroom Interactions

Another way to assist novices in using expert thinking is to embed that thinking in classroom interactions. A good example is the unusual way my class reads document sets. Here I modify the reciprocal teaching procedure first described by Brown and Palinscar to reflect the strategies historians use when reading primary sources.[26] The procedure uses group interaction to enable students to read together in ways they could not read on their own.

The key is the disciplinary specific division of labor. Each student or pair of students becomes a particular type of question or questioner. Then, within the role, each asks questions of the class about the document we are reading. Thus, discussion ensues.

The beginning questions are common to any classroom reading procedure, as students identify confusing language, define difficult works, and summarize the key points. The remaining roles are specific to the discipline, encouraging students to pose questions expert historians might ask. Using historians' heuristics, students ask their classmates:

- Who made the source, and when it was made?
- Who is the intended audience for the source?
- What is the story line within a source?
- Why they produced a source and the purpose it served?
- Whether other evidence supports the source?
- Whether other evidence contests the source?
- Whether the source is believable?
- What is the story line that connects all the sources?

As they ask questions, classmates return to the documents, make journal entries, and discuss their answers. Thus, in this structured manner, the class raises multiple questions that guide everyone's reading and discussion of text.[27]

This activity is initially awkward and time consuming with its role assignments, complex questioning, and discussion. It is different from cooperative learning where content divides tasks. Here it is the complex thinking that divides the task. This structured activity recognizes that, while individual students cannot perform complete, complex historical analysis of a document or a document set, as a group they can. The activity does not lower disciplinary standards or allow novices merely to mimic experts. As a group, students participated in the complex, authentic activity "where initially the adults and the artifacts bear a large part of the load, but where children come to be fuller participants (that is competent readers) over time."[28] Using these roles challenges the students' habit of treating historical text as they do other text.

Discussion

Do any of these techniques improve students' understanding of history? Though I am excited and enthusiastic about this cognitive approach to history instruction, I cannot yet make definitive statements about its impact on student thinking. However, analysis of student journal entries reveals three areas of change in student thinking. I offer these not as research conclusions but as suggestions of the effect an epistemic approach might have on student cognition.

First, at the end of the year, students reported a noticeable and positive difference between this approach to learning history and other approaches. For example, Sara wrote that she was "surprised" by the "way we learned history in this class."

> I thought it would be like past history classes where you memorize facts, people and dates which have little significance if you don't understand them. Also, I thought it would be like performing events in history, working in groups, *which I hate*, and have a "parrot-like" repetition all of the time. We didn't do anything like that. It was *interpreting* history. We made it relevant because we interpreted events not memorized them. (SW, 6/7/96)

Another student explained that most of her prior courses "just taught us what happened," while this course "explored further into things like cause, effect and significance. You cared about how we thought and how we interpreted history" (RG, 6/7/96). Other comments support this,

> [H]istory came alive for me by having us develop our own interpretations of the past. (DR, 6/7/96)

> It was the first time in my life that I studied history from all viewpoints and interpretations and not just the interpretation of the author of the book. (ET, 6/7/96)

> I learned that the history books can be wrong, and that I can even interpret some things myself if I don't agree. This is the only year history became interesting to me. (WS, 6/7/96)

Second, students gave more complicated definitions of history at the end of the term than they did at the beginning. In initial entries, no student mentioned historical interpretation or the historian's part in constructing history. However, a more dynamic view of the discipline defined their closing entries, one student wrote, "History is the interpretation and organization of facts. Historians have a unique job in picking dates that split things"(WS, 6/7/96). Students placed thinking as the central element in the study of history; one noted, "I think history is the study of the way people thought, reacted to problems and reacted toward themselves and others" (JT, 6/7/96). Some students reported that history involved an approach to knowledge: "The process went sort of life this—1) decide if the subject/person/event is significant 2) analyze how it effected [*sic*] each institution 3) give our interpretation insight on the subject" (PG, 6/7/96).

Finally, a preliminary analysis of student work shows that students used their developing skills and understandings to handle text in a more sophisticated manner. For example, after using the "tools" I have discussed to work through multiple primary sources on the fourteenth-century plague epidemic, students offered complicated criticisms of their textbook's treatment of the same event. Students' criticism ranged from the textbook's failure to include evidence of human agency, that is, the book's account "can lead to the misconception that people did nothing to try and protect themselves" (SW, 2/28/96), to the textbook's omitting documentation; one student complained that the book "needed to add . . . many more references to outside sources" (KC, 2/28/96). One of the most surprising complaints the ninth-grade students lodged concerned the shortage of facts found in the text; one noted that "one weakness in the way the textbook addresses the Black Death is that it leaves out many details that contribute greatly to the story" (ES, 2/28/96). Students' observation that a textbook needs more details is indeed an unanticipated benefit of this approach to teaching.

While I am still investigating the impact of this approach to teaching on student thinking, I am more confident about the productive changes it generated in my thinking. For example, the focus on expert, novice, and pedagogical knowledge opened new avenues for reflection and understanding. With this heightened need to locate student thinking in relationship to "expert" thought, I began to read student work and to listen to student talk with a new, almost anthropological intensity. More accurately, I used my *historian's skills* of contextualizing, corroborating, and sourcing to read student journals or attend to classroom conversation.

Similar change marked my approach to instructional design, enactment, and "real time" pedagogical modification.[29] Using research as a teaching tool thus opened new opportunities to understand teaching and learning history within the classroom. In turn, this new understanding presents new questions for investigation. Here, again, I find myself poised between worlds—this time, research and practice—with questions aimed in both directions. For example, within the classroom, as we would expect, there was variation in student response to this approach to teaching history. Some students seemed overwhelmed by such active mental processes, even when I used mediating tools; other students quickly stopped using the scaffolds, finding such cognitive tools cumbersome or constraining. Do some students need "scaffolds" to help them use the scaffolds? What other bridges might help them make sense of the complexity that historical thinking demands? Though I have read interesting pieces on how student understanding of time or causation develops, little in my instructional design reflects this literature. It probably should, as I suspect it might help vary and complicate the scaffolding tools. Or, consider the variation in attitude I observed as students deepened their understanding of the constructed nature of historical accounts. Some students embraced a productive skepticism that invigorated their approach to the world around them; others used the ideas to sustain a cynical relativism. We need to explore how these understandings develop.

While I have been arguing that an environment rich in historically grounded scaffolds enables deeper thinking, I have no idea what happens when students move into other settings. Does any of this have staying power, or is it merely contextualized to "that is how we studied history in our freshman year"? How do students negotiate teachers' epistemological differences? Would students benefit from more investigations into the structure of other disciplines, creating images that promote comparison?

Finally, how might other practitioners best use the insights gathered from research probes into how historians, history students, and history teachers think? Conversely, what can researchers learn about practice by the ways teachers adopt, translate, or ignore findings? How might we represent research findings and classroom practice in ways that engage these communities in greater collaboration?

Such questions sit, like the history classroom, at the intersection of several intellectual worlds. As a practitioner, I have found great value in moving from one world to another. The continued interaction among historians, cognitive researchers, and history teachers likewise promises to enrich the work of all, especially the history students in our classrooms.

NOTES

1. Joyce Appleby, Lynn Hunt, and Margaret Jacob, *Telling the Truth about History* (New York, 1994); Marc Bloch, *The Historian's Craft*, Peter Putnam, tr. (Manchester, 1967); R. G. Collingwood, *The Idea of History* (Oxford, 1946); Louis O. Mink, *Historical Understanding* (Ithaca, NY, 1987); Peter Novick, *That Noble Dream: The "Objectivity Questions" and the American Historical Profession* (Cambridge, 1988).

2. Peter N. Stearns, *Meaning over Memory: Recasting the Teaching of Culture and History* (Chapel Hill, NC, 1993).

3. See also Denis Shemilt, "The Caliph's Coin: The Currency of Narrative Frameworks in History Teaching," this volume; Peter Lee and Rosalyn Ashby, "Progression in Historical Understanding among Students Ages 7–14," this volume.

4. Diane Ravitch, "The Educational Backgrounds of History Teachers," this volume.

5. Samuel S. Wineburg, "On the Reading of Historical Texts: Notes on the Breach between School and Academy," *American Educational Research Journal,* 28(3) (1991), pp. 495–519; also see Isabel Beck and Margaret G. McKeown, "Outcomes of History Instruction: Paste-up Accounts," in M. Carretero and J. F. Voss, eds., *Cognitive and Instructional Processes in History and the Social Sciences* (Hillsdale, NJ, 1994), pp. 237–256; M. A. Britt et al., "Learning from History Texts: From Causal Analysis to Argument Models," in G. Leinhardt, I. L. Beck, and C. Stainton, eds., *Teaching and Learning in History* (Hillsdale, NJ, 1994), pp. 47–84; Mario Carretero et al., "Historical Knowledge: Cognitive and Instructional Implications," in Mario Carretero and James F. Voss, eds., *Cognitive and Instructional Processes in History and the Social Sciences* (Hillsdale, NJ, 1994), pp. 357–376; Gaea Leinhardt, Isabel L. Beck, and Catherine Stainton, eds., *Teaching and Learning in History* (Hillsdale, NJ, 1994); Linda S. Levstik and C. Pappas, "New Directions for Studying Historical Understanding," *Theory and Research in Social Education,* 20(4) (1992); Charles A. Perfetti et al., "How Students Use Texts to Learn and Reason about Historical Uncertainty," in Mario Carretero and James F. Voss, eds., *Cognitive and Instructional Processes in History and the Social Sciences* (Hillsdale, NJ, 1994), pp. 257–284; Peter Seixas, "Students' Understanding of Historical Significance," *Theory and Research in Social Education,* 22 (1994), pp. 281–304; Denis Shemilt, "The Devil's Locomotive," *History and Theory,* 224 (1983), pp. 1–18; James F. Voss and Mario Carretero, "Introduction," in Mario Carretero and James F. Voss, eds., *Cognitive and Instructional Processes in History and the Social Sciences* (Hillsdale, NJ, 1994),

pp. 1–14; Samuel M. Wineburg and Suzanne S. Wilson, "Peering at History through Different Lenses: The Role of Disciplinary Perspectives in Teaching History," *Teachers College Record*, 80(4) (1988), pp. 525–539; Samuel S. Wineburg, "Historical Problem Solving: A Study of the Cognitive Processes Used in Documentary and Pictorial Evidence," *Journal of Educational Psychology*, 83(1) (1991), pp. 73–87; Samuel S. Wineburg and Suzanne M. Wilson, "Subject-matter Knowledge in the Teaching of History," *Advances in Research on Teaching*, 2 (1991), pp. 305–347; Samuel S. Wineburg, "The Psychology of Learning and Teaching History," in D. C. Berliner and R. Calfee, eds., *Handbook of Educational Psychology* (New York, 1993).

6. Peter Seixas, "When Psychologists Discuss Historical Thinking: A Historian's Perspective," *Educational Psychologist*, 29(2) (1994), p. 107.

7. Paul Gagnon and the Bradley Commission on History, eds., *Historical Literacy* (Boston, 1989); National Center for History in the Schools, *National Standard for History: K–4* (Los Angeles, 1994); National Center for History in the Schools, *National Standards for United States History: Exploring the American Experience* (Los Angeles, 1994); National Center for History in the Schools, *National Standards for World History: Exploring Paths to the Present* (Los Angeles, 1994); National Center for History in the Schools, *National Standards for History: Basic Edition* (Los Angeles, 1996).

8. Robert B. Bain, "Assessing the World History Standards: A Teacher's Perspective," *Education Week* 14(22) (February 22, 1995), pp. 35–36; Robert B. Bain, "Beyond the Standards War: Politics and Pedagogy in the National History Standards Controversy," *Ohio Council of Social Studies Review*, 32(1) (1996), pp. 36–40; Robert B. Bain, "Teaching History as an Epistemic Act: Notes from a Practitioner," paper presented at the American Historical Association Annual Conference, New York, January, 1996.

9. Wineburg, "On the Reading of Historical Texts"; Samuel S. Wineburg, "The Cognitive Representation of Historical Texts," in G. Leinhardt, I. L. Beck, and C. Stainton, eds., *Teaching and Learning in History* (Hillsdale, NJ, 1994), pp. 85–136.

10. See Samuel Wineburg, "Making Historical Sense," this volume; Linda S. Levstik, "Articulating the Silences: Adolescents' and Teachers' Conceptions of Historical Significance," this volume.

11. Peter Seixas, "The Community of Inquiry as a Basis for Knowledge and Learning: The Case of History," *American Educational Research Journal*, 302 (1993), pp. 305–324.

12. Beck and McKeown, "Outcomes of History Instruction"; Britt et al., "Learning from History Texts"; Carretero et al., "Historical Knowledge"; Juan Delval, "Stages in the Child's Construction of Social Knowledge" in Mario Carretero and James F. Voss, eds., *Cognitive and Instructional Processes in History and the Social Sciences* (Hillsdale, NJ, 1994), pp. 77–102; Wineburg, "On the

Reading of Historical Texts"; Wineburg, "The Cognitive Representation of Historical Texts."

13. Jerome S. Bruner, *The Culture of Education* (Cambridge, MA, 1996); Michael Cole, *Cultural Psychology: A Once and Future Discipline* (Cambridge, MA, 1996); Roy D'Andrade, "Cultural Meaning Systems," in Richard A. Shweder and Robert LeVine, eds., *Culture Theory: Essays on Mind, Self and Emotion* (New York, 1984); J. Lave and E. Wenger, *Situated Learning: Legitimate Peripheral Participation* (Cambridge, 1991); Barbara Rogoff and Jean Lave, eds., *Everyday Cognition: Its Development in Social Context* (Cambridge, MA, 1984); Richard A. Shweder, *Thinking through Cultures: Expeditions in Cultural Psychology* (Cambridge, MA, 1991); Schweder and LeVine, eds., *Culture Theory*; Lev S. Vygotsky, *Mind in Society* (Cambridge, MA, 1978); James V. Wertsch, *Vygotsky and the Social Formation of Mind* (Cambridge, MA, 1986).

14. James T. Bruer, *Schools for Thought: A Science of Learning in the Classroom* (Cambridge, MA, 1993).

15. Vygotsky, quoted in Cole, *Cultural Psychology*, pp. 110–111.

16. Roland G. Tharp and Ronald Gallimore, *Rousing Minds to Life: Teaching, Learning, and Schooling in Social Context* (Cambridge, 1988).

17. Lev S. Vygotsky, *Mind in Society* (Cambridge, MA, 1978); H. Gardner, *The Unschooled Mind: How Children Think in Schools and How Schools Should Teach* (New York, 1991).

18. G. Williamson McDiarmid, "Understanding History for Teaching: A Study of the Historical Understanding of Prospective Teachers," in Mario Carretero and James F. Voss, eds., *Cognitive and Instructional Processes in History and the Social Sciences* (Hillsdale, NJ, 1994), pp. 159–186.

19. Shemilt, "The Devil's Locomotive."

20. Cole, *Cultural Psychology*, 183.

21. Ibid.

22. Wineburg, "Historical Problem Solving."

23. Peter Elbow, *Writing with Power: Techniques for Mastering the Writing Process* (New York, 1981).

24. Beck and McKeown, "Outcomes of History Instruction"; Gaea Leinhardt et al., "Learning to Reason in History: Mindlessness to Mindfulness," in Mario Carretero and James F. Voss, eds., *Cognitive and Instructional Processes in History and the Social Sciences* (Hillsdale, NJ, 1994), pp. 131–158; Wineburg, "The Cognitive Representation of Historical Texts."

25. Wineburg, "The Cognitive Representation of Historical Texts"; Wineburg and Wilson, "Subject-Matter Knowledge in the Teaching of History."

26. Ann L. Brown and Annemarie S. Palinscsar, "Inducing Strategic Learning from Text by Means of Informed, Self-control Training," *Topics in Learning and Learning Disabilities*, 2 (1982), pp. 1–17; Bruer, *Schools for Thought*; Cole, *Cultural Psychology*.

27. For examples of the way technology might be employed to support students' use of sophisticated strategies to read historical documents, see Robert B. Bain, "Embedding the Structure of the Discipline in the Technology," paper presented at the American Association of History and Computing, Cincinnati, Ohio, April 1998, and M. Anne Britt et al., "The Sourcer's Apprentice: A Tool for Document-Supported History Instruction," this volume.

28. Cole, *Cultural Psychology*.

29. The most obvious example of such new instructional design can be seen in the Web site and electronic conferences I created to teach world history during the 1997–1998 school year. See Bain, "Embedding the Structure of the Discipline in the Technology," or visit the World History Project Web site at http://www.beachwood.k12.oh.us.

Chapter 18

Making Connections

The Interdisciplinary Community of Teaching and Learning History

Christine Gutierrez

This is the hardest thing of all to make you understand.
. . . I tell you that to let no day pass without discussing
goodness and all the other subjects about which you
hear me talking and examining both myself and others
is really the very best thing that a man can do, and that
life without this sort of examination is not worth living.
—Socrates[1]

In the late afternoon of Wednesday, April 29, 1992, uprisings and riots ex-
ploded in South Central Los Angeles following a jury's acquittal of four po-
liceman accused of brutally beating a motorist, who had been stopped after a
high-speed chase. The action was videotaped by a witness from a nearby
apartment balcony. That all of the policemen and the jury were white and
the motorist black seemed to make all the difference.

Thomas Jefferson High School's Humanitas Academy, where I teach, sits
less than four miles from the intersection where the melee began. The school
was closed immediately and remained so for several days. For the next two
nights, my Humanitas teaching team and I tried to call all of our students to
make sure that they were all right. It mattered that we spoke with the stu-
dents because Humanitas is a community, one of students and teachers
making connections together, connections of an interdisciplinary nature and
connections between what we teach and learn in the classroom with how we
live our lives.

Five days later, classes resumed, and my American Studies Humanitas history students and I began grappling with what was happening in Los Angeles, trying to make sense of the jury's acquittal, the angry and chaotic rioters, the burning of businesses, the National Guard's presence, the city-wide curfew, the numerous deaths, the looting.

After about an hour, we had a break. One of my male students, Alfonsus,[2] waited until almost everyone had left the room and then approached me rather slowly. Hesitantly, in a low voice, he said he needed some help. He proceeded to tell me that he was worried because he had been joking about having looted during the riots and now some of the Humanitas students were mocking him or sneering at him. I listened and shook my head. At first, I was unsure about what to say, unsettled by Alfonsus's remarks. I knew I could only respond honestly, forthrightly, person to person; he would expect no less from me.

I commented that looting was not a joke. Alfonsus agreed. I told him that the best thing would be for me to bring the issue to the Humanitas class as a whole because, as he knew, we are a community, and problems such as this one need to be dealt with in the open. Having worked with me for eight months, he appreciated that I would be discreet.

When everyone returned several minutes later, we continued our discussion about the riots' causes and dimensions. I asked the students what they thought about the looting. Some students justified it, saying that some people were so poor that it was the only way that they could finally get many things they usually did without, extra boxes of Pampers, cases of Cokes, batteries, etc. Many asserted that most looters were just exploiting the opportunity to get away with stealing.

When I raised the specific problem that one of their colleagues felt troubled by folks' thinking that he may have been one of the looters because he had been kidding about it, some nodded. Others started to wonder aloud what the big deal was. A few said that it really did not matter whether he had been looting or not because they knew of other Humanitas students who had. This was not some vivid simulation in my history class. This was life in South Central Los Angeles.

My stomach churned. Seventy-five students and I needed to confront this personal admission head on. I realized all that I had been seeking to teach my Humanitas students about history in general, about United States history in particular, about themselves inevitably, had converged in a moment of truth. I needed to redirect the critical thinking about the Los Angeles turmoil to the inner reality of the choices that my students had made.

When I spoke, my anger and disappointment were evident. I said very sternly that it was not okay that any one of our Humanitas students had looted—for whatever reason. I said very clearly that we hold very high standards in Humanitas and that that was the purpose of our community of scholars—to understand the big questions of humanity—humanities—through our study of history and other disciplines. I admonished them to think about what we had been teaching them about ethics, social justice, critical thinking, philosophy, and so on. They knew what stealing was; they knew that, no matter what anyone else was doing or saying, looting was wrong.

I let them know that, for those who had looted, they had failed a critical test. I insisted that the looters needed to come forth to me personally, in private, admit what they had done, and figure out with me what their restitution should be. The room was quiet.

By the time I finished, our media artist had joined us. I asked that she monitor the group so that I could take a little walk. She later came out to report that the students were very sorry. She added that she wondered whether I should have shown them such anger. (My tone of voice had clearly communicated my ire.) I said I thought it was appropriate that the class witness my anger and disappointment because my response fit the situation.

When we resumed class, I explained to the students why I had responded so angrily to finding out that some of them had looted. I stressed that our work as a community of scholars is meant to help them not only to understand history better but to understand themselves better. I reminded them that we had always taught them to think for themselves as individuals so that they could be stronger community members and leaders. Being responsible to a community of peers, they could be more conscious of their actions and take responsibility for them.

After class, two young men spoke with me and admitted that they had looted. I listened, and together we discussed what to do next.

The preceding story sets an important context for this essay. It illustrates what it can mean to teach and learn history by making distinct, explicit, and continuous connections in a high school class that formally recognizes itself as a "community of scholars," while drawing upon the interdisciplinary nature of history and historical thinking to understand and use those connections well. The story also reveals what happens when I take responsibility as a history teacher to help adolescents respect their role in a certain time, place, community, and culture. The goal of helping students see themselves as the "historical beings" Sam Wineburg addresses in chapter 16 of this book underlies all my work. This essay is my reflection upon aspects of that work, particularly how a formal recognition and maintenance of students' community connectedness works hand in hand with a specific contextualization tool and media literacy. As primarily a social constructivist, I work with youths in my classroom, or, frankly, in the many places and milieus I consider my "classroom," to cultivate their verve and acumen so that they will study history for the questions and truths it can show us in our own lives.

For more than ten years in South Central Los Angeles, I have been teaching history in a very large, comprehensive secondary school, Thomas Jefferson High School, an urban setting that each year educates 3,500 young people, low income and minority: Latino, African American, and Cambodian-American youth. My teaching has been mostly in an interdisciplinary program called Humanitas,[3] which commits to teachers and students making connections together in a "community of scholars." One of our primary goals is to build a classroom community connected to the community at large so that students can excel academically, express themselves honestly, and become leaders, in obvious and subtle ways. Ultimately, I am interested, with my colleagues, in providing learning contexts within which teenagers are affirmed for internalizing processes of historical thinking in order to act nonviolently, ecologically, and democratically, conscious of who they are and the power they have to direct their lives and solve problems with others. I intentionally set out to help young people grapple with the meaning of their own lives as they make meaning of past lives because the discipline requires it and our study inspires it.

Echoing two other voices expressed in this text, James Wertsch, who provokes our consideration of how to work with a people's beliefs, and Veronica Boix-Mansilla, who establishes criteria that can demonstrate a rich, complex application of history to contemporary problems, I seek to dig with students into history to see its truths and to hold its mirror up to ourselves. In short, for me, the teaching and learning of history are epistemic acts of cognitive, affective, and metacognitive development invigorated by human relationships and humane, ecological, and democratic purpose.

The Humanitas Approach

Humanitas itself has a twofold purpose: to ensure that a heterogeneous group of students benefits from humanities education and that teachers benefit from enriched collegial professional development. The program offers thematic, interdisciplinary, team-taught, and writing-based curricular and instructional experiences that integrate the humanities with the social sciences, natural sciences, fine arts, and, at times, mathematics. Philosophy permeates the curriculum. Intellectually vigorous, Humanitas's culture of inquiry at Jefferson High engages students in a three-year college-preparatory program that begins with teachers modeling respect for oneself and for others in a team that critically thinks and problem solves.

We have paid particular attention to empowering youth. We have created a community of scholars at an inner-city school to provide a stimulating intellectual and caring learning environment. The context within which I teach is important because the Humanitas approach has assured me of the need and wonder of establishing formal community parameters to support teaching and learning. A recent book, *How People Learn,* by the National Research Council, attests to the important role one's community plays in developing expertise, let alone in substantial transference. I am deeply interested in the way such transference can lead to a transformation of young lives; hence, I am fascinated by the ways the instructional strategies I use to guide students in making meaning appear to refine their sense of sense and inner power. Furthermore, these strategies interact dynamically with their honing their sense of community. Service learning, in my case often intermixed with media literacy, imbues a spirit that gives one's scholarship a meaning beyond the classroom. There are risks involved in such endeavors, reasonably encouraged and guided. My Humanitas teaching at Jefferson has convinced me of ways that my history teaching can and needs to ground adolescents in a secure and honest sense of self challenged and enriched by an historical acuity.

Although this is clearly significant for inner-city minority students, who confront conditions of violence, gangs, poverty, negative stereotypes, and marginality, it is just as important for all students whose postmodern lives are moving at a faster and faster pace and whose spiritual strength is threatened by alienation and materialism. Being honest about the social, economic, and political realities children and teens face these days raises the stakes for what I do in the classroom. As I write this essay, the Littleton, Colorado, high school killings and the deaths and destruction in places like Kosovo and Rwanda are painful reminders of the state of things, of our fractured state of beings. Considering the inequities that exist between places like Harlem and the rest of Manhattan only heightens my sense of urgency. Yet, the delight and talent of youth encourage my hope.

Two dimensions of connections have served my teaching and students' learning well:

1. Community connections inside and outside the classroom that draw extensively on the interpersonal and intrapersonal intelligences
2. Interdisciplinary connections that derive from the complexity of historical knowledge and made robust by my team teaching.

In my history class, these connections converge significantly. As they do, they reinforce the cognitive processes of historians and their capacities, working with diverse colleagues, to deal with complex questions. It is fascinating to consider how these forces manifest themselves in my students' work, including the making of an HIV/AIDS video as a public service announcement (PSA). The interdisciplinary community, proffering a rich context for teaching and learning, is the foundation that I present first.

Within it I use a tool I have come to call the *context boxes*. In the preceding essay, Robert Bain challenges teachers to design history courses that proceed from the practices of historians. My own approach includes inventing or adapting tools that pull together features of historical thinking. The contextual box, which I give students in our opening unit on epistemology, is a critical semantic map and scaffold that helps them understand both the discipline's structure and their role(s) in a community. Media literacy, which leads up to the PSA, also offers robust experiences for critical thought and self-understanding. Together, as I discuss here, my context boxes and media literacy appear to be important in brightening student attitudes toward social studies and facilitating interactions that help empower and educate youth. Subject-matter particulars may change, but the structure and the tools I employ in my class remain consistent, modified, and refined as needed.

Our Interdisciplinary Community of Scholars

With backpacks and books or nothing more than hands in the pockets, young folks traipse into class. Ana slips in hesitantly; Robert saunters in confidently; Luz and Jose stroll in chatting; or Heidi bounces in smiling. They carry into history class a lot of preconceived notions about history and about their role as students. They come with questions about the work, which they usually state aloud, and questions about themselves, which they usually keep quiet. Herein stir the vitality, intelligence, talent, uncertainty, and inquisitiveness that will mark them as young scholars, apprentice-historians. I know I need to capitalize on these qualities not only to develop their historical acumen but to show them how such knowledge and rationality can help them take control of their lives. Teens are invested in experimenting with and asserting their identities as they try to figure out who they are and how they fit in, whether they stand out or just belong. Feeling secure can be tough. The ways we think about the past can have a tremendous impact on the ways students think about themselves. I find it is important to validate this self-reflection and self-understanding as features of the processes I use both to scaffold their historical thinking and to help them grapple with the meaning of their lives. If history education, indeed, education in general, is to affect lives for the better, let alone be respected by students, then it needs to be intentionally connected to what goes on outside the classroom and school. Service learning is valuable not only for its contributions to academic depth and community enhancement; it is invaluable as a source of strength and purpose for a young life.

As the lives of our ancestors have proceeded within contexts, I have found that making connections in a community of scholars yields a deep sense of historical empathy and positive attitudes toward oneself, others, and history. In effect, the purpose of the community of scholars is to proffer a safe, interesting, and challenging setting in which to learn. It also sets the context of learning history by manifesting the contexts of history. Each individual student and teacher makes connections by being responsive to and responsible to a larger whole. This in turn builds bonds of trust and a consciousness of our interdependence. Students begin to learn what role beliefs play in this scholarship. They can come face to face with those who agree and those who disagree with them and deliberately wrestle with their ideas in a forum, making visible the process by which consensus or conflict can be handled well.

In huge schools like mine, anonymity usually prevails. Peer groups often negatively influence students. The Humanitas community counteracts this negativity by creating an alternative peer group whose members connect with one another. In the community of scholars, students know one another and their teachers well. They learn that others care about them. They feel they belong to some place and to a group that is secure and stable. A case study done at Jefferson Humanitas in 1991 showed that the Humanitas students come to school at a much higher rate of frequency than non-Humanitas students. A small learning environment personalizes the learning experience. Our community and interdisciplinary connections deepen the personalization.

When conflicts occur, we deal with them openly, face to face. People who trust can confront differences without things inevitably exploding. We want our students to know they can differentiate between a person and his ideas. One of our most important norms is that one can disagree with someone without disdaining the person. Whether it is a matter of controversy, racial uncertainties, adolescent cliques, personal animosity, or frustration of almost any kind, we tackle the conflicts, as well as other problems as a community, in their entirety or in smaller parts. Wertsch asks whether we can teach beliefs. In the interdisciplinary community, I realize that I purposefully tap and exercise interpersonal and intrapersonal intelligences to unmask beliefs and to continually build community among class colleagues, which then extends beyond the classroom.

I do have training in conflict resolution. My confidence about embedding it right in the thorniest of discussions or small-group interactions stems from my own professional development in this area. However, I also am clear that if I am not working on my own conflicts, conscious of my own biases, reflecting on my own difficulties, "my issues," my ability to dig with young thinkers into historical intricacies wanes. Weaving affective understanding into teaching and learning has been essential. Dispassionate investigation need not, cannot ignore the truth that passion stirs somewhere. How to handle it within legitimate structures of discourse is the question. Taking time—time to think; time to listen, to oneself and others; time to imagine; time to reflect; time to respond—cannot be underestimated, especially as affective domains matter to historical inquiry. Unfortunately, taking time remains an untended feature of "higher-order thinking."

Ironically, Fred Newmann's research on classrooms that exhibit the six indicators of thoughtfulness may influence a lot of teachers like me, but then we find ourselves confronting pressures of a high-stakes testing culture promoted by our current accountability mismeasures. Although they need not do so, as such pressures lead teachers to focus on the abstracted test scores, many teachers and administrators turn back to content-based education. In places like Jefferson, these are the folks who are not in collegial communities, who find themselves at a loss when trying to deal with the fact that the majority of our students score in the first, second, or third stanine on standardized tests. My Humanitas group buffers this re-action. However, the reality is these low stanine levels. Our way of con-fronting it is to have interdisciplinary thematic units that engage young people in a culture of critical literacy. Scholastic scaffolds must be affec-tive scaffolds not only to improve dispositions toward the discipline but to give teens two oars with which to steer through the white waters of learning and living.

Flexibility and Self-Evaluation

As a "community of scholars," Humanitas teachers and students carefully consider philosophical or historical ideas, concepts, and questions—our themes—from different times in the past: Epistemology, Greek Idealism, Romanticism in the American Mind, Racism and Its Legacy, Roots of Multiculturalism in the United States, Majority Rules versus Minority Rights, and Social Darwinism. Many of these issues continue to confront us today. Themes are discussed as teachers sit down together and cull through their respective course expectations, what most people today call high standards, and any recent findings, including those on students' needs, that invite the use of new materials and practices. We incorporate into our lessons ideas we gather by constantly reading, by paying atten-tion to contemporary conditions and problems, and by observing stu-dents in varied interactions, sometime in the homes we visit. We try to formulate our overarching year's theme as an issue that not only under-lies the particularly interdisciplinary concerns but that directly relates to the students.

For example, after two years, my team, which usually consists of three teachers (one each in history, literature, and science) noticed a serious weakness in our program. Our eleventh graders were too often saying that "the white people" were at fault or indulging in the "poor-me-I-am-a-victim-of-oppression" perspective. We wondered what we could do to contend with this vulnerability. We wanted to shatter what we acknowl-edged to be a seductive myth. Radically attuned to exposing prejudices and oppression, we want our students to know that structural conditions and forces interact with individual choice to maintain oppression. With-out blaming the victim, we worried about how to enrich the analysis. Over several weeks we pondered this question. The problem crept into small and large areas of our ongoing discussions. I started to look at it as a problem of history and focused on how I had framed the problem of oppression. I suspected that too little had been done to elucidate the transactions within oppressive situations. I had remembered my psychology readings about situational behaviors. I knew how a person could take on the personality of any institution as he or she came to identify more and more with his or her role in that institution and/or got satisfaction or rewards for doing so. I had studied this concept in college and had taught about it years earlier in a psychology class. In college I had also been struck by the conditioning experiments that tested how much pain one person would inflict on another under certain conditions. Philip Zimbardo's prison experiment still intrigues me. It is interesting now to recall how this knowledge insinuated itself into my reconsideration of the lessons we had taught on oppression and related concepts. My team and I talked a lot about our thinking about the messages that the students hear simply by living in South Central Los Angeles. We decided to examine explicitly what we had presented in a less direct fashion: the condition that emerges as a colonization of oneself and one's spirit, which victims of oppression can internalize.

First, we changed our year's theme, which is our overarching frame of reference. From "Image versus Reality of the American Experiment," we shifted to "Individual Rights and Responsibilities in a Multicultural Democracy." We simultaneously refined our curriculum and instruction and our meaning of engaging students. This happened because our curricular thinking proceeds from a knowledge of who our students are and what we are helping them to become.

Teaching as a Team

While it can only briefly be sketched here, teacher collaboration is vital to the Humanitas approach. As our *Humanitas Teachers Center Handbook* indicates, we expect teachers to work together for critical inquiry and for interdisciplinary exchange. I, like Bain, see the enormous value of having one's history course scrutinized like any other rendition of history, and teacher teams play a vital role in this process. We meet two or three times a week to discuss teaching issues, student work, and larger intellectual issues. We hunt new materials in all relevant fields. We actively explore best practices. In district-wide Humanitas Summer Academies, we meet with other teams and hear from university scholars. While much of our coursework is prescribed, we work hard to shape and lead the course design. Most teachers across the district know that to be a Humanitas teacher takes a lot of time and means a lot of extra work. Most involved agree that it means staying challenged and interested in teaching.

Over the years, we have developed protocols that involve a series of reflective questions to help us examine our efforts more candidly and efficiently. Along with the student work, which we often grade together, these questions stimulate our thinking and document what we know to be occurring in our classes. The reflective questions fall into five categories: what we teach (and why); who our students are; how we teach processes of learning and metacognition; how we attend to our community of scholars; and how we know what students have learned. Within the first category, a supporting critical query we pose is "How do concepts, ideas, and topics in each discipline require interdisciplinary connections to be deeply understood?" An example is weapons of war. History, science, and literature merge here as the nature of war is constrained or expanded by the technology of weapons, the effects of which are so often heard in poetry, prose, or song. Our interdisciplinary curriculum substantially deals with such a topic in no less than three classes and through a multitude of disciplines. History alone will necessarily interlock with anthropological, archeological, political, economic, geographic, and psychological understandings. Literary and scientific realms may coalesce. It ends up that students progress in their capacity to discern and comprehend multiple causality and to analyze complex conditions or forces alive in history as we study within an interdisciplinary context. This aids in what Boix-Mansilla calls "building an informed comparison matrix."

Course Goals

Each of us needs to be careful that we do not make mush of history or of the other fields that come into our classrooms by not distinguishing one discipline from another. An interdisciplinary teacher is effective only to the degree that he or she knows a discrete discipline really well. Not all the curriculum can or should be interdisciplinary, given the necessary standards of rigorous inquiry.

What are the goals of our teaching? My team stresses three considerations: first, the kinds of human beings we are developing; second, the roles that a responsible human being plays in a democracy; and, third, the ecological and peaceful quality of the society we help shape. More specifically, our ends are to educate:

- Humane individuals, nonviolent, ethical, rational, and compassionate
- Scholars who value interdisciplinary thought
- Critical thinkers, rigorous, independent, and honest
- Problem solvers, deliberately dealing with a problem's roots and interdisciplinarity
- Workers, reliable and reasonable in their individual or collaborative endeavors
- Community activists, socially and ecologically conscious in their efforts.

This is not a course in which they will collect facts or memorize and recall events. This is an adventure of internal and external cognitive and affective (yes, I use these terms with students) practices to ferret out truths, to construct meaning of the past, to appreciate the impact of it on us as historical beings, and to narrate our stories and those of others. From this beginning, my students know that I expect them to develop healthy habits of being that strengthen themselves and their community.

I tell them that we expect them to meet high standards of scholarship and to live up to high standards of ethical behavior, often higher standards than those that many adults meet. To this end, I realize, our study of history is a cultural and epistemic experience in which a sense of individual responsibility, spiritual consciousness, and human relationships are as germane as readings, inquiry, research, analysis, and interpretation. For them to internalize healthy lessons of history, I need to be very explicit about and supportive of the idea and practice that scholarship matters in how my students shape their lives each day.

When my team realizes that our year's course of study should contend with new material, given changes in our students or contemporary challenges, we begin to investigate and share our findings. Our inclusion of issues related to HIV/AIDS is such a case. We saw in the late 1980s and early 1990s how much the disease was affecting society, how it had tested the scientific community, and how it had sparked a new literary genre. Most important, we witnessed in the lives of our students how HIV/AIDS had become a new horror. Some friends or family members suffered. We learned that poor and minority communities were at particular risk. Teenagers, with their sexual experimentation, are especially at risk of

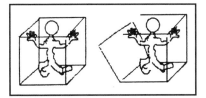

Figure 18.1. The context boxes that
frame our thinking and being

being infected. Since we were already having our students attend our
local AIDS walk, we decided to integrate the topic as one of several year-
long contemporary issues on which we would keep checking. I see our interdisciplinary units as spokes of a wheel that link to a hub of ideas,
within which sits the axle of critical inquiry, including affective and cognitive elements. The wheel moves forward as we keep the spokes true in
relationship to the hub and axle. One of these ideas in this hub involves
taking personal responsibility for dealing with what one learns from history and applying it to an effort to make sense of the world around one
and for making choices. Having a topic like HIV/AIDS as part of the hub
leads to our asking, "How do a virus like HIV and a disease like AIDS affect our society, and what do we do about them?" Long before I initiate
such a question, I introduce a way for individuals to get a historical sense
of things in general, and themselves in particular, by using what I call the
context boxes.

On the first day in our American Studies history class, I tell my students, "This is a class about you. Yes, it is about the history of the United
States, but it is fundamentally also about you." Like a Greek chorus, this
refrain reverberates throughout all of our experiences as we learn and do
history together. I make this assertion not only because I understand that,
ultimately, historical study is a tool for knowing oneself but also because
each of us is an "historical being," to use Sam Wineburg's illuminating
concept. I introduce the diagrams in Figure 18.1 to illustrate the structural components of history's discipline: the conditions, forces, time,
place, culture, community, and ideology that affect the individual. I want
students to have a tangible tool with which to contextualize history by sit-
uating historical actors, including themselves, within such a box. Generally, the boxes are also a tool for handling the dynamic complexity of historical causality, helping students make sense of themselves as historical

beings and of their relationships and learnings in our interdisciplinary community.

On the first day of class I draw the diagrams on the board, and the students copy them into their critical thinking notebooks (a wonderful daily tool whose analysis will need to wait for another essay). I am giving them what Jerome Bruner calls an iconic representation of the knowledge about the discipline's structure and simultaneously of the knowledge we will draw from many sources. I am translating these into a form more accessible to a wider audience, while creating a mental map in students' minds. The boxes serve as a cognitive strategy that calls to mind the hiker's map John Dewey uses as an analogy for the process of a student's learning. This map shows the connections between cause and effect, past and present, thought and action, humans and the environment, individuals and groups, time and place, as well as the connections between people and the forces or conditions of their times, places, and communities. When cast in an interdisciplinary light, these connections becomes clearer, more interesting, and certainly more relevant to our scholastic obligations, including our obligation to meet today's standards. Students become nimble in seeing interdisciplinary connections as inherent complexities of knowledge and of knowing. The students anticipate new possibilities and generate new questions of where to look for sources or pieces of the historical puzzle.

Because I want students to appreciate the role the individual has in making history, which extrapolates to themselves, the second drawing shows the individual pushing against a side. I intend the diagram to empower students. My course is not about a deterministic history. In discussion, in their notebooks, and in small groups, they begin to play with the diagrams, putting themselves into the boxes and identifying the current conditions and forces that frame their lives and the ways they contend with them. They begin to realize that history does not just "happen" but occurs as a dynamic transaction between the individual and the contexts within which one lives. In short, I want students to acknowledge the numerous interlocking features of the contexts that help shape and define us and the contexts with which a historian must reckon conscientiously. In this way my work clearly reflects Sam Wineburg's conception of "historical beings." He addresses the importance of having teachers be aware of students' efforts to make sense of themselves, a point my diagram is intended to address.

Unfortunately, history can be so rarefied and abstract that it turns into a shallow and vacuous study of "dead people." To avoid this, students need to wrestle with the historian's narrative and data in terms of the underlying human thoughts, feelings, and action. By showing how people exist within contexts marked by conditions and forces of time, place, and community, a history teacher can prod students to examine their own contexts. "What would they have done in another time?" I ask. Such a required reflection comes to mean, "What do I do in these times?" By implication, history students can begin to value being more conscious of the decisions they make.

The boxes necessarily refer to converging interdisciplinary connections. For example, technology is a force; the environment is the place; the oral tradition represents a condition, and so forth. Thus, my collegial teamwork enriches historical complexity and scaffolds the historiography of what we teach. Moreover, as the box on the right depicts, as one pushes down (dare I say breaks through?) the side(s) of the box, one can develop a mature sense of freedom in acting on what one knows. Paradoxically, within the limits of this structure, knowledge is liberated, and so, too, the student's learning. With structure there can be an unfolding of information in a coherent and logical fashion that manifests the principles of the discipline. To Bruner, those fundamental principles facilitate a transferability of knowledge, indeed, an application of learning outside the classroom. Students who can exercise the learning for themselves and apply the knowledge for themselves are free. The context boxes sharpen historical methodology. They also give rise to richer self-reflection. Most important, when used later, they clarify what happens to knowing when one ignores context.

Bain discusses the problem (and hope) of designing and teaching history courses on the basis of the kind of cognition historians exercise. At Humanitas, we start by comparing and contrasting the methodologies of various disciplines. Students investigate how we know anything, what we mean by critical thought, how we find and what we do with multiple sources, how we deepen our corroboration, what we mean by intelligence, how we each possess a range of multiple intelligences, and, most important, how our collaboration in an interdisciplinary community of scholars enables us to deal with the complexity of knowledge and its purposes in a democracy.

In an interdisciplinary American Studies community, it is particularly enlightening to study the debates about intelligence in the United States.

Exploring philosophical and scientific concerns that have influenced these debates, such as Social Darwinism and theories of natural selection, pragmatism, and relativism, helps Humanitas students understand how intellectual capacities have been defined, categorized, and explained. The history lesson becomes a means of grappling with their own intelligence, recognizing how sociology, philosophy, and science can, at different times, be liberating or limiting constructs. The Humanitas students are challenged to see their capacities for what they can be, not how they may be delineated by others. Intrapersonal intelligence plays a vital role here. I introduce Howard Gardner's theory of multiple intelligences early on when I present the context boxes as part of the opening thematic interdisciplinary unit on epistemology and the ways we know in history, literature, and science. Through questionnaires, narratives, exercises, and games, students construct profiles of their intelligences and learning styles. I want students to know that the historian needs to be conscious of his or her own perspective about things because he or she will interpret evidence and infer meaning(s) on the basis of it.

Building Historical Awareness and Critical Skills

Needless to say, I have to observe students very closely to assess their levels of trust and forbearance. Our first week includes a lot of early examinations about the ways roles operate in society, beliefs and biases, facts and opinions, and the ways that historians need to detect the emotional content of a source to appreciate its trouble spots and insight. The point is to discern how roles, ideology, emotions, and biases can lead to undisciplined affective responses that filter, possibly even distort, perceptions. We use masks and other devices to help students see the limits of adopted roles, like cheerleader or silent type, and the responses and stereotypes the presentation of roles can elicit.

Students need to get comfortable with identifying their feelings, stepping outside their beliefs in order to understand things better. They see how significant but troublesome emotions can be in the study of history; like Wineburg's young cohort, my students have commented on the value of understanding emotions. If the group shows high levels of trust and respect, I will tackle head-on how their own beliefs about themselves and/or what others think about them filter the way they look at the world and how that affects their actions.

In those opening days, I am careful to reestablish the norms of historical inquiry and those of our community of scholars, which the students began to examine as tenth graders, but I want to pursue a deeper level of metacognition as well. This is reinforced by my Humanitas colleagues. While I am presenting the graphics shown in Figure 18.1, I am refining students' historical skills and heuristics (e.g., collecting data from multiple sources, working with primary documents, weighing evidence, analyzing, making inferences, writing accounts) at the same time that I begin working on the power of beliefs. I set up the mask interplay as an episode of perceptual conflict, but it is not the only event I create to bring to the fore multiple ways of seeing or interpreting. Like Bain, I want students to wrestle with the multiplicity of voices and views in discerning "what happened," but I start by asking how beliefs affect our seeing and then later knowing what happened. Students review, or learn, general critical thinking questions that they need to apply throughout their inquiry: What do we know? How do we know it? Are there other ways of seeing or knowing this? What is the context? How does this fit into a big picture? What does it mean? What are the implications?

Along with these, the students discuss other epistemological queries, which the historian uses: How do we find out? How have I gathered and processed or thought about this information? What do these sources mean? Which sources agree? How do they differ? What is signficant? What are the features of the primary document? What is the purpose of the primary document? Who was the intended audience? Whose point of view is expressed? Whose perspective is missing? What difference does this knowledge make today? How do we talk about or present our knowledge? How do our beliefs affect what we know and think?

As I continue to draw upon and strengthen intrapersonal intelligence still other inquiries help: What difference does it make in my life? What do I believe? Why do I believe this? How do I feel about what I am discovering? Why do I feel this way? Metacognitive queries work side by side with the cognitive and affective ones. Each helps students maneuver through their later investigations, their research, and their experiences with me and my team, moving from classroom to classroom, considering themes and often a philosophical question or idea, in multifaceted ways. I hope to engender in them the confidence to use these skills when they find themselves confronted by unexpected challenges in life.

Inevitably, the serious and sensitive challenge of how one handles beliefs in a history class confronts me daily. I see what I do as an issue of unmasking, challenging, and cultivating beliefs grounded in responsible scholarly standards and those of the community within which we work and live. In this way, it is my responsibility to help young thinkers consider carefully and see the world around them honestly and responsibly, aware of what they bring as the observer to their studies as young historians *and* to their understandings of themselves as historical beings.

In this way, I weave experiences of getting to know one another with early processes of historical inquiry, beginning with the context boxes. This takes time. In fact, time is an interesting ally of learning we too easily take for granted. Just as the historical discipline depends on scholars' being distanced enough in time from the event under study to pursue inquiry in a detached, dispassionate manner, a young person needs time in class to deal with personal beliefs and feelings. These must be acknowledged, exposed, and worked with in order for the person to become aware of how they affect how she or he sees the world. Left unacknowledged, beliefs and feelings can fester, like a thorn beneath the skin. In my classroom, I embrace my students' multiple perspectives, including the affective, as an integral part of our doing history. That is where my teaching begins—with unveiling for youth what they believe so that they can begin to develop a sharp and lucid sense of collecting, assessing, evaluating, and interpreting the evidence of their historical study.

In the first week, I set out to make it clear that our exploration into the past will help reveal and, in fact, will depend upon the students' knowledge and understanding of themselves. I assure them that understanding what they believe and why they do so, as well as knowing how they think, what they may feel, how they regard themselves, what motivates them, how and why they act in different situations, and how they perceive the world and their role in it will enable them to make reasonable sense and complex interpretations of the past. Trusting themselves and one another strengthens their capacity to assess and weigh multiple sources and multiple perspectives. In becoming historians, they must be aware of and set aside their biases.

They need to appreciate historical actors as humans dealing with hope and fears, attitudes and feelings. This kind of historical empathy relies on the students being conscious of their own emotions at play. However, the trick is to realize one's feelings, to understand them, and to allow them not to sully but to inform and elucidate their interpretations. I make it clear that at times this work will appear messy to them, uncomfortable and difficult; sometimes it will involve unsavory, possibly painful, truths about themselves and their community or society. This, like the writing and studying of history, is often delicate business, as it should be.

As the course progresses, we apply the task of self-informed interpretation and the habits gained in dealing with historical sources and biases to contemporary exercises as well. Projects involving media literacy allow this kind of application. Roughly speaking, media literacy is the critical reading and analyses of media, the varied genre, the infrastructures, the technologies and purposes. Media literacy aims at deconstructing how and why information is packaged and communicated and the impact its subsequent delivery has on culture and consumers. In our opening epistemology unit, features of media literacy appear. Actually, in a neat way, the masks activity presents one element of media analyses. The masks become a tangible reminder that all sorts of masks or filters may screen our seeing, thinking, and knowing, in much the same way that a medium operates—"coming between" the recipient and the message. In a way, historical accounts have much in common with media—both rely on selection and interpretation of sources that get made into a story. I tell students to consider their history text on the spectrum of media genre, for publishing is one institution of the print media.

The media literacy exercise is a very public use of historical thinking. It may also reveal an appropriation of an historical narrative. It certainly helps make sense of one's own historical being. Wineburg emphasizes how compelling media images are as teachers or sources of what students know about history. This is an essential lesson I want my students to learn in order to understand how media create culture. They deconstruct images from television, commercials, films, magazines, billboards, and textbooks to discern the underlying messages and the production tricks that manufacture a sense of reality, which one literary critic calls "faction," the mixing of fact and fiction. When that mixture intentionally distorts perception, the intended purpose must be rigorously exposed. For images, as Wineburg nicely points out, linger as long-lasting, often unconscious, authorities. Media literacy instills in adolescent consumers the skills to break down these media images and to be conscious of their impact on a person and the culture. The deconstruction of historical images, political cartoons, posters, illustrations, and photographs, along with those on television, movie screens, and in headlines, is a recurring theme in our studies.

My goal is to encourage the documentation of as many perspectives as possible, imagining and uncovering evidence from numerous sources and generating as many preliminary, tentative anticipations as possible before we determine which interpretations are most valid. This means helping students to be patient in their thinking, to suspend their judgment until they have opened their eyes to many views, attuned their ears to many voices, sensitized themselves to see what part of a story may be missing, emboldened themselves to question assumptions and to challenge authorities so that they can handle the fragile equilibrium of historical inquiry and interpretation. The most challenging work is to sift through the assemblage and to organize the stories of the past into honest, reasonable, and meaningful interpretations.

Conclusion

I *have* to require social action in my history class, and, fortunately, my Humanitas interdisciplinary community facilitates and encourages my doing so. I am countering the forces and conditioning of television, the market, and advertising. Too often, these generate in youth an attitude that all one can be is someone to fit in, consume, and be entertained. American anti-intellectualism and corporate marketing collude in sending double messages. The average student has little incentive to pursue learning deeply; the overachieving pupil is captivated by grades, while the dropout is cruising through life. However undeveloped their skills, however unconvinced of the importance of working hard, adolescents crave more from their learning and generally respond positively when authentic tasks are asked of them (even if it is cool to moan and groan). When I ask Humanitas students to do more with their knowledge outside the classroom and school, they tell me it makes them feel important. Applying historical knowledge to improving society—especially for the long-term sustenance of our democracy—does not happen automatically, as if by osmosis or spontaneous generation. I need to build it into my curriculum and include it in the course requirements and student evaluations. My students' habits of being need this validation.

Denying or ignoring the effects of one's thought and action contradicts this basic historical principle. Ultimately, this denial can alienate us, and history can become too facile. Worse, it becomes too easy to deny that our decisions and actions ever really matter, that they can shape and influence our politics, society, and economy. It becomes too easy to see ourselves as powerless, let alone discern the embryonic history breathing around us. The drama in the inner city of Los Angeles may make more visible the making of history, but, even in the quietest of villages, much history lives. Without understanding the effect a person has through his or her actions, it becomes far too easy to become apathetic. If our choices and actions do not count, we have no need to weigh them by any humane or ethical standard. How we live our lives does affect the unfolding of history.

What does this matter? Ruth responds, "By just exposing me to the reality of life in communities I never found out before [*sic*] has taught me to look at things in a new perspective. I felt that I learned more this year than any other years about my communities and other communities around me, plus I also learned about myself." Did she learn history deeply enough? If one indicator is whether she got a sense of her own historical being, her own historical acting, perhaps so: "I also realize that when I succeed, I can come back to my own community and give it a hand so that young kids will wake up to see a better future."

Valuing young people as thinkers means that I use overarching philosophical frameworks to ground their thinking and the structural dimensions and processes of the discipline to guide and challenge their cognition, putting them into the role of historian. Respecting them as individual human beings means that I validate and support their affective as well as their cognitive responses, getting them to reflect about their feelings in conjunction with their ideas, developing their metacognitive capacity. Embracing them as members of a community means that I attend to and mediate their socialization and relationships, affirming the democratic purposes of their history education and expecting them to use their academics to contribute to their communities. My responsibility is to reveal their place in history and their value and power as human beings.

They begin to understand that developing their inner power involves using what they learn in the classroom to take control of their lives and to be positive forces for good. Most important, students who make such connections develop habits that enable them to believe in a strong future vision. They see that society needs and wants them involved, creatively, intellectually, actively, to build and sustain a strong and just democracy. As we, history teachers, design our courses in terms of the practices of historians and work with students connected to themselves and one another in communities, the teaching and learning of history become transformational epistemic acts.

NOTES

I have learned to take reasonable risks and to pursue deep and innovative scholarship for the sake of youth development and democracy because I have had generous students, mentors, teammates, and other colleagues in the Humanitas program. My first teammates, the late Roland Ganges and the late Jim Martin, and my initial coordinator, Cathy Nadler, proved to be invaluable allies in showing me how to move on the current paths of my teaching within an institution like the Los Angeles Unified School District. Our media artist in residence, Gina Lamb, provoked me to open my eyes in new ways to respect students' voices and to see the creative and cognitive potential of video and other technology in the classroom. She also taught me why media literacy is essential to a democratic education.

1. Plato, "Socrates' Defense (Apologia)," trans. Hugh Tredennick, in *The Collected Dialogues of Plato*, ed. Edith Hamilton and Huntington Cairns (Princeton, 1971), p. 23.

2. All names of students are pseudonyms.

3. A teacher-driven senior high school reform, Humanitas is based on an early-1980s prototype developed in a magnet school setting. Since 1986, thanks initially to a grant by the Rockfeller Humanitas and the support of the Los Angeles Educational Partnership, Humanitas has been offered throughout the Los Angeles Unified School District (LAUSD), first in seven schools, including my own, and currently in more than thirty.

Chapter 19

A Case Study of Developing Historical Understanding via Instruction
The Importance of Integrating Text Components and Constructing Arguments

James F. Voss and Jennifer Wiley

The purpose of this chapter is to review a set of studies concerned with enhancing student learning and understanding of history.[1] The studies have focused primarily on two questions: whether presenting segments of a history text separately (as multiple texts) produces better performance than presenting the segments as a single text and whether writing an argumentative essay about a historical topic produces better performance than writing other types of essays, such as a narrative. The interaction of these two factors was also of interest. Before providing the rationale for the research, however, we need to consider the concepts of learning and understanding as we are using them.

Learning and Understanding

Learning

From a psychological perspective, the concept of learning is most frequently the acquisition of particular information or the development of some type of skill by an individual, although the term may also be used in relation to the acquisition or change of beliefs, attitudes, or other concepts. In the context of history, the acquisition might consist of information about the American Civil War, the development of skill in writing historical arguments, or a change in one's attitude about the policies of the United States toward American Indians during the settling of the West.

Relatively standard types of evaluation are employed in the classroom to determine whether a student has learned the information under study. These include multiple-choice, completion, and short answer tests, as well as exams requiring the student to write longer essays. Students may also be required to write papers on topics related to the subject matter under study. For the purpose of the research reported in this chapter, the term "learning" will refer to the ability to recall or identify correctly the contents of a text. Specifically, we measured learning by determining the number of correct answers given by participants to questions about the text contents and by asking participants to verify whether particular statements were true according to the text contents.

Understanding

There is less precision and agreement in the use of the term "understanding" than there is for the term "learning." Most psychologists would probably agree that the term "understanding" implies not only knowledge of a given object, issue, event, or person but also knowledge of components, causes, or underlying operations that pertain to the issue in question. There can be differences in what two or more people understand about the same issue, yet all may feel that they "understand" that issue. This arbitrariness correctly suggests that what constitutes understanding, or how well something is understood, is open to debate.

At an intuitive level, if a person says she understands how a car runs, we think she knows the parts of the car and how they are involved in the car's operation. If a person says he understands another person, we think he knows the person reasonably well and is able to tell what is producing a particular aspect of the other person's behavior. If a person states that she understands the American Civil War, we think she means that she has a substantial knowledge of the war, what produced it, how and why it was fought as it was, and why it concluded as it did, along with perhaps knowledge of the war's consequences and an awareness of any controversies that exist with respect to any of these topics. However, in the case of history, no matter how the person describes such an understanding, someone else may state that the war is not really properly understood unless one considers some other factor(s) that have not been considered or not been considered appropriately.

In order to describe how we measured understanding in our research, we first need to consider the theoretical basis of the work. When an individual reads a text, the person develops what Kintsch has termed a situation model.[2] This model is a mental representation of the text contents that takes into account what the individual already knows about the topic of the text. Thus, if a person reads that in the year 2000 the Democrats will nominate Senator Dianne Feinstein of California for vice president, the person's mental representation may include not only this statement but the fact that California has more electoral votes than any other state and that Feinstein's nomination may help the Democrats to carry the state in the November 2000 election.

Two points may be made with respect to a situation model and a person's knowledge. As would be expected, people with more knowledge about a particular topic typically produce a more developed representation. Also, knowledge utilization is important. It is not sufficient just to have the knowledge; it must also be accessed and used.

At a more molecular level, the situation model may be considered as a node-link network structure, with the nodes representing the concepts and the links denoting the relations between concepts. Moreover, there are different types of links, that is, different types of relations. For example, there may be a link indicating that Stonewall Jackson was a general in the Confederate army. This link also may point to a category membership, indicating that there were a number of Confederate generals. Another type of link is causal; these links indicate a causal connection, such as "Lee lost the battle because he overestimated the strength of the Union troops." A number of expressions in English portray some level of causal relationship. These terms include "influences," "produces," "leads to," "causes," "is due to," and "is attributable to." Such expressions not only cue the reader to the relation; they also provide a means of obtaining an approximation of the structure of the overall text. Viewed in this context, understanding is assumed to refer to the type and extent of the node-link structure or, correspondingly, to the nature of the contents of the mental representation that a person has and utilizes in a given context. Having a better understanding in this context requires having a good sense of the causal relations and other relationships that affect the topic in question.

Thus far, we have considered the idea of a mental representation or a situation model and its underlying structure. We now turn to the issue of process. We assume that when individuals read a text or perform any of a number of other tasks, they may process the incoming information either at a relatively shallow or superficial level or at a deeper level. In terms of the effects of such processing differences, superficial processing leads to a less developed situation model; it is as if much of the information a person has in memory about the topic in question is not activated when the text is read, and the memory information therefore is not linked to the input, nor does it become part of the mental representation of the incoming information. On the other hand, deeper processing presumably activates more related information, and a more extensive mental representation is therefore developed. The deeper processing should then lead to a representation with more causal relations and connectives. An important point regarding superficial and deeper processing is that more superficial processing should lead to a substantial knowledge of the surface structure of the text, but it should not lead to a relatively substantial understanding. On the other hand, deeper processing should produce both a substantial knowledge of the text structure and a more developed understanding.

Given these considerations, we now consider the five measures of understanding employed in the present research. Three types of measures were obtained via analyses of the written essay. The essays were first analyzed for their overall organization. Using a method of analysis developed by Meyer,[3] each essay was categorized according to whether it primarily listed information with minimal focus or was more analytic, having a thesis or conclusion, and was organized in relation to that conclusion. The second occurrence was taken as a measure of better understanding.

The second essay measure involved connectives. The number of times connective words were used in each essay was taken as a measure of understanding; the connectives included inferences, temporal links, conjunctions, and causal links. In addition, the number of causal connectives alone was determined for each essay. A greater number of causal connectives was assumed to indicate better understanding. Since the number of all connectives was in substantial agreement with the number of only causal connectives, we will discuss only the results obtained for the causal connectives.

A third essay-related measure was sentence origin. Using a procedure employed by Greene,[4] we placed each sentence of each essay in one of three categories: borrowed, added, or transformed. Borrowed sentences were those taken directly from the text. Added sentences were statements that had no text content. Transformed sentences either had content that included both text content and additional information the reader brought into the text situation or brought together two units of the text that had been previously unconnected. Transformed sentences were assumed to depict better understanding because they showed a rephrasing of the text material and an integration of what the person already knew with the text contents.[5]

The fourth and fifth measures of understanding involved verification of factual data. To determine the fourth measure, we presented individuals with a statement after they had read the text and asked whether the contents of the statement could be correctly inferred from the text contexts. There were ten correct and ten incorrect statements. For the principle verification task, the fifth measure of understanding, we asked individuals to compare the historical issue in the present research, the Irish potato famine of the nineteenth century, to four other events that varied in similarity to the potato famine in a surface and/or a deep manner. The stock market crash of 1929 was regarded as not similar in either way, the Black Plague, because of its natural causes and its loss of life, was regarded as having surface similarity, (the loss of life in that event, however, occurred at all levels of society). Recent outbreaks of tuberculosis were seen as having both surface and deep similarity, with disadvantaged people being victimized more than the advantaged. The post–Civil War poll tax was assumed to be similar to the famine at a deep level, since poor populations were the victims in both cases, but dissimilar on the surface, because the tax caused no deaths. We were interested especially in answers to the poll tax item because we assumed that those who observed the similarity between it and the famine would have greater understanding of the events. Individuals were asked to rate each of the four test items on a scale of 1–10 according to how similar its causes were to those of the Irish potato famine.

Rationale and Procedures for the Present Studies

Rationale

A number of efforts have been made to enhance learning and understanding in history. These include improving textbooks,[6] using multiple documents,[7] providing quality instruction,[8] and asking students to generate "their own histories."[9] Thus, an important question is, What type of manipulations or interventions would be expected to facilitate learning and understanding? On the basis of the theoretical issues that have been discussed, a goal of an instructional procedure should be to produce a deeper processing of the to-be-learned information, a processing that includes an integration of text contents and the reader's knowledge. The two manipulations of the present research were selected with this goal in mind.

As previously mentioned, one manipulation employed in the present studies was presentation of a textbook chapter as a single text in its standard narrative form and presentation of the same text in a multiple-source format in which the text was divided into eight segments, presented in a random order as separate sources. In both conditions, individuals were asked to read all of the text.

The rationale for this text manipulation was our first hypothesis: that the multiple-segment condition would yield deeper processing than the single-text presentation because the reader in the multiple-segment condition would need to integrate the eight sets of content in order to develop a coherent text structure, while in the standard-text condition the structure was already present in the text.

The other instructional procedure we studied consisted of having different individuals write different types of essays. There were three types in the first study: a narrative, an argumentative essay, and a historical essay, with "history" left undefined. The instructions were identical in all three conditions, except for the insertion of one word, "narrative," "argument," or "history." In some of the other studies, explanatory and summary essays were also requested. The focus of the present discussion is, however, a comparison of the process of writing a narrative versus that of writing an argumentative essay.

A second hypothesis tested by the essay writing manipulation is that writing an argumentative essay would require more and deeper processing of the material than writing a narrative, because the former requires more rearrangement and reorganizing of the text material than the latter. Indeed, extensive processing should be required when the multiple-source text version is read and an argumentative essay is written. The point constituted our third hypothesis: that understanding measures would be of the highest magnitude in the multiple-source, argumentative essay task.

As to the learning measures, which would require only a surface comprehension of the text contents, we hypothesized that learning would not differ among the conditions, since a reasonable surface comprehension was expected in all cases. This constituted our fourth hypothesis.

Materials and Procedures

The historical set of events chosen for the studies was the nineteenth-century Irish potato famine. The text for all of the five studies described the religious, political, sociocultural, and agricultural factors involved in the famine and the resulting population decline in Ireland that occurred in the mid-nineteenth Century.

In all studies, individuals were given two packets. The first contained materials that asked them to read one of the two versions of the text, the single text or the multiple-segment version. The contents of the two versions were identical except for the difference in order and the need to include a few sentences in the multiple-segment condition to provide a sense of flow. These sentences did not contain any causal or explanatory information. The separate "segments" consisted of a map; biographical accounts of King George III and Daniel O'Connell; brief descriptions of the Act of Union, the Act of Emancipation, 1829, and the Great Famine; census data on population size, the death rate, and the rate of emigration between 1800 and 1850; economic statistics on crop prices, rent costs, and distribution of land holdings; and occupational breakdowns for the years between 1800 and 1850. The excerpts were taken from a number of texts and constructed into a textbook–like chapter.[10]

When writing the essays, individuals always had access to the text they had read. This procedure was followed so that the essay writing would not be dependent upon memory. In other words, we were interested in how the writer would use the contents of the essay, not in how well the person could remember the text contents in writing the essay.

The second packet contained materials for testing. Depending upon the study, some packets contained a number of completion questions to measure learning and a sentence verification task in which individuals indicated whether each item of twenty appeared in the text contents (ten did and ten did not). The inference and principle verification items, intended to measure understanding, were also included in the packet.

Findings and Their Implications

In general, the most important finding of our studies was that reading from multiple segments combined with writing an argumentative essay yielded deeper understanding of the material than any other condition in which text format and essay type were manipulated. This result supports Hypothesis 3 and is consistent with the idea that presentation of multiple texts and the writing of an argumentative essay requires more processing than the other conditions. The question of whether the multiple-segment condition produced better understanding than the single-text condition and whether writing an argumentative essay produced better understanding than writing a narrative essay may be answered in the affirmative, although with qualifications.

Regarding the overall organization data, that is, the writing of a listing versus an analytic essay, in general, the multiple-segment condition yielded more analytic essays than the single-text condition. Furthermore, more analytic essays were written in the multiple-segment, argument-essay condition than in any other condition, while more listing essays were written in the single-text, narrative-writing condition. These findings support the general idea that, with respect to understanding, there is a relationship between the way information is presented and the particular task involved in using the information.

With respect to the causal-connective measure, the proportion of causal connectives was greater in the argument condition essay than in the narrative essay condition. While the single-versus-multiple segment variable did not yield a significant difference, the multiple-segment argumentative-essay condition yielded the greatest proportion of causal connectives, up to a third of the connectives used.

These excerpts from one participant's essay are typical of an analytic essay that contained a number of causal connectives.

> There are several reasons that led to the sharp decrease of the Irish population between the years 1846–1850. They include the great famine, which had a devastating effect. . . .
>
> Another reason causing the decline of population was the Catholic Emancipation in 1829. George IV granted Catholics the same right to worship as the Protestants, but raised the qualifications for voting. These were based on property value, and this caused the voting population to fall from 100,000 to 16,000.
>
> Death rate per 1000 people was a whopping 50, more than double the mark set by the population in the 5 years previous. . . . Also, the immigration rate in Ireland was off the charts. In 1850 alone, 250,000 people left the Emerald Isle compared to 1838 when only 15,000 left.
>
> The population in Ireland decreased in the years 1846–50 because people were being persecuted for their beliefs or did not have a strong voice in government.

In contrast, the following listing essay lacks causal connectives.

The lives that were being lost somewhat made the significant change in Ireland's population. In 1846 to 1880, it was all about survival for Ireland's population. The overlapping cold and what winters didn't make anything better for Ireland's population. There were people struggling to survive off bad crops. The decrease in average shows that there were less food supplies, and to top it off the crops that were bad were being produced were regularly being taxed. The feeling under the ruling of the United Kingdom may have affected the population of Ireland.

The multiple-segment condition and argument-writing task tended to yield a higher proportion of transformed sentences than the single-textbook condition or the narrative-writing condition. However, the greatest proportion of transformed sentences was obtained when the multiple-segment and argument-writing conditions were combined. The proportion of added sentences varied little according to the essay type or presentation format. However, the proportion of borrowed sentences was greater in the narrative-essay condition than in the argument-essay condition, especially in the single-text condition. This finding supports the idea that the construction of narrative essays involved less processing that was necessary in the argument-essay condition.

In relation to the inference verification task, students who read from multiple segments and wrote argumentative essays were best at recognizing inferences that followed from the text.

The principle verification data, which required the participant to recognize the similarity between the famine and other events, indicated that individuals who wrote argumentative essays from multiple segments were more likely than individuals who wrote narrative essays or who wrote from single texts to rate the poll tax as more similar to the famine than the other events. These results support the idea that understanding is facilitated by writing an argumentative essay from multiple segments.

Turning to the learning measure of recall, which was obtained in one study, the primary finding was that, while participation in the single-text narrative-essay and the multiple-text argumentative-essay conditions did not differ in the number of correct items recalled, they both demonstrated better recall than did participants in the other conditions. This finding suggests that, when reading a narrative text, readers develop a narrative representation of the contents. When they are then asked to write a narrative essay on the subject, a type of resonance occurs, making the task somewhat easier and reducing the amount of processing required. This congruence also is consistent with the relatively high number of borrowed sentences in this condition.

The sentence verification data, which also are a measure of learning, produced better recognition in the narrative-writing tasks than in the argument-writing task, especially when students wrote from single texts. This suggests that students who wrote narratives from single sources engaged in more extensive processing at the textbase level. In other words, writers of narratives were more concerned with being accurate in relation to the text than in developing their own models of the situation. However, if asked to write an argumentative essay instead of a narrative, individuals need to construct the argument on the basis of a narrative representation, which requires considerable processing of the text content.

In the multiple-segment condition, the reader is able to develop a narrative essay with a relatively small amount of processing. But, if asked to write an argumentative essay, the writer finds the representation narrative of little help; especially in the multiple-segment condition, substantial processing is needed. These notions suggest that individuals, to understand or make sense of events, are predisposed to place them in a chronological, narrative form and that writing an argumentative essay requires deliberation or processing that are not present in the narrative.

We wish to note three other findings. In one study, results supported the account of representation development that we have given. All participants read the multiple-segment text and subsequently rated each sentence of the text for its importance to the overall text contents. Half of the individuals wrote narratives, and half wrote argumentive essays. For each type of essay, half of the participants rated the sentences before writing their essays, and half rated them after writing them. We found that the advantage in understanding in the argument essay condition, compared to the narrative condition, occurred when the ratings in both conditions were performed after the essay writing. However, when the ratings were done before the essay writing, those who wrote argumentative essays demonstrated no advantage with respect to understanding. Specifically, considering the number of causal connectives, the argument condition yielded a mean of 7.8 before the ratings but 5.4 afterward. The narrative essay yielded means of 4.9 and 5.4 for ratings before and after essay writing, respectively. This finding indicates that taking time to rate sentence importance interferes with the construction of an argumentative essay but not with the construction of a narrative essay. This raises the interesting possibility that argumentative essay writing involves considering the study contents in relation to a standard of importance different from that used in a text-based narrative. In other words, an argument structure may attribute importance based on supporting and opposing reasons to the claim rather than on utility in reconstructing the narrative.

The second and third results were obtained in the fifth study in the series. Two additional procedures were employed in that study that were not part of the other studies. One of these consisted of studying student perception of the narrative- and argumentative-essay tasks. This procedure was employed in order to understand better the differences we had found in essay writing in the earlier studies. Students were asked to state what they understood to be narrative- and argumentative-essay tasks. Their perceptions of the tasks were classified into two categories, using a keyword procedure. One class included essay descriptions using terms such as "story-like," " one-sided," "descriptive," and "writing your opinion." The other class included terms involving presentation of "two sides" or "both sides," "defending," "backing up," "interpreting" facts, or "proving." The former list was regarded as perceiving a more one-sided and descriptive view, a relatively simple view, whereas the second class was regarded as perceiving two sides and the need for evidence, a more complex perception.

The results indicated that individuals who wrote analytic, as opposed to listing, essays were more likely to have complex views of essay writing rather than a simple view. The more complex view was also positively related to having a greater number of transformed sentences in the essays and a greater proportion of correct inference verifications and principle verifications. These results point to the important conclusion that for text understanding to be maximized via writing essays, student knowledge of essay structure and especially of how different viewpoints or perspectives are related and can be incorporated into the essay structure is critical.

The other procedure added to the fifth study involved asking individuals to read two essays about the Irish potato famine. The rationale behind this change is this: The results have indicated that, when a student writes an argument from multiple materials, a causal or complex model that considers multiple sides of an argument is more likely to be developed. From this result it may be inferred that a person who develops such a complex, causal model that incorporates both sides of an issue may also be better at detecting bias in another account. To test this notion, students were presented with two additional essays after they completed the reading and writing tasks. One essay was an abbreviated version of a lecture given by the Reverend John Hughes at the Broadway Tabernacle on March 20, 1847, and published by the *New York Times* on March 21, 1847. The title of the lecture was "A Lecture on the Irish Question"; in it, Hughes argued that both the English and the Irish were responsible for the effects of the famine. The second document was an editorial by Thomas Campbell Forster, published in the *London Times* on March 15, 1847, which suggested that the Irish had brought on the famine by themselves. The Forster article in particular was quite a biased account of the famine. On a scale of 1–10, students rated their agreement or disagreement with each article.

While we found no significant differences in the level of agreement with the two essays as a function of argumentative- or narrative-essay writing, those students who perceived the writing task as more complex were more likely to disagree with Forster's editorial, suggesting the observation of bias in the essay. We did not find significant differences between the two groups of participants in their ratings of the Hughes paragraph. The bias ratings found in the Forster essay, however, suggest that those individuals who were developing a more complex, causal representation of the famine were more likely to perceive bias in the Forster essay and to disagree with it.

Instructional Considerations

What does this research suggest about instruction in history? A number of points are noted. First, understanding is a function of the nature of the information processing that takes place both during reading and during performance of a task, such as writing. Moreover, the processing that takes place is related to the depth of understanding that is achieved. Learning the text contents per se is possible with relatively superficial processing, as well as with deeper processing, but understanding occurs only with deeper processing.

Second, deeper processing is facilitated by the individual's prior knowledge, of the specific topic, related topics, and history in general and by a more advanced level of general information and thinking skills, such as knowledge of essay structures. Furthermore, such knowledge needs to be utilized in particular contexts in order to facilitate processing.

Third, having individuals use multiple sources—even segments of several secondary accounts—and write argumentative essays constitutes a combination of procedures that helps to maximize processing. When students' perception of the writing task included the need to integrate information from multiple materials into an argument with two sides, the students were more likely to transform and integrate the presented information. Moreover, in doing so, students developed better causal models of the potato famine and a better understanding of its causes, as evidenced by their better performance on the inference verification and principle identification tasks. Furthermore, the development of their own complex causal models allowed students to see the bias in another account.

Other research on learning from multiple materials has also indicated that reading multiple sources can facilitate historical understanding, for example, by encouraging the comparison of contents across texts, making students aware of the importance of source information, and producing the recognition of inconsistencies and biases within texts. Some studies go beyond the present exercise in deliberately involving different perspectives, but the results of using multiple segments of information are clearly important in their own right.[11] It is also desirable to have students construct and synthesize their own histories from documents, which can help students develop an understanding that history is more than "someone else's facts."[12] And, especially when they are asked to write problem-based essays from multiple materials as opposed to a historical narrative, students are more likely to compare and cite information from the various sources in their essays.[13]

The present results are also related to the idea of integrative complexity.[14] Measurement of integrative complexity involves a content-free procedure in which a text segment is analyzed in terms of whether it considers two sides of an issue or only one. The measure has been used extensively in political science with documents and speeches, and results generally show that integrative complexity is greater when issues are analyzed more thoroughly, and lower when one-sided and sometimes dogmatic views are stated in the text. This measure fits well with the present findings, since one would expect the perception of the writing task as requiring a two-sided or integrated approach to be related to greater complexity of material. The measure could conceivably provide a means to evaluate student development in writing argumentative discourse.

NOTES

1. Jennifer Wiley and James F. Voss, "The Effects of Playing Historian upon Learning in History," *Applied Cognitive Psychology*, 10 (1996), pp. 563–572; James F. Voss and Jennifer Wiley, "Developing Understanding While Writing Essays in History," *International Journal of Educational Research*, 27 (1997), pp. 255–265; Jennifer Wiley and James F. Voss, "Constructing Arguments from Multiple Sources," *Journal of Educational Psychology* (1999).

2. Walter Kintsch, *Comprehension* (Cambridge, 1998).

3. Bonnie J. F. Meyer, "Prose Analysis: Purposes, Procedures, and Problems," in Bruce Britton and John Black, eds., *Understanding Expository Text* (Hillsdale, NJ, 1985), pp. 11–64.

4. Stuart Greene, "Students as Authors in the Study of History," in Gaea Leinhardt, Isabel L. Beck, and Catherine Stainton, eds., *Teaching and Learning in History* (Hillsdale, NJ, 1994), pp. 137–170.

5. Carl Bereiter and Marlene Scardamalia, *The Psychology of Written Composition* (Hillsdale, NJ, 1987).

6. Isabel L. Beck and Margaret G. McKeown, "Outcomes of History Instruction: Paste-up Accounts," in Mario Carretero and James F. Voss, eds., *Cognitive and Instructional Processes in History and the Social Sciences* (Hillsdale, NJ, 1994), pp. 237–256.

7. Charles A. Perfetti, M. Anne Britt, and Mara C. Georgi, *Text-Based Learning and Reasoning* (Hillsdale, NJ, 1995).

8. Samuel S. Wineburg and Suzanne M. Wilson, "Subject Matter Knowledge in the Teaching of History," *Advances in Research on Teaching*, 2 (1991), pp. 305–347.

9. Tom Holt, *Thinking Historically* (New York, 1990).

10. J. Mokyr, *Why Ireland Starved: A Quantitative and Analytical History of the Irish Economy, 1800–1850* (London, 1983); J. M. Goldstrom and L. A. Clarkson, eds., *Irish Population, Economy, and Society: Essays in Honour of the Late K. H. Connell* (Oxford, 1981); K. S. Bottingheimer, *Ireland and the Irish* (New York, 1982); R. D. Edwards, and T. D. Williams, *The Great Famine* (New York, 1976); Charles Sidman, "From the Act of Union to the Fall of Parnell," in Harold Orel, ed., *Irish Society and Culture: Aspects of a People's Heritage* (Lawrence, KS, 1976); E. E. R. Green, "The Great Famine," in T. W. Moody and F. X. Martin, eds., *The Course of Irish History* (Cork, 1984).

11. Charles A. Perfetti " Sentences, Individual Differences, and Multiple Texts:

Three Issues in Text Comprehension," *Discourse Processes*, 23 (1997), pp. 337–355.

12. Holt, *Thinking Historically*.

13. Greene, "Students as Authors."

14. Philip E. Tetlock, "Integrative Complexity of American and Soviet Foreign Policy Rhetoric: A Time Series Analysis," *Journal of Social and Personality Psychology*, 49 (1985), pp. 565–585.

Chapter 20

Historical Understanding
Beyond the Past and into the Present

Veronica Boix-Mansilla

[B]y liberalizing the mind, by deepening the sympathies, by fortifying the will, history enables us to control, not society but ourselves—a much more important
thing it prepares us to live more humanely in the present and to meet rather than foretell the future.

—Carl Becker (1915)[1]

Introduction

A fundamental challenge underlies history education. While students explore the actions of individuals and societies in the past, most educators
hope that what they learn will somehow inform their ability to make
sense of the world they inhabit.[2] Yet, the relationship between past and
present in history education remains broadly unexplained. What are the
major stumbling blocks that students and teachers find as they begin to
utilize what they know about the past to interpret the present? How can
an understanding of the rise of Nazi Germany and the Holocaust prepare
students to make sense of recent tragic events such as the mass murders
in Rwanda, Bosnia, and Kosovo? Most important, how can we, as educators, assess students' ability to link past and present in ways that are respectful of the discipline of history and personally meaningful?

Attempting to examine the present through the lens of history carries
with it important risks. Left to their "unschooled minds,"[3] students (and
teachers) will likely exhibit the "sins" of anachronism and decontextual-

ization. They may fail to properly historicize such constructs as "prejudice" or "propaganda" and remain unable to capture the unique ways in which "prejudice" or "propaganda" have changed form and meaning over time and across societies. In addition, linking past and present in history education may reinforce students' intuitive inclinations to interpret the past through the lens of their everyday contemporary experience. Unschooled in the discipline of history, students may believe that they can "know" the lives of people in the past in the same way they "know" their contemporaries. Conversely, they may come to believe that understanding the lives of individuals and societies in the past yields immediate understanding of people and societies in the present. Both stances are "illusions of understanding"; they may satisfy the standards of truth of the unschooled mind, but they fall short of disciplinary standards of historical understanding.

Simplistic linkages between past and present in history education impose additional threats to historical understanding. Teachers and students may succumb to the temptation to put history to the service of particular moral, social, or political values. No matter how desirable such passions may be (e.g., democracy, respect for human rights, or appreciation for national identity), subordinating history education to values in this manner often requires that historical accounts be simplified, indeed reduced, to a collection of facile "myths" about one group or one person's "heritage," "identity," or "culture." Thus conceived, historical accounts may become unimpeachable dogmas and moral "lessons" to guide present actions.[4] Within this moral framework, the disciplinary skepticism that might lead one to legitimately question the validity of historical accounts is mistakenly perceived as an affront to the values that such an account is said to embody. Subordinating history to values education undermines deep historical understanding when it forces teachers and students alike to lose sight of the meticulous process by which understanding of the past is established and revised by historians, no matter how difficult and morally problematic the past may be.

Misconceptions of this kind abound both in students' intuitive historical understandings and in their efforts to interpret the present. By linking past and present in history education and by challenging students to use what they know about the past to make sense of current events, teachers address a pivotal aspect of historical understanding. They embark with their students on the task of navigating the tension between the feeling of familiarity and the feeling of estrangement from the human beings whose lives they attempt to understand. In referring to such tension, Wineburg alerts us to the fact that "neither of these poles [familiarity and distance] does full justice to history's complexity, and veering to one side or the other dulls history's jagged edges and leaves us with cliché and caricature" (p. 490).[5]

Faced with the challenge of preparing students to use what they learn about the past to think better about the present while avoiding cliché and caricature, teachers are left with two pedagogical options. They may chose to teach the past carefully and rely on the hope that students eventually will appropriately bring to bear historical knowledge and analytic tools when they confront novel social or political processes in the future. Alternatively, teachers may scaffold students to make such connections by giving them multiple supervised opportunities to do so, identifying students' difficulties, and orienting their efforts.

In this chapter, I examine the possibilities and challenges inherent in assessing and scaffolding students. If helping students use their understanding of the past to interpret the present is one of our goals for history education, we must find valid indicators that allow us to assess the degree to which students are moving in the desired direction. In other words, we must explore how students "use history" successfully and when they fail to do so with disciplinary rigor. Bearing this challenge in mind, I examine a series of criteria and standards that may help teachers discern when students are using their understanding of the past appropriately to examine comparable processes in the present.

Broadly speaking, particular developments in the past may be linked to contemporary events in two major, though not mutually exclusive, ways. A narrative link portrays the past as antecedent to the present under study, relating it by threads of continuity and change over time. The present appears as evolving from the past, and such a developmental process provides the body of the historical narrative. A comparative link contrasts past and present as somewhat discrete cases. The unfolding of events in each of the cases is compared across societies as examples of "totalitarization" or "genocide." As Peter Stearns proposes, underlying both a narrative and a comparative approach is the skill of identifying continuity and change, similarities and differences among periods or societies. However, a comparative approach proves more demanding because it requires consideration of two particular processes of change over time.[6]

In this essay, I focus mainly on the comparative link. I examine a series of assessment criteria that emerge from analysis of students' work in which they apply what they know about the Holocaust to a media account of Rwanda. I begin by describing the challenge of understanding the Holocaust and comparing this genocide with the one that took place in Rwanda in 1994. I propose four criteria to assess students' ability to use the Holocaust as a lens to explore the Rwandan case, and I illustrate these criteria with successful and unsuccessful examples of students' work. I conclude with an analysis of the possibilities and challenges of using historical understanding as a lens to examine contemporary processes in history classrooms.

Understanding the Holocaust

The Holocaust, the systematic murder during World War II of European Jews and other minorities, resists simple explanation. Understanding this dramatic historical episode entails becoming knowledgeable about (a) the social and human experiences that shaped (and were shaped by) the period, and (b) the fabric of disciplinary modes of thinking by which such experiences are established and interpreted. As students learn about the events that culminated in the Holocaust, they gain a sense of the range of forces that made possible the unleashing of genocide in Europe between 1941 and 1945. Key occurrences such as Hitler's ascension to power, Goebbels' propaganda, the passage of the Nuremberg Laws of 1935, Kristallnacht, and the adoption of the "Final Solution" are not isolated units of factual information. Rather, they are embodied in historical interpretations of the period that give them meaning.[7]

Naturally, narratives about the Holocaust vary. They do not embody an exact correspondence with the events as they took place.[8] Instead, they are driven by different questions and interpretive frameworks, establish different bodies of evidence, and consider different actors' points of view in order to propose distinct explanations of how and why things "seem to have happened."[9] For example, a great body of historical work (e.g., Dawidowicz, Jaeckel, and Nolte)[10] focuses on Hitler's ideology of hatred and his blueprint for mass murder as the driving force of the Nazi's anti-Jewish politics. Other historians (e.g., Broszat and Mommsen, and, more recently, Goldhagen[11]) reject this hypothesis and propose that Jewish extermination emerged within the chaotic structure of a polycratic government system and a culture of "eliminationist anti-Semitism" in the Third Reich.[12]

For most historians, accounts of the Holocaust are validated when they survive the scrutiny of their community of peers—scrutiny that embodies contemporary standards for historical inquiry (e.g., a disposition against careless interpretation of sources, monocausal explanations, and unilateral accounts).[13] Likewise, in the best history classes, students are given multiple opportunities to explore currently held accounts of the past and to engage in historical modes of thinking. They examine social, political, and cultural developments by determining their historical significance;[14] building multicausal explanations and considering various historical actors' points of view;[15] weaving together historical narratives and discerning among competing accounts;[16] and interpreting sources to establish evidence.[17] Given the nature of historical knowledge, students demonstrate their best understanding of the Holocaust when they master events and broader interpretations about the period *and* when they are able to engage in the habits of mind and standards of thinking that have proven most powerful in determining whether and how things happened in the past.

Beyond the Holocaust: The Rwandan Genocide of 1994

During the past five years, Americans have been confronted with extensive media accounts of the mass killing of Tutsis by Hutus in Rwanda and the impossibility of reconciliation between these two groups. Such reports have provided opportunities for students and their families to use what they have learned about totalitarian regimes and genocide in Nazi Germany to make sense of the incomplete, fragmentary, and partisan information presented to them. Important questions emerge as the tragic experience of Rwanda (or Kosovo) enters our collective consciousness. Would an in-depth study of Nazi Germany enhance students' ability to look deeply into these more recent cases of genocide? What misconceptions would students elicit in such a complex attempt at transfer?

Like post–World War I Germany, Rwanda in the early 1990s experienced a sustained progression of state-sponsored mass murder of innocent members of a minority group. While distant from each other in time and space, both societies experienced the preconditions, development, and consequences of genocide, as defined by Article II of the United Nations Genocide Convention. In potentially genocidal societies, ancient conflicts between groups are harbored in the collective memory. Such hatreds may lie beyond the manifest beliefs of a people at a particular time but remain alive, tacitly, in the songs, rituals, humor, and everyday customs handed down from previous generations. In pregenocidal periods, indicators of an exaggerated sense of "the other" abound, where "otherness" can be defined as ethnic, cultural, religious, or economic difference. During such periods, political or economic crises typically find a bureaucracy and business leadership under the direction of the undemocratic elements of society. These crises build on religious leaders and educators who fail to stress cooperation or respect and monolithic media that present a distorted view of history in the hope of establishing a new social order. Conditions of this sort deepen the economic and political fractures, precipitating mass killings.[18]

While common features across cases of genocide are interesting to the social scientist, they are insufficient to the historian who seeks to discern the unique path taken in each instance of genocide.[19] Generic characteristics of potentially genocidal societies play out according to the particular material and social contingencies within which they operate. For example, while Germany and Rwanda both operated with an exacerbated sense of "other," the distinct meaning of "otherness" in each case impacted the development and reach of the resultant genocide differently.

In Europe, anti-Semitism was rooted in the perceived theological and psychological need to differentiate Christianity from the religion from which it had separated.[20] During the twentieth century, and under the pressures of the Treaty of Versailles, hyperinflation, and the progressive ungovernability of Germany under the Weimar Republic, the Nazis built on an existing anti-Jewish sentiment to gain access to power. They transformed "otherness" into an "unredeemable" trait by adopting a biological definition based on "race." Thus defined, Judaism served as the basis for a ghastly, coherent, and single-minded ideology demanding the total elimination of stateless Jews who were unable to counterattack as a cohesive unit.[21] The technology that allowed the Nazis to carry out their total elimination plan—modern railway networks and gas chambers established for the sole purpose of murder—responded to the country's industrialized status. Its systematic nature and efficiency responded to the way such technology was used to "protect" Germany from the biologically defined "Jewish threat."

In Rwanda (as well as in Burundi, and in parts of Uganda and Tanzania), the tensions between Tutsis and Hutus were long-standing. While no reliable record of precolonial Rwanda remains, analysis of the oral tradition suggests that Hutus and Tutsis arrived in Rwanda in distinct and successive immigration streams (with the Hutu groups having settled there several centuries ahead of the Tutsi). Hutus descended from the Bantu people, Tutsis from the Nilotic people, and each group had its particular customs and physical archetypes. Over time, these two groups came to share language and religion; they intermarried and lived intermingled with each other, sharing the same territory in small chiefdoms. Historians and ethnographers have highlighted the limitations of the term "ethnicity" and the controversial expression "tribal rivalries" to characterize the differences and tensions between these two social groups.[22] They propose, instead, that differences and tensions stemmed from their differing economic status and political placements within those chiefdoms. Tutsis were herdsmen and thus considerably wealthier than their Hutu neighbors in a country where cattle were perceived by both groups as a most valuable possession. Hutus, on the other hand, typically were agriculturists. Hutus were not allowed to own cattle, a symbol of wealth, power, and good breeding.[23] Although some Tutsis worked the land and some Hutus did indeed own cattle, the term "Tutsi" became synonymous with political and economic power and prestige, and Tutsis and Hutus defined themselves in opposition to each other. Such perceptions of self and other changed over time.[24]

Under colonial rule, Germans, and later Belgians, utilized racial theories to justify the social stratification that they found upon their arrival. They saw Tutsis, whose physical archetypes are tall, thin, and more "white looking," as a race of warrior kings. Hutus, more commonly shorter and darker, were seen as natural subordinates.[25] Hatred between the Tutsi rulers and the Hutu majority grew with progressive incidents of violent oppression committed by Tutsis against Hutus. After the Hutu revolution of 1959, the racist ideology that had dominated the colonial period was not destroyed but merely turned on its head. The Tutsis (many of whom sought refuge in neighboring Uganda and Zaire) became the symbol of old economic and political oppression and the scapegoats for all social injustices.

By 1991, exiled Tutsi-armed groups were reentering the country in an attempt at initiating a civil war. In most cases, these were the sons of the original exiles, many of whom had never lived in postindependence

Rwanda. In 1994, the economic crisis trigged by the fall of the coffee market and the assassination of Rwandan President Habyarimana left the country in the hands of the most radical Hutus, who openly incited mass murder of all Tutsis as a move of "self-defense." Opportunistic looting, deadly beatings, and machete assassinations of armed as well as innocent Tutsis and "moderate Hutus" spread across large parts of the country. The "incomplete" and unsystematic character of the Hutu genocide corresponded to the political and economic content of the perceived "Tutsi threat" in agrarian Rwanda.

In sum, while an extreme sense of "other," rooted in long-standing differences and conflicts, is observable in both interwar Europe and late-twentieth-century Rwanda, the definitions of "otherness" and the contexts in which such definitions took root were distinct, as were the implications for the nature of the two genocides that unfolded. In Germany, millions of stateless, landless, and unarmed Jews, unable to defend themselves in any systematic manner, became victims of a stepwise progression toward mass murder. The enviable German technological capacity of that time was tragically put in service to the Nazi policy of total elimination of (what they saw as) the "Jewish threat" to the biological pool of the nation. In Rwanda, by contrast, the "Tutsi threat" was evidenced by visibly armed groups returning to the country in 1994 and rooted in centuries of Tutsi political and economic domination. Indeed, systematic killing of Hutus by Tutsis had taken place in neighboring Uganda in 1972. The predominance of theft and the disorderly machete killings instigated by deadly agrarian metaphors (e.g., "cleaning the bushes") reflected the political and economic definition of "otherness" in agrarian, preindustrial Rwanda and the long-standing history of violence between the groups in the region.

Well-framed comparisons between past and present genocides recognize important commonalties but do not seek to assert identity between cases. On the contrary, comparisons provide the background against which particular qualities of separate instances are brought to light. By highlighting specific commonalties and differences, historical comparisons are necessarily selective. Conclusions drawn from a comparison depend to a great degree on the terms compared. Consider, for example, two explanations for the weak democratic edifice of the Weimar Republic that resulted from two distinct comparisons.

On one hand, compared with its Dutch and English counterparts, the German liberal bourgeoisie during the years preceding the rise of

National Socialism surfaces as relatively limited in size, power, and liberal qualities. Historians have argued that the "premodern" aristocratic orientation of the German upper bourgeoisie was a key threat to the sustainability of the democratic spirit of the Weimar Republic.[26] On the other hand, compared to the preindustrial or quasifeudal social organization that prevailed in Rwanda, the characteristics of the dynamic German bourgeoisie, interested in science, scholarship, arts, and culture, appear particularly modern. The "premodern" character attributed to it by historians in the first comparison loses ground and explanatory power as a precursor to the Third Reich. Instead, other typically modern coexisting factors emerge as defining the unique qualities of the German path toward genocide. For example, Germany's social unrest resulted from a rapid process of industrialization. Its long-standing bureaucratic tradition gave way to public trust in an authoritarian welfare state. Its militaristic path to forming a nation-state was accompanied by the growing prestige of the military. Overlapping in the end of the nineteenth century, the factors that set the conditions for the emergence of National Socialism were clearly absent in premodern Rwanda.

In sum, historical comparisons are more than algorithms to identify similarities and differences. They prove helpful to shed light on the particular qualities of specific historical developments by placing them against the background of other developments of the kind. Because comparisons are always selective, they invite scrutiny of the very terms on which a comparison is built. Changing the partner compared (e.g., German social organization against its Dutch and its Rwandan counterparts) makes this selectivity visible and lessens the distortions that necessarily result from single comparisons.

Using the Holocaust to Think about Rwanda

How can we assess students' ability to use their growing understanding of the Holocaust to guide their inquiry into Rwanda, a genocide about which they likely know very little? With this question in mind, a group of middle school teachers, teacher educators, and researchers collaborated in the development of a performance assessment task for middle school teachers and students to use after an in-depth study of Nazi Germany and the Holocaust. Members of the group were associated with Facing History and Ourselves and Harvard Project Zero.[27] Heated debates preceded our decisions to use Rwanda as a comparison case and to choose *Forsaken Cries* (an Amnesty International documentary on the history of Rwanda) as a source of information about Rwanda. We also deliberated about the type of tasks that would best reveal the most important qualities of students' understanding of this period of European history and their ability to transfer such understanding to a present case of genocide.

Our choice of Rwanda as a contemporary comparison case was grounded in a series of historical-pedagogical arguments. First, it was the differences between Germany and Rwanda that were most striking. As noted, the premodern Rwandan organization contrasted sharply with its modern German counterpart. The military nature of the Tutsis' return differed significantly from the helpless position of Jews and other minorities in a changing Germany. The immediacy and the speed of the Rwandan genocide was opposed to the slow stepwise progression that characterized the Holocaust. The presence of interested colonial sponsors who supported both Tutsis and Hutus was a direct contrast to the lack of such postcolonial conditions in Germany. We hoped that such sharp contrasts would alert students to the risks of assimilating the present case (Rwanda) uncritically into an unrevised representation of the past one (Germany), and vice versa.

We also valued the contrast between life in rural Rwanda and our students' lives in urban or suburban Boston, Massachusetts. We hoped that such a contrast in life styles would raise their skepticism about projecting their local values and world views onto a contemporary case of genocide. We wanted to avoid the illusion of understanding that takes place when local and personal experiences are used as the sole blueprint for understanding the world.

The choice of Rwanda as a comparison case was not without risks. We feared that the contrast between Rwanda in the 1990s Germany in the 1930s, on one hand, and the students' own lives, on the other, would render Rwanda's experience inexplicable or esoteric. As one student carelessly put it, "Rwanda was all a crazy mess"—a stance that is likely to undermine their efforts to make sense of this dramatic process.

The choice of the Amnesty International documentary was as promising as it was controversial. The documentary had been released a few months earlier by public television, and some of the students had seen at least parts of it. We wanted the assessment-task to create an authentic situation for transfer. The fact that students would recently have had access to the TV documentary supported the authenticity of the task. We hoped that showing the documentary in class once, with just a few interruptions and a very brief background on Rwanda, would create conditions comparable to those under which students had watched the documentary at home, without a rich context in which to place the information provided by the program. In addition, some students knew that Amnesty International was a human rights organization dedicated to denouncing violations worldwide. We hoped that students would consider the source of the video in their assessment of its account of Rwanda. Finally, the documentary was short and could be shown in one class period.

On the other hand, we were aware of the challenges of presenting Rwanda through this medium. Some participants in our group thought that the few but ghastly scenes of the genocide in the video were too horrifying to be shared with eleven- and twelve-year-olds and an infallible invitation to parental complaint. For other participants, the video's strong activist agenda was manifest in the history of Rwanda narrated by an anonymous voice and in the interview excerpts where expert analysts spoke in support of the interpretations put forth in the narrative. The video's purpose and its use of language and images risked overriding any attempt on the part of students to engage in a critique of it as a source.

The Rwandan assessment task illustrates the risks and possibilities of asymmetrical comparisons, comparisons in which the parts compared are not attended with equal precision and depth. The teachers with whom we worked dedicated between six and ten weeks to the study of the Holocaust and barely three days to the introduction and analysis of the situation in Rwanda. Our goal was clearly not to teach Rwandan history. That would have required additional time and work on the part of students, time our teachers did not have. Instead, we sought to provide a manageable and authentic context in which to explore what students were able to do when presented with an opportunity for transfer. Would they be able to identify relevant grounds for complex comparisons? Would students question their source and actively pursue alternative interpretations of what had happened in Rwanda? Would they be skeptical of the illusion that they could understand all genocides by understanding one?

 The task was designed to assess the sense-making apparatus that students counted on as they confronted an unscaffolded situation in which to use what they had learned. We asked students to write about the conditions that had allowed the Holocaust to happen and the characteristics that they would expect to find in an African society on the verge of committing genocide. Students were advised to consider similarities and differences between the cases; to keep in mind that genocides like the ones in Germany and Rwanda are complex social processes; and that no one simple explanation can do justice to the depth and multifacetedness of the experience.

Once generally informed by the video and by a chronology of events included in the task, students were asked to hypothesize about the reasons that, in their opinion, the Hutu majority may have engaged in a brutal mass killing of Tutsis in 1994. Students were advised to bear in mind that historical phenomena result from a combination of factors, rather than from any single cause. They were also reminded that to understand why this genocide occurred, one needs to focus on the particular characteristics of Rwanda. In a second portion of the task, students were asked to propose what they thought might be important similarities and differences in the use of propaganda in Germany and in Rwanda. In this case, students were again advised to recognize that similarities and differences exist between the cases. They were asked to take into account the content of propaganda (use of language, calls for action, justifications), as well as the technological medium (radio, film, loudspeakers) used in each case. In a third portion of the task, students were provided a biographical sketch of a Rwandan Tutsi woman and were asked to hypothesize what options were available to her at different points in the genocidal process. Students were alerted to attend to how changes in a society over time may affect people's options at different moments in the process. They were asked to consider the actor's perspective as they assessed her options over time. After each portion of the task, students proposed questions raised by their hypotheses and suggested empirical inquiry strategies that might help them address these questions. As they did so, they were instructed to think about how an expert historian would go about resolving the questions at hand.

The task was tested among twenty-five eighth graders (ages 12–14) and ten ninth graders (ages 13–15) in a public and a private school in the Boston area respectively. All students had taken the Facing History and Ourselves curriculum and responded to the task in writing toward the end of the unit. Students worked on the task for three forty-minute periods in the public school and two forty-minute periods in the private one. Analysis of students' responses yielded a four-level assessment rubric for each section of the task. Prior research or students' conceptions of historical accounts, causality, perspective taking, and historical significance informed the development of the rubric by suggesting progression models to describe levels of understanding. Two independent raters assessed students' responses and discussed their analyses to enrich the assessment criteria.

Assessing Students' Understanding of the Rwandan Genocide

Examining students' ability to use their knowledge of the Holocaust to inform their thinking about Rwanda confronts teachers with the challenge of defining the criteria by which such transfer should be assessed. Our analysis of students' work on the Rwanda assessment case converged on four such criteria. Successful students were able to (1) build an informed *comparison base* between both cases of genocide; (2) recognize *historical differences* between them; (3) appropriately apply *historical modes of thinking* to examine the genocide in Rwanda; and (4) generate *new questions and hypotheses* about the Rwandan genocide. In the section that follows, each criterion is explained and illustrated with students' work—their misconceptions and unwarranted inferences as well as their sophisticated comparisons and distinctions. Toward the end of the next section, I highlight some understandings that students might develop by way of deepening their ability to use what they have learned about the Holocaust to make sense of Rwanda. I also suggest teaching designs that might foster such understandings.[28]

Building an Informed Comparison Base

The first criterion we used to assess how students use their understanding of the past to guide their thinking about the present stemmed from the fact that historical analogies require a factual basis for comparison.[29] What sort of events took place in Germany that might be relevant in trying to understand Rwanda? The *comparison base* criterion referred to the degree to which students had built a rich (rather than oversimplified) representation of such types of events. It assessed, for instance, the degree to which students were able to consider a variety of interrelated factors that led to the Holocaust, which may have informed their exploration of Rwanda.

Students' ability to identify such factors ranged in accuracy and informative power. Before watching the documentary on Rwanda, students like Andrew[30] exhibited an oversimplified version of the conditions that allowed the Holocaust to happen. He focused solely on the power of ideas, without contextualizing his account in the specific historical events and processes that preceded the Holocaust and provided fertile ground for eliminationist ideas.

> The followers of Hitler passed on the idea to other racist groups who hated the Jews and other groups. They put the idea into the Jews head that they are terrible human beings. They put crazy and outrageous ideas into people's minds scaring other groups who stood up against these ideas.

Andrew's intuitions about the conditions that might be expected in pregenocidal Rwanda were limited by his perception of the Holocaust.

> If you put ideas into people's head things will happen. Ideas lead to actions. If you do this slowly people will feel the same way you do especially if you have a lot of power, if you have power people will listen to you.

His account was generic and excluded any reference to contextual factors or to variables other than "ideas." He situated his analysis against the background of an everyday-life logic by which contemporary people (such as "you," referring to his reader or to anyone else) convince others, particularly when in power.

On the other end of the spectrum, some students held rich, substantive knowledge about the interrelated conditions that led to the Holocaust (i.e., the social, political, cultural, and economic long- and short-term conditions) and the particular contexts in which these conditions played out. Typically, these students were equipped with a richer set of working hypotheses about Rwanda before watching the documentary. Gina's description exemplifies this point:

> In Eastern Europe there was already antisemitism, pre-Hitler. After the Weimar Republic failed, the citizens needed a strong leader to follow.
>
> [In Rwanda] I would expect to see bred-in prejudice, which had been there for hundreds of years. From this the people would have a sense of righteousness in discriminating against others. I would also expect to see a weak government, so that a rebellion would be inevitable. I would expect unhappy citizens; underpaid, maybe or treated poorly—maybe some crisis like in the economy. I would expect some people in the society to display prejudice, and form a sense of belonging for others who would join in the group. I would expect for discrimination to be acceptable—part of their way of lives.

In a similar vein, after watching *Forsaken Cries*, Alfred used his understanding of propaganda in Nazi Germany to inform his explanation of why propaganda "worked" in Rwanda. In his reflections he went beyond the fragmented images provided by the video. His account suggested that he had built a rich comparison base from which to analyze propaganda. For instance, Alfred drew on video information about the language used to refer to Tutsis and offered an interpretation of how such dehumanizing language supported the killings:

> People used a lot of propaganda in Rwanda to lead to genocide. Hutus called the Tutsis rats and cockroaches, two animals generally thought of as bad, very bad, and difficult to get rid of. . . .

He went beyond the documentary's images of Belgian anthropologists measuring Hutus' and Tutsis' physical traits and spontaneously contextualized such practices as part of eugenics studies (a term not used in the video) and interpreted them as early official propaganda.

> But I think the very beginning of propaganda was when the Belgians measured the Rwandans skulls, brought in eugenics, and separated the people. They indoctrinized people into believing they were truly divided. The Tutsis didn't necessarily think they were better, but the Hutus felt very belittled and oppressed.

He concluded with a personal interpretation of the role of the sociocultural context as a contributing force to the success of propaganda in Rwanda.

> I think one reason propaganda worked so well is because of the fact that the discrimination was so widespread and felt so vividly. The need for propaganda was maybe minimal, and the propaganda just added to the people's rage.

Recognizing Historical Differences

One of the greatest risks in inviting students to use their understanding of the Holocaust to guide their thinking about Rwanda involved the likelihood that, despite the striking differences between the cases, students' comparison would minimize defining distinctions between the two processes. In doing so, students would build the illusion of "understanding Rwanda by understanding the Holocaust." In comparative history, underscoring distinctions is a condition of validity.[31] Because a perfect fit between historical processes never exists, a comparison between past and present processes is valid as long as the past is not used as a simplistic blueprint to interpret the present.

The second assessment criterion, historical differences, examined the degree to which students exhibited healthy skepticism regarding apparent similarities between the cases. In their open reflections after watching the video, some students, impressed by the similarities between the cases, failed to recognize distinctions. Consider Laura's reaction:

> It [Rwanda] is *so* much like the Holocaust! There is hierarchy, there are killings there are so many comparisons. The Nazis are like the Hutus and the Jews are the Tutsis.

Other students, by contrast, pointed directly to perceived distinctions between cases. Kathy, for example, highlighted the openness of the Hutu oppression and the alternating nature of the role of victims and perpetrators between Hutus and Tutsis over time—two distinct features of the Rwandan genocidal path.

> It is very hard to imagine how a genocide could happen again (after the holocaust) [*sic*]. One thing that I really picked up on, was how in the Holocaust people waited so long to respond. If the signs were so obvious in Rwanda, why didn't they respond sooner. Hadn't they learned from Germany? Another thing about the UN backing out: If they had stayed this might not have happened. Were they being threatened in Rwanda? Maybe they were afraid of favoring one side. The Hutus were doing wrong things, but so were the Tutsis. It seemed like big events happened every time the Hutus and the Tutsis switched power.

Similarly, in her comparison of propaganda, Gina went beyond identifying common patterns across cases (e.g., dehumanizing language, threat, and fear) to highlighting unique aspects in each case of genocide. She recognized that propaganda in Germany was subtler and more organically embedded in national institutions than in Rwanda (where open, violent, anti-Tutsi discourse increased dramatically in a matter of months in early 1994).

> In both cases [Germany and Rwanda] (a) people are compared to insects: something people dislike and want to get rid of. Somethings that are useless and parasitic [*sic*].

> In Germany propaganda was more widespread; taken for granted. They used it not only on the radio, etc. but also in school and art. This was not

used in Rwanda, or at least not portrayed [in the video]. This strategy made the propaganda more feasible. It made the prejudice seem standard and okay. Very clever. . . . Propaganda in Rwanda seemed much more open and straightforward. They did not hide their purposes or goals. The propaganda did not seem so much a general strategy as a pep talk before the "big rebellion."

In addition, Gina sensed a contrast in the general level of education in each society and the ways in which propaganda was geared toward a rural audience in Rwanda.

Applying Historical Modes of Thinking

As mentioned in the introduction to this chapter, history provides not only a body of substantive knowledge about the past but also a collection of modes of thinking that can be applied in examining societal and individual experiences over time. An in-depth study of the Holocaust challenges students to build multicausal explanations of events such as the Final Solution; to confront conflicting narratives; to consider various historical actors' points of view; to examine evidence; and to attend to continuities and changes over time. Students demonstrate an understanding of such modes of thinking when they apply them to their analysis of and further inquiry into contemporary events like Rwanda. At their best, students develop a healthy skepticism toward monocausal explanations, oversimplified accounts, single points of view, insufficient evidence, and anachronism.[32]

Consider the challenge of building multicausal explanations. To assess students' ability to do so, the Rwanda assessment task confronted youngsters with a chronology of events preceding the Rwandan genocide and a question to be addressed: "Why do you think so many Hutus may have participated in the mass murder of Tutsis?" To respond to this question in a rigorous way, students needed to move beyond naïve monocausal or linear explanations (i.e., explanations in which several causes are linked consecutively). Instead, they needed to consider a variety of causes (long and short term, structural, intentional, and unintentional) that affect one another as well as the final result.[33] Consider the following examples of causal explanations of varying degrees of sophistication:

> They did what their leader told them to do. Maybe their leader was a good speaker like Hitler. *Monocausal explanation:* Sonia

The Belgians divided them into Hutus and Tustis. Hutus and Tutsis hated each other and so the Tutsis killed the Hutu president. That made the Hutus angry so they participated in the massive killing. *Linear explanation:* Mauro

A big factor is the way Belgium [*sic*] divided the Hutus and the Tutsi. Since the Tutsi had all the power and the Hutus had none it made the Tutsi look evil and greedy in the eyes of the Hutu. This stereotype continued even after the Hutus claimed power. Even though it was Belgium that divided them the Hutus needed a scapegoat that was closer to them like the Nazis targeted the Jews instead of the Allies who created the Treaty that made life rough for them. Not only that but when the Tutsi returned to Rwanda a depression took place. Although this was because of the drop of coffee prices it was all that was needed to rekindle the hatred. Of course this wouldn't have made all the Hutus hate Tutsi. That is what propaganda is for. The Hutu fanatics used many propaganda tricks such as radio air time and names such as cockroaches for the Tutsis. *Complex explanation:* Jennine

The Rwanda assessment task also asked students to demonstrate their ability to use historical modes of thinking when it challenged them to describe how they would further investigate this and other aspects of the Rwandan genocide. It assessed the degree to which students would be able to grasp the constructed, uncertain, and provisional nature of knowledge about contemporary historical processes. It sought to shed light on whether students would be able to distinguish "what is" the case from "what one can legitimately say" about the case, provided certain historical modes of thinking are put to work.[34] On one end of the continuum, students would design a strategy for inquiry that was rooted in the rituals of schooling (e.g., synthesizing, memorizing, asking teachers as sole sources of knowledge, reading textbooks and encyclopedias). Mauro, for instance, described his strategy to find out more about the reasons for Hutu participation in mass murder as follows:

I would get all the written info I could about the genocide and research and memorize it. Then after memorizing it, I would visit as many survivors as possible and get their side of the story. After this I would compare what the people said happened with what I know really happened.

In his mind "all the written information" embodied "what really happened" in Rwanda. Triangulating such information against the survivor's oral testimonies would not affect the already established account of what "really" took place.

In some cases, students elicited a more sophisticated conception of the nature of historical inquiry. For example, Alfred exhibited the beginning of a healthy skepticism regarding the constructed nature of historical "facts." He understood the importance of considering various historical actors' perspectives, although he still held a simplistic belief about how such perspectives could be gathered.

> I would talk to: (a) a Rwandan historian (b) a Tutsi refugee (c) a Hutu extremist (d) a Hutu who was opposed to the genocide (e) someone in the UN. I would talk to them and gather the facts I could. Many of the "facts" would be terribly biased and wouldn't do much good, but the different points of view would be good sources.

Toward the upper end of the continuum, students like Mara were able to recognize the intrinsically limited nature of historical knowledge.

> I would talk with survivors, victimizers, bystanders and people from outside the country. I would try to look at the problem for all sides and would read up on it by researching in libraries. . . . I would never be able to have total knowledge on the subject without being there. Even then I wouldn't completely know because I couldn't know all the sides to the story.

Searching for Generativity

Comparisons between past and present events are informative when they transcend mere taxonomy of similarities and differences and suggest perspectives that neither the past nor the present could yield by themselves. The present presents itself to us in an immediate fashion. It is such immediacy—such illusion of familiarity—that makes understanding the present a difficult task. We cannot know present circumstances in the way we know past ones because we lack the perspective gained by hindsight. In the present we still don't have the "end of the story," as it were, since significant events linked to the story are still unfolding. History makes available to us a repertoire of comparable past experiences through which we interpret current processes and assign them meaning. The Holocaust defined for subsequent generations the meaning of the term "genocide," a term we now use to characterize the events in Rwanda. By providing analytical categories and textured pictures of past experiences, history provides working hypotheses to explain present processes, attribute significance to particular people and events in them, and shed light on aspects that might otherwise remain unattended. Without the power to generate new questions and hypotheses to orient their further exploration, students' efforts to use historical understanding to interpret contemporary events risk becoming a dull algorithmic endeavor.

This fourth and last assessment criterion focused on students' ability to raise questions and establish working hypotheses and interpretations that went beyond the information given in the video. As with earlier criteria, students' performances on this criterion also varied in sophistication. For some, the Rwandan documentary raised basic questions of clarification, strictly linked to the information provided by the video: "Who killed the president?"; "How did they kill the president?"; "Why was the presidential security working with the Hutus?"; "Why did France give Hutus weapons?" These questions failed to probe more deeply into central aspects of the Rwandan genocide and showed no apparent connection between Rwanda and the Holocaust.

Toward the other end of the spectrum, some students inquired about the long-term roots of the conflict, the nature of Habyarimana's leadership, and the role played by propaganda.

> Was the Hutu president nominated by vote by the people, or was his goal to be president of the Hutu people and he kind of weaseled himself into [the] presidency? Basically, was he a good man?

> How popular was the Hutu president? Was he only liked by the extremists or did he have national approval? Was he a good leader or did he have dictatorship qualities?

> Was the genocide known by everyone in the country? Because in Germany the Nazis' killings were not known everywhere.

> Why did the UN leave? Was it in their best interest? Was it difficult to decide who to support? Isn't the UN's job to prevent civil wars (or any wars) and large amounts of injustice?

Some students' questions revealed attention to specific historical modes of thinking. Some sought alternative points of view not presented in the video. Others showed skepticism toward the slightly idealized portrait of precolonial Rwanda that the video proposed. In most cases, successful inquiries were informed by hypotheses stemming from their understanding of Nazi Germany and the Holocaust.

> Was it really true that before the Belgians came, the Hutus and the Tutsis thought that they were equal and get opportunities, and get along [as

suggested by the video]? Didn't they think that they were better than one another?

Was the large amount of hatred towards Tutsis shared by all (most) Hutu? Was the time of peace [portrayed in the video] really peace, or just an uneasy happy medium?

Enhancing Students' Understanding

Assessment situations like the one I have described provide opportunities for students to make their understanding public—to demonstrate their understanding to themselves and to others (teachers, peers, school authorities, parents). They also provide rich opportunities to advance students' understanding, not only because they ask students to use what they know in novel situations, enriching the meaning of what they know, but, most important, because, informed by students' performance, teachers are in a better position to further their learning. Public understanding allows teachers to identify students' achievements, difficulties, and misconceptions and to design additional learning experiences especially geared to address understanding challenges.

Most students in our study were able to think about substantive aspects of the past—the various conditions that contributed to the totalitarization of Germany, the stepwise progression toward mass murder, the actions and dilemmas faced by individual rescuers. In most cases, they recognized the complexity of the past by highlighting the multiple causes that led to the Holocaust, recognizing how conditions in Germany changed over time or considering perpetrators', victims', and bystanders' perspectives in their descriptions. However, with a few exceptions, students failed to recognize the constructed nature of the very account on which they were grounding their hypotheses and interpretations about contemporary Rwanda. Students tended to treat the Amnesty International video as an epistemologically unproblematic portrait of Rwandan history. They rarely engaged in what Sam Wineburg calls "sourcing heuristics"—the ability to inform our interpretation of a source by examining its context of production.[35]

How can teachers help students, in Denis Shemilt's words, understand *the past* (i.e., the lives of people and societies in times gone) *and* understand *history* (i.e., the disciplinary thinking processes and criteria by which accounts of the past are produced and validated)?[36] Specifically, how can teachers help students understand the constructed nature of historical accounts like the one portrayed in the video documentary? The multiple teaching approaches that might follow the Rwanda assessment task are rooted in a few challenges central to teaching history for disciplinary understanding: understanding precisely how students conceptualize historical accounts; problematizing students' naive conceptions; and making the historian's narrative craft visible to students.

Teachers may engage students in a conversation about the degree to which the Amnesty International video is believable. Students may learn about Amnesty International as an organization and identify claims or scenes in the documentary that reflect its allegiances and political purposes. They may compare the story told in the documentary to alternative conflicting accounts of Rwandan history. At first, as Peter Lee and Ros Ashby report in this volume, students are likely to reduce differences in accounts to "the way authors tell the story" or to an undesirable "author's bias." Teachers may problematize such beliefs by posing dilemmas: "How can there be two conflicting stories about the same bit of the past?"; "If two historians are using the same sources and they do not lie, how can their stories be different and both be true?"[37]

To bring such epistemological conflicts closer to home, students may be asked to compare the explanations they proposed about why Hutus may have participated in the mass killing of Tutsis in 1994. Alternatively, they can compare individual narratives about a school event experienced by all. Confronted with differences among accounts, students may propose a series of criteria to determine what counts as "truth" in writing narratives about past events. It is at this point that teachers may begin to make the historian's craft visible to students. They may address notions such as historical significance, use of primary and secondary sources, sourcing heuristics, or the role of guiding inquiry questions and temporal frames in the construction of historical narratives.

The work undertaken after the Rwanda task should help students understand that narratives are humanly constructed, that they embody particular world views, that they are written with a contemporary audience in mind, and that they seek to be faithful to life in the past. Ideally, students will have access to historians and their accounts of the challenges and decisions they need to make in the process of establishing "truth about the past" (even if imperfect and provisional). By sharing their challenges, reflections, and expertise with young students, historians may help them perceive that the work that students carry out in their history classrooms is important to society beyond the confines of their school. Interaction with men and women who dedicate their lives to investigating the past humanizes children's perceptions of the discipline, rendering the process of learning a more intrinsically meaningful task.[38] One hopes that such interaction will help students develop a disposition toward healthy skepticism—not only vis-à-vis the narratives of the past that they encounter but also with respect to their own interpretations and hypotheses about contemporary events.

Understanding and Assessment Revisited

In what ways can an in-depth study of Nazi Germany and the Holocaust inform students' understanding of contemporary Rwanda? As members of their cultures, students acquire collections of beliefs about how past societies worked, what people were likely to have experienced, and how a society came to be the way it is today. Beliefs about the past are embedded in cultural artifacts such as monuments, films, and commemorative holidays. They are organically intertwined with common sense and everyday life. Prior to careful instruction, students' predisciplinary sense of the past is typically ill shaped and unquestioned. Frequently, stories about the past are dogmatically believed as part of a society's foundational myths or heritage.[39]

Students' naive beliefs set the background against which they interpret contemporary events. Against such a background, they are likely to reduce the Holocaust to Hitler's demented plan and the Rwandan genocide to stereotypical African tribal rivalries. Counteracting such naive perceptions, history education informs students' efforts to interpret contemporary events by providing them with well-grounded accounts of processes like the totalitarization of Germany. Such accounts demand careful analysis of multiple causes and points of view, serious consideration of supporting evidence, and delicate temporal distinctions. Even if fallible, history provides an alternative superior to the naïve, rather unconscious, and distorting sense of the past that students are likely to espouse as grounding for the examination of the present.[40] In sum, history prepares students to examine the present by undermining the myths, oversimplifications, and distortions embodied in popular views of the past.[41] In so doing, a careful study of the past prepares students to be skeptical about the possibilities of knowing events past and present. At the same time, it enhances their confidence in the epistemological tools that communities of experts have developed as our contemporary societies' best attempts to investigate the lives of individuals and societies as they change over time.

In exploring the relationship between past and present in history education, a question is often raised. If history does not repeat itself, how can a substantive understanding of events like the Holocaust inform students' views of contemporary events like Rwanda? Understanding the past does not ensure understanding of the present. Rather, it triggers informed questions and hypotheses that only a careful exploration of the contemporary world can resolve. Conversely, contemporary concerns may inform valuable questions and hypotheses about the past, which only careful exploration of the past may unravel. While it is indeed legitimate to let concerns from one time dictate the questions to be explored about another time, it is entirely unacceptable to let anachronistic views determine the answers to such questions.[42] Students must recognize that passage of time has changed material life and world views between then and now. Moreover, they need to recognize that human and social experience is unpredictable and embedded in particular contexts.

The development of the Rwanda assessment task was triggered by two important concerns. First, our exploration responded to the worrisome distance between the analytical capacities that are valued in contemporary societies at large, on the one hand (e.g., the ability to interpret an unfolding ethnic conflict or to decide about conditions that demand international intervention to protect human rights), and the type of skills increasingly favored by current national and state assessments, on the other (manipulation of fragmented facts). As Howard Gardner eloquently states it

> Understanding [of the multiple worlds students inhabit] will never come about through the piling of facts. It can only emerge if students have the opportunity to tackle authentic problems; to use their skills appropriately in plausible settings; to create projects, alone and in cooperation; to receive feedback on these endeavors and ultimately to become willing productive thinkers.[43]

By challenging students to use their understanding of the past to make conjectures about a contemporary development, the Rwanda assessment case aims at providing students with such *authentic problems* and *plausible settings* to exercise and develop *culturally valued understandings* with the help of their teachers.

The second concern driving our study stemmed from two important limitations embodied in the collection of assessment strategies and criteria available to teachers as alternatives to "standardized" or "objective" tests. First, most of the so-called alternative or authentic assessment literature has focused on tools such as rubrics, performance tasks, and portfolios emphasizing the mechanical rather than the substantive challenges involved in eliciting, valuing, and reorienting students' understanding. A preoccupation with measurement (explicitness of criteria, multiplicity of formats for students' expression) has obscured the difficult question of which qualities of disciplinary understanding we aim to assess and support.[44] Second, the alternative assessment tools typically proposed are so idiosyncratic and admittedly tightly linked to particular curricular experiences that they become limited as instruments for comparisons among children across schools and social groups. Responding to these concerns, our project aimed to produce a task rich in options in order to open room for students with a wide range of experiences learning about Nazi Germany and the Holocaust. We attempted to develop a collection of explicit assessment criteria that were so central to the discipline of history on the one hand (e.g., understanding change over time, multiple causality, multiple perspectives) and to that particular period on the other (e.g., conditions that allowed the Holocaust to take place, the role of propaganda, victim's experience over time) that teachers committed to teaching *history* as well as the *past* would perceive as valuable a lens through which to examine and share students' work.

The assessment challenge we set for our project was multifaceted. We aspired to develop an assessment case that would shed light on culturally relevant outcomes of good history education; that would engage teachers and students in a careful reflection about understanding in the discipline; and that would allow for comparisons beyond particular curriculum units and schools. In the end, the degree to which we were successful in our attempt will be determined by the way in which teachers come to appropriate the themes highlighted by this assessment case. The task's success will depend on the extent to which teachers see it as a springboard for deeper scholarly inquiries into their discipline and for more enlightened analyses of their students' understanding—a challenge that stands at the very center of the remaking of the teaching profession.

NOTES

This chapter was written with the generous support of Thomas H. Lee and the Louise and Claude Rosenberg, Jr. Family Foundation. I would like to thank my colleagues at Facing History and Ourselves and the teachers in our project for their thoughtful critiques throughout the development of the ideas here proposed. I am particularly grateful to Greg Cope, Doc Miller, and their students for their full engagement in this exploration; Edouard Boustin and Barbara Brown for their careful assessment of my representation of Rwanda; Paul Bookbinder and Richard Hovannissian for their insights on historical comparisons; and Lisa Bromer and Wendy Fischman for their editorial comments. My special gratitude goes to Howard Gardner and Alan Stoskopf, for their clear-sighted comments on previous drafts, and to the editors of this book, Peter Seixas, Peter Stearns, and Sam Wineburg, for their generative recommendations and their visionary invitation to explore the interaction between history and memory in scholarly work, cultural life, and education.

1. Carl Becker, Dial 59 (September 2, 1915): 148.

2. See B. von Borris, "Methods and Aims of Teaching History in Europe: A Report on Youth and History," this volume. See also J. Appleby, L. Hunt, and M. Jacob, *Telling the Truth about History* (London, 1994); and G. B. Nash and C. Crabtree, *National Standards for History* (Los Angeles, 1996).

3. In his book *The Unschooled Mind: How Children Think and How Schools Should Teach* (New York, 1991) Howard Gardner defines the "unschooled mind" as the robust collection of naive and often misconceived theories about the natural and social world that children develop early in life and that are difficult to replace with more disciplined understandings.

4. See P. Seixas, "Schweigen! die Kinder! Or, Does Postmodern History Have a Place in the Schools?"; J. Wertsch, "Is It Possible to Teach Beliefs, as Well as Knowledge about History?"; and S. Wineburg, "Making Historical Sense," this volume. For a more detailed treatment of the distinction between history and memory and between history and heritage, see also J. LeGoff, *History and Memory* (New York, 1992), and D. Lowenthal, *Possessed by the Past: The Heritage Crusade and the Spoils of History* (New York, 1996).

5. For a careful analysis of the tension between familiarity and distance in historical understanding, see Seixas "Conceptualizing the Growth of Historical Understanding," in D. Olson and N. Torrance, eds., *Handbook of Education and Human Development*, (Cambridge, MA, 1996), and S. Wineburg, "Historical Thinking and Other Unnatural Acts," *Phi Delta Kappan* (March 1999), pp. 488–499.

6. See P. Stearns, "Getting Specific about Training in Historical Analysis: A Case Study in World History," this volume.

7. M. Marrus, *The Holocaust in History* (Hanover, NH, 1987).

8. See G. R. Elton, *The Practice of History* (London, 1969); J. Appleby, L. Hunt,

and M. Jacob, *Telling the Truth about History* (New York, 1994); and P. Seixas, "The Community of Inquiry as a Basis for Knowledge and Learning," *American Educational Research Journal*, 30(2) (1992). See also R. Bain, "Into the Breach: Using Research and Theory to Shape History Instruction," and P. J. Lee and R. Ashby, "Progression in Historical Understanding," this volume.

9. Elton, *The Practice of History*.

10. See L. Dawidowicz, *The War against the Jews 1933–1945* (New York, 1975); E. Jaeckel, *Hitler's Weltanschauung: A Blueprint to Power*, Herbert Arnold, tr. (Middletown, CT, 1972); and E. Nolte, *The Three Faces of Fascism: Action Française, Italian Fascism, National Socialism*, Leila Vennewitz, tr. (New York, 1966).

11. See W. Lacqueur, *Fascism: A Readers' Guide, Analysis, Interpretation, Bibliography* (Berkeley, CA, 1976); D. Goldhagen, *Hitler's Willing Executioners: Ordinary Germany and the Holocaust* (New York, 1996).

12. Goldhagen, *Hitler's Willing Executioners*.

13. J. Appleby, L. Hunt, and M. Jacob, *Telling the Truth about History* (London, 1994); and P. Seixas, "The Community of Inquiry as a Basis for Knowledge and Learning" *American Educational Research Journal*, 30(2) (1992). The reaction to Goldhagen's eliminationist anti-Semitism hypothesis illustrates the predisposition among historians against monocausal explanation as a standard for scholarly work. For an overview of critiques and positions, see Franklin H. Littell, ed., *Hyping the Holocaust: Scholars Answer Goldhagen* (New York, 1997); and N. Finkelstein, *A Nation on Trial: The Goldhagen's Thesis and Historical Truth* (New York, 1998).

14. See, in this volume, L. Levstik, "Articulating the Silences: Teachers' and Adolescents' Conceptions of Historical Significance." See also P. Seixas, "Mapping the Terrain of Historical Significance," *Social Education* 61 (1997), pp. 22–28.

15. See R. Ashby and P. J. Lee, "Children's Concepts of Empathy and Understanding in History," in C. Portal, ed., *The History Curriculum for Teachers* (New York, 1987), pp. 62–88. See also R. Ashby, P. J. Lee, and A. K. Dickinson, "How Children Explain the Why of History: The Chata Research Project on Teaching History" *Social Education*, 61(1) (1997), pp. 17–21.

16. For an excellent treatment of this topic see, in this volume, R. Bain, "Into the Breach: Using Research and Theory to Shape History Instruction," and P. J. Lee and R. Ashby, "Progression in Historical Understanding." See also P. J. Lee and R. Ashby, "None of Us Was There: Children's Ideas about Why Historical Accounts Differ," in S. Ahonene et al., eds., *Historiedidaktik, Nordisk Konferens om Historiedidaktiks, Tampere* (Copenhagen, 1999), pp. 23–58.

17. See, in this volume, M. A. Britt, C. Perfetti, J. Van Dyke, and J. Gabrys, "The Sourcer's Apprentice: A Tool for Document-Supported History Instruction"; and G. Leinhart, "Lessons on Teaching and Learning in History from Paul's Pen."

18. See H. Fein, "Genocide, Terror, Life Integrity, and War Crimes: The Case

for Discrimination," as well as R. Hovannissian, "Etiology and Sequelae of the Armenian Genocide," in George J. Andreopoulus, ed., *Genocide Conceptual and Historical Dimensions* (Philadelphia, 1994). See also P. Bookbinder, *Weimar Germany: The Republic of the Reasonable* (New York, 1996).

19. See M. Marrus, *The Holocaust in History* (Hanover, NH, 1987).

20. See S. Friedlander, *Nazi Germany and the Jews: The Years of Persecution* (New York, 1997); and D. Goldhagen, *Hitler's Willing Executioners*.

21. For a historiographic accounts of the possibilities and limitations of including the Holocaust in comparative history see Marrus, *The Holocaust in History*.

22. See P. Gourevitch, *We Wish to Inform You That Tomorrow We Will Be Killed with Our Families: Stories from Rwanda* (New York, 1998); S. Hameso, *Ethnicity and Nationalism in Africa* (Commack, NY, 1997); and A. Klinghoffer, *The International Dimension of Genocide in Rwanda* (London, 1998).

23. See G. Prunier, *The Rwanda Crisis: History of a Genocide* (New York, 1996); and P. duPerez, *Genocide: The Psychology of Mass Murder* (New York, 1994).

24. D. Newbury, "Understanding Genocide," *African Review*, 41(1) (April 1998), pp. 73–97.

25. J. H. Speke, *Journal of the Discovery of the Source of the Nile* (Edinburgh and London, 1863).

26. For an overview of this thesis, see J. Kocka, "Asymmetrical Comparison: The Case of the German Sonderweg," *History and Theory*, 38(1) (1998), pp. 40–50. For further reference, see L. Krieger, *The German Idea of Freedom* (Boston, 1957); and G. L. Mosse, *The Crisis of German Ideology: Intellectual Origins of the Third Reich* (New York, 1964).

27. Facing History and Ourselves is a nationwide organization dedicated to the teaching of history and social responsibility. In this collaboration FHAO was particularly interested in exploring the challenge of providing good disciplinary history education to teachers and students *and* fostering civic values such as democracy and respect. Project Zero is a research and development organization based at THE Harvard Graduate School of Education and dedicated to research in teaching, learning, assessment, and development in the arts and other disciplines. In this collaboration HPZ was particularly interested in examining the challenge of assessing students' ability to use knowledge to understand the world around them in ways that were culturally relevant and rigorous.

28. For a previous attempt to examine the possibilities of using history as a frame of reference to look at the present, see P. Rogers, "The Past as a Frame of Reference," in Christopher Portal, ed., *History Curriculum for Teachers* (London, 1987).

29. C. Maier, *The Unmasterable Past: History, Holocaust and German National Identity* (Cambridge, MA, 1988).

30. All names are pseudonyms.

31. Maier, *The Unmasterable Past*.

32. For a careful overview of historical modes of thinking, see P. Seixas, "Conceptualizing the Growth of Historical Understanding," in D. Olson and N. Torrance, eds., *The Handbook of Education and Human Development: New Models of Learning, Teaching, and Schooling* (Cambridge, MA, 1996).

33. See J. Voss and M. Carretero, "The Collapse of the Soviet Union: A Case Study in Causal Reasoning," in Mario Carretero and James Voss, eds., *Cognitive and Instructional Processes in History and the Social Sciences* (Hillsdale, NJ, 1994).

34. See P. Lee et al., eds., *The Aims of History: The National Curriculum and Beyond* (London, 1992). See also J. Tosh, *The Pursuit of History: Aims, Methods, and New Directions in the Study of Modern History* (London, 1991).

35. See S. Wineburg, "Historical Problem Solving: A Study of the Cognitive Processes Used in the Evaluation of Documentary and Pictorical Evidence," *Journal of Educational Psychology* 83 (1991), pp. 73–87.

36. See the essay by Denis Shemilt in this volume. See also P. Seixas, P. Stearns, and S. Wineburg, "History, Memory, Research, and the Schools: A Report on the Pittsburgh Conference," *Perspectives* (March 21, 1999).

37. These questions were used by Peter Lee in his study of children's conceptions of why accounts differ. For an extended report on developing conceptions of accounts, see Lee and Ashby, "None of Us Was There," pp. 23–58.

38. For a careful description of the importance of linking expert mentors with students in schools, see H. Gardner, D. H. Feldman, and M. Krechevsky, *Building on Children's Strengths: The Experience of Project Spectrum* (New York, 1998).

39. H. Gardner and V. Boix-Mansilla, "Teaching for Understanding in the Disciplines—and Beyond," *Teachers College Record* 96(2) (Winter 1994), pp. 198–218.

40. For an extended analysis of the relationship between memory and history relevant to this point, see J. LeGoff, *History and Memory*. See also E. Hobsbawm, *On History* (New York, 1997).

41. For a careful analysis of the corrective function of history see J. Tosh, *The Pursuit of History.*

42. For an analysis of the relationship between past and present in the history of the discipline see J. L. Gaddis, "The Nature of Contemporary History," occasional paper for the National Council for History Education, Westlake, Ohio; and A. Stoskopf, "The Uses of History: Then and Now," unpublished paper prepared for Facing History and Ourselves, Brookline, MA, August, 1998.

43. H. Gardner, "Foreword," in David Allen, ed., *Assessing Student Learning: From Grading to Understanding* (New York, 1998), p. viii.

44. For an analysis of qualities of disciplinary understanding see V. Boix Mansilla and H. Gardner, "What Are the Qualities of Deep Understanding?" in Stone Wiske, ed., *Teaching for Understanding: Linking Theory with Practice* (San Francisco, 1998).

Chapter 21

Getting Specific about Training in Historical Analysis
A Case Study in World History

Peter N. Stearns

Student capacity in relatively demanding tasks of historical analysis can be improved within a single semester college course, the improvement speeded up with explicit exercises, its extent measured, and further steps planned. This essay discusses the goals and methods involved in the context of a freshman world history course required of most first-year students at Carnegie Mellon. The students overall are relatively able. They include liberal arts and professional students, who enter the course with widely different levels of history experience and interest. The course, conducted in large (300-person) lectures spiced by a once-a-week discussion section,is usually favorably evaluated.

This essay describes one set of analytical skills and the commonsensical but nonstandard procedures to accelerate students' learning of those skills. The result is a case study of what can be done to further students' lasting capacities in historical analysis. We hope that our work, suitably adapted, of course, to other specific settings, will be of real use to other teachers of history. The story is also meant to illustrate how I as a history teacher and researcher was able to interact with specialists in more formal learning studies to improve what students took away from my course, in terms I had defined as important. It thus illustrates possible collaborations that can be widely pursued; this is the excuse for what might otherwise seem an excessively narrow and personal account. It's important to talk about general findings and possibilities regarding history learning, but it's also important to examine some explicit, accessible experiments in the genre.

The players in this study have been numerous. They include myself, as principal instructor in, indeed designer of, the course about twelve years ago, when it was inserted into the University's general education program. They also include a number of graduate teaching assistants, whose collaboration and suggestions, amid some extra (limited, but undeniably additional) evaluation chores, have been essential. They include people from the University's Center for Innovation in Learning, which seeks to apply lessons from cognitive psychology to college-level instruction, mainly in the sciences but in other areas as well—people not explicitly schooled in history learning research, but active contributors nevertheless. And they include several graduate students who were especially assigned to the collaboration and to the development and testing of relevant exercises.

A bit of background on the course, designed particularly to show why explicitly analytical learning goals became important: I have been interested in changing history teaching virtually all my professional career, but my concerns long focused on content, as I pushed for more social history topics and then, additionally during the past fifteen years, for a world history approach. Only gradually did I realize how these enthusiasms needed to be balanced by more explicit attention to the kind of historical thinking I depended on in my own life, as citizen as well as historian. I still eagerly defend these coverage reforms, since I believe that they offer students more relevant information, insights, and perspectives, but on the whole my focus has shifted. I believe the major history teaching and teacher training debates must be redefined to include much more commitment to issues of habits of mind. This commitment is compatible with various coverage formats, even ones more conventional than those I espouse, but it requires a genuine reconsideration of priorities so that historians no longer relegate habits of mind to eloquent preface in their discussions of curriculum, followed by chapter after chapter of discussion of coverage necessities.

Required world history courses so tempt instructors into coverage zealousness that they particularly warrant some caution. Ross Dunn's essay in this volume suggests important curricular points in world history, and my own sympathies are with his emphasis on global forces, though I would offer as a modification attention to civilizations and comparisons of civilizations. But it is the very lure of coverage enthusiasm (of whatever stripe, in the world history debates) that helped generate my own desire to right the balance by greater attention to how students handled history, and not simply to how data were presented to them. I tried to recognize the problems Ross Dunn encounters, regarding the capacities students bring to world history but also to go a bit further in studying them and, above all, in trying to improve them. It is true, as Dunn also suggests, that we need more research on student dispositions to world history, research comparable to that on assumptions about national histories, but we need not wait for the results of such research to venture some promising experiments.

The world history course, with its characteristically mammoth (usually at least 1,200 pages) textbook, is usually focused on providing students with a wide range of information about various societies in world history and, in the better courses, various global processes, such as technological diffusion and disease transmission. Because world historians have such a vast factual field and because they are still battling the heritage of a disproportionate emphasis on Western civilization, even in courses sometimes labeled world history, the crusade to cover different peoples, the various major religions, and eras before the rise of the West can be militant, as well as factually daunting (one reason that world history texts are usually even larger than Western civilization texts). Lists of "must-know" facts can swell, and assessment vehicles can easily deteriorate into memorization checks, particularly when the courses are also burdened with sizable enrollments. Where is the place for working on analytical skills as one data point crowds another?

The question is even more apt at the college level than at the high school level in the United States, though it applies in both contexts. The college world history course, which is becoming increasingly common in both two- and four-year institutions, is often the last history course non-majors will take—the final shot at firming up some enduring habits of mind. High school world history is usually taught in the tenth grade, and is often followed by a course in American history—though this is no excuse for ducking the challenge to lay a foundation for thinking skills that should be built upon by the next history offering.

All world history courses, obviously, must be highly selective; one veteran in the field long urged that the instructor's first obligation was to "dare to omit." Yet, selecting, on the one hand, and ruthlessly pruning, on the other, in order to focus on essentials, including how to think historically, need not be the same thing. In order to clear the way for what I view as essentials, I operate my world history course (uncharacteristically confined to a single semester) with three coverage goals in mind. The first is to provide some coherent data (on almost any topic over time, though it makes more sense to pick topics with the other two goals in mind) on which exercises can be based. Historical analysis is empirically formed; it cannot float above some available (if not always remembered) facts, and it must include knowledge of how to use and to assess facts. Second, I admit that there are a few (genuinely few, no more than two or three a week) essentials that people operating in contemporary society "ought" to know about world history: something of the nature of Confucianism and Islam, of slavery and its justifications, of the industrial revolution. Third, and this relates to the second goal, I want students to emerge my course with an international—that is, nonethnocentric but also not purely national—perspective. This means they should know the origins and the evolution of the major global forces that shape all societies, in-cluding our own. It also means that they should know, with examples, that cultures other than their own have functioned very well, that their own culture or society has some problems or deficiencies that other soci-eties or cultures can note (although they have their own problems), and that it has often made sense, historically and now, to criticize Western so-ciety—and in some respects, to praise it. The goal of developing perspec-tive is ambitious; it requires the presentation of some data (it would be useful to experiment with how much), but it does not require that every world society and period be covered in detail.

Once factual needs are defined in terms of a finite, manageable num-ber of essentials and perspectives, there is then time to work on analytical capacities that also use the same factual cores. I thus move on to habits of the mind, so often relegated to sincere prologues to the teaching of his-tory and then overwhelmed by coverage requirements.[1] Here I must go back briefly to my own little story. My early teaching approach to world history assumed that students possessed several capacities. I expected that students could select data according to their relevance to an argu-ment and then construct an argument; I expected that they could build essays (at least given time) that would introduce an analytical problem and then argue a point of view coherently, selecting confirming data and dealing with major factual anomalies. I should note that when I intro-duced this particular history course I had not taught freshmen for twenty years, so I had a lot of learning of my own to do; I should also note that I enjoy the challenge precisely because, if teaching is properly done, one can induce so much fruitful change. Needless to say, before moving to my qualified joy, I was disappointed, given what I had expected. I faced what many instructors face: relatively able students who "do the work," who confuse a question about explaining the Indian caste system or comparing it with social inequality in Greece with a question that invites them to parade whatever they know about India; students, in other words, who confuse data dumps with focused analysis. My initial temerity was even greater: I assumed that students should be able to learn how to compare key features in one society with those in another, if not in the first requested exercise, at least in the second. Here, too, I met disappointment. I did find that most students could do this at the end of the course, which pleased me once I adjusted my expectations but which meant that my other analytical goals had to remain on the sidelines. (The ability to make comparisons, I should note, is not a capacity that pleases all world historians, some of whom like to bypass a civilizational framework; but I will argue later that it is a central historical capacity, whatever one's approach to the issue of civilizations.)

My problems, in sum, were several. I encountered relatively able students who could not consistently move from descriptive, memorized presentations of data to selectivity and analysis and whose idea of comparison was to talk about one society, then another (often introducing data that were not germane to the comparison in any event) and who would then assume that the job was done. They discussed, for example, the role of mountains and forests in one society without considering whether the other society had mountains and forests, too—without demonstrating, in other words, that the factor their reading had highlighted in one case was in fact relevant in a comparison of that society with another. They also sometimes made factual mistakes, which was annoying but which was neither the most common nor the principal point. The majority of students, except the most able, found it hard to think in analytically appropriate terms.

Gradually, of course, I learned some techniques that helped a few more students. First, I would offer instructions and guidance: If your introductory paragraph isn't comparative, if it charges off dealing with only one society, then you are not well launched. In a binary comparative set, both societies should be seriously mentioned in the first paragraph. If the first part of your paper deals only with China and the second part only with India, you've done something wrong: You haven't structured the paper in a way that will allow you to compare the two adequately. What I was attempting here was of course to use mechanics to help induce better conceptualization, which is putting the cart before the horse, but it did help sometimes. Equally obvious, it did not lead to consistent improvement in students' comparative capacities; what would click for one assignment might strike no sparks the next time around. That is, I had too little assurance that a student who did one comparative exercise well had developed ongoing skills and would handle the next comparison correctly from an analytical standpoint. There was no assurance of transferability of skills within the semester itself, much less after it had ended.

Because of the students' lags in grasping comparative fundamentals, I was ready for some outside help. My problem was simple: I had relatively bright students who just could not think through how to organize data to answer comparative questions that were usually fairly simple and who could not predictably conduct a good, sequential argument or select materials to that end. I decided that these problems bothered me a lot more than students' really annoying factual errors about Buddhism or their distressingly common tendency, after the classical period, to assume that India and the Middle East fused. (I still work on these confusions, too, but it's a question of priorities, partly because these errors usually reflect simply sloppy habits that are relatively easy to correct.)

I worked at a university, Carnegie Mellon, that prides itself on its applications of cognitive psychology, and it had set up a learning-enhancement center. Here was an obvious recourse. Two asides: I also knew that history learning research existed, from my contacts with scholars such as Wineburg, Seixas, and Voss, and I had profited from several findings, though more diffusely than I wished. And, I worried, and still worry, that the "revolution" in cognitive research, along with the new "national priorities" of math and science, would so privilege more quantitative disciplines that history would lose ground, through no fault of its own, simply because it had not married the latest pedagogical fashions. So, while I wished to obtain help, I had an additional agenda, wanting history to be at the front lines of learning advocacy and a leader in the application of relevant learning research.

Back to the narrative: I had people to consult about my concern that a good, sensibly selective world history course was proceeding more slowly and uncertainly than I desired. My new colleagues in the field of cognitive psychology spent more time catching on to history's peculiar pedagogical flavors than I wished—meetings were long and frequent—but they did catch on and began to formulate ideas that would continue to inform our collaboration.

The first spark—we had no grant money, so that tinder was absent—proved crucial, on both sides of the collaboration. The learning folks asked me what my main goals were in terms of what students should take from the course. I don't think I had ever formulated my curriculum in this way, which is an admission of inadequacy, but in fact I did have goals and was able to respond: I knew what I wanted students to be able to do at the end of the course that they had not routinely been able to do at its outset (beyond just parroting back facts).

My response flowed partly from my exercise plans, including the early comparative paper assignments, and from my disappointments, but also from my own joy in historical thinking. It was not, as a result, highly dependent on the usual rationalizations for world history. I wanted students to be able to develop fact-derived arguments better; I wanted them to be able to make comparisons sooner than they generally seemed able to do; I wanted them to be able to assess change over time; and I wanted them to be able to evaluate relevant history-social science theory—to test it factually, often in a comparative context—as in the world economy approach.

Two interventions here. First, it was crucial to my new colleagues that I have a definite and finite answer. I had cognitively relevant goals—like people who do not know they speak in prose, I had not known this—and I suspect most history teachers have such goals. The point here is that it's vital that the goals be explicit and available. It was valuable for me to put the goals on the table, and such explicitness was certainly vital to any collaboration with the learning experts. At the same time, a focus on analytical aims helped all participants generate a common vocabulary, shorn of some of the jargon (offputting if only because unfamiliar to historians) that cognitive research sometimes involves. We could all agree that defining what capacities students should develop quickly and be able to repeat (even in assessments outside the bounds of the course) constituted a fruitful first step.

Second, however, my response was flawed, even though it turned out to be useful. I didn't include some goals that are in fact important in my course, such as facility in handling primary materials. The course uses such materials regularly, particularly as the basis for the weekly discussion sections, and significant history learning research applies, as the essays by Britt, Perfetti, Van Dyke, and Gabrys and Voss and Wiley in this volume discuss, but I was too ignorant to bring all this in, and the omission continues to invite further attention. I also did not place much emphasis on evaluating and reconciling divergent interpretations, though I value this as a history learning outcome (assessing theory is, however, related). And, I was simply unaware of the work that has gone into improving student capacity to assess factual reliability and biases, to figure out how to know historical materials more accurately.[2] I still lack a position on this: World history materials, derived from textbooks, are not the best testing ground for these vital habits, and I continue to hope that students can bring into their college work some solid achievements from their high school studies. But the point bears watching. Clearly, I did not venture a full list of the goals I would seek in history learning more generally, kindergarten through college, and others might prefer a different set of priorities. But the further point is that I made the choice to emphasize certain analytical skills in this particular course, a choice that can be criticized but that has the merit of being both definite and finite. Historical habits of mind are wide-ranging, and the whole edifice cannot be built in a semester. The priority is to get at least some sense of where one particular course fits within a larger analytical edifice, to be explicit, and to have real goals beyond coverage, while at the same time not pursuing too long a list of goals. In the long run, of course, the goals of history learning must transcend a single course to include a larger program that stretches from the years before college to college and, for highly motivated history students, to the history major itself.

Working on comparisons focused our initial efforts. The approach developed was simple, though it took some time to elaborate, and it is still evolving. Beyond explicit identification of mechanics, it consisted of two basic maxims: break down the capacity into its component skills in relation to the data involved (see also the emphasis on "decomposing tasks," in chapter 22), and repeat it frequently. Before this collaboration, our world history course had always imposed an early quiz, requiring brief comparisons ("cite three differences between the upper class in Rome and in classical India") and a short initial comparative paper. I had assumed that these exercises, suitably graded and commented upon, would suffice to teach students the necessary comparative skills, except for hopelessly idle students. I was wrong, which is why systematic incapacities to compare were still showing up three months later. Exactly why comparison posed such problems remains a bit of a mystery. Many students, dealing with admittedly unfamiliar data, simply found it difficult to escape the ingrained habits of relying on descriptive summaries, adapted from textbooks or even documents, in order to rearrange data more radically so that they were actively and comparative juxtaposed. Identifying concrete exercises that helped students accomplish this reconceptualization of data, repeating these exercises, and gradually increasing their complexity addressed the most common failings.

The specific remedy involved adding some homework assignments that required students to show similarities and differences (i.e., to make comparisons) for specific topics derived from the text. These assignments helped students chart factors by highlighting relevant data from the reading and also helped them see when similarity or difference was likely to be the main point (see Appendix 21.1). These exercises were repeated frequently throughout the first two-thirds of the course and were expanded to encompass standard essay and examination exercises and discussion section topics.

I had two anxieties about these exercises, and I should have had a third. First, I feared able students would reject them, and the course, as mickey mouse. They did not, on the whole. Able students reported that the exercises (which could look quite different one from the other when they were used with different materials) helped them highlight data and learn to analyze. My second worry was that the extra grading (even on a pass-fail basis) would prove too demanding for my hardworking teaching assistants, but in fact the evaluation can be accomplished fairly quickly (an extra forty-five minutes for a section of twenty-five students, including brief comments), and templates can be distributed with the evaluations to reduce the need for commentary. The benefits, in terms of better essays and more lively class discussions (the exercises also encourage doing the reading in advance, a really prosaic point but far from irrelevant), help compensate as well. What I should have realized was that students would too often convert analytical charts to note-taking practice and so fail to distinguish between requests for differences and requests for similarities, simply putting down data for their own sake. But this problem can be addressed through more explicit instructions (see Appendix 21.1, exercise 1).

Explicit identification of analytical goals, with equally explicit exercises that reinforce methods of thinking, works. Over the past five years, students in the course have become much more facile at making comparisons. This impressionistic conclusion—the fact that we can move on to other types of assignments much sooner than before—has been confirmed by two years of before-and-after testing, using comparative data sets. Students improve their ability to handle unfamiliar comparative exercises massively within the course framework (second-week pretest, thirteenth-week posttest), and, more important, they improve in that ability to a level well above that of comparable Carnegie Mellon students who have not taken the course. The gap is striking, and really pleasing (see Appendix 21.2).

There are two other points. First, why do the exercises work? This whole procedure has been based on learning research but not on research specifically in history, so my answer must be tentative, though I hope it will contribute to such research. Having students break down the topical features of a society (e.g., culture, politics) and then juxtapose them against those of another society allows students to repeat the basic procedures of comparison in radically different settings. Both the repetition and the process of analyzing a society differentiate this practice from otherwise more demanding but occasional essays. The exercises force student to reorganize and recombine their readings into the comparative categories—a first step toward selectivity, toward choosing facts to answer questions. The practices also involve every student, unlike the randomness that often characterizes even the best-run discussion section. And, since they are easy to evaluate, they can be returned quickly to the students and even used as one of the bases for a discussion section. The second point is that measurable teaching success of this sort is immensely satisfying, much like a creative work of scholarship. Having students move ahead rapidly and become capable of setting up an analytical problem that would have been impossible just a month before is tangibly rewarding. In this sense, the later confirmation that we obtained through control group tests was redundant—the students' progress was already clear in the daily classroom.

But the procedures we developed for advancing comparative capabilities did not form the end of the story. We applied the same techniques of breaking down data into relevant, finite categories to theory testing, asking students, for example, to chart premodern African politics and to juxtapose that with the kind of political structures that would be predicted by world economy theory for such a peripheral economy. With comparative techniques under their belts, most students responded strongly, despite some reluctance to believe that a high-powered theory, clearly written, might in fact be overdrawn and merit debunking.

We also applied the same procedures to learning how to deal with issues of change over time, another analytic skill that is central to the course—indeed, to my mind, the quintessential historian's conceptual tool. I worried initially that we had devoted so much time to comparison that we might run out of energy before addressing this even more crucial but possibly more elusive category. Among other things, students by definition cannot begin addressing issues of change at the outset of the course, since they have no baseline against which to measure change. But then, ridiculously belatedly, the obvious point dawned: The basic capability is the same as for comparison; the only difference is one that compares similarities and differences (continuities and changes) over time rather than across societies. Exercises to foster this skill can therefore be constructed in precisely the same ways as those for making comparisons and yield the same kinds of gains in student aptitudes (see Appendix 21.3).

As we realized that students could grasp conceptual issues and frame answers better and faster, we made some of the later assignments in the course more complicated. We asked, for example, for comparison of degrees of change in two societies, essentially calling for a three-dimensional chart (one that so far we have left it to students to construct). We will try to figure out how to facilitate the capacity to handle this kind of analytical exercise more fully in future (see Appendix 21.4).

Finally, we needed to deal with causation, the remaining point on my initial list of analytical goals for the course. Assessing historical causation is an inexact art, of course, but it is not random. It involves tolerance for disagreement, but it also entails the capacity to distinguish relevant factors from the clearly irrelevant—and also, usually, the ability to blend several factors, rather than rely monocausal simplifications. The capacity is fundamental to the larger assessment of historical change, even though it cannot be handled, as it can in some sciences, through deliberate replication.

As we worked through exercises to enhance the students' conceptualization of change, comparison, and theory assessment in the course, I assumed that the talents involved in assigning causation would follow along, particularly since we often set exam questions in this mode and achieved satisfactory results. I was wrong. Initial control-group testing revealed that students who had not taken the course improved as much on causation exercises (which was not much) as those who had worked with us for fifteen weeks and who had displayed such marked gains in comparison.

The lesson I learned is this: In contrast to change, causation is a distinct conceptual category, unrelated to comparison; while it's great to have goals, if they are not taught recurrently and explicitly, with data broken down into relevant categories, they will not necessarily take hold. Even students who are able to handle exam questions well because they know the material may demonstrate no skills at abstraction.

In response to this lesson, over the past year we have introduced some exercises, plus a mid-term essay assignment, that focus explicitly on handling causation issues, and the results have again been measurably favorable. Students now do significantly better than the control group when asked to identify causation issues by analyzing unfamiliar materials. Explicit exercises, with materials broken down, work here too, though the results are not yet as good as those for comparative analysis. (There are several possible reasons for the gap: The skills may be harder to come by; the tests may be less well designed; or the exercises may be too sketchy, in contrast to our better-developed comparative materials.) (See Appendix 21.5).

Finally: so what? Discussion of efforts to improve students' ability to engage in historical thinking must address why history is to be taught and learned at all. The suggestions I have sketched, applied to world history, have been deliberately mixed. I have suggested that we teach the subject so that students become familiar with some facts that educated people in contemporary society should know (e.g., to have some recognition of what Islam means amid a growing Muslim minority in their own midst and growing Muslim assertiveness in the world at large) and to gain some factually derived global perspective as well. But we must teach it also so that students will have some understandings and capacities that they can regularly apply to new data and issues, understandings that will help them as citizens and workers. Knowing how to compare and assess change is relevant to working at a host of jobs in addition to developing a broader civic competence, and we should not be modest in our fledgling claims that we can improve this capacity and demonstrate progress through formal assessment. (The same capacity, parenthetically, underlies the ability to evaluate analogy, an ancillary goal we work on, informally so far, in the world history course.) Assessing change and causation, comparing different social patterns, is part of understanding how people behave, and this is relevant, even crucial, even in the highest-tech environments.

Obviously, the experience drawn from one course, with intriguing but limited assessments made within six months after students completed the course, is suggestive at best. We need to think of fuller assessments, further out in time (particularly if, as we hope, we can construct curricula that build on and extend students' initial gains). Other tasks await. What we've been doing with college freshmen might well be doable a bit earlier as part of high school history, with suitable adaptations. Experiments in this direction would be a vital part of an appropriate sequencing of capacities that enables us to build on established gains while solidifying these gains. Too many students reach college believing, rightly or not, that the history they have had to date (and usually disliked, though sometimes loved) was purely descriptive, involving nothing more challenging than memorization. We need to push some explicit sequenced analytical exercises down to the high school level. The same lessons apply to training teachers: We lament too often those teachers who have had so little history that even coverage decisions come with difficulty. We should also check prospective teachers' degree of comfort with thinking historically, because this training may be harder won than the capacity to keep a day ahead in the textbook.[3]

The specific project I've been engaged in is small, an early step at best, although we have had encouraging results. Even in this little byway, students continue to delight and disappoint, sometimes sliding back and sometimes, toward the end of the course and with no apparent sequential mediation, producing penetrating causation analyses. The gains are real, but of course the fluctuations in teaching outcomes persist among them.

Debate about world history teaching in recent years has focused on issues around coverage and perspective (usually the dominance of Western civilization, sometimes the balance to be struck between global and civilizational approaches). Worthy discussions all, at least to a point. But, while these debates will continue, as Ross Dunn eloquently demonstrates, they will probably begin to fade, at least in their starkest incarnations—witness the virtually universal adoption in state curriculum standards, at least in name, of world history as a necessary component. It's time, then, for a new debate to open on how to ensure appropriate improvements in students' analytical capacity within the world history curriculum. A variety of approaches need testing, but the desirable conclusion—that feasible world history learning goals are compatible with constructive pedagogy—can already be ensured.

The modest pedagogical changes I have described need amplification and, certainly, further assessment. Essays in this volume demonstrate how important it is to be careful about claiming analytical progress. I believe we have shown that students can acquire truly useful, widely applicable habits of mind more quickly and more certainly as a result of careful and explicit training than they otherwise would and that the gains show up on assessments after the training has ceased. But, we need to extend the monitoring and (and this project is under way) build on our findings by actively using the acquired capacities in the next history course students encounter. We hope that the results will bear out the claims ventured here.

What is clear, even within the bounds of a modest, ongoing program, is that teaching goals belong on the agendas of university history departments, along with (though not instead of) more orthodox kinds of research. Research and development on student learning have clear results, and they are interesting besides. In this sense, I view my efforts as a bit of a template. It involved collaboration across standard boundaries, by history teachers and graduate students initially a bit put off by the styles and claims of cognitive science. It involved paying a lot more attention to the prosaic aspects of the teaching process, increased study of what my own teaching involved, than I had been accustomed to venture. But, the results paid off, at least in terms of my satisfaction with my own course and with how students could navigate analytical tasks by the course's conclusion. The gains were worth the commitment involved—and the commitment, as well as some of the specific exercises, is eminently replicable.

Appendix 21.1

Early Comparative Homework:

1. Gender Relations in China and India (week 3 of course)
(based on source readings as well as text)
Instructions: Remember that comparison involves two steps, the identification of key features and the assessment of the degree of similarity or difference between these features.

Fill in the grid, on roles and statuses of women:
Differences: China only
Differences: India only
Similarities: common to both

(Note: verbal instructions remind the students that since both societies were patriarchal, similarities should be numerous; this is meant to control what is otherwise a natural tendency to list undistinctive gender features for China simply because this is the first slot on the sheet; the caveat works pretty well.)

2. (a week later) Comparing the Islamic Middle East and China
Students have already been introduced to social, political, cultural, and economic categories for grouping information about one society.
Islamic Mid East: Main features (social, cultural, economic, political) (the chart asks for highlights in each category)
     China: use the chart to compare similarities in each category
     China: use the chart to note differences in each category

Appendix 21.2

Test Results

An average of 68 percent of all students improved their scores by an average of 33 percent from a pretest to a posttest that used unfamiliar (sometime fabricated) comparative materials; no more than 5 percent of students experienced a decline in scores. Another pre- and posttest administration yielded an average score of 9.8 points out of 15 possible on the pretest and 11.8 out of 15 on the post-test. The tests asked students to select an important similarity and an important difference from two descriptions of historical societies, and a piece of information that was irrelevant to comparison.

On the tests (based on unfamiliar reading passages that offered comparative materials, followed by questions about similarity, difference, and irrelevance to comparison), the control group answered 47 percent of pretest questions and 57 percent of the posttest questions correctly; the text students who took the course answered 42 percent of the pretest questions and 68 percent of the posttest questions correctly.

Appendix 21.3

Theory Testing and Change Over Time—Extending Comparison

A homework exercise in week 8 of the course asks students to chart the political and economic features that a core society and a peripheral society are supposed to have and then to chart the political and economic features of early modern Britain and early modern sub-Saharan Africa. The difference in fit, based on a comparative assessment, is striking (e.g., Britain is a core, but with relatively weak government; West African government stronger than world economy position would predict) and the students are then asked to write up their main conclusions in a short paragraph. (A subsequent exercise asks for a similar analysis of developments in nineteenth-century Latin America, assessed against predictions drawn from both world economy and modernization theory, to see which fits best or whether neither fits.)

An exercise in week 9 asks students to compare political, social, cultural, and economic features of Russia before and after Peter the Great's introduction of reforms to deal with change and continuity. The usual grid is employed for categorizing brief highlights. Then students are to write a paragraph explaining what features he sought most to change and what his motivations for emphasizing these features rather than others might have been.

Appendix 21.4

Comparing Two Societies and Change (week 13)

Students are asked to chart enduring traditional cultural features in twentieth-century Japan and twentieth-century sub-Saharan Africa (i.e., features that are roughly the same in 1990s as they were as in 1900—comparative similarities) and then to do the same for features that have changed, using the now-familiar grid format in which brief highlighted notes are listed on a chart. They then are asked to write a paragraph about how helpful modernization theory is for explaining difference between patterns of cultural change in the two cases. The charts work well, but blending the comparative results into the theory assessment produces more mixed results.

Appendix 21.5

Causation Exercises

Our materials for causation exercises are sketchier than for the other exercises, since this is a category under development. In week 2, we ask students to pick among several possible causes for the primary emphases of Confucianism—influence from other regions, Confucius's distinctive genius, the political situation in the Zhou dynasty, and demands raised by peasant protesters, with specific reference to pages in the text. They are then asked to choose among a similar set of outcomes to determined what Confucianism helped cause. Another exercise, used in the weekly discussion section, lists potential causes of European feudalism (frequent wars, Christianity, Roman tradition, nature of weaponry, strong monarchies); students are to pick the two most relevant causes and show why the others aren't as important. Later, using Carlo Cipolla's short book *Guns, Sails, and Empire* (New York, 1996), we ask students to select the most plausible explanations for European expansion post-1450 from a list of possible causes: religion, population growth, problems in the balance of trade, fear of Chinese power, technological change, new weaknesses in Asia, use of the steam engine in manufacturing, and political rivalries in Europe. In class, they note why some of these factors work as causes, and why some do not.

We also now devote our second outside essay to a causation question such as this: Given their somewhat similar positions in the world economy, why did Latin America and sub-Saharan Africa develop such different political structures in the early modern period? (Students handled the descriptive comparison very well; their handling of the causation part of the question was admittedly shakier at this point in the course).

NOTES

My thanks to several colleagues: Montserrat Miller, Michael Neiberg, Jeff Suzik, Fred Reif, and Richard Hayes. Assessment was supported by a grant from the Hewlett Foundation.

1. Earlier stages of this project are discussed in Montserrat Miller and Peter N. Stearns, "Applying Cognitive Learning Approaches to History Teaching," *History Teacher* (1995); *National Standards for World History* (Los Angeles, 1994). For an eloquent and informative discussion of the controversy, albeit one with little reference to learning skills, see Gary B. Nash, Charlotte Crabtree, and Ross E. Dunn, *History on Trial: Culture Wars and the Teaching of the Past* (New York, 1997).

2. Rosalyn Ashby and Peter Lee, "Children's Ideas about Testing Historical Claims and the Status of Historical Accounts," paper presented at American Educational Research Association conference, New York, 1996.

3. S. M. Wilson and S. S. Wineburg, "Peering at History from Different Lenses: The Role of Disciplinary Perspectives in the Teaching of History," *Teachers College Record*, 89 (1988), pp. 525–539.

Chapter 22

The Sourcer's Apprentice
A Tool for Document-Supported History Instruction

M. Anne Britt, Charles A. Perfetti, Julie A. Van Dyke, and Gareth Gabrys

History offers a literacy environment as rich as any a student is likely to encounter prior to college. The study of history centers on documents—letters, treaties, notes, official records, diaries—as well as textbooks. Instruction that makes good use of this rich text environment has the potential to support broad-based literacy skills that may extend beyond history classrooms to other cases of text learning, reasoning, and writing. This potential is acknowledged in the recommendations of the National Standards for United States History concerning historical thinking skills, which "enable students to evaluate evidence, develop comparative and causal analyses, interpret the historical record, and construct sound historical arguments and perspectives on which informed decisions in contemporary life can be based."[1]

High, literacy-rich standards in history education offer many possibilities for going beyond simple transmission of consensual narratives. A basic high standard requires that students demonstrate more reading of more sources, more informed analysis, and more writing than is currently common. The call for higher standards can embrace much more than these requirements, but they constitute a reasonable minimum. The narrative is the starting point. Literacy—thinking, reasoning, and writing about history via the use of documents—is the trajectory. Thus, the National Standards also suggested that teachers capitalize on younger students' interest and skill in learning from narratives, but only as a starting point to be cultivated and developed into more sophisticated literacy skills. The Standards report introduces its description of historical skills this way:

> Children should also have opportunities to compare different stories about a historical figure or event in order to analyze the facts each author includes or omits, and the interpretations or point-of-view communicated by each—important early steps in the development of students' abilities to compare competing historical interpretations of events.[2]

These goals embody reasonable standards that, apparently, are far from being met. Only 10 percent of twelfth graders test at or above the proficiency level, which includes the ability to use historical evidence to support positions and to write arguments that reflect an in-depth grasp of issues and that refer to sources.[3] The standards are thus high as well as reasonable, and need for some correspondingly higher effort by students and teachers is implied.

Use of sources relates closely to capacity for handling conflicting viewpoints. Currently, average students have few opportunities to learn by reading multiple texts on the same topic and by discussing controversies of interpretation. According to Ravitch and Finn, these activities are not routine in typical history classrooms. These authors summarize eleventh graders' view of history instruction as follows:

> [T]he typical history classroom is one in which they listen to the teacher explain the day's lesson, use the textbook, and take tests. Occasionally they watch a movie. Sometimes they memorize information or read stories about events and people. They seldom work with other students, use original documents, write term papers, or discuss the significance of what they are studying.[4]

Although many teachers encourage interpretative activities, textbooks continue to dominate the curriculum.[5] In fact, only 39 percent of the twelfth-grade students in the 1988 National Assessment of Educational Progress (NAEP) history assessment claimed to have read material from a source other than a textbook.[6] Current textbooks provide very little opportunity to learn the interpretative skills required by the National Standards. In an effort to simplify the presentation of events, textbooks often gloss over controversial interpretations, possibly conveying to the student that interpretations are facts. Furthermore, history textbooks tend to omit qualifiers, terms of uncertainty, and signs of authorship (i.e., indicators that the author is giving an opinion), features that are standard in works by historians.[7]

In what follows, we assume, and argue for this assumption only summarily, that reading multiple accounts of common events should be an integral part of high school history instruction. We describe an ongoing project, built on this assumption, which has theoretical, experimental, and instructional components. We refer to sources in terms both of primary documents and of historians' accounts, for both types generate some common issues including diversity of viewpoint. Although here we emphasize the instructional components, the theoretical and empirical components are important. We begin with a summary of these components, as developed through our research. We then describe a computer-based learning environment, the Sourcer's Apprentice (SA), that we developed to assist students in acquiring evidence-seeking and evidence-evaluation skills and to foster students' awareness of document type and document privilege in historical research.

Learning by Reading History Texts

Students require various skills and representational abilities to read a set of historical documents, evaluate them, and construct their own interpretation of the described events. The most basic demand on a reader of history texts is the construction of a simple narrative account of some event. We have found that, after a first reading of a history text, students appear to learn the central events of a story and connect these events with simple causal or temporal links.[8] In some ways, this is similar to what very young children learn from reading fiction.[9] A useful method of describing this knowledge is as a Causal-Temporal Event Structure. The Causal-Temporal Event Structure is a graphical structure in which nodes represent events and connectors represent either causal or temporal links between events. This structure has proved very useful in capturing what students recall and summarize about a single narrative text.[10] Because constructing these types of representations is compatible with the cognitive abilities of even young readers, most history students should have little problem obtaining the basic story from a historical text. Frequently, this level of ability (with the additional learning of many details) is all that is demanded of them in the high school history class.

The demands on the student become significantly greater, however, when the student is presented with either an additional text (e.g., multiple texts) or a single text that does not conform to a narrative structure (e.g., an historian's argument, a treaty, military correspondence). Each of these cases place special demands on the student that may cause learning difficulties unless the student receives explicit instruction and environmental support. In the next section we describe the representational structure, in addition to a single Causal-Temporal Event Structure, necessary to understand multiple texts. Then we briefly review the empirical results pertaining to students' limited ability to construct such a representation.

Learning from Multiple Texts

Integrating information from multiple documents introduces a complexity to history learning that is absent when one is using only a single narrative. When reading two texts on the same topic, it is not enough to simply construct a single Causal-Temporal Event Structure. At the very least, the reader must construct a representation of each author's text. However, a single representation that incorporated information from both texts would be more beneficial to a true understanding of the events discussed. For a student to form a single coherent representation of the situation, he or she must create an additional level of structure that can resolve any discrepancies between the individual representations. We call this additional structure the *Documents Model*.[11]

DOCUMENTS MODEL

A documents model, shown in Figure 22.1, has two components: the *situations model* and the *intertext predicates*. The situations model is similar to the Causal-Temporal Event Structure in that nodes are linked to express the relationships between events. The difference is that the situations model is a model of both the overlapping and the unique information from all texts read about the topic (i.e., all described situations). We consider this situations model to be mostly a cumulative and integrative representation of the situation described by all the texts read on this topic, within certain constraints. For instance, in the cumulative situations model in Figure 22.1, the boxes represent the events (e.g., *U.S. military arrives*), and the solid arrows represent the relations between events. Some events were mentioned by only one author: *U.S. recognizes Panama* was mentioned only by LaCosta and *Panama gains independence* was mentioned only by Clark. Other events were mentioned by both authors: *U.S. military arrives* was mentioned by both Clark and LaCosta.

The situations model is elaborated with an intertext model to indicate

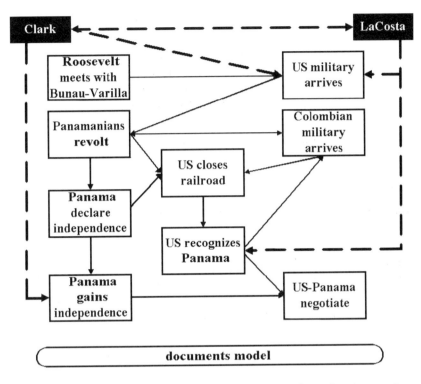

Figure 22.1. Documents' Model representing a segment of Text from two authors (Clark and LaCosta). Representation of situation (boxes and solid arrows) and Intertext links (dotted lines) to a Document Node (shaded rectangle).

that selective events are marked for their source origin. The intertext model allows connections to be made between sources and from a source to its content. These relations (see the dotted lines on Figure 22.1) are referred to as *intertext predicates* and represent links from documents to other elements. In this model, we also include representations of entire documents (see the shaded rectangles on Figure 22.1), referred to as *document nodes* (e.g., LaCosta).

The intertext predicates enable document-to-content links that indicate which author mentioned a particular fact. For example, in Figure 22.1 two intertext links from LaCosta's document node show that he mentioned two events: *U.S. recognizes Panama* and *U.S. military arrives*. The intertext predicates also enable links between documents to indicate the relationship between different authors' documents. For example, in Figure 22.1 there is a link between the document node for LaCosta and the node for Clark. Document-to-document links are generally used to indicate whether an author's text supports or opposes the other author's texts.

Document nodes can be more or less elaborated, depending on the reader's expertise and the reader's goals in reading the document. A fully elaborated document node includes information about the document's source (e.g., who the author is), the document's content (e.g., the main point of the document), and the author's rhetorical goals in writing the document (e.g., author's intentions).

A Documents Model enables the reader to represent multiple authors' versions of the same events. As is common in historical interpretation, authors often disagree over the causal significance of a particular series of events. For example, one author may suggest that Event Y occurred because of Event X, whereas another author may discount the relevance of Event X, arguing instead that Event Z had a greater causal impact. Representing the source of an event or causal relation by a intertext predicate enables the reader to qualify aspects of the situations model, thereby allowing otherwise discrepant information to be incorporated into a single coherent representation.

LIMITS ON DOCUMENTS MODEL CONSTRUCTION

There is some evidence that the ability to construct a Documents Model may be beyond the ability of many high school students. Wineburg found large differences between expert historians and high school students in the use of the Corroboration Heuristic, that is, the tendency to make direct comparisons of information learned from several documents.[12] This heuristic enables a reader to check a historian's interpretation of a cited primary document or compare arguments on opposing sides of a controversy and can be represented by an intertext predicate such as agrees/disagrees with or supports. Although Wineburg found that experts used this skill often, his Advanced Placement (AP) high school students rarely used it. While it is still an open empirical question whether secondary students are able to form intertext links during reading (e.g., noting corroboration among sources), there are reasons that we would expect this skill to be less developed in high school students than in college students or experts. First, high school students have little experience reading multiple texts on a shared topic. Second, high-school students have less experience using documents as evidence in written arguments. Third, high school students have limited experience evaluating sources when they are reading argumentative essays. College students, on the other hand, clearly do form links from events to sources and can use these links when writing an essay to present one author's version of the events.[13]

Students are similarly limited in their ability to construct elaborated document nodes (i.e., representations of source information). Indeed, in order for a student to represent the source of a document in some detail, they must know about sources in general and historical sources in particular. Wineburg found that, when studying a document, expert historians use a Sourcing Heuristic wherein they examine the source of a document before working through the content of that document. The AP high school students he studied, however, did not show this behavior, and college students appeared to represent only some of the important characteristics of documents and their sources.[14] In a recent study, Rouet, Britt, Mason, and Perfetti asked students to read a variety of documents to come to an informed opinion regarding four controversies.[15] After finishing their reading, students were asked to rank the documents in terms of their trustworthiness and usefulness and to provide a short justification for each ranking. Classification of the 672 justifications showed that students attended to more than the content of the document. They frequently mentioned features of the author (e.g., author's credentials, motivations or participation in the events) and features of the document type (e.g., when it was written) and made comparisons among the documents (e.g., authors agreed or disagreed). This is just the type of information that students would need to encode in order to create an elaborated document node during studying.

Presenting students with problems can improve their document use and evaluation skills. In several studies with high school and college students, we found that, when students are presented with controversies to address in essays, both their sense of document privilege and their use of documents in providing arguments improve.[16] For example, we asked several groups of students (history graduate students, psychology graduate students, college students, AP high school students, and regular high school students) to read excerpts from primary documents, historian accounts, and a textbook to learn about an historical controversy.[17] The graduate, college, and AP high school students all recognized the importance of primary documents and mentioned both source and content when judging a document's source. They were all able (to varying degrees) to reason about sources in a semisophisticated way under optimal circumstances. This was not true of the regular high school students.

Although they were able to judge primary documents as most trustworthy and frequently used document content to justify their ranking, the regular high school students judged the textbook as most useful and rarely used the source of the document to justify their ranking. Thus, unlike the other four groups, regular high school students were limited in their ability to reason about sources even under optimal circumstances.

The potential for enhanced document use is seen in a large-scale study by Spoehr, who found that high school students in a hypermedia intervention program showed higher history performance than comparison students, including better use of evidence in essay arguments.[18] Thus, although students show limited document awareness, they also show a potential for better use of documents and better learning outcomes with procedures that promote and support document use.

Representing Nonnarrative Information

The special demands of learning from texts in history are not limited to issues of multiple document representations. Reading beyond the textbook exposes the student to unfamiliar genres and text structures that stretch the student's narrative approach to texts. One text type of specific importance is the historian's essay, which presents an argued interpretation. For students to fully understand and evaluate such essays, they must form an Argument Model for each author's argument, a mental representation of the interrelations of claims, support, evidence, and sources.[19] However, even among college students the ability to detect and understand arguments is incomplete. Britt, Marron, and Perfetti found that half of the students had difficulty spontaneously detecting an argument, and one-quarter failed to detect or represent arguments.[20]

The need for providing students with training and practice in document-based learning in history thus raises the general issue of how to support students' reasoning with and about multiple documents. In the next section, we describe the principles guiding the design of the Sourcer's Apprentice (SA). In following these principles, derived from cognitive theories of learning, the SA environment (a) has students learn by solving problems with richly integrated sets of documents, (b) supports construction of expert representations such as documents and argument models, (c) creates an interface by decomposing the task into necessary elements, (d) supports transfer by using a real world environment and providing several problems

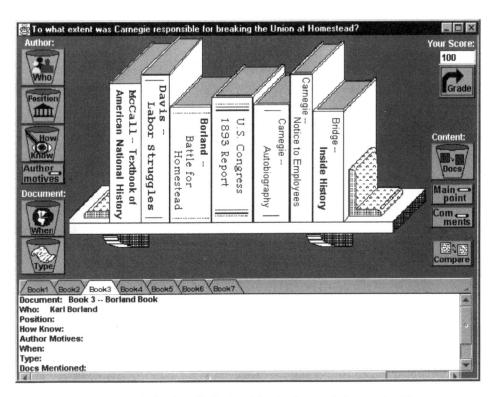

Figure 22.2. Example Bookshelf displayed by the Sourcer's Apprentice. Notes are displayed for Book 3. Note the problem statement at the top of the screen.

of very different types, (d) provides students with explicit and interactive instruction on the relevant skills, (e) motivates student engagement through challenges and immediate feedback. After a discussion of the design principles, we describe SA from a user perspective. We conclude with a report on an effectiveness study that shows that the Sourcer's Apprentice can raise some components of students' document literacy.

Principles for the Design of a Document-Based Learning Environment

We believe that students who do not spontaneously display the requisite skills and orientations toward texts can, given a supportive environment, begin to develop them. The Sourcer's Apprentice was designed to provide high school history students with opportunities to practice the kind of document-based reasoning exhibited by expert historians.[21] With the Sourcer's Apprentice, students view a computer screen that displays a bookshelf of excerpts from several documents of various types (see Figure 22.2). Their task is to learn about an historical controversy by reading these excerpts. They are given explicit instruction in attending to features of the source and elements of the author's argument. Also present on the screen are structured note cards that provide further support for the students' efforts to attend to sources and arguments. To motivate engagement, students are given points for filling in these note cards. After reading and filling in the note cards, students are asked several comprehension questions. Finally, they write an opinion essay on the controversy in which they support their claims by citing documents. The note cards, but not the excerpts, are available during the writing process.

Our goal was to create a simple coached-apprenticeship system that would provide students with the support they need to interact with documents in a more authentic way.[22] Although such systems typically are technically complex, the Sourcer's Apprentice is an example of how a coached-apprenticeship system can be implemented in a very simple way. We have incorporated the following six general cognitive principles in designing the Sourcer's Apprentice.

Principle 1: Learn by Solving Problems

Providing problems for the learner to solve has proven to be an effective means for teaching procedures in math and physics.[23] Several theories of learning have advocated using problem solving as a way to acquire a cognitive skill or concept. The Cognitive Apprenticeship approach proposes that problem-solving activity be situated in as authentic a context as possible, thereby ensuring a sense of "real world" application for the to-be-learned skills and concepts.[24] Instructional techniques such as modeling, coaching, and fading are then employed to support students' learning in a complex environment.[25] Working in an authentic, problem-solving environment supported by coaching and structured practice should enable students to acquire flexible procedures and concepts, thus allowing them to apply the knowledge when the need arises.

The Sourcer's Apprentice attempts to incorporate several elements of Cognitive Apprenticeship instructional methods. First, it requires an authentic, problem-solving activity central to historical literacy: a simplified version of the history research paper. When writing a research paper, students are asked to read books, take notes, extract relevant information, and synthesize this information into a coherent essay. Problem-solving activity of this sort, however, requires a very active role for the student, who must apply new procedures and concepts during the learning process. The cost for such active learning is a high cognitive load and possibly also learning impasses. To counter excessive cognitive demands, support must be provided during initial learning states. In designing the Sourcer's Apprentice, we provided structured note cards for each document and buckets for dragging and dropping text from the documents into these note cards. Separate buckets for each source feature provide an important memory aid to free up resources during the early phases of learning.

The apprenticeship approach also allows students to have several experiences with deep learning in the subject matter. The cost of depth, of course, is that it requires time to study a specific problem or topic. Whether "depth" or "coverage" is to be emphasized in a high school history course is a difficult question for which there is no cost-free answer. However, even with standard full coverage as a goal, we suggest that some deeper learning, requiring real time, leads to intrinsically rewarding student achievement that cannot be duplicated with more shallow teaching events.

Principle 2: Support Expert Representations

One characteristic difference between expert and novice problem solving is the form of the representation experts and novices develop.[26] Differences in the type of problem representation correspond to different success rates in problem solving. An expert's knowledge is more highly organized and interconnected than a novice's.

The specialized representations required to learn from multiple texts—a Documents Model (i.e., document nodes and intertext predicates) and an Argument Model—need to be supported by various intermediate representations created by learning activities. Note taking, a critical part of historical research, is an explicit intermediate representation that supports acquisition of these models. Specific attention to relevant aspects of the source and document (see earlier discussion of the sourcing heuristic) is another learning strategy that promotes formation of Documents Models and Argument Models. We have noted that many students do not apply this strategy spontaneously. The Sourcer's Apprentice supports the acquisition of this sourcing strategy by providing special buckets for each source and document feature (e.g., who wrote the document, when it was written). In effect, it combines note taking and sourcing into a single activity in which students enter information on their note cards by dropping information into the bucket for that feature. Likewise, buckets are provided for each important element of an argument, highlighting information necessary for constructing an Argument Model. A series of comprehension questions provide additional support for these representations. The Sourcer's Apprentice includes questions to direct the student's attention toward constructing an elaborated Causal-Temporal Event Structure (e.g., "What demands did the Homestead labor union make in 1892?"), a Documents Model ("Which author mentioned Carnegie's Autobiography?"), and an Argument Model for each historian's account (e.g., "What reason did Professor Wilson offer for believing that Carnegie intended to break the Union?"). Working through several questions of each type helps students build all three types of representations.

Principle 3: Decompose the Task

Task analysis is a bedrock of the cognitive approach to determining what should be taught and how that learning should best be accomplished. Complex intellectual skills can be more easily grasped if one first decomposes them into their elements and then develops an understanding of how these elements function together.[27]

In designing the Sourcer's Apprentice, we began by decomposing Wineburg's expert heuristics as well as those skills identified as necessary to comprehend an historical argument.[28] Then we incorporated these components directly into the Sourcer's Apprentice interface (e.g., buckets and structured note cards). For instance, to support the application of Wineburg's corroboration heuristic, the Sourcer's Apprentice allows side-by-side comparison in which a student can open two documents on the screen simultaneously. Comparison of information across documents can be vertical, as when the student checks an historian's interpretation of a cited primary document, or horizontal, as when the student compares arguments on opposing sides of a controversy. Thus, vertical comparisons are made across different levels in the hierarchically structured document set, whereas horizontal comparisons are made at the same level. In order to help the students make clear, meaningful comparisons, we allow the side-by-side comparison of only two documents at a time.

Decomposition at the level of the interface shows students the importance of each component and allows them to focus on each during learning. Additionally, because learning from problem solving requires high cognitive load, separate buckets for each source feature provides an important memory aid during the early phases of learning.

While we are suggesting a decomposition of the skill, this is only a first step in trying to help students learn to attend to the appropriate information. Eventually, once the skill of identifying elements is automatized, students must be taught how to look at the source as whole. Without teaching them what to pay attention to, we have no chance of helping them evaluate the source as a whole. But, it is critical that we not stop there. Thus, during the tutorial section on source evaluation, the student learns about the importance of looking at a source feature in context of the other features.

Principle 4: Support Transfer

Creating transfer is critical to the production of flexible knowledge that can be applied in various "real world" situations. In some respects, only routine, highly structured procedures can be learned without the expectation of transfer, and we believe this type of learning to be the exception rather than the rule. Transfer, while hard to accomplish, can be shown to occur under certain circumstances. For instance, Singly and Anderson found that transfer is dependent on how closely the practice environment and the target environment map onto each other.[29] Druckman and Bjork suggest that providing variability in problem type during practice will increase transfer.[30]

One aspect of the interface that supports transfer is the direct mapping of surface features with the objects in the real world. Students select books from a bookshelf and take notes on a screen section that resembles note cards. These are independent, and the note cards are available whether the student is studying, answering questions, or writing the essay. We expect these activities to enhance transfer to a real library setting, since graphically and functionally they so closely resemble the actual objects and actions in the library setting.

We designed the Sourcer's Apprentice with the assumption that performing multiple varied practice exercises that provide exposure to a wide range of examples allows students to abstract the essence of the heuristic or concept without absorbing context-specific but irrelevant information. In learning and reasoning from historical documents, skills, heuristics, and concepts must be flexible and transferable to many different settings; they must be abstracted principles. We believe that this flexibility can be promoted by having students solve several very different problems including controversies from military, social, and economic history. This ensures that the type of documents also will vary. For example, treaties and military correspondence are common primary documents for military history, whereas speeches and letters may be more common in social history. By reasoning from documents of different problem types, students can begin to understand the privilege of primary documents and how they function in historians' arguments. This will become abstracted in their minds, and thereby transferable, only after they have had many exposures to different problem types.

Principle 5: Provide Explicit Instruction

Direct instruction is a standard method for providing declarative knowledge quickly. Instructor- controlled verbal explanation and description can ensure that important requisite knowledge is available to the student at exactly the necessary moment. Guided instruction that provides opportunities for students to practice applying the material can allow students to test their knowledge before proceeding.

Document literacy skills such as sourcing, corroboration, and argument comprehension can be explicitly taught to students in the form of a short, incremental tutorial. Instruction for each skill involves three incremental levels: identifying, using, and evaluating the component information. For example, a tutorial intended to teach a student enough about attending to source information during reading should help the student to identify source and document features (e.g., who, why, when, and type). Then, the tutorial can help the student understand how this source information is used in problem solving (e.g., citing information in an essay). Finally, the student can be taught how to evaluate this source information (e.g., judging the trustworthiness of a source). All direct instruction is presented in the context of the controversy and is available to students later during problem solving.

Principle 6: Motivate Engagement

Motivating students to spend more time on a task, to work harder, and to value their learning process is an important goal that, when achieved, results in performance gains. Malone and Lepper have identified twelve factors that affect an individual's motivation.[31] We discuss four of the most important factors: challenging goals with uncertain outcomes, performance feedback, (limited) student choice, and fantasy supporting learning.

Challenging goals have been found to improve performance on both simple and complex cognitive tasks.[32] Meaningful success is a by-product of both setting and meeting challenging goals. Such goals, however, must be balanced with assurances that success is in fact possible. Otherwise, there is a risk of diminishing a student's self-esteem and motivation.

A balance between risk and assured success can be partially achieved through the provision of encouraging, informative feedback. Immediate feedback that provides corrective information can be beneficial for learning.[33] It prevents learners from wasting time unproductively on erroneous solutions and can be used to ensure success for all skill and knowledge levels. Furthermore, immediate feedback assures students that they are "on the right path," allowing them to proceed more confidently down that path. The timing of feedback can also be critical; it is not beneficial to provide immediate feedback that interferes with progress through the environment. On the other hand, one of the benefits of computers is that they can provide immediate feedback, which is impossible for a teacher who is working with twenty-five students all of whom work at different paces. Thus, we can take advantage of the feedback capabilities of a computer while not impeding learning.

Student control over choice can also be easily supported by computer environments. There are two ways to allow students to have some control while not interfering with learning. First, we can allow students to proceed at a user-determined pace, pushing ahead or working more slowly depending on their needs. Losing one's place and becoming bored are less likely with self-pacing than when each student is held to some average pace. Second, we can allow students to determine their document selection order. This enables students to follow their own interests and to set their own immediate subgoals.

The final factor shown to affect motivation is the use of fantasy supporting learning. While much of the first generation of educational software tried to capitalize on this motivating factor, we believe that it failed to target the critical component—the to-be-learned target skills or concepts—as part of the fantasy. The bells and whistles either interfered with or were irrelevant to learning in many of these programs. Rather than depend on incidental learning, the software designer should ensure that any fantasy used to make the task more fun and engaging reinforces target skills or concepts.

Game environments are motivating for students and can be effective, pro-vided that the game conditions map onto specific learning goals.

When designing the Sourcer's Apprentice, we incorporated all four mo-tivating factors. In an effort to help students learn to read and reason from a variety of documents, we created an environment that closely matched the surface structure of the target behavior in the "real world." The environ-ment supports selecting books from a shelf, taking notes, answering ques-tions, and writing an essay with the documents and notes available. Thus, we minimized fantasy at the global level, believing this should increase transfer to other situations, such as going to a library and writing a research paper. Instead, the motivating game component centers on the local level of helping students focus on important elements in the readings and include them in their notes. The fantasy is that the students are detectives trying to find important information for later use. This fantasy provides motivation at the level of performing necessary subgoal satisfaction. A critical feature of our motivational component is that the payoff is contingent on the stu-dent's building and using a model of the discourse. Students cannot succeed at this game unless they read and comprehend the situation described in the texts as well as the source information.

In the SA environment, when students drag and drop an answer into a bucket, they receive immediate feedback. Incorrect answers result in in-cremental hints, with the ultimate hint ensuring that every student can complete all parts of the task correctly. Because the point system results in points lost for answering incorrectly, the students are highly motivated to respond without relying on the hints that follow an incorrect response. While it may seem worrisome to give points to students in history, imply-ing that there are simple and correct answers, we limit points to those sit-uations where there is a correct answer. For instance, the author's name either is or is not Andrew Carnegie. Other source features that are more interpretive rather than factual, such as the author's motives, are not scored by dragging-and-dropping responses.

We opted to give students a large degree of freedom in how they work through the controversy. They are free to go at their own pace, select docu-ments in any order, reread any documents, and fill in the notes in any order. They also decide when they have learned enough to write their essay, know-ing that their note cards will be available but not the books themselves.

Now we turn to a detailed description of the environment and materials used in the Sourcer's Apprentice, followed by presentation of results from a study of the effectiveness of the Sourcer's Apprentice in two classes.

Sourcer's Apprentice Environment

Sourcer's Apprentice is a Java application that promotes evidence seeking and evidence evaluation in students while developing an awareness of document type and document privilege in historical research. While we intend to extend the environment to the skills of content integration and argument comprehension, the present version focuses on the skill of sourcing. The SA has three components: *content modules, study environment*, and *skills tutorial*.

Content Modules

On the basis of our previous research, we created content modules that center on a historical controversy and include hierarchically structured sets of excerpts from real documents. We define controversies as historical events for which historians offer conflicting interpretations. The controversy for the Homestead steel strike module is: "To what extent was Carnegie responsible for breaking the Union at Homestead?" Students are given the controversy and excerpts from seven documents. They are told to read the books and take notes so that they can write an essay on this controversy using only their notes.

A document set comprises several relevant documents that address the controversy and have certain highly constrained features. The first document is a textbook excerpt that provides an overview of the situation, characters, and conflict. The next two documents are historians' interpretations of the events. These documents provide opposing accounts of the events and use primary documents to support their arguments. Finally, there are four primary documents that can be used as evidence to support one of the two accounts. Two of these primary documents were specifically mentioned in the historian's accounts, so the student has a model for citing and using primary documents as evidence. The student then has to relate the other two primary documents to the problem statement by themselves.

We have created five modules, each centered on a controversy. These include:

1. Lexington-Concord controversy: "To what extent were the British responsible for the events of April 19, 1775?"
2. Panama Canal controversy: "To what extent were Roosevelt and his administration responsible for the 1903 revolution in Panama?"

3. Salem witch trial controversy: "What was the primary cause of the Salem witch trials?"

4. Homestead steel strike controversy: "To what extent was Carnegie responsible for breaking the Union at Homestead?"

5. Vietnam War controversy: "What was the Gulf of Tonkin resolution, and why did Lyndon B. Johnson push Congress to pass it in August 1964?"

These modules have been used and evaluated in a classroom setting. The first two modules (Lexington-Concord and Panama Canal) are presently used as the transfer pretest and posttest. The Salem witch trial module is used as a tutorial to directly teach students to develop skills for learning from historical documents.

Study Environment

The Sourcer's Apprentice main environment screen is shown in Figure 22.2. The controversy statement is always present in the top of the portion of the screen. Prominently displayed in the center of the screen is a "bookshelf" containing seven books, starting on the left with a textbook, followed by two historians' accounts, and ending with four primary documents. At the bottom of the screen, and available at all times, are "note cards" for each document. These note cards are structured to aid in appropriate note taking during the study period. Along the sides of the screen are buckets for each important source feature. These are separated into features of the author (i.e., WHO: who wrote it, POSITION: what the author's position is, and HOW KNOW: how did the author know the information he or she was writing about), the document (i.e., WHEN: when it was written, and TYPE: what type of document it is), and content (i.e., what documents does it mention). To insert text into the note cards, a student selects a phrase from the author, document, or content page and drags it into the appropriate bucket. Notice that intermixed in the set of buckets are three rectangular "buttons." One button relates to a feature of the author (i.e., AUTHOR MOTIVE: what the author's motives are) and two relate to the content (i.e., MAIN POINT: what the document's main point is, and COMMENTS: important things mentioned in the document). It is not possible to limit all note card information to phrases that can be selected and dragged, so we have included buttons for inputting student-initiated text. The student must click on these buttons to insert text into the note cards.

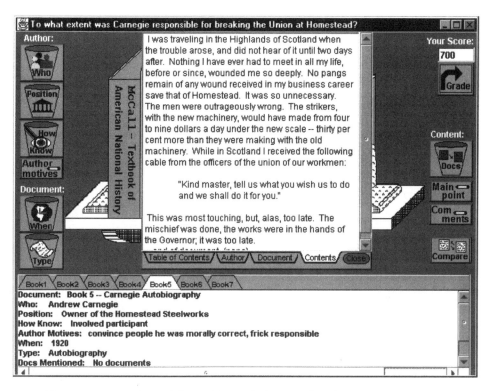

Figure 22.3. Here Carnegie's autobiography is opened to the contents page. Note the four tabs at the bottom of the open book each corresponding to a page in the book.

Students can open a book by clicking it in the bookshelf. An opened book is shown in Figure 22.3. Each book has four pages in the following order: title page, author information page, document information page, and content page. A student can change pages by clicking on the corresponding tab at the bottom of the page. The book in Figure 22.3 is currently opened to the content page. The excerpts are all very short, but if they were longer than the screen length provided, the student could scroll down to view more text. The author page provides detailed source information about the author's credentials and motives. The document page explains the type of document it is, who publishes it, and when it was written. Much of this information is provided on the inside cover of actual books.

Recall that the students' task is to learn about each document's source from the author and document pages and then to read the content page to learn what this document contributes to the controversy. While they are reading, students fill in the note cards for each book so that information will be available later when they write their essay on the controversy. Figure 22.4 shows how information is inserted into a note card. A phrase is selected from a page in the book by clicking on it. The phrase is then highlighted as shown in Figure 22.4. It can then be dragged into one of the buckets on the side of the screen. In this figure the phrase "is a historian who specializes in labor unions and their effects on business" is being dropped into the "How know" bucket. If the correct phrase is dropped into the bucket, an abstracted form of the information is inserted into the note card. Notice that the previous dropped phrase resulted in the fourth line of the note card changing to include the phrase: "Scholar in area." The student's score in-

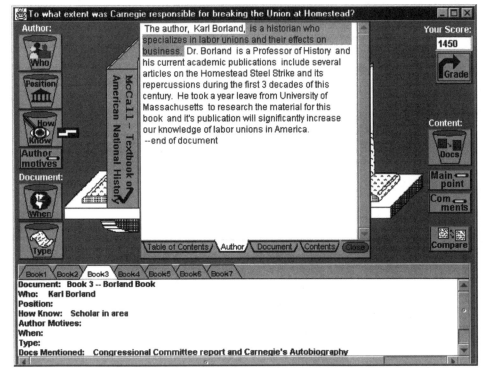

Figure 22.4. Filling in the note cards. To fill in the note cards, students highlight text from the author page and drag it to a bucket (sides of screen). When they drop the phrase into the bucket, an abstracted version is then inserted into the note card, and their score is increased (top right).

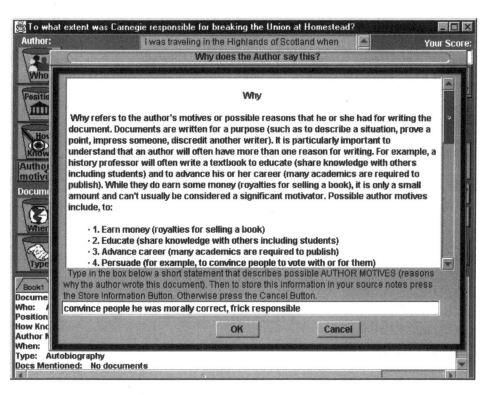

Figure 22.5. Scrollable Help screen for the Author Motives button. Each bucket and button have a help screen associated with them to provide detailed instructions for that source feature. Buttons have an additional field on the help screen for directly typing in text to insert into the note cards.

creases by 100 points and is displayed in the top right corner of the screen. If, however, a student drags an incorrect answer into a bucket, the student loses 50 points and is given graduated hints until he or she selects a correct response.* The hints vary from vague (e.g., "An historian would probably have an opinion on that point") to very specific (e.g., "Carnegie mentions that information in the last paragraph of his autobiography").

Students can obtain direct instruction on any of the note card features by clicking on the corresponding bucket or button. Figure 22.5 shows the Help screen for the Author Motives button, which appears when a students clicks

---

* In version 1.0 no hints were given. In the original version (0.5), hints were given and the students were more satisfied with that aspect of the earlier version. Hints have been re-instituted in the current version.

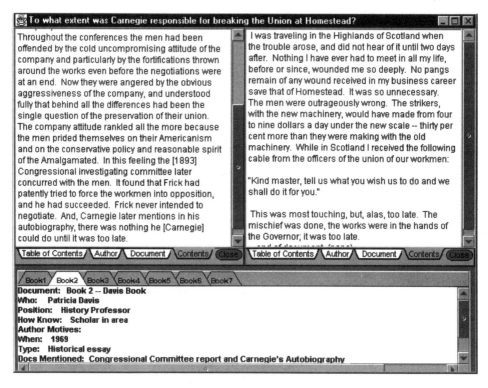

Figure 22.6. Comparing document information. The Sourcer's Apprentice allows side-by-side comparison in which a student can open two documents on the screen simultaneously. The main document, Davis's book, is opened on the left, and the additional document, Carnegie's autobiography, is opened on the right.

the Author Motives button. This scrollable window explains the feature from three perspectives: identifying, using, and evaluating the component information. Help information of this type is available only when a student specifically asks for it, in contrast to hints, which are given when a student makes an error.

The Sourcer's Apprentice allows side-by-side comparison in which a student can open two documents on the screen simultaneously. Students can click the "Compare" button shown in Figure 22.2 to display a second document next to the already opened document. The main document, Davis's book, is on the left in Figure 22.6. The book that is opened on the right is Carnegie's autobiography, which is mentioned in the last sentence of Davis' book. Students can compare Davis's summary of Carnegie's excerpt with Carnegie's actual excerpt.

When students have completed their note cards and integrated all the content into a coherent answer to the controversy, they move on to the questions screen. Students receive several questions of each of the following type: source (e.g., "Which document was written the earliest?" or, "Who thought that Andrew Carnegie deliberately left Pittsburgh to avoid having to take responsibility for the negotiations?"), content (e.g., "What was Frick's first action when the contract was about to end?") and argument (e.g., "What is one reason used to support the claim that Carnegie was responsible for the breaking of the Union?"). These questions are presented in a small window at the bottom of the screen shown in Figure 22.7. To answer a question, the student drags a phrase from one of the books into the

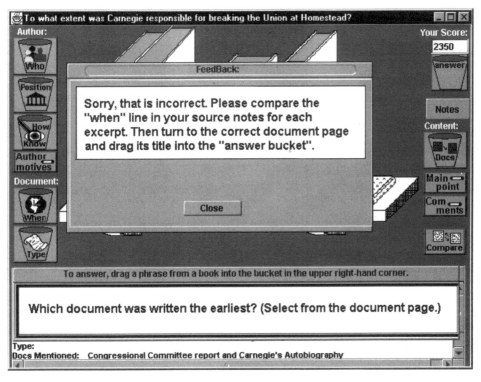

Figure 22.7. Comprehension question environment with feedback. Content, source, and argument questions are presented in a small window (bottom). Students drop answers into a bucket. If the answer is incorrect, a feedback screen appears (center), providing a hint. This feedback screen also appears during the filling of the note cards.

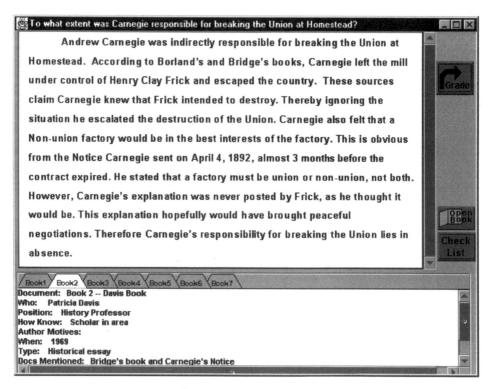

Figure 22.8. Essay environment. When the questions have all been answered, the student receives the final essay environment. The text shown in the essay field is an actual student's answer to this controversy. The note cards are available for review during the writing phase.

answer bucket in the right-hand corner. If the answer is correct, the student receives 300 points. If it is incorrect, the student receives fewer points and gets the next in a series of graduated hints.

When the questions have all been answered, the student receives the final essay environment shown in Figure 22.8. The bookshelf is no longer available. It is replaced by a large screen that includes a field where the student can insert text.* Note cards are available during this writing phase and the student can flip through these cards using the tabs on the top. The text entered here is an actual essay from an advanced placement student working on the Homestead Module.

* Students have an option of using a sheet of paper to write their answer if typing is too difficult or frustrating.

Skills Tutorial

To ensure that students begin their problem solving with the requisite knowledge, the Sourcer's Apprentice begins with a short tutorial on sourcing and understanding arguments. An example screen from the tutorial is shown in Figure 22.9. Students page through the text and occasionally are asked specific questions that they must respond to before continuing. The tutorial provides direct instruction at three incremental levels: identifying, using, and evaluating the component information. Practice follows immediately after each of these three levels. For instance, when teaching the students about sourcing, SA first describes critical features to help the student identify each feature. Then it describes the

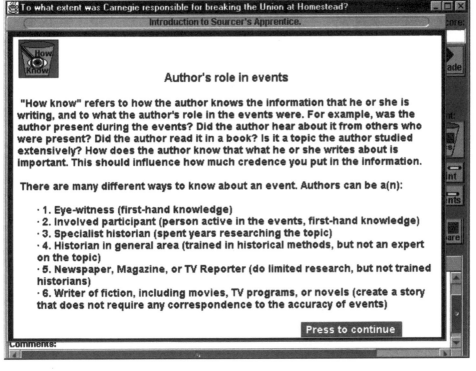

Figure 22.9. Skills Tutorial. Several screens, such as this one explaining the author's role in events, provide direct instruction on the sourcing and understanding arguments. Students page through this short tutorial by pressing a button (bottom right).

conditions under which sourcing would be most useful when writing an essay. Finally, students are taught how to evaluate sources for their trust-worthiness. Ideally, the tutorial should be embedded in the context of a separate module, forcing students to transfer what they learn through explicit instruction.

Classroom Study

Recently, we evaluated the Sourcer's Apprentice in two schools. To examine SA's effectiveness, we looked for improved performance on a posttest transfer problem (Panama Canal) compared to pretest performance on another problem (Lexington-Concord). We are currently analyzing the student essays for evidence of SA effectiveness but will not present that data here.

Participants

In each school, an eleventh-grade history teacher used the Sourcer's Apprentice in one class while another of the teacher's classes served as a control. The teacher from School A (from a small town) had two classes of eleventh-grade regular economics classes, resulting in ten complete participants from the experimental class and nineteen from the control class.[34] The teacher from School B (from a small suburban city) had two classes of regular American history classes, resulting in eight complete participants from the experimental class and seven from the control class.

Procedure

The general procedure was the same for both schools. On the first day, all students were given a pretest. On the next two to three consecutive days, the experimental students received the SA tutorial on sourcing and a single module. The control students stayed in the classroom engaging in regular classroom activities. On the final day, all students in both conditions received the posttest.

The formats for the pretest and posttest were designed to be equivalent and each took thirty-five minutes to complete. The topic for the pretest was the 1775 battle at Lexington and Concord and the topic for the posttest was the acquisition by the United States of the right to build a canal in Panama. For both tests, students were given a booklet with six documents that included source information at the bottom of each page. They were told that they could take notes on a one-page sheet and that they could use these notes later when answering questions about the documents. When they were finished studying, students received several questions, including source questions (e.g., which document was written earliest, which document was the least trustworthy), a short-answer controversy question (i.e., "To what extent were the British responsible for the events of April 19, 1775?," "To what extent were Roosevelt and his administration responsible for these events?"), and a short-answer situation question (i.e., "What happened on the Lexington Green on April 19, 1775?," "What happened in 1903 to enable the United States to get a canal in Panama?").

The experimental classes from both schools received training and abbreviated tutorial instruction on a single module. School A received the Homestead steel strike module and School B received the Vietnam module. Students were first provided training on the use of the environment and training in sourcing. Students in school A were given the tutorial in groups of five each due to computer malfunctions, whereas students in School B received this instruction individually. Following training, students were given minimal background information on their module. For both schools, this preparation was completed in a single period (forty minutes).

Students from school A worked with their module for the next two forty-minute periods over two days. They read the seven documents and filled in the note cards for each document. Then, they answered several content and source questions using the drag-and-drop procedure (Figure 22.7). Finally, they were given their note cards and asked to write an essay on the controversy for homework.

In school B, students began working on their Vietnam module immediately after tutorial instruction. For most students, this amounted to about twenty minutes of work on the module. They had thirty minutes the next day to complete the module. They read the seven documents, filled in the note cards, and answered several questions. Because this is the first group of students to use the Vietnam module, we needed to get student's open-ended responses to the content and source questions. For this reason, students answered these questions on paper rather than using the drag-and-drop procedure.

Finally, on the last day, all students were given the posttest in their regular classroom. Students were not explicitly told that this posttest was related to the computer activity on the previous couple days. Thus, any evidence of transfer is due to students' determination that the skills taught and practiced using SA should be used on the task, and not the result of hinting.

Results

Only the post- minus pretransfer test results are considered here. Scores for these tests were computed by counting the number of source features mentioned in the student's notes for each document and adding this to the number of source questions answered correctly. For both schools, the pretest performance did not differ between groups. Of a possible 70 points, the means for the experimental and control groups at School A were 13.2 and 15.6. The means for the two groups at School B were 13.3 and 16.6. The experimental group improved significantly more than the control at both schools. The mean difference score between pretest and posttest scores was positive for experimental groups (School A mean = 2.9; School B mean = 10.3) and negative for the control groups (School A mean = -2.7; School B mean = -3.4). As the negative control group results suggest, students had more difficultly with the Panama Canal test than with the Lexington-Concord test.

Conclusion

This study provides preliminary evidence that the Sourcer's Apprentice is an effective tool for teaching regular eleventh-grade history students document-based literacy skills. Even with exposure to an abbreviated form of the program, use of the Sourcer's Apprentice resulted in significantly better performance on a transfer task. We expect that providing a more intense intervention would be even more beneficial for students.

Discussion

Our study of SA's effectiveness is encouraging but limited. On the one hand, given the brevity of the tutoring (twenty minutes), it is very encouraging to find evidence that students responded to the instruction by making increased use of documents when they took notes. On the other hand, effectiveness should ultimately be measured in a more naturalistic setting. Our next step in evaluating SA effectiveness is to give students the opportunity to demonstrate their increased document literacy on a library research paper. We hypothesize that after exposures to the various tutorials, including practice in the environment, students will write papers with more document citations, clearer use of claims and evidence, and more references to primary documents.

In addition to effectiveness, it is important to inquire about SA's usability. Do students find it interesting to use? Too difficult? In a recent classroom study using the SA environment, we had six college students from the University of Pittsburgh and eight high school students (a different class from School B) use SA and then complete a survey, giving their opinions of its usability. More specifically, they rated on a scale from 0 (negative) to 9 (positive) how they felt about different aspects of SA. Students found SA to be easy to use (medians 8.0 and 9.0) and educationally valuable (medians 8.5 and 8.0). Furthermore, they thought the tutorial was useful (medians 7.5 and 7.0), but high school students were less interested in our choice of topic selected—the Homestead steel strike (medians 7.5 and 6.0). These survey results suggested that students find the environment helpful and easy to use. The real questions, however, concern what the students learn about how to approach history texts and questions about history. There remains much to learn about these questions.

These effectiveness and usability results pertain only to SA's sourcing tutorial and practice environment. Our next step in developing the Sourcer's Apprentice is to create tutorials for two additional document literacy skills: content integration and argument comprehension. This will entail creating a component in which students learn to identify important elements of each skill and practice these skills in terms of SA interface. Content integration, for example, is critical to learning from multiple documents, but it is not the type of skill with which high school students have a great deal of practice. In a recent study of eleventh graders, we found that students asked to read a historical narrative from a single integrated text learned better than students who read the same material from two texts.[35] In the two-text condition, the students were required to integrate the events themselves. Students who read two texts with only comprehension instructions made more errors, recalled less information, and provided less integrated answers to questions. More encouraging, however, were the results from students in the two-text condition who were explicitly instructed on how to integrate the material. They performed as well as students given the single integrated text. This strongly suggests that students will not create an integrated representation of information across texts unless given assistance and instructed to. This is precisely the type of instruction and practice that SA can provide.

Our extension of the Sourcer's Apprentice to teach students to integrate information across documents will certainly be illuminated by other works from this volume. For instance, Lee and his colleagues researched young children's developing awareness of causation in history. They analyzed seven-, eleven-, and fourteen-year-old students' responses to probes about causes and explanation in history. They found that younger students tended to produce single, shallow interpretations of causes, whereas older students tended to produce multiple, complex interpretations.[36] Clearly, limits on students' understanding of important concepts in historical analysis will impact their ability to learn to integrate information across documents. Developmental limits on the ability of students to understand the multiple causation in history will inevitably limit their ability to construct an integrative representation of events based on material from multiple texts. The task, however, may be influential in this integration process. Voss and Wiley, in the study reported in this volume, found that providing students with multiple documents in an argumentative writing task influenced the degree to which they transformed the information, especially if the students understood the task to be requiring integration.

Ultimately, we think that the Sourcer's Apprentice could be used in history class as a "history lab." Throughout the year, students would visit the lab to learn and practice document literacy skills. Each session could include a fifteen-minute interactive tutorial on skill (e.g., sourcing, content integration, argument comprehension). Then, students would be given approximately one hour of practice on the skill in the context of learning in depth about a historical event that corresponds to the period of history they are presently studying in class. This ensures that instruction time, a valuable commodity, is maximally used. To learn and practice each skill for the first time should only take one and a half hours, spent primarily on learning content. When a skill has been practiced once, the student would move on to the next skill. After working through all three skills, students could visit the lab to practice all three skills with the same module. This is important because it is unclear how many exposures are necessary, but we suspect two or three will be more beneficial than one. Thus, for only five blocks out of a school year, students could learn in depth about five modules and get multiple exposures to three document literacy skills.

A final note about the focus of the Sourcer's Apprentice on multiple short excerpts: We have opted to provide students with very short excerpts so that they can practice literacy skills on a variety of documents of differing types and within the constraints of a high school class setting (thirty- to fifty-minute periods). Additionally, it is a common practice for historians to include embedded excerpts of this length in their books and essays. We acknowledge that selecting text can have a significant impact on the meaning on the text. Furthermore, there is no reason that the Sourcer's Apprentice must be confined to short texts. Nor are we suggesting that a detailed analysis of a single text such as the Declaration of Independence would not be valuable in the classroom. We are merely providing an environment to enhance single-text analysis in the high school history classroom.

NOTES

1. National Center for History in the Schools, National Standards for United States History: Exploring the American Experience (Los Angeles, 1996), p. 2.

2. Ibid.

3. National Assessment of Educational Progress, *NAEP 1994 U.S. History Report Card: Findings from the National Assessment of Educational Progress* (Princeton, NJ, 1996).

4. D. R. Ravitch and C. E. Finn, *What Do Our 17-Year-Olds Know? A Report on the First National Assessment of History and Literature* (New York, 1987), p. 194.

5. S. J. Thorton, "Teacher as Curriculum-Instructional Gatekeeper in Social Studies," in J. P. Shaver ed., *Handbook of Research on Social Studies Teaching and Learning* (New York, 1991), pp. 237–248.

6. National Assessment of Educational Progress, *The U.S. History Report Card: The Achievement of Fourth-, Eighth-, and Twelfth-Grade Students in 1988 and Trends from 1986 to 1988 in the Factual Knowledge of High School Juniors* (Princeton, NJ, 1990).

7. A. Crismore, "The Rhetoric of Textbooks: Metadiscourse," *Journal of Curriculum Studies*, 6 (1984), pp. 279–293.

8. M. A. Britt, J. F. Rouet, , M. C. Georgi, and C. A. Perfetti, "Learning from History Texts: From Causal Analysis to Argument Models," in G. Leinhardt, I. L. Beck, and C. Stainton, eds., *Teaching and Learning in History* (Hillsdale, NJ, 1994), pp. 47–84.; C. A. Perfetti, M. A. Britt, J. F. Rouet, M. C. Georgi, and R. A. Mason, "How Students Use Texts to Learn and Reason about Historical

Uncertainty," in M. Carretero and J. F. Voss, eds., *Cognitive and Instructional Processes in History and the Social Sciences* (Hillsdale, NJ, 1994), pp. 257–283; C. A. Perfetti, M. A. Britt, and M. C. Georgi, *Text-Based Learning and Reasoning: Studies in History* (Hillsdale, NJ, 1995).

9. N. L. Stein and C. G. Glenn, "An Analysis of Story Comprehension in Elementary School Children," in R. O. Freedle, ed., *New Directions in Discourse Processing* (Hillsdale, NJ, 1979), pp. 53–120.

10. C. A. Perfetti, M. A. Britt, and M. C. Georgie, *Text-Based Learning and Reasoning: Studies in History* (Hillsdale, NJ, 1995); T. Trabasso and P. van den Broek, "Causal Thinking and the Representation of Narrative Events," *Journal of Memory and Language,* 24 (1985), pp. 612–630; P. van den Broek and T. Trabasso, "Causal Network versus Goal Hierarchies in Summarizing Text," *Discourse Processes,* 9 (1986), pp. 115.

11. C. A. Perfetti, J. F. Rouet, and M. A. Britt, "Towards a Theory of Documents Representation," in H. van Oostendorp and S. R. Goldman, eds., *The Construction of Mental Representations during Reading* (Hillsdale, NJ, 1999).

12. S. S. Wineburg, "Historical Problem Solving: A Study of the Cognitive Processes Used in the Evaluation of Documentary and Pictorial Evidence," *Journal of Educational Psychology,* 83 (1991), pp. 73–87.

13. M. A. Britt, C. A. Perfetti, R. L. Sandak, and J. F. Rouet, "Content Integration and Source Separation in Learning from Multiple Texts," in S. R. Goldman, ed., *Narrative Comprehension, Causality, and Coherence: Essays in Honor of Tom Trabasso* (Mahwah, NJ, 1999).

14. Ibid.

15. J. F. Rouet, M. A. Britt, R. A. Mason, and C. A. Perfetti, "Using Multiple Sources of Evidence to Reason about History," *Journal of Educational Psychology,* 88 (1997), pp. 478–493.

16. C. A. Perfetti, M. A. Britt, and M. C. Georgi, *Text-Based Learning and Reasoning: Studies in History* (Hillsdale, NJ, 1995); J. F. Rouet, M. Favart, M. A. Britt, and C. A. Perfetti, "Studying and Using Multiple Documents in History: Effects of Discipline Expertise," *Cognition and Instruction,* 15(1) (1998), pp. 85–106; and see note 15.

17. M. A. Britt, J. F. Rouet, and C. A. Perfetti, *Evaluation of Source Information in Learning with History Documents,* paper presented at the annual meeting of the American Educational Research Association, New Orleans, LA, April 1994.

18. K. T. Spoehr, "Using Hypermedia to Clarify Conceptual Structures: Illustrations from History and Literature," paper presented at the annual meeting of the American Educational Research Association, San Francisco, CA, April 1992; K. T. Spoehr and L. W. Spoehr, "Learning to Think Historically," *Educational Psychologist,* 29 (1994), pp. 71–77.

19. M. A. Britt, M. A. Marron, and C. A. Perfetti, "Students' Recognition and Recall of Argument Information in History Texts," unpublished report, 1994.

20. Ibid.

21. See note 12.

22. C. Gabrys, A. Weiner, and A. Lesgold, "Learning by Problem Solving in a Coached Apprenticeship System," in M. Rabinowitz, ed., *Cognitive Science Foundations of Instruction* (Hillsdale, NJ, 1993), pp. 119–147; A. M. Lesgold, S. P. Lajoie, M. Bunzo, and G. Eggan, "SHERLOCK: A Coached Practice Environment for an Electronics Troubleshooting Job," in J. Larkin and R. Chabay, eds., *Computer-Assisted Instruction and Intelligent Tutoring Systems: Shared Issues and Complementary Approaches* (Hillsdale, NJ, 1992), pp. 201–238.

23. M. T. H. Chi and R. Bjork, "Modeling Expertise," in D. Druckman and R. A. Bjork, eds., *In the Mind's Eye: Enhancing Human Performance* (Washington, DC, 1991).

24. A. Collins., J. S. Brown, and S. E. Newman, "Cognitive Apprenticeship: Teaching the Crafts of Reading, Writing, and Mathematics," in L. B. Resnick, ed., *Knowing, Learning, and Instruction: Essays in Honor of Robert Glaser* (Hillsdale, NJ, 1989).

25. Ibid. See also J. S. Brown, A. Collins, and P. Duguid, "Situated Cognition and the Culture of Learning," *Educational Researcher*, 18(1) (1989), pp. 32–41.

26. M. T. H. Chi, R. Glaser, and E. Rees, "Expertise in Problem Solving," in R. Sternberg, ed., *Advances in the Psychology of Human Intelligence*, vol. 1 (Hillsdale, NJ, 1982), pp. 17–76; A. M. Lesgold, P. J. Feltovich, R. Glaser, and Y. Wang, "The Acquisition of Perceptual Diagnostic Skill in Radiology," Technical Report No. PDS-1, University of Pittsburgh Learning Research and Development Center (1981); J. Larkin, "The Role of Problem Representation in Physics," in D. Gentner and A. L. Stevens, eds., *Mental Models* (Hillsdale, NJ, 1983), pp. 75–98.

27. J. R. Anderson, *Rules of the Mind* (Hillsdale, NJ, 1993); K. A. Ericsson and H. A. Simon, *Protocol Analysis: Verbal Reports as Data,* 2nd ed. (Cambridge, MA, 1993); A. Newell and H. A. Simon, *Human Problem Solving* (Englewood Cliffs, NJ, 1972).

28. See note 12.

29. M. K. Singley and J. R. Anderson, *Transfer of Cognitive Skill* (Cambridge, MA, 1989).

30. D. Druckman and R. A. Bjork, eds., *In the Mind's Eye: Enhancing Human Performance*, Committee on Techniques for the Enhancement of Human Performance, Commission on Behavioral and Social Sciences and Education, National Research Council (Washington, DC, 1991).

31. T. W. Malone and M. R. Lepper, "Making Learning Fun: A Taxonomy of Intrinsic Motivations for Learning," in R. E. Snow and M. J. Farr, eds., *Aptitude Learning and Instruction*, vol. 3 (Hillsdale, NJ, 1987), pp 223–253.

32. H. R. Strang, E. C. Lawrence, and P. C. Fowler, "Effects of Assigned Goal Level and Knowledge of Results on Arithmetic Computation: A Laboratory Study," *Journal of Applied Psychology*, 63 (1978), pp. 29–39; P. Earley, T. Connelly,

and C. Ekegren, "Goals, Strategy Development, and Task Performance: Some Limits on the Efficacy of Goal Setting," *Journal of Applied Psychology*, 72 (1989), pp. 107–114.

33. J. R. Anderson, C. F. Boyle, and B. J. Reiser, "Intelligent Tutoring Systems," *Science*, 228 (1985), pp. 456–468; E. L. Deci and R. M. Ryan, "The Initiation and Regulation of Intrinsically Motivated Learning and Achievement," in A. K. Boggiano and T. S. Pittman, eds., *Achievement and Motivation: A Social-Developmental Perspective* (New York, 1992); M. W. Lewis and J. R. Anderson, "Discrimination of Operator Schemata in Problem Solving: Learning from Examples," *Cognitive Psychology*, 17 (1985), pp. 26–65; J. E. McKendree, "Effective Feedback Content for Tutoring Complex Skills," *Human Computer Interaction*, 5 (1990), pp. 381–414.

34. Complete participants are those who were present for the pretest and the posttest and for at least one day of treatment.

35. M. A. Britt, S. R. Goldman, and C. A. Perfetti, *Content Integration in Learning from Multiple Texts*, paper presented at the meeting of the Society for Text and Discourse. Vancouver, BC, Canada, August 1999.

36. P. J. Lee, A. Dickinson, and R. Ashby, "Researching Children's Ideas about History," in J. F. Voss and M. Carretero, eds., *Learning and Reasoning in History* (Hillsdale, NJ, 1998), pp. 227–251.

Postlogue

This volume is intended to encourage wider understanding of how history education and learning can be studied and, through study, advanced. Collectively, though admittedly with some differences in emphasis, the essays argue that there is far more to the discussions of history curricula than bitter debate over which facts to cover and what identities to highlight. They present a case for goals of a different order. The essays also argue that there is more to innovative history teaching than the latest hot technology. Though technology can help interest and inform students, and can even improve their analytical skills, its use never automatically solves the problems posed by more traditional historical texts.

Collectively, finally, the essays contend that, although improving history teaching and history learning is difficult, it is possible—though degrees of optimism vary widely, given past experience with reform. Students are not tied to a set developmental pattern that makes carefully planned interventions futile. Indeed, research on history learning suggests that there are vital distinctions between modes of understanding that students naturally acquire but at their own pace—for example, a sense of sequence in time—and modes of understanding that can be fruitfully taught to advance analytical ability and enhance its durability.

Precisely because of the new opportunities before us, the essays also point to a series of vital tasks for the future. There is far more to be done than has been accomplished to date in this marriage between educational research and analytically oriented history teaching. The Pittsburgh Conference, indeed, set two goals: first, discussion of the current state of the art, to the benefit of educational research and history teaching alike, and second, the establishment of a basis for crucial new steps. This Postlogue sketches parts of the agenda before us.

We continue to suffer from certain blind spots, which learning research and/or explicit intervention have not yet penetrated. Despite the surge of world history courses, for example, researchers have not explored students' assumptions and their impact on learning, as has been done for national histories. Are there gaps comparable to those in U.S. history, between frameworks students bring to world history courses and standard school paradigms (and how do frameworks vary by cultural background?)? Findings from experienced teachers provide a start here, as Ross Dunn's essay suggests, but the need for more formal probes is obvious.

We also need more attention to the ways students develop analogical thinking in history—how they identify models from one historical case and apply to others. Historians have explored analogical thinking, such as the enduring power of the Munich model, but not how the same patterns are conveyed in schools, and with what effects. Here, indeed, is one of the most common scenarios for historical thinking, particularly in public life, but there is little systematic inquiry into analogy's role in history teaching and learning, or into how assessment of analogy can be improved. Veronica Boix-Mansilla's work suggests that student capacity to apply analogies may be advanced through explicit lessons, but much wider-ranging experiments and assessments are desirable.

Even where existing work is more advanced, additional connections are vital. British pedagogy has demonstrated that student abilities to handle conflicting interpretations can be fruitfully accelerated. Can these findings, and appropriate intervention techniques, be joined to the tensions between student assumptions and classroom emphases that Sam Wineburg and Linda Levstik examine? We know that some conventional interpretations in national history bounce off certain student groups because of the interpretations' lack of fit with histories learned outside the classroom. Can we figure out how to pull in both the curricular and the extracurricular versions of history, while improving student capacity to assess their validity through imaginative exercises in interpretive conflict? Certainly, we need more attention to the teaching implications of the student-classroom disputes, which are now too often unacknowledged. Here is a clear case where the results of learning research can be brought into greater interaction with guidance for effective teaching, even as the research itself proceeds.

Progression, or dealing with history learning tasks sequentially, is another obvious challenge. There is a fair amount of agreement on desirable history thinking goals. In addition to effective writing and the capacity to develop arguments based on empirical evidence, students can profitably advance their capacities tp assess and use various forms of primary materials; they can learn to weigh conflicting interpretations; they can formulate increasingly complex comparisons and comparisons' close kin, assessments of change and continuity over time; they can explicitly identify causation issues; and, finally, they can learn something about analogy. This is a challenging list, but it is not in principle unmanageable. But, when and in what order are these capacities best addressed? How can one capacity be maintained when another is added? Here, both learning research and explicit teaching experience come up short. Even the British work, which is concentrated on younger students and offers less than a full skills package, has not yet moved fully into the area of sequencing, though Lee and Ashby's comments on progression are an important start. In the United States, the pervasive tendency to view each history course in isolation, sometimes failing even to carry an analytical sequence through a single yearlong course, has inhibited imaginative experiments with what students can do over time. The new emphasis on historical habits of mind hardly suggests the kind of rigorous sequencing common in mathematics, but it may not prove to be a totally different animal. Certainly, questions of progression in historical understanding warrant the same kind of thought that has recently been applied, say, to chronological coverage sequencing in a multiyear U.S. history program in the schools.

Finally, we need mechanisms for assessment, again over time. Several articles in this book, including the Voss and Wiley essay, point the way, but the efforts must clearly be extended. Not only individual teachers but broader educational jurisdictions must develop assessments to determine how capacities to handle documents or to deal with interpretive conflicts are developed and maintained. Too often, even in otherwise imaginative courses, we fall back on memorization tests for final evaluations in history, sending clear—and misleading—signals to students about what really counts. Too often, we simply do not know what students can do analytically on the strength of a prior history course when we start them on the next one. Too often, finally, we launch teaching experiments, with new materials, perhaps a new technology, now perhaps a new exercise to promote comparison or causal analysis, but with no clear and explicit evaluation at the end. Assessment usefully joins ongoing research on student learning with a program of analytical goals and active interventions: to determine what students can pick up and what they retain.

Does society want students more capable of applying historical skills and perspective to political and social issues? The essays in this volume reflect a belief that the capacity to think historically enhances an ongoing understanding of how human societies work. Skills in using data or assessing the nature of change are vital for many types of jobs, in an information-rich, fast-paced work environment, and certainly for civic life. Programs to promote historical thinking offer a far richer promise for a polity than mere memorization of national historical icons. To the extent that the goals involve greater curricular challenge and rigor, they can appeal across political divides. And, ultimately, of course, the premises can themselves be assessed. If we gain a measurably more historically alert citizenry, we can evaluate the results.

Obviously, a reorientation to a greater commitment to training in historical thinking and the use of learning research requires a host of practical adjustments. We need to train history teachers better. We need to make sure they take history courses, an old plea now making some headway, but also we need to make sure that the courses teach historical thinking and its pedagogical underpinnings. (And we need to evaluate the results.) We should use the new opportunities in considering history learning to enhance our appreciation of what history teaching involves, how its challenges and complexities relate to the more familiar components of conventional history research in making history teaching more discussible and assessable. Happily, in the new history learning movement, the capacity to make history teaching more interesting and more worthy of collegial commitment and study matches the capacity to make it more effective. Barriers of routine and institutional lethargy are considerable, from history departments to textbook producers to public testing programs. But, the prospects for a reconsideration of how and why to teach history are at least as substantial.

Crucial to a commitment to thoughtful, research-based history education, analytically conceived, are three needs. First is the need for ongoing communication between educational researchers and history teachers, to the benefit of both groups. History teaching publications and Web sites need regular enrichment from educational research and provide an opportunity for discussions by both researchers and teachers on the implications for history pedagogy. The international component can be vital, as well. It is disturbing that even English-language projects are so little known beyond their countries of origin. One of the goals of the Pittsburgh Conference was to redress this gap. Other developments, such as the growing Canadian interest in research-based history education, further highlight the need for regular communication and exchange.

Second, the need for pedagogical experiment is obvious. We know enough about learning issues and successful interventions to devise imaginative applications. Can college-level enhancement of students' comparative skills, for example, be adapted to secondary schools? Can school-based exercises in handling sources be picked up and extended in college courses? Can we begin to work more systematically on analogical thinking? The questions and opportunities are increasingly obvious.

Finally, and relatedly, we need classroom flexibility, including serious relief from overwhelming textbook coverage and memorization drills. Robert Bain's essay suggests how courses can be readjusted to encourage greater thoughtfulness about historical thinking. We need wider opportunities, more chances to convert portions of the history class into the equivalents of laboratory sessions where, as in science, students explicitly learn basic methods of the discipline—the components of historical thinking—in single courses and across multiyear curricula. A reorientation of this sort does not conflict with a reasonable agenda of coverage and identity goals, but it requires space of its own.

Contributors

Rosalyn Ashby is Lecturer in Education at the University of London Institute of Education, where she is responsible for the coordination of the History PGCE and course leader for the master's degree in history education. After teaching history in secondary schools, she was appointed to the post of Project Officer for the Cambridge History Project and became History Adviser for the Essex Education Authority. She was Research Officer for Project Chata and published numerous articles with other members of the Chata team. She is currently finalizing her doctoral study on children's approaches to testing historical claims.

Robert B. Bain recently joined the faculty of University of Michigan's School of Education after teaching high school for twenty-six years. His research includes history teaching, professional development, and history of education.

Veronica Boix-Mansilla is a research coordinator at Harvard Project Zero. Her work focuses on the development of disciplinary understanding among students and on the challenges that teachers face in assessing and enhancing such understanding. She has published several papers that address students' understanding in history, science, and literature. Her current research involves a comparative study of adolescents' beliefs about the acquisition of knowledge and the unveiling of "truth" in history and science.

M. Anne Britt received her Ph.D. from the University of Pittsburgh and is currently an assistant professor of psychology at Northern Illinois University. Her interests include both theoretical and applied issues related to learning and reasoning from multiple texts. Along with her colleagues Gareth Gabrys and Charles Perfetti, she has designed a Web-based learning environment to help students learn from multiple history documents.

Ross E. Dunn is Professor of History at San Diego State University, where he teaches African, Islamic, and world history. He also serves as Director of World History Projects at the National Center for History in the Schools, UCLA. His publications include *The Adventures of Ibn Battuta, A Muslim Traveler of the Fourteenth Century* (1986). He is coauthor of *History on Trial: Culture Wars and the Teaching of the Past* (1997). He served as founding president of the World History Association.

Gareth Gabrys has a master's degree in cognitive psychology from the University of Pittsburgh. He is currently a software developer and user interface designer with Philips Speech Processing.

Christine Gutierrez, a native of Los Angeles, is a peace educator. She taught for twelve years in the Los Angeles Unified School District and for eleven years in the inner city at Thomas Jefferson High School and currently teaches in the suburbs at Palisades Charter High School. Presently, as a Carnegie Fellow, Cris is documenting her work as a teacher-scholar to understand the ways in which developing democratic and ecological competencies collaborate with scholastic achievement and self-understanding.

Peter Lee has responsibility for research in the History Education Unit in the Curriculum Studies Group at the University of London Institute of Education. His interests include the philosophy of history and research into students' understanding of history. Major projects in which he has been involved have been the Cambridge History Project and Project Chata (for both of which he was Codirector) and the Youth and History Project (for which he was UK national coordinator). Publications include *History Teaching and Historical Understanding* and *Learning History* and, more recently, numerous papers on aspects of the Chata research. He is currently one of the editors of the *International Review of History Education.*

Gaea Leinhardt is a senior scientist at the Learning Research and Development Center and Professor of Education and Program Chair in Cognitive Studies in the School of Education at the University of Pittsburgh. She conducts quantitative and qualitative classroom research on teaching and learning in subject matter areas (mathematics, geography, and history). She has written and published widely in major educational journals and edited two books, *Analysis of Arithmetic for Mathematics Teaching* and *Teaching and Learning in History.*

Linda Levstik is Professor of Social Studies at the University of Kentucky. Her research interests include the development of historical thinking and learning in children and early adolescents. She is coauthor, with Keith C. Barton, of *Doing History: Investigating with Children in Elementary and Middle Schools* (Erlbaum) and, with Christine Pappas and Barbara Kiefer, of *An Integrated Language Perspective in the Elementary School* (Longman).

David Lowenthal is Professor Emeritus of Geography at University College London and Visiting Professor of Heritage Studies at St. Mary's University College, Strawberry Hill, Twickenham, England. He is the author of *The Past Is a Foreign Country* (1985), *The Heritage Crusade and the Spoils of History* (1996), and *George Perkins Marsh: Prophet of Conservation* (2000).

G. Williamson McDiarmid has taught history and English literature in Greek, British, and rural Alaskan schools. He has also taught history methods at Michigan State University and at the University of Alaska Anchorage. He served as Codirector of the National Center for Research on Teacher Learning (NCRTL) at Michigan State. Currently, he is Director of the Institute of Social and Economic Research at the University of Alaska Anchorage and Professor of Educational Policy.

Desmond Morton is Director of the McGill Institute for the Study of Canada, Professor of History at the University of Toronto, and the author or coauthor of thirty-three books on Canadian political, military, and industrial relations history.

Gary B. Nash is Professor of History at the University of California, Los Angeles. He is Director of the National Center for History in the Schools and was cochair of the National Center for History Standards Project. He has served as President of the Organization of American Historians and has won numerous awards and honors. He has written or edited eighteen books, the most recent of which is *Forbidden Love: The Secret History of Mixed Race America* (1999).

Charles A. Perfetti is Professor of Psychology and Linguistics and Senior Scientist at the Learning Research and Development Center, University of Pittsburgh. His research in the cognitive psychology of reading and text understanding has been published in some 130 articles and books, including a monograph on history learning, *Text-Based Learning and History: Studies in History* (Erlbaum, 1995).

Diane Ravitch is a historian of education. She is Research Professor of Education at New York University and holds the Brown Chair in Education Policy at the Brookings Institution, where she edits the annual "Brookings Papers on Education Policy." She was Assistant Secretary of Education 1991–1993. She is the author of six books and the editor of a dozen books.

Roy Rosenzweig is College of Arts and Sciences Distinguished Professor of History and Director of the Center for History and New Media at George Mason University. He is the author, coauthor, or coeditor of many books, including *The Park and the People: A History of Central Park*; *Eight Hours for What We Will: Workers and Leisure in an Industrial City*; *Experiments in History Teaching*; *Presenting the Past: Essays on History and the Public*; and *The Presence of the Past: Popular Uses of History in American Life*.

Peter Seixas is Associate Professor in the Department of Curriculum Studies at the University of British Columbia. He taught social studies in Vancouver schools over a period of fifteen years prior to moving to UBC. His research and teaching interests lie in history education and in the relations among universities, schools, and popular culture in the construction of historical understandings.

Denis Shemilt has worked at the University of Leeds for more than twenty-five years and since 1986 has been head of the School of Education at Trinity and All Saints, a constituent college of the University. In 1974, he became Evaluator of the Schools History Project 13–16 and, in 1985, Codirector of the Cambridge A-Level History Project. Recent years have been devoted to educational management, which, in the nature of things, has tended to displace and to substitute for real work.

Peter N. Stearns is Provost of George Mason University, having previously taught a large world history course at Carnegie Mellon University, Pittsburgh. He has written widely on teaching issues and on experiments to further learning outcomes in world history. Past Vice President of the American Historical Association (Teaching Division), he is the winner of the Doherty educational award and the ED Smith teaching prize at Carnegie Mellon. His most recent book is *Battleground of Desire: The Struggle for Self-Control in Modern America*.

Julie A. Van Dyke is pursuing her Ph.D. in cognitive psychology at the University of Pittsburgh's Learning Research and Development Center. Her research focuses on language comprehension at the sentence and text level, including work on emotion in reasoning processes, recovery from garden path sentences, and learning from multiple texts. She is currently compiling a large database from eleventh-grade U.S. history students in the Pittsburgh City Schools who have used the Sourcer's Apprentice as part of their classroom instruction.

Peter Vinten-Johansen, Ph.D., is Associate Professor of History and Adjunct in the Department of Teacher Education, as well as at the Center for Ethics and Humanities, at Michigan State University. He writes on topics in the history of medicine and health care, historical pedagogy, and European intellectual history. He is part of an interdisciplinary team of scholars currently writing an intellectual biography of John Snow, the pioneering anesthetist and epidemiologist. His translation of Johann Ludwig Heiberg's 1826 vaudeville, *The April Fools*, was published by Wisconsin Introductions to Scandinavian Studies in 1999.

Bodo von Borries, with a doctorate in history, has served as a high school teacher and, since 1976, as a professor of education (mainly learning and teaching history) at Hamburg University. His research and publications deal with the analysis of textbooks, films, and novels; innovative school topics (e.g., materials on women's, children's, colonial, and environmental history); and empirical studies on historical consciousness of children and adolescents.

James F. Voss received his Ph.D. from the University of Wisconsin and is Professor (now emeritus) of Psychology and Political Science and Senior Scientist at the Learning Research and Development Center at the University of Pittsburgh. He has interests in the study and teaching of learning, reasoning, problem solving, and decision making, especially in the areas of history and international relations.

Shelly Weintraub is a Teacher on Special Assignment with the Oakland School District, Oakland, California. She is responsible for social studies curriculum and staff development. Prior to taking this assignment in 1990, she taught social studies in the Oakland schools for fifteen years. She has been a consultant for the Bay Area Writing Project and has won numerous teaching awards.

James V. Wertsch is Professor and Chair of the Department of Education and Professor in the Program on Social Thought and Analysis at

Washington University in St. Louis. Among his publications are *Vygotsky and the Social Formation of Mind* (Harvard University Press, 1991) and *Mind as Action* (Oxford University Press, 1998). His research is concerned with language, thought, and culture, with a special focus on the role of textual meanings for the formation of identity.

Jennifer Wiley is Assistant Professor of Psychology at Washington State University, Vancouver, Washington. Her research interests are in psychology and education, especially learning from text and Web environments.

Sam Wineburg is Professor of Educational Psychology, College of Education, and Adjunct Professor, Department of History, at the University of Washington, Seattle. He was a member of the fifteen-person commission that produced the report *How People Learn: Brain, Mind, Experience, and School* (National Research Council, 1999). He has published numerous articles and chapters on historical cognition and consciousness in journals such as *Cognitive Science, Phi Delta Kappan, American Educational Research Journal, Perspectives, History Teacher,* and the *Journal of Educational Psychology*. With Pam Grossman, he is the author of *Interdisciplinary Encounters: A Second Look* (Teachers College Press) and of the forthcoming *Historical Thinking and Other Unnatural Acts* (Temple University Press).